**teach**<sup>®</sup>
**yourself**

**good study skills**

# teach yourself®

## good study skills
bernice walmsley

For UK order enquiries: please contact Bookpoint Ltd, 130 Milton Park, Abingdon, Oxon, OX14 4SB. Telephone: +44 (0) 1235 827720. Fax: +44 (0) 1235 400454. Lines are open 09.00–17.00, Monday to Saturday, with a 24-hour message answering service. Details about our titles and how to order are available at www.teachyourself.co.uk

For USA order enquiries: please contact McGraw-Hill Customer Services, PO Box 545, Blacklick, OH 43004-0545, USA. Telephone: 1-800-722-4726. Fax: 1-614-755-5645.

For Canada order enquiries: please contact McGraw-Hill Ryerson Ltd, 300 Water St, Whitby, Ontario, L1N 9B6, Canada. Telephone: 905 430 5000. Fax: 905 430 5020.

Long renowned as the authoritative source for self-guided learning – with more than 50 million copies sold worldwide – the **teach yourself** series includes over 500 titles in the fields of languages, crafts, hobbies, business, computing and education.

*British Library Cataloguing in Publication Data:* a catalogue record for this title is available from the British Library.

*Library of Congress Catalog Card Number:* on file.

First published in UK 2006 by Hodder Education, 338 Euston Road, London, NW1 3BH.

First published in US 2006 by The McGraw-Hill Companies, Inc.

This edition published 2006.

The **teach yourself** name is a registered trade mark of Hodder Headline.

Typeset by Transet Limited, Coventry, England.
Printed in Great Britain for Hodder Education, a division of Hodder Headline, 338 Euston Road, London, NW1 3BH, by Cox & Wyman Ltd, Reading, Berkshire.

The publisher has used its best endeavours to ensure that the URLs for external websites referred to in this book are correct and active at the time of going to press. However, the publisher and the author have no responsibility for the websites and can make no guarantee that a site will remain live or that the content will remain relevant, decent or appropriate.

Hodder Headline's policy is to use papers that are natural, renewable and recyclable products and made from wood grown in sustainable forests. The logging and manufacturing processes are expected to conform to the environmental regulations of the country of origin.

Impression number    10 9 8 7 6 5 4 3 2 1
Year                 2010 2009 2008 2007 2006

## Acknowledgements

Thank you to the Teach Yourself team at Hodder for their friendly help and guidance. I must also thank my husband William for his continuing support and patience.

## Dedication

This book is for all those teachers and tutors who have helped me to enjoy studying throughout my life.

**contents**

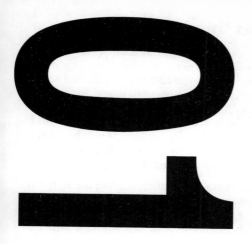

# 01

# introduction

**In this chapter you will learn:**
- how you can use this book to develop your study skills
- how you can gain more confidence
- how positive thinking can help you.

# Who should read this book?

University and mature students, apprentices, driving test entrants, i.e. anyone who is a learner – in short, anyone who needs to learn can gain from some – or all – of the tips and ideas contained in this book, but it will be especially useful for people who are often referred to as 'mature students' and those people approaching independent study for the first time. This would include both new learners and returning learners. It will be useful to anyone who has had difficulties in focusing on their studies in the past or who has no idea where to start with a new course.

In many cases, students will be starting out on a new path in their lives and will need some guidance along the way. If you're a first-year undergraduate or have not studied for some time, you may be surprised by how independent in your studies you will be expected to be. If you've been at school up until this point in your studies or your last experience of studying was some time ago, you will find that, although help and support will be available to you, you will need to find out a lot of things for yourself and develop your own way through your studies. Or it may be that you're aiming at a one-off event such as the written portion of the driving test or a work-based seminar. Or maybe you're trying to gain a work-based qualification such as a national vocational qualification (NVQ) where your competence is assessed 'on the job'. Everyone will find slightly different ways to study and will choose their own path, using their own combination of study skills, tools and aptitudes. This book is designed to help you to develop the skills you need, provide you with the necessary tools and to help you to find, develop and use your own blend of aptitudes to ensure that you are successful in your studies.

# How to use this book

This book can be used in a number of ways. You could decide that you are going to improve all areas of your study skills before you start your course and will be prepared to sit down and read this book from cover to cover. Alternatively you could already have noticed a particular area or two of weakness in your study skills and for this you will be able to dip into the book for the appropriate chapters to help you out. You may also need to keep this book by you as you go through your course, using it as you come up against problems.

One thing to remember is that you will not become an expert student overnight. The process of learning study skills must be taken at a speed to suit you – your existing level of skills, your priorities, your current commitments. You may be able to spare the time and effort to read straight through this book in one sitting but this will not mean you have mastered all the study skills discussed. This takes time and plenty of practice, as you need to learn the skills then try them out on the different types of assignment you're tackling to see how you can use them best.

To use this book effectively, you will need to become familiar with the layout. Check out the contents list now. You'll see that each chapter deals with one broad area of study skills – there's a chapter on note taking, for instance and one on effective reading. If you know that you have problems in any of these specific areas, then this will help you to focus on them quickly and easily. Next, if you flick quickly through the chapters, you will see that they all open with a short section starting 'In this chapter you will learn' followed by a few bullet points giving a summary of the expected learning outcomes of that chapter. This tells you where you can expect to be if you use the information contained in that chapter. This is followed by fairly short sections on all the topics contained in the subject being dealt with in the chapter. The subjects are broken up into short sections like this to make them easier to deal with.

This helps in two ways – first, it breaks the information down into more easily digestible chunks and, second, it gives you sub-headings that you can skim through and then zero in on the particular information that you need. At the end of each chapter you will find two sections – a summary and a quick revision test. The summary can be helpful either by giving you a quick revision of what you have learned as you come to the end of the chapter (and of course, if you see something in the summary that you think you've not really got to grips with, you can then go back and read that section again) or by helping you to see what's in the chapter before you read it to help you to decide if the information you need is in there. Throughout the chapters you will find quizzes and questionnaires to help you assess your current level of skills or to find out your attitudes to areas of study, checklists and plenty of 'top tips' to help you save time and effort in your studies.

Whatever your current level of study skills and whichever way you decide to use this book and at what point in your studies, this book will help you through your course by improving your study skills and giving you more confidence as you go along.

## What are study skills? Can they be learned?

Many students fail to do as well as they are capable of doing because they lack vital skills that will help them to learn. They are capable of learning but don't know how. These are study skills. The term 'study skills' covers a variety of techniques that can be learned that will make your studying activities easier and more effective. These techniques include note taking, reading, writing essays and reports, planning, revising for examinations and sitting examinations.

Study skills also encompass the habits that are necessary to become successful at studying. These habits establish patterns in your study timetable and ways of doing things that will help you to make the most of your study time. Of course, all these skills, habits and techniques have different components that will be used at different times. Effective reading, for example, can be split into planning, skimming, speed reading, setting goals and developing a reading strategy and you will need all these components if you are to become proficient at reading to learn. Even if you already have one or more of these skills, you will be able to improve by following the advice and tips given in this book. In effect, you will learn how to learn. The major tasks that you will undertake as a student – writing essays, revising for and sitting exams, giving a presentation – all require a combination of study skills. You will need to bring together the right techniques and habits and to have these skills at a sufficiently proficient level for success. While you are becoming proficient at the individual skills, you will also be developing the ability to combine the different skills as required.

Let's take the example of note taking. This is a very important study skill and one that you will find very difficult to manage without. In the Chapter 04 on note taking you will find different ways of recording what you have learned from lectures or from your reading. Why not try them all? One will be sure to be more suitable for you than others and you will probably find that you will be able to use different methods in different situations. For instance, if you're brainstorming ideas prior to writing an essay, you may find it useful to use a spider diagram, jotting down ideas as they come into your head and then linking them up and organizing them into a suitable essay plan. If you're reading a difficult text and want to summarize it for future use or revision, you may want to use a highlighter pen to pick out the important bits in the text. If you currently have problems with note taking – perhaps you find it difficult to decide quite what you should be recording or you only know one method of taking notes, then reading this chapter will help you to develop your note taking skills so that you can take notes that are easy for you to understand (after all, it's not important that other people can understand them – just you), organized and, above all, relevant.

Of course, you will already have lots of skills that will be useful in your studies and, as we said, study skills are, like any other skill, made up of several elements. It might be that you are already a relatively fast reader and very self-aware so that you know what your strengths are and can make sure that you play to these strengths. In this case you will be well on the way to developing your effective reading skills. Or you may be very organized and able to keep to deadlines. As you can no doubt imagine, this will help when it comes to writing essays. There is a whole host of other skills that you may have acquired throughout your life and that you would not usually consider to be study skills in quite the same way as reading or note taking would be readily accepted as study skills. Nevertheless, these skills and aptitudes, such as being able to work independently, stamina, an analytical mind and ability to concentrate, will undoubtedly help you in your studies.

## Check your skills

Knowing what skills you already have is very important, as this will enable you not only to make the most of these existing skills but also to identify where you need to improve. So now, let's look at how you can identify the skills that will help you in studying. Sometimes it can be difficult to identify our own abilities and to see what we have to offer in any situation. Somehow, we let our natural modesty deny all the qualities that we possess, so it can be a good idea to go through this exercise with someone who knows you reasonably well and whom you can trust to be honest with you. Perhaps you can pair up with another student on your course for a discussion about this exercise so that you can, in turn, help them to discover their own skills sets.

Look at this list and, being as honest with yourself as possible, mark off all the skills you already possess, i.e. where you feel that the area mentioned is where you can give a reasonable performance:

- I am able to be succinct – useful for both note taking and essays.
- I am organized – vital for efficient studying.
- I am able to take instructions from others – something you will inevitably have to do at several points during your course.
- I am good with numbers – many courses contain some element of number work.
- I am self-disciplined – always a useful skill when you have deadlines to meet.
- I am able to write letters and reports – you may have learned this at work and it will help with the writing you will need to do to complete a course of study.
- I am computer literate – a vital skill if you want to produce high-quality reports and essays or to use the Internet for research.
- I am able to learn from my mistakes – some people tend to ignore their mistakes and problems and will therefore not find it easy to improve.
- I am determined to succeed – determination to keep going will help you through the difficult times in your course.
- I am good at problem solving – a valuable skill in many areas of your course from the initial planning to working out how to pass your exams.
- I can read quickly – if this is not a strong point for you, check out the chapter on effective reading skills.
- I have an ability to concentrate even under difficult circumstances – this could enable you to study at odd moments in crowded places or when you have other problems on your mind.
- I am willing to ask for help when I need it – everyone needs help sometimes, so don't be afraid to ask for it.
- I am a good negotiator – this might help in group work or when you need to come to an agreement about deadline extensions.

- I am a team player – an obvious advantage if you're working in groups.
- I am confident when speaking in public – many courses require you to give an oral presentation.
- I am very creative – this might help you with design elements of your course and the presentation of your assignments.
- I am not frightened of making decisions – some people find themselves paralysed when a decision about their studies is needed so the ability to make decisions can save time and torment.
- I am good at putting my point across in a debate – this will help not only in group work or online debates but also in putting essays together as an essay can be a bit like a debate with yourself.
- I find it easy to set priorities – a vital skill when planning your study timetable.
- I can read and understand complex information – an obvious help for a higher level course.
- I can manage my stress levels – stress can be debilitating and adversely affect your results so managing it is important.
- I can set goals for myself – goals will help you get to where you want to be so this is an essential skill.
- I am highly motivated – this will lead to your meeting assignment deadlines and will enable you to keep going even when things get difficult.
- I manage my time well – good time management at all stages of your course is essential.
- I can weigh up an argument easily – arguments are the backbone of many academic texts and also of the assignments you will have to produce.
- I can organize information into a logical order – when you are writing essays or reports or note taking this will be an indispensable skill.
- I can find information from different sources – this will help with research.
- I am good at seeing how things work – this means that your level of understanding of many types of text or principles will be high.
- I work well under pressure – with any course there will be times when pressure increases such as when assignments are due or at examination time.

- I can keep going until a task is finished – having stamina can be important when you're studying as there may be times, for example, when you are facing an assignment deadline but you have been late home from work or the children are sick, when you will need to keep going even though you are tired. You may need to work late into the night on a complicated piece of work. For that you need staying power and determination.
- I am able to work independently – this is a vital attribute to have when you are learning as a mature student as you will not be 'force fed' all the necessary elements of your course but will have to find things out for yourself.
- I have plenty of self-confidence – having confidence in your own abilities will help you to achieve just about anything.
- I am able to think analytically – a useful skill when you're reading academic texts or preparing essays and reports. Then you will have to be able to weigh arguments for and against a view put forward.

Were you surprised at just how many skills might be involved in studying? And surprised at how many of them you already possess? These are all elements of the main skills you need to help you in your studies so you will need to master many of them over the course of your studies.

So, as you can see, study skills are vital and the ones that we do not already possess can certainly be learned. If you follow the advice in the appropriate chapters in this book and do the exercises and the revision tests, you will certainly be able to improve your study skills.

## Study smarter – not harder, or longer

Many people believe that, to be a successful student, it is necessary to study into the night, making endless notes, reading until your eyes hurt. This is not true. Of course, to pass exams and to get good coursework scores requires plenty of work but it should not be necessary to abandon all other things in your life or to do so much studying that you feel exhausted. With the right skills, applied in the right way, studying at any level can be easier than that. Lots of things can help you to cut down on the amount of time that must be spent and on the effort that must be made to ensure good results. These include:

- Making your notes brief and to the point – see Chapter 04.
- Reading more quickly – see Chapter 03.
- Being more selective in what you read – see Chapter 03.
- Planning – and more planning – see Chapter 02.
- Managing your time – see Chapter 02.

Confidence is a very important element of working smarter. You need to know – and have complete belief in this – that you can succeed. For this level of self-belief to be developed, you need to learn the skills and to understand how all the components of these skills will ensure that you can do what you are setting out to do. You need to know, without any doubt, where you are going and how you are going to get there. Can you visualize yourself reaching the end of your course? Do you see yourself bathed in glory, completely satisfied with your performance and then going on to get that job you were aiming at, or all your family finally convinced of your potential? Being able to visualize success is an important part of achieving it and is just one more study skill that you should practise often.

Of course, most people who start a new course of study worry about their abilities. They are afraid that they will fail. They are intimidated by all the unfamiliar things that they will be required to do – meeting new people in new places, reading academic texts, studying independently, writing assignments and sitting exams to name but a few. But why are we all so afraid? Feelings of fear when facing something different are normal – almost everyone is scared when they first go to university or take their driving test for example. It might appear, as you go onto the university campus for the first time or walk into the driving test centre, that everyone is calm, self-assured and comfortable in his or her surroundings. We can see that this is not the case if we examine our own reactions in this situation.

What do we do if we're almost paralysed with fear as we walk into a new situation? Do we turn to the person next in line to us and burst into tears, saying 'I'm so frightened that I'm thinking of not doing this course. It's impossible. I just can't do it'? No, of course we don't. We stand there appearing calm and self-assured – just like everyone else! We're all putting on an act. However, we must work hard to ensure that these feelings that we are hiding so well are not allowed to affect our chances of success. We might not let the outside world see how we feel but you can be sure that inside, these insecure thoughts are having an effect. This is where the power of positive thinking comes into its own.

> **Top tip**
>
> Prepare a few motivational statements for yourself – maybe 'I am a hardworking, conscientious student' or 'I know I am going to succeed' – and repeat them to yourself at every opportunity.

# The power of positive thinking

There are plenty of self-help books on the market that will help you to develop a sense of self-belief and set you on the right path to building your self-confidence. The essence of positive thinking is that you can achieve more if your thoughts are positive ones than if they are negative ones. It is believed that our internal voices are continually criticizing our performance and sabotaging our chances of success. When our minds are oriented in this way, we are set up to fail. If we can retrain ourselves to think positive thoughts and to believe that success is possible – no, that success is *assured* – then we will indeed be successful.

There are several ways in which it will be useful to engage in positive thinking during your time as a student and the first of these that we will take a look at is to envisage positive outcomes. Do you see yourself passing your course? If not, then change your thinking right now. If you weren't capable of passing it is highly unlikely that you would be on the course at all. Set yourself some positive goals now. State them positively and in as much detail as you can muster. For example, you might say 'I'm going to pass this course in the top ten per cent of the class' or 'I am capable of meeting all my assignment deadlines this term.'

Visualization is a really important skill in the area of positive thinking and is often used by athletes. Do you think that they stand at the starting line, waiting for the gun to fire, with the thought that they will lose? That they see themselves coming last in the race? No, of course they don't. They use visualization repeatedly, seeing themselves breasting the tape, achieving their own personal best times, going at just the right pace at all the points in the race until they break through into the lead just before the finishing line or they visualize being way out in front all the way. The reasoning by all the top athletics coaches and sports psychologists is that positive thinking and visualization work and are vital elements in an athlete's training regime. The same is true for students. Picture yourself getting top results or emerging from the driving test centre waving your pass certificate or getting the promotion at work that you're working towards and you will significantly enhance your chances of success. Play the scenes of your success like a videotape in your head – pushing the rewind button as often as you can – and you will come to believe it. Your confidence will soar and, as if by magic, your results will improve.

A second way in which positive thinking can help you in your studies is by looking at your fears in a different way. This will help to diminish them. Let's go back to that queue where everyone is feeling afraid of what is to come in a new situation. When you accept that everyone feels fear when they're attempting something new, you can see fear as something that is just part of being human. It is nothing to be ashamed of – it's just normal. Accept that and get on with your life. Of course, that doesn't make the fear go away. Can you think of anything that always makes fear go away? There is only one way. Fear will, without fail, disappear when we do whatever it is we're frightened of. We can feel terrified of leaping into the unknown, but once we've made the leap and become accustomed to the new situation, we're no longer afraid. So, next time you're feeling frightened of something, don't try to live with the fear, instead *face the fear* and it will vanish.

Positive thinking can also help with the choices you make. Every time we're faced with a situation – a good experience or otherwise – we have a choice as to how we look at it and, in turn, this dictates how we deal with it. If you get a bad mark for an assignment do you then think that it was the end of the world and it just proved you right in thinking that you couldn't get the hang of this subject? Or did you get the same mark and think 'So, what were the good bits in that essay? And what can I learn from what went wrong?' These two very different points of view will have different consequences. If you think it's a disaster, you're unlikely to make much improvement and might even be tempted to give up the course. If you can think positively and use all experiences – good or bad – to benefit you, you will be able to make improvements, in this case to your essay writing skills, and get a better mark next time.

Here are some tips to help you to think positively:

- Think of some positive statements about yourself – I am hard working, I am a good student, I am good at this subject, I can write essays that get the message across. Be sure to state these in the positive, i.e. not 'I am not lazy, I am not a bad student,

I'm not bad at this subject or I think I can write essays' and so on.

- Write these positive statements down and keep them where you can see them while you're studying.
- Learn to assess your own work. Do not allow yourself to think that passing or failing is a matter of luck or, worse, that you are doomed to failure because your work is simply not good enough. Discuss your marks with your tutors and understand what you have done wrong and, more importantly, what you have done right. Initiate discussions with other students about how they tackled assignments and then assess what you have done. Continuous improvement is possible by learning about your own work in this way and that will send your confidence soaring.
- Meet up with some positive people. We all know people who drag us down. They voice our fears – 'Do you really think you can cope with all that studying as well as your job?' or 'What are you studying for, it's a waste of time.' When you're feeling vulnerable, keep away from these people and seek out instead some people who will talk you up. They might say 'Well done you, starting a new course takes courage' or 'Education is never lost, anyway it sounds really interesting.'
- Mind your language. Try to use positive words and think positive thoughts. This will cause a subtle change in how you feel and in the choices you make.
- Accept responsibility for yourself and what happens to you. Don't be a victim, forever thinking 'That always happens to me' or 'I'm just unlucky.' Instead, if something goes wrong, accept that it's happened and find out what you can do to make sure you do things better next time.

Positive thinking has been proved to be beneficial in all areas of life and for all sorts of people – including students – so try out some of these ways of using positive thinking and increase your confidence.

Working smarter – rather than harder or longer – is a vital skill for all students to learn, whatever their personal circumstances. You need to learn how to make every minute that you spend on your studies count. Your studying must be effective, so strategies like planning, time management, active learning and motivation are vital for success. So, don't just sit there staring at your books and notes and not making any progress – that is not effective study. Get organized, know your learning style, set your goals, engage with your notes and books and get great results – quicker.

> **Top tip**
>
> If you find it difficult to settle down to study, limit your studying time to just 10 minutes. If, at the end of that time you do not feel you've made progress, go and do something else. Plan your next study period into your schedule immediately.

# Summary

In this chapter you have learned:

- How to use this book to improve your study skills – either by reading it from cover to cover, doing all the exercises, tests and quizzes as you go along or by dipping in at appropriate points to learn specific skills as and when you need them.
- About the wide range of skills that you will need to study effectively – many of which you will already possess and others that you will be able to master with the help of this book.
- How to appreciate what it means to work smart and where you will find information to help you do this.
- Some ideas on how to build your confidence, as this will help you in your studies. Positive thinking is the main tool in getting more confident in your abilities.

# Quick revision test

1 Name three study skills that you will learn about in this book.
2 What are stated at the start of each chapter?
3 What is the essence of positive thinking.
4 What makes fear go away?
5 Why are the subjects in each chapter broken up into short sections?

# 02

## getting organized

**In this chapter you will learn:**
- how to manage your time
- how to make some space for studying
- how to get an overview of your course.

# Introduction

Getting organized is essential for successful study. Managing your time, getting your space set up properly and setting goals will bring dramatic improvements to your studies. Also, understanding what motivates you and managing your stress levels will help to make life easier and your studying more effective. So, let's look at the first thing you can do to get yourself organized.

# Making a space for studying

Having your own space for studying and getting it organized will have many benefits. First, it will make your studying seem real. If you have been putting off starting some serious work on your course, you may find that having a desk set up with all your bits and pieces will finally motivate you into sitting down and getting on with it. Second, you will find it so much easier to pick up where you left off. If you don't have to waste time putting things away and then getting them out again when you next come to study, you will get so much more done and feel better about doing it. Other benefits include impressing on your family and friends that this business of studying is important to you, you will get fewer interruptions because it will be obvious that you are studying if you are installed at your desk and also being at your workspace is likely to put you in the right frame of mind for studying.

Having convinced ourselves of the usefulness and advantages of having an organized workspace, let's look first at some of the practical elements of getting organized. If you are continually having to clear a corner of the kitchen table for space to study or cannot find your calculator because last night you studied in a different place, then you will waste a huge amount of time getting ready to study rather than, if you had an organised space for study, being able to plunge right into your work without wasting valuable time. Of course, life is not always perfect and it may be that you are simply unable to earmark a space that is solely for your use when studying. Maybe you must share a space with other students or you must put everything away after each studying session so that the space can be used for something else. In this case, make sure that you are able to store your books, notes and equipment safely. Clear out a nearby drawer for this purpose, or, at a pinch, you could buy a large plastic storage box and use that. Ideally, though, you need to get your hands on your own exclusive space, so let's look at this in a bit more detail.

Your first priority must be to decide on your space for studying. Where will it be? Ideally, it will be a space of your own where you will be able to get organized and then leave your things ready for you to come back to them after each break in your studying. In considering the space you have, your *minimum* requirements should include:

- A writing surface with plenty of space for your books, papers, pens etc.
- At least one bookshelf.
- Room for your computer if you have one.
- A light in the correct place – not shining on to your computer screen or into your eyes – that is suitable for reading by.
- A chair at the correct height for your computer and for your desk for writing. Remember that you will be spending some time in this chair so it should be comfortable and support your back.

Your setup will, to a certain extent, depend on whether or not you have a computer. Most people do these days but it may be that you have decided that you can manage with the facilities provided at college, university, at work or in libraries.

---

**Top tip**

Keep your working space tidy and well-organized. If it always looks a mess then you will be far less likely to want to come back to it.

---

Having created an efficient space for your study area, you will now need to organize it so that everything is to hand. Make sure that you have plenty of files so that your notes and handouts can be filed away in a way that makes it easy to find them when you need them. Simply piling everything up and hoping that you will be able to lay your hands on them at some future date will not save you time in the long run. You will lose vital pieces of information and waste precious time and patience shuffling through papers over and over again.

Other things that you will find useful – or even essential – to keep in this area will include:

- Course books – some you will have had to buy and others you will be able to borrow from a library.
- A diary or wall planner so that you can note the dates on which assignments are due.
- Plenty of A4 paper – plain copier paper if you are using a computer and lined, punched paper for handwritten notes.
- Ring files – it's a good idea to use a different coloured ring file for each different subject that you're studying.
- A dictionary and a thesaurus.
- A calculator.
- Assorted items of equipment such as a stapler, a hole punch, glue and sticky tape, correcting fluid, ruler, highlighters, pens and pencils, small notepads, spare disks for your computer, scissors and so on.

You should find a space for all these things when you are setting up your study area. Don't just put them on the workspace, thinking you'll get organized later – do it now and save yourself lots of time and frustration. Keep the space tidy by filing loose notes as soon as you've made them (use A4 paper rather than reporter's pads or notebooks to make this easier) and putting everything away when you've finished for the day.

If you have a computer as part of your studying setup, you will need to organize that too. The first – and most important – piece of advice about working with a computer is to *back up your files*. Keep backup copies of everything that you've saved to the hard drive and also of anything you have on floppy disks. Don't be tempted to leave this job – it's vital. Just imagine how you would feel if your computer crashed and you lost that essay you'd just spent days researching, organizing and writing. Work out how many hours it would take you to rewrite that piece of work (and add on the time you would spend desperately searching your hard drive in an attempt to get it back). It would take a lot longer than getting organized would, right? Then back up your files! Apart from making sure that you have backup copies of all your work, there are other things you can do to ensure that you keep your computer and all the hard work you do with it in tip-top order:

- Use a separate disk for saving each subject.
- Keep your disks safe in a storage box, with all the disks suitably labelled.

- Use a different folder on your hard drive for each subject that you are studying. Within these folders you can then use sub-folders for assignments, notes etc. There is more advice about using your computer to learn in Chapter 09.
- Name files on the hard drive so that you immediately know what is in that file. Don't be tempted to use dates and very abbreviated titles – you'll forget what is in the file and waste time opening them to check them out when you're looking for a particular file.

Whether it's your computer or your desk and your notes, the most important thing to remember is that getting it organized – and keeping it that way – will save you time.

## Making time for studying

In addition to finding and organizing the physical space for studying, you must also consider how you will find and organize the time in your schedule. We all have the same 24 hours in a day – that's 168 hours every week – but some people seem to find the time to do far more than others. The reality is that we have choices as to how we spend our time in just the same way as we all have choices about how we spend our money. Some habits and personality traits become a drain on our time resources and it is these that we need to change if we want to spend our time wisely. We can all achieve more if we learn a bit about time management and then put what we have learned into action. Use this checklist to see if you have too many drains on your time resources.

Tick each box that applies to you:

1 I am easily distracted. ☐
2 I am often late for appointments. ☐
3 I have not set myself achievable goals. ☐
4 I do not understand what motivates me. ☐
5 I check my e-mails more than twice a day. ☐
6 I frequently put things off. ☐
7 I chat for hours on the phone – even when I have a deadline to meet. ☐
8 I frequently stop when I am working to make a cup of tea or coffee. ☐
9 I read absolutely everything I am told to read. ☐
10 I don't keep a diary. ☐

Give yourself one mark for each answer you have ticked and add up your score and check it as follows:

*If you scored 1 or 2*: You don't have much of a problem with time management when you are studying. Read the remainder of this section to pick up a few tips to help you and then simply keep going.

*If you scored 3 to 5*: You have a few issues with time management and will benefit from putting some of the advice that follows in this section into practice.

*If you scored 6 to 8*: Your lack of time management skills will be causing problems, so read the remainder of this section carefully and, most importantly, take action. Do not put it off.

*If you scored 9 or 10*: You need some help to manage your time. You are probably not managing your time at all and will be wasting a lot of it. Read the advice that follows then make some changes to your routines.

Before we look at time management in a bit more detail, here are the basics of improving how you manage your time:

- Do not procrastinate.
- Set achievable goals.
- Keep track of your time.
- Stay focused.
- Get organized.
- Plan to succeed.

Although we all have the same number of hours to spend, many of us have extra demands on our time and it can be incredibly difficult to juggle all these demands. It may be that you have a small child – or several – who need care on a daily basis, an older family who have hectic social lives and you are their taxi service, a challenging teenager to deal with or an elderly relative to care for. Or you may have a stressful job with long hours that leaves you feeling drained when you return home. However, whatever your commitments, you have decided to pursue a course of study so you need to learn to juggle your commitments so that you spend your time to the best possible effect. Having chosen to study, you must give that your best shot or it will have been a waste of time to start the course. So, what can you do to decide how to allocate your time effectively and to lessen your responsibilities so that you have more time available for your studies?

# Time-saving tips

## How do you spend your time?

Find out how you spend your time now. Unless you know *exactly* what you are doing with the 24 hours you have available to you every day, then you will not be able to make any effective changes. Write down everything you do from getting up to going to bed – cleaning your teeth, feeding the dog, travelling, sitting doing nothing – absolutely everything. This is known as a *time audit*. If you can do this for a whole week, you will find that this is a very enlightening exercise. Then add up how much time you spend on regular tasks and pastimes such as sleeping, travelling, working, eating and so on.

Subtract all these chunks of time from the 168 hours in a week and see what you're left with. Invariably there will be a leftover period and this is how much time you already have available – without making a single change to your daily life and habits – to spend on your new task of studying. Now look at exactly what you are doing during a week and how much time you're spending on non-essential things. Do you need to spend half an hour every day reading a newspaper? Could you group all your phone calls together on one evening and limit the time you spend on each? Could you go food shopping once a week instead of two or three times? Revising your habits in any of these areas could yield a couple of hours every single week – enough time to write a report or plan out an essay.

## Make a plan

Get a large day-to-a-page diary or make yourself a 24-hour planner on your PC and put all your commitments in it – include work, exercise, sleep, and your family duties, a little 'slack' where you'll be able to catch up on things that have slipped a little or take longer than you thought and don't forget to add your social life. Now you should be able to see just where you will be able to allocate time to your studies. Look carefully for those times when you have not planned anything specific to do. Look also for the things that you are planning in but which are not essential or errands that could be grouped together to save you time. Could you get up an hour earlier or go to bed later to enable you to fit in everything you want – or need – to do?

Then write in all your assignment deadlines and exam dates and plan in all the extra time you will need to spend on your studying at these times. Now, write in your studying schedule where you can fit it in. Actually writing it down – as you would a dental appointment or family visit – will make it seem more like a commitment. If you can make this plan visible to your partner and children or others who feel they have a call on your time – then you will have an even greater chance of making your plan work. Alternatives to using a diary or your PC to record your activities and to plan your time could include A4 paper in a loose-leaf file, an electronic organizer or a specially designed time management planner. You must choose the method that works best for you.

## Plan both long term and short term

You could start with a general academic year planner where you will get an overview of what's ahead of you, then move on to planning for the term to come and work your way through to a monthly plan and then go into real detail on a weekly study planner.

## Create new habits

Use your diary to record each time you succeed in following your new habits. At first, all changes in behaviour require thought but if you do it for three or four weeks consecutively (and make an effort to record it, which reinforces the habit) you will soon find that you can do it automatically.

## Set some rules

If everyone who is affected by the time you will have to spend on your course knows what is expected of them, it will be a lot easier to keep to your plans and to meet your goals. Rules you might like to consider could include 'Nobody to interrupt me while I'm studying unless it is really urgent.' You may have to review this rule and give some guidelines as to what you consider to be urgent if you find that you are interrupted for demands for snacks or help in finding lost possessions. What *you* decide regarding what is urgent is what everyone will have to abide by. Another rule that might help is that 'Everyone picks up and puts away their own belongings.' Even very small children are capable of doing this, so don't hesitate. You have different priorities now and waiting on everyone will not fit in with your studying. Make rules too that you will have to follow such as no studying after midnight (unless you're a night owl) or no studying on Sunday afternoons if this is usually a time that you spend with the family.

## Steal a few minutes

Grab small chunks of time whenever you can. A lot can be achieved in small time slots. If you have a 20-minute bus journey every morning, then make sure that you use this time to move your studying efforts forward. Plan an essay, read an article or a chapter of a set book or make a few notes about something you read the previous day. If you drive to work or back from the school run, record tapes of revision notes so that you can listen to them as you drive. You may find that you are unable to concentrate for the whole of the tape but that, if you play it often enough, you will absorb plenty of information and will have avoided wasting your time in a traffic jam. You could also read in the bath or in your lunch hour at work. You will soon find that if you can snatch a few minutes in this way every day you will have achieved a lot without too much disruption to your life by the end of the week.

## Delegate

It is almost always true to say that you are not the only person who can deal with the tasks you have taken on. Do you drive your son or daughter to various activities every evening? Could you share this task with another child's parents? Take turns at this task (or delegate it to your partner, perhaps) and you will have several hours extra to enable you to get stuck into an assignment for your course.

## The 80:20 rule

This rule says that 20% of your time will be spent on productive work while the remaining 80% will be spent on tasks that are lower priority, unproductive or unnecessary. You must find your 80% and cut out as much of the work in that 80% as you possibly can. If you are fanatical about keeping your house clean, for example, decide how often you really need to dust or vacuum – could you miss this job out occasionally and allocate the time you've saved to studying? Do you watch television programmes that you haven't specifically chosen to watch – you just sit there after your favourite programme has ended and continue to watch until it's time for bed? Cut out those programmes and how much time will you have freed up? Do you have a lie-in on weekend mornings? Could you have a lie-in on either Saturday or Sunday rather than both? Or could you set a slightly earlier time to get up than at present but still giving you a little extra time in bed?

## Get organized

If everyone in the family could write their social commitments down on a wall planner, it will save time that you currently spend asking everyone what they're doing at the weekend or it may stop your daughter surprising you with a request to collect her from a friend's house just when you'd started a complicated piece of work for your course. Another way that getting organized will save you time is that you will not waste time looking for things on a regular basis if your cupboards and drawers are tidy and everything put back in place after use.

## Talk to your family

Explain to them what you are trying to achieve and how important your studying is to you. It is essential that you enlist their support if you are to achieve your aims. If you have previously spent all your spare time catering to their needs it may be difficult at first for them to accept that you will sometimes have to put their requirements second and that you will be spending time doing something for you, but if you can make them understand the situation and ask for their help in achieving your goals, most family members will be cooperative. Ask them how they think they can help you – you may be surprised at some of the ideas they come up with and with the level of support they are prepared to give you.

## Introduce changes gradually

Do not make the changes all at once, as this will be far too painful both to you and to your family. If you need help to run the house then have a week where your family helps with one small job. When you've got that up and running, introduce another change at home. This also applies at work. If your aim is to leave on time every evening instead of working late, you may need to leave on time on one day per week for a while and then start cutting down on the time you work on other days until you have reduced your hours to a more manageable level.

## Make good use of lists

Each week, make a list of all the things you plan to achieve that week – research goals, progress towards an assignment and so on – and then cross off each item as and when you have completed it. Not only is this an organized approach that will prevent you from forgetting some vital task but it can also be very satisfying to cross things off the list. It will give you a sense of achievement and keep you motivated.

## Review your progress regularly

Keep track of how closely you've stuck to your plans and how much progress you've made towards your goals. If you're going off track you need to find this out as soon as possible and then take corrective action. There is little point in making elaborate plans with every assignment noted down, revision time planned in and time blocked out for lectures if you ignore the plan and make little or no progress and then only realize this when you fail your exams at the end of your course. You need to know about problems and rectify them or get help.

## Don't put it off

We are all guilty of some level of procrastination but if we want to achieve anything in our lives, we must get on and do it. This rule of 'do it now' applies to the things we must do to manage our time as well as to the tasks we must do to complete a course of study. It helps if you understand why you are putting something off and the most common reason associated with starting an essay or other assignment is the fear of failure. Conquer your fear of failure (if you don't start, you'll never, ever finish) and make a start.

---

### Top tip

In your efforts to save time, do not be tempted to eliminate completely the activities that relax you. Keeping yourself fit, healthy and relaxed is essential to allow you to work to your full potential.

---

If you're still looking for just a bit more time to save, take a look at your study methods and see where you could work more efficiently:

- *Never rewrite.* Your notes don't need to be super-neat, so don't waste time writing them out again. Write assignments directly on to your computer rather than writing them first in long hand (remember you can use the cut and paste facility later if you need to change the order around slightly).
- *Focus.* Don't work on things that will not take you closer to your goals or spend too much time on relatively simple, short assignments.
- *Be brief.* Your notes should not be a word-for-word repetition of what the lecturer has said or a rambling essay on a book or article you've read. They should be short, so use lots of headings and write in keywords and phrases rather than complete sentences.
- *Be tidy.* If you know where all your notes are and they're filed away in a logical order, you won't waste time searching for one piece of information or for the notes you know will help you to complete an assignment. File your notes away as soon as you've made them so that the filing task doesn't get out of hand.
- *Make filing easy.* Use a separate piece of paper for every topic so that you can file them in a logical order and then file them in a lever arch file so that you can extract them as needed.

## Understanding your learning style

The way we learn differs from person to person and many ways of classifying learning styles have been tried. One of the most popular analyses of ways we learn centres on the senses we use to absorb information – the *primary learning pathway*. It is helpful to find our own learning style as this will ensure that we can look out for ways to learn that are appropriate for us and will make learning easier. The three learning styles that have been defined by psychologists working on neuro-linguistic programming (NLP) projects are:

- Visual – this is where learning is sight based.
- Auditory – here the primary sense involved in learning is hearing.
- Kinaesthetic – this involves the sense of touch.

Try this quick quiz to discover your learning style. A lot of the clues to defining our learning style can be found in the things we say or how we tackle everyday tasks. Read these questions and decide which answer you would be more likely to give:

1   When checking the spelling of a word you would say:
    a   That looks right.
    b   That sounds right.
    c   That feels right.

2   If you're trying to reassure someone that you understand what they are saying to you:
    a   I can see what you're saying.
    b   I hear what you're saying.
    c   I feel that I understand what you're saying.

3   If you're buying a new piece of furniture or equipment for your home, what would influence your decision the most:
    a   How it looks.
    b   The description given by the salesperson.
    c   How it feels when you touch it.

4   What would be most useful to you if you were trying to assemble this new item of furniture of equipment?
    a   A video of it being assembled.
    b   Recorded instructions.
    c   Trying to do it yourself.

5   What would help you to understand a mathematical problem?
    a   Diagrams about how it can be solved.
    b   Listening to someone's explanation of the solution.
    c   A model of how it all fits together.

6   If you're trying to understand some new computer software, would you:
    a   Read the manual that came with the software.
    b   Ask a friend to come over and tell you how they use it.
    c   Sit at the keyboard trying it out.

7   If you were choosing a book to read for pleasure, what would make you buy?
    a   The look of the cover.
    b   A friend talking about it and saying it was worth reading.
    c   The book feels heavy and glossy.

8    How are you most likely to give someone directions to your home?

    **a** Writing the directions down.

    **b** Telling them which roads to take.

    **c** Drawing them a map.

9    Think back to when you were at school. Which sort of lessons did you most enjoy?

    **a** Where the teachers drew diagrams or gave us a textbook.

    **b** Where the teacher told us about a subject.

    **c** Practical sessions.

10   Where would you be most likely to find a review of a film that makes you want to go to see it?

    **a** In a newspaper or magazine.

    **b** On the radio or from a friend telling you about it.

    **c** On the TV.

Now add up all your a's, b's and c's and check out the styles below.

*If you got mostly a's*: Your learning style is visual. You learn best by seeing things. This might be by reading books or by watching television or educational videos. Anything you can do to enhance the visual impact of your learning materials will improve your learning experience and help you to remember what you have learned. For you, it will be a good idea to use different coloured highlighters and pencils when making your notes and to make sure that you include plenty of spider diagrams (more about these in Chapter 04), tables and graphs in your revision materials.

You will know that you are a visual person if you say things like 'I see what you mean' or 'I can't see what the problem is.'

*If you got mostly b's*: Your learning style is auditory and the most important sense that you use in learning is that of hearing. You will learn best by discussing things with fellow students or listening to audio tapes or lectures. Debates will help you tremendously and you could try explaining something that you find difficult to understand to someone else who has no knowledge of the subject. Your revision can be helped along by recording yourself reading your notes out loud (keep them brief or you'll spend too long doing the recording) and then playing the tapes back to yourself repeatedly.

The things that you will say that will show that hearing is your primary learning pathway include 'Sounds OK to me' and 'I hear what you're saying.'

*If you got mostly c's*: Your learning style is kinaesthetic. This means that the sense of touch is most important to you. Practical learning sessions will help you to retain information so you should make sure that you take part in as many experiments as you can and get hold of practical objects in connection with your studies that you are able to feel and touch.

The clues in the language you use that show that touch is most important to you include 'It feels good to me' or 'That touched a nerve'.

Although everyone will have a dominant sense that dictates their learning style, the very best approach for all students is one that uses a combination of all senses to get the message across. Individual students will need to be aware of their own preferences and then play to their strengths as we have just detailed, while using materials that combine all the learning styles. Now that you know what is likely to work best for you, seek out the type of materials that suit you and will help you to retain the information you will need to be successful in your studies.

Do not, however, let knowing your learning style blind you to all the other ways to learn. If you concentrate exclusively on methods that you think will suit your way of learning you may miss something that would really help you. It is important, while knowing and catering for your learning style, to experiment with different methods of learning. We are all a mixture of styles and personality traits and these can change according to our mood and what's going on in our lives so we must remain open minded about learning methods.

## Motivation

The single most important factor in whether or not you will find a course enjoyable and productive is motivation. If you are highly motivated and genuinely want to make a success of your studies, then chances are you will. If you really want to improve your study skills, then reading this book and putting its principles into practice will ensure that you arm yourself with a set of skills that you can use in whatever course of study you choose to undertake. Of course, you must do more than acquire study skills – you must be prepared to put in the work that will make the most of these skills and ensure that you can complete your course of study successfully.

Some people seem to be motivated to do things and it is difficult to see how they have achieved this motivated state. Partly this is probably because of their personalities – these fortunate people are usually optimists who have high levels of self belief and determination to achieve. Typically, they will see any problems that may crop up as challenges to be overcome or as opportunities to show what they can do. But if you are a little unsure of yourself and can see only difficulties when you contemplate your new course of study, then you need to build your self confidence (take a look back at Chapter 01 for some more tips on confidence) and work on your motivation.

Motivation is often all about our reasons for wanting to achieve something, so examining why you want to take – and pass! – your course will help with focusing on and increasing your motivation. If you can identify positive outcomes that really matter to you and keep working towards these rather than just forcing yourself into the drudgery of studying you will be on the way to becoming more motivated. Complete this quick quiz to help you identify your motivating factors.

Here is a list of possible reasons you may have for taking your course. Pick the five most important reasons for you:

- To get a specific job.
- To use it as a stepping stone to further qualifications.
- To gain promotion at work.
- To earn more money.
- To learn about a subject that I find interesting.
- To change my life.
- To improve my prospects.
- To gain control of my life.
- To prove to myself that I can achieve something.
- To prove to my family and/or friends that I am intelligent.
- Because all my friends are going on to further education.
- To get a better social life.
- To make up for wasting my educational opportunities when I was younger.

Now put your five reasons in order of importance and think about them carefully. Knowing just why you're doing something is usually enough to supply motivation – especially if the reasons are compelling enough and that you can see how the course will serve you.

---

**Top tip**

Keep this list of your motivational factors somewhere where you can see it. Make sure that you look at it frequently during your studies, as it will help to get you through the inevitable rough patches.

---

One thing getting in the way of your motivation may be stress. We'll look at how we can keep this under control in the next section.

## Managing stress

There are many different stresses involved in studying. You may be a student away from home and finding it difficult to study independently for the first time or you may be a mature student with myriad demands from your family or your employers on your mind. You may feel that the course of study you have taken on is beyond your capabilities or you may be feeling that you have nowhere to turn to for help with the work you have to do. Some of the causes of stress may not be related to your study. You may have money worries or one of your close family members may be ill. Whatever the cause of your stress, the important thing is not to let it overwhelm you.

A low level of stress can have a positive effect on your ability to study. If you were not bothered in the slightest by a looming deadline for an assignment, it is highly unlikely that you would produce the best work that you could, and on time. If, by the same token, the assignment is on your mind for several days before it is due and you worry about meeting the deadline, then you are more likely to deliver a competent piece of work on schedule. What is not desirable is an excessively high level of stress. If you are really affected by the amount or difficulty of work you have to produce or the deadlines that you must adhere to, then you may display some or all of the following symptoms:

- Becoming irritable and easily upset.
- Having difficulty sleeping.
- Eating, smoking or drinking too much in an effort to calm your nerves.
- Spending too much time (i.e. all your spare time) studying.
- Thinking that everyone is doing better than you.
- Becoming clumsy.
- Feeling sick at the thought of an assignment.

If you feel like this, you must get help. These are all symptoms of stress and it must be managed so that it is not allowed to affect your health. Wherever and however you are studying there will be sources of support available. You must search them out. If you are at university there will be a whole range of support services. Your first port of call should usually be your tutor. He or she will be able to deal with specific difficulties you may be having with any of the course material and may also have experience in dealing with more general stress.

Your student union will usually have officers able to offer support and, of course, all these services will be confidential. If you are studying a work-related course then the course tutors or your boss/personnel department may all be able to offer support. If you are doing a distance-learning course, you will still have a tutor who will be responsible for offering you help to complete the course successfully. Whichever route you take, the important thing is to get help before it becomes a serious issue. If you allow the problem to get gradually worse and perhaps move from being something that causes you the occasional twinge of discomfort to something that is in danger of seriously damaging your mental and physical health, then by that time your coursework will have suffered and you will find it increasingly difficult to get yourself back on track. If the situation has become serious, apart from seeking help from your tutor or others involved in your studying, you may need to approach your doctor for help with coping with the symptoms of depression or stress.

It is well-known that severe stress can affect memory and brain function as energy is diverted to deal with the stress. If you think that you are suffering from relatively mild stress and want to take steps at a very early stage to help yourself, then you should consider the following:

- Make sure you get enough sleep – an hour spent having a nap (occasionally!) will be beneficial and you must try to get a regular six to seven hour's sleep at night, as this is when the brain will refresh itself.
- Plan in some activities that you find relaxing – reading a book for pleasure or listening to music will pay dividends in terms of making you more relaxed and refreshed ready for your studying task.
- Getting organized will make you feel less stressed – put some of the ideas given in the next chapter into practice.
- Get to know yourself – consider what causes you to feel stressed. Keeping a note of times when you feel most stressed will highlight these occasions and then you can make plans to deal with them. It helps to jot down your feelings about these stressful times and situations and then to note your options for resolving the situation. You can then decide, in a calm, unstressed way, how to deal with things that bother you. Taking an organized approach to your stress like this will mean that you can make steady progress through your course without letting stress build up.
- Deal with the most important things first. If you have a number of things on your mind that are beginning to bother you, you could list them, prioritize them according to urgency and importance and then deal with them one by one. You will find that dealing with just one thing at a time – and knowing that this is the highest priority – will immediately take the stress out of most situations.
- Realize that you are not the only one. Most of your fellow students will be feeling anxious about all sorts of things – including the very same things that are worrying you. They will be wondering what everyone else thinks of them, whether everyone else is finding the course easier than they are, whether they will be able to cope with the workload, whether they will meet their next assignment deadline and so on. Many students, especially mature students with family responsibilities will also be worrying about their finances, childcare facilities, family reactions to their studies, finding the confidence to make friends, job commitments and so on. The solution to this is to get together, if at all possible, with other students. Form a support group, a study group, a social group or an online group – any one of these will help you to realize that your worries are common ones and you will benefit from others' experience.

- Get some exercise – getting outdoors for a while or doing something that uses up energy (it could be going to the gym, jogging or walking, gardening, swimming or even a bit of housework) will make you feel better and more relaxed. Getting plenty of exercise will also ensure that you sleep well to boost memory.

- Try meditation – if you can learn how to do this you may be able to think more clearly and see your way through your temporary difficulties. A simple way to start is to sit quietly and simply focus on your breathing. Breathe in, breathe out and keep doing this until your mind is quiet. If thoughts intrude, acknowledge them and let them go, then go back to concentrating on your breathing. If you persevere, you will find that you become relaxed. There are many books about meditation that you could try if this is the sort of thing that you feel would help you.

- Eat well – aim to keep your blood sugar level in good balance to ensure efficient brain functioning. Eat a wide variety of foods including plenty of fruit, vegetables and whole grains.

- Drink plenty of water – if you wait until you're thirsty before you drink, then you are probably already dehydrated. Dehydration can affect your ability to remember and to concentrate. Don't be tempted to drink too much coffee instead of water – caffeine can give you an initial boost but will soon cause a lack of concentration.

Stress can be helpful if it gives you the impetus to get up and get going. If it gets beyond that then you should take action. If it's mild then you can help yourself but if it is severe than you need to tap into the support that will be there for you in various forms. If it becomes more acute it will rapidly affect your coursework and will usually result in your missing deadlines and suffering a lack of concentration – neither of which will enhance your chances of getting a good result from your studies. Make sure that stress does not affect your result. Severe stress is not inevitable; it can be managed so that you keep your stress levels under control.

# Getting an overview of your course

Often when you first start a new course of study, your enthusiasm is high and you just want to dive right in. You rush out and buy the set books, perhaps mark your assignments on your shiny, new wall planner and enter the exam dates in your diary. But you shouldn't. Your first task should be to get an overview of your course. This will put you in the driving seat as it will help you to prepare for what is to come and if you take control at this very early stage, you will find that your motivation and energy for the course will soar. You will be able to see clearly where you are going and what your goals are.

How can you take control in this way? If you're lucky, there will be an easy way to get an overview of your course. Often your course tutors or designers will have prepared a summary of the course that details the required learning outcomes. It may also have a paragraph or two that give the aims of the course. Don't be tempted to ignore these paragraphs, as they are very important. Knowing what you are aiming for is vital. As soon as you're accepted on to a course you should find out if a booklet of this kind has been produced and, if so, get hold of a copy without delay. This will be your map for your studies. It tells you where you are going. You will then be able to work out how you are going to get there.

Your next step in gaining an overview should be to find out exactly how the course is going to be assessed. It may be that the only thing that matters in whether you are judged to have passed or failed the course is the mark you get in the examination at the end of the course. Alternatively, your coursework may also be taken into account or even the entire course mark may be based on the marks you get for your assignments. When you know how the assessment works, you will be able to see where the bulk of your time should be spent. If the course is based on continual assessment, then you will have to make sure that every single piece of work that you complete – whether it be an essay, a report, a computer-marked assignment or a presentation that you have to do – should be as good as you can make it. In this case there will be no room for coasting along during the year and then revising furiously for the end-of-year exam. Having said that, coasting is not a good idea even if the course result depends solely on the exam. In this case, steady progress, understanding all the different aspects of your course and sorting out problems as you go along will get you the best results and be far less stressful. However, if the course result does depend on how you do in the final examination then you will obviously need to plan in time for the extra revision involved.

There are various other sources of information that will help you to get an overview of your course and give you plenty of clues as to how you should be tackling your studies. These include past examination papers, timetables and assignment details. It is important that you combine all these additional sources of information about your course with what you have found out about the expected learning outcomes and assessment. Go through all the materials you have collected and highlight or make a separate note of how each session, assignment or exam question ties in with each of the learning outcomes. It can be a good idea to write each of the learning outcomes on a separate sheet of paper then seek out and add to each sheet all the things that contribute to that particular learning outcome. For example, you may take the first of your learning outcomes then add any exam questions or assignments that directly relate to that outcome and also note on this sheet of paper the points in the course where you will learn the things you need to know to achieve that outcome. Having done this it will become clear just how you are going to get from where you are now to where you want to be at the end of the course. *Do not rush this task.* You will find it useful and productive to allow yourself plenty of time to reflect on the journey you are about to take. If you can think clearly now and get straight in your mind the way in which you will tackle your studies, it will pay dividends later.

Gaining an overview of a course is an important part of becoming an effective learner and is therefore an essential study skill to master. You should do this before you start any other work on your course so that you can see what you are aiming at and how you are going to get there. Your goals will become clearer and you will have developed a map through your studies for yourself.

## Summary

In this chapter you have learned:

- That having a study space for yourself can have many benefits including making you more productive, getting fewer interruptions and getting you into the right frame of mind.
- The most important thing is to get organized – in your study space, in your time management and with your computer (back up files frequently!).

- How to manage your time – including finding out how you spend your time now, planning your schedule using a diary or wall planner, developing and reinforcing new habits, using short blocks of time to study, discussing your needs with family and friends in an attempt to limit interruptions and gain some time for study, using lists, stopping procrastination and reviewing your progress regularly.

- How to discover – and make the most of – your own learning style. This could be visual (where learning is sight based), auditory (where the primary sense involved in learning is hearing) or kinaesthetic (involving the sense of touch).

- The five most important reasons you have for taking your course to discover what motivates you.

- About the symptoms of stress and how to manage your stress levels during your studies. Ways include getting organized, getting enough sleep and relaxation, exercising and learning relaxation techniques such as meditation.

- How to get an overview of your course so that you can see what you are aiming at and how you are going to get there. This includes a summary of the learning outcomes, method of assessment, past exam papers and details of assignments and timetable.

## Quick revision test

1 Name three of the things you need to arrange – as a minimum – for your study space.
2 What is the most important thing to do on a regular basis when using a computer for study?
3 Give two ways that you can save time while studying.
4 Name the three different learning styles discussed in this chapter.
5 Give two symptoms of severe stress.

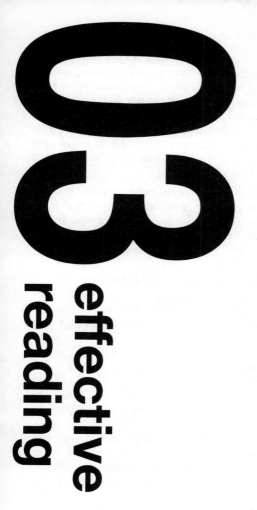

# 03 effective reading

**In this chapter you will learn:**
- the difference between reading for pleasure and reading to learn
- how to plan your reading tasks
- how to speed read or skim texts to save time.

# Introduction

Reading is central to any studying task so it is vital that you do it as effectively and efficiently as you possibly can. Now, if you're saying 'But I can read already!', you must take into account that being able to make sense of words on a page is not the same as learning from your reading. There are a number of reading strategies that you can adopt to ensure that what you read is useful and appropriate to your course of study and also that you read in an organized way and retain a lot of what you read so that you can use it in the future.

If you have problems with reading – perhaps because of dyslexia or some other difficulty – get help early. Your tutors will have ways to make things easier or will be able to point you in the direction of some practical help and support.

# How reading for study is different from reading for pleasure

Learning is an active pursuit. It is not something that just happens. When we read to learn, we need to actively gather information, make sense of it and organize it so that we can use it effectively to get the best return from the time we invest in our study. And, of course, in most cases we need to memorize certain aspects of what we have read so that we can use the information to help us pass exams. Reading for pleasure, by the same token, is something that we can do while we're relaxing; we can let a favourite book or the morning's newspaper just wash over us and we don't necessarily remember any of it. Mostly we make no effort at all to remember it; we just take the pleasure from it. When reading for pleasure we may choose newspapers, magazines, romantic, historical, mystery or thriller novels and non-fiction books featuring subjects of particular interest to us. We read things that appeal to us for a variety of reasons and then we let them go.

In contrast to this, reading for study means that we have to read totally different materials and make a concerted effort to remember them. We may have an endless list of books recommended for our course of study, journals, magazines and articles that develop points relevant to the course, newspapers, course books and also research materials from the Internet – and we may not have chosen to read any of these things had we not been doing this particular course of study.

Studying will be infinitely easier if we can engage with our subject and have a genuine interest in at least part of it. When we take part in academic reading we are aiming to increase our knowledge of the subject and we also have the aim of passing our course of study. At first this will seem like an impossible task but it does become easier as we become more familiar with what is required of us. Academic reading is done in stages. First, we read to gain a general understanding of our subject and some background knowledge. As we learn more and add to this background knowledge, we move on to developing the ideas that are new to us and then to finding different opinions and arguments about different areas of our subject.

As academic reading is different from reading simply for pleasure, we must approach the task in a different way. We need to have a strategy, to set goals for our reading and to have ways of knowing whether we have achieved what we set out to do. For this we need to plan and this is the topic covered in the next section.

## Planning your reading task and setting goals

If you are reading to study, you will need to have a reading strategy to ensure that you get the most from your hard work. Do not just pick up a book from the recommended reading list for your course, start reading at page one and then plough painfully through the book until you get to the end. This will be time consuming, boring and not very effective. Before you set off on your reading journey, you need a map to show you where you are going – and you will have to make this map yourself. Ask yourself where you want to be at the end of your journey. Your answer to this question must be as specific as you can make it and tailored to the text you are reading and the course you are taking. Try not to answer the question of where you want to be by saying something like 'I want to know a bit about X or Y' or 'I have to broaden my knowledge of A or B.' Better replies would be 'The course requires a detailed knowledge of this process so I have a reading list to get me to that point' or 'I need to know this writer's opinion on X and I believe that this article will give me this.'

There are a number of things that must be taken into account when putting your map together:

- An overview of your course. What are the main topics that you will have to master? Are some more important than others? Do you have examples of the assignments you will have to complete and copies of past examination papers?
- What are the planned learning outcomes for your course? If you are unsure about this, ask your tutor.
- Is there a recommended reading list? This list will have been put together by your tutors or the people who designed the course and it may or may not be thought necessary to read in its entirety. It might be desirable to read all the books on the list but it will quite often not be possible and you will need to be selective about what you read.
- What do you know already? Is this a subject that you have already studied at some level? If so, you may have a different starting point with your reading map than someone who is coming to the subject with no knowledge at all.
- Try to get hold of the assignments you will have to complete and to compile a list of the most likely exam questions – this will make your journey far more predictable.

---

**Top tip**

Don't forget to check the date of publication of any books and texts that you need to ensure that you are getting up-to-date information.

---

With your current level of knowledge as your starting point and the stated learning outcomes as your finishing point, you will need to plot your route through the topics to be covered. You will need to take into account the amount of time that you will be able to allocate to your journey and the assignments that you will have to cover – the stops along the way. It is at this point in developing your strategy that you will have to pay close attention to how you allot your available time for study to the various tasks you will have to undertake – of which reading is just one. If you have any doubt about how to do this, turn back to the section on time management in Chapter 02.

There are also more specific reading tasks and these also need to be planned. For example, if you are reading a number of articles to find alternative arguments to include in an essay, you will read differently to if you are trying to find just the right quote to finish that essay. If you are trying to gain an overview of a topic, then that will again be a different reading task. For each reading task you will need to ask questions such as the following to clarify your goals:

- What information am I looking for?
- Is this information in the text I am about to read?
- How will I use this information?
- Do I need to remember this and in what level of detail? Don't make the mistake of thinking that your goal in reading a text is to remember it. Your primary aim should always be to understand it and then to retain enough in your mind about the ideas that the author of the book or article is trying to get across. Making notes – *active learning* – will usually help with this. If you can work with the ideas, think about them and compare them with other views you may have read, then you will have achieved one of your reading goals.
- Exactly how will reading this help me with the stated learning outcomes? **NB** If you're not sure whether the article or book you are about to read will help you reach your goals, you must ask yourself why you're reading it.

Now, you've set yourself a strategy, know what you're aiming for and how you're going to get there, how will you carry out the actual reading tasks?

## Speed reading

Most students complain that they do not have time to read everything that is expected of them. This is undoubtedly true and it is necessary to be selective about what we read. We must read the most important texts and maybe just skim the remainder so that we understand what information is contained in them – more about skimming later.

Even when we have pared down the amount we have to read, it will still be important to read quickly, so how can we improve our average reading speed? Here are a few things you can do to read more quickly:

- *Get comfortable.* If you are relaxed when you sit down to read, your level of comprehension will improve and your reading speed will increase when you understand what you are reading.

- *Read with a purpose.* Decide what questions you want to answer from reading this particular text and ignore sections that do not add to this answer.

- *Focus on groups of words rather than on each individual word.* This will mean that your eyes will be jumping along the lines, resting on a few words at a time so that you understand the sense of the text without even seeing some of the words. By doing this the number of times that your eyes pause and fix on a word will reduce and will make the reading task quicker. With practice, you will find that not only do you get better at this but also you will stop noticing many of the smaller, 'joining words' such as 'and', 'the', 'but' or 'because'. This will not affect the meaning of the sentences too much.

- *Notice words that will give you a clue as to the direction of the argument.* Words such as 'however', 'although' and 'nevertheless' signal that a change of ideas is imminent while words such as 'also', 'moreover' or 'in addition' let you know that the argument is being developed. A conclusion is usually signalled with words like 'consequently', 'to sum up', 'therefore', 'thus' and, of course, 'in conclusion'.

- *Use a guide.* Moving your finger fairly quickly down the page (just keep your finger on one side of the text and move straight down – don't try to track every word as this will usually have the effect of slowing you down) can help you not only to keep your place in the text but also will speed you up as you try to keep pace with your finger. You could also try using a sheet of paper as a tracker.

- *Move your eyes forward continually.* Lingering on a word or group of words will slow you down and interrupt your rhythm. Also going back in the text to check something that you might not quite have caught will slow you down considerably, so you will have to resist this temptation.

- *Don't move your lips!* Many people say the words to themselves as they read – or even read out loud – but this, too, will slow you down.

- *Practise.* Spend some time every day reading as fast as you can and you will soon improve your average speed.

Improving your reading speed is essential to effective study so this is something that you should pay particular attention to. However, sometimes reading slowly is necessary too. It is not desirable to race through every bit of information that you are given to read as sometimes you will need to read more carefully than speed reading allows. This could include when you are reading a text with detailed instructions or really densely packed information. It would also include situations where you are required to closely analyse texts. So, work hard at increasing your average reading speed but remember that there will be times when it is more appropriate to read slowly.

You may be in the habit of quickly assessing the information in a text by checking the beginning and end and running your eye over the text. This is not speed reading, it is skimming. This is a very useful skill to have and in the next section we will look into how this is done.

---

**Top tip**

Adjust your reading speed in line with the type of text you're reading and your aims in reading it.

---

# Skimming

This is also known as *selective reading* and means that you do not read a book from cover to cover but simply select the bits that you need to read in order to find particular information or to judge whether or not the text is suitable for your purpose.

To skim a book, start with the front and back covers. The book title and subtitle will obviously tell you the subject matter contained in the book, while the back cover blurb will usually indicate the level of student at whom the book is aimed and more detail about what is covered in the book. Next, look at the contents page. If you do not find what you are looking for here, try the index.

Next you can start on the chapters. Perhaps from your check on the contents and index you will have decided that only one or two chapters are worthy of your time and attention. Read the first and last paragraphs of each of the chapters that interest you. This is where the main ideas and conclusions will usually be found. If there is a summary at the end of each chapter read this too.

At this point you should have got a great deal of useful information out of a relatively small amount of reading. You will have gathered the main points and ignored the supporting facts and arguments that are often contained in the body of each paragraph. Sometimes, of course, it will be necessary for you to read the whole thing to find these supporting facts but you will often find that skimming will produce sufficient information and save you spending hours reading a lot of detail. Alternatively, it can prove to you whether or not it will be worth your investing the time needed to read the whole text.

It is useful to make brief notes as you skim a text as it is easy to forget information acquired at this speed.

# Active reading – developing a reading strategy

To read effectively and to put our reading time to the very best use possible, we must add an active element to it rather than letting the words flow over us. We need to engage with the text and make sure that we get just what we need from it. To do this we must ask questions continually and react to the answers. A word here about marking books. Unless the book is yours (and you find it acceptable to make marks in books – many people find it almost impossible to put even a pencil mark in the margins) you should not mark a book but make photocopies of relevant sections and then be interactive with those copies. Here are some of the questions that you should ask as you read:

- What is the main point of this book, chapter, essay or article? Look for clues before you begin by checking the contents page, the back cover blurb or the title and sub-heading in the case of an article or essay.
- What is the main idea in this paragraph? This is usually contained in the first sentence or so. Highlight or underline the two or three words that encapsulate this idea.
- Does this answer the questions that I have on this topic? You should prepare a list of questions that you want to find the answers to before you start to read. If the text you're reading will not answer your questions you are probably wasting your time and should move on to something else.
- How does this compare with what I already know about this topic? Is it introducing a different argument or adding to what you have already learned or maybe it contradicts what you thought was correct? You will have to decide, as you read, how this new information relates to your existing knowledge and how you will mesh this with current ideas.

You may find that if the viewpoint presented is not what you expected you will have to do some further reading to ensure that you can present a balanced case.

- Is the evidence valid and convincing? In most academic texts, the author is making an argument and you will need to decide, in the light of what you already know and from the evidence the author presents, whether he has made his case.
- What is the author's conclusion? This will, of course, be in the final paragraph or chapter and you may find it useful to find it and underline it.

Write down your questions and keep them by you as you read. To complete your active reading task, you will need to quickly reread the text, making notes as you go. Your underlinings or highlighting will help you in this, as they will draw you to the important points. By reading actively and interacting with the text, you will find it much easier to remember the useful bits.

Let's look at how this active reading works in practice by examining how we might deal with reading an article.

## Exercise

Read the following text on choosing a training course, underlining or highlighting the answers to your questions as discussed earlier.

### What is a good training course?

*The answer to that question is simple – and complicated! Put simply, a good training course is one that meets all your requirements. Viewed in more depth, a good training course is one that will be effective – but defining that effectiveness can be quite difficult. You will need to do a lot of research so that you know what skills you already have within your organization and also that you know what training is available – and at what price – outside your company. When you have done this, you will then be in a position to choose your training. Use the checklist that follows to help.*

### Course choice checklist

- *Does the course content match the training need that you have identified? Will successful completion of the course enable your delegates to be able to do what you want them to do?*

- *Will the content keep your delegates interested? If you feel that they may be bored by parts of the material, take care – a bored delegate will not learn much and probably will not ultimately make a more effective employee.*
- *Is it going to be cost effective? i.e. will the benefits justify the costs?*
- *Does the course use the appropriate method of delivery? A course that is very practical and 'hands on' may not necessarily suit a very academic subject with delegates who are senior managers in your organization. Similarly, a course based on listening and then completing written exercises may not be appropriate for practical skills training, with delegates who feel uncomfortable with written materials.*
- *Is the venue convenient and suitable? You must take into account possible costs of accommodation and travel as well as the size and layout of the training rooms.*
- *Is the course the right length? If it is an event of more than a day or two, can the business continue while the delegates are on the course? Will you have to organize temporary cover for any of the trainees' positions? Is the length appropriate for the subject matter?*
- *If you are considering an external course, do you know the training provider? If you have had previous, good experiences of the provider you are proposing to use, then you will be able to purchase a course with confidence. If you don't have personal experience of the training provider, do your research carefully.*
- *Does the course fit in with the culture of your organization? It may be that the training provider in question has a different approach to the subject from that of your business. For example, a course on disciplinary procedures may take a hard line towards minor transgressions. Managers returning from such a course to an organization with a much more lenient view of staff behaviour would find it difficult to put into practice what they have learned. This match between the culture of the organization and the approach of the training is important – unless your aim is to change your organization's culture, of course! In this case, the course will be just one part of your strategy for change.*

*Of course, any training solution that you decide on must meet the objectives set for the training at an affordable price. If you have neglected to set specific objectives, then you will be unable to tell whether the training course that you propose is going to be suitable, so read the earlier section about objectives and make that the very first thing you do after you have gathered all your information about the need for training in your organization.*

*Having set your objectives and obtained sufficient information about the training needs, you will be in a position to differentiate between a good course, i.e. one that is good quality and closely matches your needs, and a bad one.*

*From a delegate's point of view, a successful course is one that is not boring and that teaches them something useful. Obviously only the latter part of this view ties in directly with the objectives of the company paying for the training. However, it is essential that the delegate's needs are taken into account in assessing the effectiveness of a course. It is unlikely that a bored trainee will gain the maximum amount of usable knowledge from any training so the course should be structured so that the delegate's interest is maintained. A good training course will therefore contain a variety of different elements and learning methods.*

How did you find that task? Did you get the gist of that short section of a book on training? Figure 3.1 gives an example of the way you might have marked up the text. In this example the text has been marked up by showing the keywords and phrases in bold type. You might choose to underline or highlight the text.

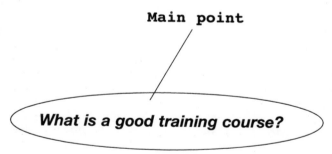

Main point

What is a good training course?

*The answer to that question is simple – and complicated! Put simply, a good training course is one that **meets all your requirements**. Viewed in more depth, a good training course is one that will be **effective** – but defining that effectiveness can be quite difficult. You will need to do a lot of research so that you* know what skills you already have within your organization and also that you know what training is available – and at what price – outside your company. When you have done this, you will then be in a position to choose your training. Use the checklist that follows to help.

## Course choice checklist

- Does the course content **match the training need** that you have identified? Will successful completion of the course enable your delegates to be able to do what you want them to do?
- Will the content **keep your delegates interested**? If you feel that they may be bored by parts of the material, take care – a bored delegate will not learn much and probably will not ultimately make a more effective employee.
- Is it going to be **cost effective**? i.e. will the benefits justify the costs?
- Does the course use the **appropriate method of delivery**? A course that is very practical and 'hands on' may not necessarily suit a very academic subject with delegates who are senior managers in your organization. Similarly, a course based on listening and then completing written exercises may not be appropriate for practical skills training, with delegates who feel uncomfortable with written materials.
- Is the **venue convenient and suitable**? You must take into account possible costs of accommodation and travel as well as the size and layout of the training rooms.
- Is the course the **right length**? If it is an event of more than a day or two, can the business continue while the delegates are on the course? Will you have to organize temporary cover for any of the trainees' positions? Is the length appropriate for the subject matter?
- If you are considering an external course, do you **know the training provider**? If you have had previous, good experiences of the provider you are proposing to use, then you will be able to purchase a course with confidence. If you don't have personal experience of the training provider, do your research carefully.
- Does the course **fit in with the culture** of your organization? It may be that the training provider in question

*has a different approach to the subject from that of your business. For example, a course on disciplinary procedures may take a hard line towards minor transgressions. Managers returning from such a course to an organization with a much more lenient view of staff behaviour would find it difficult to put into practice what they have learned. This match between the culture of the organization and the approach of the training is important – unless your aim is to change your organization's culture, of course! In this case, the course will be just one part of your strategy for change.*

*Of course, any training solution that you decide on must **meet the objectives set for the training** at an affordable price. If you have neglected to set specific objectives, then you will be unable to tell whether the training course that you propose is going to be suitable, so read the earlier section about objectives and make that the very first thing you do after you have gathered all your information about the need for training in your organization.*

*Having set your objectives and obtained sufficient information about the training needs, you will be in a position to differentiate between a good course, i.e. one that is good quality and closely matches your needs, and a bad one.*

*From a delegate's point of view, a successful course is one that is not boring and that teaches them something useful. Obviously only the latter part of this view ties in directly with the objectives of the company paying for the training. However, it is essential that the delegate's needs are taken into account in assessing the effectiveness of a course. It is unlikely that a bored trainee will gain the maximum amount of usable knowledge from any training so the course should be structured so that the delegate's interest is maintained. A good training course will therefore contain a **variety of different elements and learning methods**.*

**Conclusion?**

**figure 3.1** sample text markup

If you go on to make notes on this text, using the bold words as your guide, you would, in this case, finish the task with a few notes on the subject that look like this:

*Main point – what is a good training course?*
*Must meet all requirements and be effective*
*Match training need*
*Keep delegates interested*
*Be cost effective*
*Use appropriate method of delivery*
*Suitable venue*
*Right length*
*Check out provider*
*Does content fit our culture?*
*Set specific objectives for choosing a course*
*Conclusion – should contain a variety of different elements and learning methods*

Now you must ask yourself whether you have learned sufficient information to answer the question 'What is a good training course?' or whether you may feel the need to look up different views on the subject. And finally, to check what you have learned, check how many of the points contained in the extract about choosing a course you can remember – without using your notes, of course. Having read, marked up and then made notes about a text, asking and answering questions as you go, you should find that you retain a significant amount of the information for which you were reading the text.

Now that you have learned about reading with a purpose, you need to find out some ways to record and retain the information you have obtained from your reading, so the next chapter is about note taking.

## Summary

In this chapter you have learned:

- How reading to learn differs from reading for pleasure and how this means that you must develop a reading strategy.
- How to create a map for your reading journey – taking into account your starting point, the assignments you will have to complete along the way and the planned outcomes.

- To clarify your reading goals by asking questions of yourself such as what information you are looking for and how you will use it.
- Some tips on speed reading and skimming for information to save reading time.

## Quick revision test

1 What is usually the first stage in academic reading?
2 When you are speed reading and have decided what questions you need to answer, what should you do about the sections that do not add to your answers?
3 Name two things that you could use as guides or trackers when speed reading.
4 Should you try to read everything as quickly as possible?
5 Name two places in a book where you might discover the main point of a book.

# 04

## note taking

**In this chapter you will learn:**
- why you need notes
- different ways of taking notes
- what to do with your notes.

# When and why you need to take notes

Let's look first at the reasons why you might take notes. You may think that you have to take notes whenever and whatever you are learning because 'that's how things are'. But there are different situations in which you take notes and this may affect the style you choose to make your notes. Note taking is the traditional view of the student's work but it is not an end in itself, so when you're taking notes you need to be aware of the purpose of them. If you take a typical view of a student's work, it might mean that you make notes simply to prove to yourself – or to others – that you are working hard. They become the tangible evidence of your work rate. If you then abandon them in a pile on your desk, never to be looked at again, your work has been wasted. So, before you put pen or highlighter to paper or fingers to keyboard to take some notes, think carefully about why, *exactly*, you are making them.

One of the most common reasons for taking notes is to aid your memory. In this case, your notes will probably be brief jottings made as you read something or listen to a lecture. It is impossible for the vast majority of us to remember most of what we see or hear, so notes can be a useful way to store the facts and arguments we've learned so that we can use them later. Note making also helps the information to be assimilated. The act of writing down the most important points will help them to 'stick'.

Rather than general note taking of information for possible use later, you may be taking notes with a more specific purpose in mind. It may be that you are taking notes on a particular subject with the aim of gaining sufficient information to write an essay. Or perhaps you're making notes for exam revision. Another result of the act of note taking is that it helps you to understand what you are reading. If you have to put a complicated piece of text into your own words, you will understand it far better than if you simply read it.

Whatever the reason may be for taking the notes, it is important that you can find them and use them when necessary, so you must file them as soon as you can.

# Note taking in lectures

We're back to the traditional view of a student's work – sitting in a lecture writing down everything that the lecturer says. But, as we've seen before, that view is not a correct one – the student has to carry out many more tasks than note taking in lectures – and no one could be expected to write down everything someone said in a period of perhaps an hour or more. Note taking in lectures needs to be far more selective – and organized – than that.

Many people make the mistake that the sole purpose of a lecture is to provide material to be learned later but there is far more to it than that and this affects the way lecture notes should be viewed. During a lecture or talk given by a tutor, your prime goal should be to make sense of what you are being told. Notes may be just one element that will help you to do this.

Having accepted that it will be impossible for you to write as quickly as someone speaks and also to let your brain engage with the ideas that are being put across, then you need to develop a strategy for note taking in lectures. In developing this strategy you will have to take into consideration the following:

- Will there be any handouts to cover the contents of the lecture?
- Your way of working – do you usually take copious notes or are you a 'key points' person'?
- Do you need to take notes to stop you from 'wandering off' into your own thoughts, i.e. to keep your concentration focused on the lecture?

Your note-taking strategy for lectures should include, as a minimum, getting down on paper the broad structure of the lecture. The lecturer will often deal with this in the first few seconds of the session so make sure you're ready for it. At the other end of the lecture, the lecturer will usually summarize his or her thoughts and reach a conclusion, so this is another useful time to be giving your full concentration and making sure that you are getting it down on paper. To this outline you should aim to add at least a summary of the main points (in as much detail as you personally find necessary – don't forget that you need to be comfortable with the way of working) and also notes about the sources that the lecturer mentions. You may need to check out these sources for further information or to use them in assignments at a later date. If any questions occur to you during the lecture – maybe there is something you don't quite understand or see the significance of – then you should also jot these down. Making a note of the things you don't understand can be almost as important as noting the things you do understand. You can then ask questions after the lecture or go and find out the information for yourself in the library or in course books.

With the speed at which you will need to be making notes in lectures, you may not be able to pay much attention to the style you make them in, but do try to add some structure. Perhaps you will decide beforehand that any comments of your own will be made at the bottom of the page or to the left hand side or you may get into the habit of using diagrammatic elements such as circling important points, adding arrows and lines to link relevant bits of information. You will also probably develop your own style of shorthand so that you will be able to take notes at speed but still be able to make sense of them later.

Some students use a recorder in lectures. While this might free you from the task of making notes during the lecture and allow you to focus your attention on listening and understanding, it is not a total solution. You will still need to decide how you will use these recorded notes. If you are very disciplined, and are prepared to invest your time not just in attending the lecture but also in going through the recordings later to make notes about the key points, then recording lectures can be an effective note-taking method. You will first, of course, need to check that the recording of lectures is acceptable to the lecturer.

Whichever way of note taking you choose to use in lectures, the most important point is that they should suit you and your way of working. They should be in a form that you can make effective use of at a later date.

# Easy ways to take notes

When you're embarking on a course of study, you must be able to find easy ways to do everything – ways that make sense to you and will be in a format that will be useful to you in the future, but that aren't unnecessarily difficult or complicated or take ages to complete. Here are a few suggestions to make note taking easier:

- Highlight or underline the important bits – this is ideal for using on handouts or photocopied articles and so on but, of course, you couldn't use this method in a book unless it was yours. It is a definite no-no for books you've borrowed. When using this method, you need to be able to pick out phrases of just a few words that sum up the main idea of a paragraph then you will use a highlighter pen (you may wish to use different colours to differentiate between different sorts of information) to make them stand out. Underlining will be used in exactly the same way and here again different coloured pens can be used. A word of advice however, don't get carried away with your colour-coding system – you could end up spending more time on the system than the actual text.

- Spider diagrams are another way of making note taking easy. We will go into more detail as to how they can be made to work for you – with examples – in the next section, but briefly, they are diagrams that start with the main idea in the middle and then radiate outwards with all the subsidiary ideas and information about a subject so that the finished article looks like a spider.

- Many people develop their own shorthand system to speed up their note-taking process – especially when taking notes in lectures. This could be something as simple as shortening words – for example, 'bcos' for 'because' or 'cd' for 'could' and using common abbreviations like 'e.g.' instead of writing out 'for example' and 'i.e.' for 'that is'. If you decide to try this, it is worth remembering that our brains can interpret many words if we are given just the first and last letter or two – we can often ignore what's in the middle. Of course, if you are proficient at a recognized method of shorthand, you can use that but do make sure that you can read it easily. How awful would it be to make notes in shorthand then, when you go back to your notes many weeks later, to be unable to make sense of what you wrote?

## How to take notes that work for you

However you decide to compile and file your notes, they must work for you. It is irrelevant that they may not make much sense to anyone else or not serve their purposes. Having decided what you will use the notes for, you must find an appropriate way to make the notes that fits in with the way you work and think. If you are a very creative, visual person, for example, having an element of illustration in the notes will be especially helpful. In this case, spider diagrams will be suitable, perhaps with little drawings added.

Look at Figure 4.1 for an example of how to make notes in the form of a spider diagram:

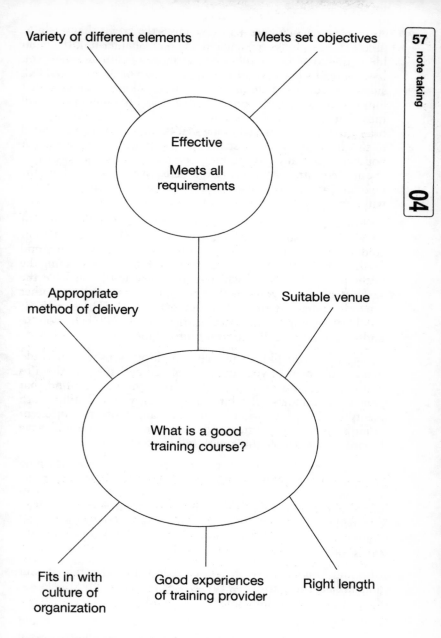

**figure 4.1** making notes using a spider diagram

As you can see in Figure 4.1 (which uses the article that was also used for the exercise on active reading in Chapter 03), the main idea – this could be the subject of an assignment or an article you have to read – has been placed in the centre of the paper and all subsidiary ideas radiate out from this – making a drawing that looks a bit like a spider or, if you make lots of connections, will radiate into drawings of several spiders. This is a good way to brainstorm an idea as each thing that occurs to you can be added to the diagram and will usually spark off your thoughts so that you will eventually have written down most of what you know about the central idea. It is also an effective way of making the links in a subject that will clarify your understanding of it and will improve your ability to remember it.

Of course, spiders are not the only way to make notes that incorporate visual elements. You could also use different coloured pens and highlighters, notes in the form of a pyramid (with the topic at the top and different sub-headings forming the lower levels, 'drilling down' into the topic until you have the amount of detail you need). You can add asterisks or other symbols to draw attention to different elements. These methods are ideal examples of active learning and will help you to understand and recall important information.

If, however, you like to use your auditory senses, you could make audiotapes of your main notes and perhaps play them to yourself over and over again. Even though you may find that your mind wanders off a bit during tapes, you will still absorb plenty of the information, as it will wander off at a different point each time you listen and, sooner or later, you will have listened to the whole thing with full concentration.

Another way that you can tailor your notes to your learning style is to use carefully written notes if you have a visual style. Here you might make notes during a lecture or while reading an article and then review them to make them more succinct. Pick out the few words (as few as you can) that sum up the ideas and arguments contained in the notes and write them down – index cards, one per topic, are useful for this.

Although you will have plenty of freedom as to the style of your note taking, there are a few things that you definitely should *not* do when you are taking notes:

- Do not write down every word said in a lecture – this could be next to impossible anyway but would mean that you were not paying real attention to what was being said. You need to give your mind time to recognize, organize and reorganize the material as you go along.

- Do not copy whole chunks of a book or article – this will be boring and may also mean that you have not fully understood the sense of the work.
- Don't crowd everything together – leave some white space (wide margins, spaces between the lines and so on) around all your notes as this will make them not only more visually pleasing but also easier to read. This applies whether you're hand writing your notes or compiling them with the help of a computer.
- Don't copy out your notes simply to make them look nice. Unless you're using the rewriting as an exercise to revise or get to grips with the material, but you already have got a legible set of notes, don't waste time copying them out.
- Don't take notes that you don't need. If you don't believe that you will use the notes, *don't make them.*

Now that you know what not to do with your notes and you've learned a few ways to make notes that work for you, here are a few things that you should do as you compile them:

- Make sure you have understood what you have read or heard before you write anything. Think about what you are writing so that you can identify the main ideas of what you are learning – the main ideas are what you should be noting.
- Keep them short – many students take copious notes that are daunting to read so they are put in a pile and never looked at again. Keep them short, relevant and useful.
- Use plenty of headings and sub-headings – these not only break up the text, making it easier to read, but also will enable you to find just what you're looking for in the future.
- Put everything into your own words – this will make the act of note taking more beneficial to you in that you will have to think about the information you are dealing with as you rephrase and summarize it.
- Listen and look out for clues to the important bits. If, for example, a text (or a lecturer) says 'The three most significant stages are …' then you need to note the three things that follow.
- Use abbreviations and make sure that you write key words and phrases rather than copying out whole sentences.
- Organize your thoughts as you write – this will result in organized notes and will also mean that you will understand (and hopefully remember) what you have written.

- Write important bits – perhaps a quotation (and its source, of course) or a useful phrase that you want to remember exactly – in a different colour.
- Remember – you must have a purpose to your note taking. Know why you are making the notes and what question they will answer for you.
- Vary your approach so that on some occasions you will take detailed notes and on others you will need very brief notes. The main thing is that they must be doing the job you want them to do.
- Note what you haven't understood. This is just as important as what you have understood. Make sure you ask questions at the first opportunity if you feel you've not understood an important point.

---

**Top tip**

If you think that you may quote from your notes at some later stage, make sure that you make a note of the source of the quotation.

---

## What to do with your notes

Unless you develop a way of making sure that your notes are easy to find when you need them, you will have wasted most of the time you spent on making them (although note making always has some benefit as it is active learning) so you will need to get hold of some files and folders and make some space on the shelves in your study area so that you can store them efficiently. Ring binders are especially useful as this will enable you to use dividers to separate the different topic areas and to add or extract notes as and when required.

It is unrealistic to think that you will ever sit down and read your notes through from start to finish at some time in the future, so filing them in topic areas (rather than as a subject from start to finish) will probably be the most useful to you. In this way you will be able to find the information you need for an assignment, when preparing for a lecture or when revising for examinations.

**Top tip**

You'll find a contents page at the front of your notes file useful. Update it each time you add to your notes.

Apart from getting your notes organized, what else should you do with them? How will you use them? As we've already said, you probably won't read them through again. Rather than reading them – which is a passive way of using your notes – you need to be active with them. You need to change them in some way that will help you to understand them while you are working on them and will also help you to remember them in the longer term. Ways of working with your notes – especially if they are linear notes (notes where everything is written down in the order in which it is said or read – line by line) could include:

- Condensing them – this is almost self-explanatory. You're making them shorter. To do this you might pick out the key words from your notes.
- Creating a different type of notes – consider converting your linear notes into a spider diagram.
- Recording the key words – if your learning style (we dealt with this in Chapter 2) is auditory, i.e. you learn best by using your sense of hearing, then recording the most important and relevant bits of your notes on to audiotapes could provide a valuable revision aid.
- Use them for another purpose – perhaps you could set yourself an exam-type question and write for 30 or 40 minutes using only the information contained in the notes. This has three distinct benefits:

  1 You will be using and digesting your notes so that you will definitely remember more from them in the future.
  2 You will be giving yourself valuable practice in essay writing or question answering to time limits.
  3 You will be able to see whether or not your notes were sufficiently detailed – or too detailed.

# Using technology to help with note taking

If you're making and keeping notes on your computer, your approach will be very similar to note taking manually – you will need to keep them short and relevant, make them with a purpose in mind and keep them organized. It is this last aspect of computerized note taking where you will see some differences and will see a benefit from using technology.

It is vital that all files stored on a computer are named and then filed in the right place. If you are careless about naming and filing your files, you computer will become like an enormous desk, overflowing with loose papers. You will waste endless hours searching for that one elusive file that you know is there somewhere but you can't recall where you put it or what you called it. If you do find yourself in that situation, try performing a search based on the approximate date when you worked on the file in question. The best idea however, is not to get into that sort of difficulty. Follow these tips for organizing your computer files:

- Name your file and decide where you will store it as soon as you create a new file.
- Choose your file name carefully. The name should tell you what is in the file so make sure you include, at a minimum, the topic covered in the file.
- Use folders and sub-folders to store your files. For instance, you may have a folder named 'Course XXX' that contains sub-folders named 'Notes', 'Assignments' and 'Research' and within those sub-folders you will have sub-sub-folders with titles based on the topics covered in the files. The important thing is to have a path of folders and files that makes sense to you and that you can follow until it leads you to exactly what you are looking for.
- Keep files small. It may be tempting to put all your notes for your entire course in one file so that you know where they are, but you will find it time-consuming and frustrating to page up and down through a very long file to find the section of these notes that covers the topic you're interested in.

**Top tip**

Make a backup copy of all your files – this applies to assignments as well as your notes. If something goes wrong, you may find that your notes are irreplaceable.

## Summary

In this chapter you have learned:

- That notes are not an end in themselves but that they can be used to develop your understanding – of a lecture, for example.
- Some easy ways to take notes – summing up the main idea of a paragraph or text by highlighting or underlining key words or phrases, or your own shorthand.
- How a spider diagram works – brainstorming a subject and making connections.
- A few ways to use your notes (after you've got them organized) – condensing them, recording them, writing exam answers with just your notes as a resource.

## Quick revision test

1 Give two general reasons for taking notes.
2 Give two specific purposes for which you may take notes.
3 What should you take into consideration when developing a strategy for note taking in lectures?
4 Where will the main idea be placed in a spider diagram?
5 Name a passive way and an active way of using your notes.

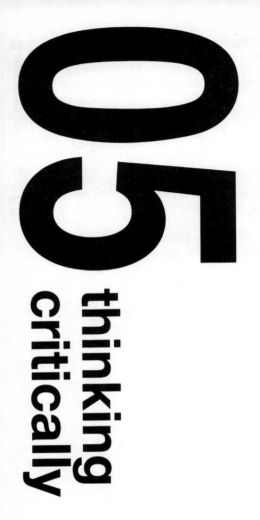

**05**

**thinking critically**

**In this chapter you will learn:**
- how to distinguish between opinions and facts
- how to evaluate an argument
- how to draw your own conclusions from your studying.

# Taking a critical approach to academic texts

When studying at a higher level, it is not sufficient to read, take notes and then repeat the information in assignments or examinations. You must develop a more critical approach to your studies. You will be required to evaluate the arguments that are presented to you and to see how the evidence presents a case both for and against a hypothesis. This is critical thinking and is an essential skill to master as it will help you to understand the material you read and to produce written work at the right level.

Of course, getting proficient at critical thinking will not happen overnight. It is a skill that will build as you practise. When you're first reading an academic text you will read it to understand the author's point of view. You will then try to find the arguments and check whether – and, indeed, where – you have met these arguments before. You will search for the evidence that the author puts forward to justify his arguments. You may then need to read the work of other authors to give you opposing or similar views. Your task then is to decide whether a strong enough case for the original arguments has been made and which view you are finding the most persuasive. It sounds like a lot of work – and of course, it can be – but your goal is to read as effectively as possible and it will happen gradually as you become more active in your reading tasks and develop your critical thinking capabilities.

All academic texts will put forward a view and, apart from understanding and remembering that view, your task will, as we saw previously, include evaluating the evidence given to justify it. You will need to decide whether or not the view being taken is reasonable and logical, given the evidence in the text and also the information that you already have at your disposal. The author of an academic text will explain his or her ideas by way of arguments and examples to illustrate the view taken. As you read it, you will be evaluating the arguments for and against the view taken by the author and deciding whether or not to accept the author's assertions. If the reasons, arguments and evidence are strong enough you will be convinced by the conclusion drawn by the author at the end of the piece.

# Finding the arguments

Now that you can see why you will be looking for arguments and points of view to evaluate, you might be wondering whether or not you will be able to find these arguments. In almost every academic text that you have to read there will be a line of reasoning and the way you will identify this is by asking questions as you read. You will not be able to take any assertion as a fact unless you have asked yourself what, why, when, where and how? An argument can appear as:

- A line of reasoning.
- A case being made.
- A point of view.
- A position being taken.

In all cases, the author will put forward reasons – evidence and examples – why you should accept his or her argument. Your job is to find this argument, i.e. what they are saying about the subject of their text and whether they are taking a positive or negative view.

Here's an exercise that will help you to find arguments and points of view in a text:

## Exercise

Read the following text and see if you can find the arguments in it.

### 'Philip Larkin – just a grumpy old man – or England's moral conscience and national poet?'

*The contents of Philip Larkin's poems are no doubt the cynical rantings of a 'grumpy old man', but it is Larkin's talent in expressing these ideas that makes his pessimistic view of English life so convincing. We are often led to agree with the poet in what he is saying, not because of a predisposition to cynicism or discontent, but because he manages to put his views across so interestingly and concisely. Looking at the five poems separately, we see that each varies in its success in expressing one of Larkin's many dissatisfactions with British society. I believe the success of each usually depends on the tone that he uses.*

*In 'Wires', Larkin uses the image of cattle to symbolize humans and the transition they go through in life, from innocence in* youth to experience. 'Young steers are always scenting purer waters' is meant to mirror the fact that young people believe that anything is possible for them, but soon find out that this is not the case, as their futures are much more predestined than they believe. Larkin employs subtle devices in 'Wires' to gently press his point across. His use of a cyclical structure, where the first line rhymes with the last line, gives the feeling of inevitability and endlessness to his perception that growing up is realising that there are boundaries to our aspirations, and that this must happen to every generation: 'Electric limits to their widest senses'. He uses the shocking image of 'muscle-shredding violence' to mark the day of realization that our range of choice and possibility is actually very limited.

Larkin is successful with 'Wires' in that he manages to express a key perception about English society in a total of three sentences. As the language and construction that he uses are both basic, the poignancy of the message is not hidden or diluted, instead remaining plain and truthful.

Compared with 'Wires', 'Going, Going' is much less successful. The effect of this poem is to show Larkin as simply discontented and nostalgic, rather than perceptive. His aggressive, didactic tone is also unappealing as it makes him appear a constantly negative critic rather than a neutral spectator. His disapproval of everything, rather than some particular things, gives his overall message less weight as he has been so offensive in making it. Larkin's comparison between old and new England is so exaggerated as to make his point practically invalid. His nostalgic fantasy of the England of times past, 'The shadows, the meadows, the lanes, the guildhalls, the carved choirs', is far too idealistic, as it fails to recognize the bad sides of life at that time.

Although Philip Larkin may be making a point that some people agree with, he is not effective in expressing his idea in a way that most people can relate to, as his approach is so pessimistic and satirical. For me, it is this poem that best shows Larkin as a 'grumpy old man', as he fails to make the poem appeal to the moral conscience of the nation because he insults them so much, calling them 'a cast of crooks and tarts'.

'Annus Mirabilis' is similar to 'Wires' in its approach. The tone is casual and rather comical, in fact. Rather than a long rambling fatalistic rant, 'Annus Mirabilis' is short and light hearted, with a message that allows us to see the dawning of the sexual revolution as both a good and bad thing. It was good, in that it made life more fun and enjoyable, but negative in that it meant people lost the sense of responsibility for their actions. In this poem, Larkin presents a much more equal argument – recognizing that 1963 was a year of enjoyment and promiscuity but also commenting that it was a gamble, as no game is completely 'unloseable'.

'Annus Mirabilis' is unlike 'Wires' or 'Going, Going' as it actually claims that things might have got better since the past in some ways! Larkin writes, 'Up until then there'd only been A sort of bargaining, A wrangle for a ring, A shame that started at sixteen.' He then contrasts this with 1963, when 'every life became A brilliant breaking of the bank, A quite unloseable game'.

In 'This Be The Verse', Larkin gives voice to a controversial concept. In his era, parents were to be respected and obeyed, not insulted. Although the title of the poem has religious connotations, the sentiments that he writes about are deeply irreligious: first, because of foul language ('They fuck you up'), second, because the Bible teaches that you must 'Honour your mother and father', and, third, because we are meant to 'Go forth and multiply' (instead Larkin suggests you 'don't have any kids yourself'). The irreverent tone of the poem makes it funny and catchy as well as being cynical and nihilistic. It is the fact that the poem does not take itself too seriously that makes the message more appealing.

'High Windows' reverts mildly back to the 'Going, Going' tone of emphasizing the transition made by every generation away from that of their parents. He shows the way that each new generation discards something that their parents valued – in the case of these 'kids', it is 'Bond and gestures pushes to one side Like an outdated combine harvester'. He also uses the word 'fucking' to imply that it is sex without emotion or bonds. It is strange that he uses the image of going '<u>down the long slide</u> to happiness' – an unusual way of putting it, as happiness is normally seen to be a journey upwards, and downwards as a decline in morality or values. Perhaps by this he is commenting that happiness comes when we forget traditions and manners, and succumb to hedonism: sex without responsibility, and life without imposed religion. By questioning whether the generation before him looked at him with disapproval, he is accepting the inevitability of change in society.

The last paragraph is in an entirely different tone to the colloquial familiarity of the first four stanzas. The lingering, transcendent image of 'high windows' is an ambiguous ending to the poem, perhaps suggesting that all we see is our own small sections of the world, like high windows from below, and that what we see is tiny compared with the whole picture. This could be saying that it is easy to be small minded but that instead we should be open to different ways of living. Alternatively it could be saying that our freedom should be framed with convention: our freedom being the 'deep blue air' beyond, and the bonds to it being like windows.

So, in deciding whether Philip Larkin is really just a 'grumpy old man' or is our national conscience, we must look at how effective his poems are. I believe that he is usually extremely skilled in expressing his (often depressing) views and it is these poems that really work. It is when his own sense of moral superiority overtakes that Larkin writes poems that elicit no empathy of agreement in the reader.

Did you immediately spot that the line of reasoning was that Larkin's ideas succeed not because they are necessarily right, but because he is so skilled in putting them into words? Or did it take you some time to identify it? There are several assumptions that you should have been questioning as you read the piece and we will be looking more closely at these in the next section when we evaluate the arguments. If you are in any doubt as to the main point of the text, go through it again, this time with a highlighter pen or (especially if this book is not yours) a pen and paper. Highlight or note down the keywords in the piece: You should end up with something like Figure 5.1. In this example the text has been marked up by showing the keywords and phrases in bold type. You might choose to underline or highlight your text.

### 'Philip Larkin – just a grumpy old man – or England's moral conscience and national poet?'

The contents of Philip Larkin's poems are no doubt the cynical rantings of a 'grumpy old man', but it is **Larkin's talent in expressing these ideas** that makes his pessimistic view of English life so convincing. We are often led to agree with the poet in what he is saying, not because of a predisposition to cynicism or discontent, but **because he manages to put his views across so interestingly** *and concisely*. Looking at the five poems separately, we see that each varies in its success in expressing one of Larkin's many dissatisfactions with British society. I believe the success of each usually depends on the tone that he uses.

In 'Wires', Larkin uses the image of cattle to symbolize humans and the transition they go through in life, from innocence in youth to experience. 'Young steers are always scenting purer waters' is meant to mirror the fact that young people believe that anything is possible for them, but soon find out that this is not the case, as their futures are much more predestined than they believe. Larkin employs **subtle devices** in 'Wires' to **gently press his point** across. His use of a cyclical structure, where the first line rhymes with the last line, gives the feeling of inevitability and endlessness to his perception that growing up is realizing that there are boundaries to our aspirations, and that this must happen to every generation: 'Electric limits to their widest senses'. He uses the shocking image of 'muscle-shredding violence' to mark the day of realization that our range of choice and possibility is actually very limited.

Larkin is successful with 'Wires' in that he manages to **express a key perception about English society in a total of three sentences**. As the language and construction that he uses are both basic, the poignancy of the message is not hidden or diluted, instead remaining plain and truthful.

Compared with 'Wires', 'Going, Going' is much less successful. The effect of this poem is to show Larkin as simply discontented and nostalgic, rather than perceptive. His **aggressive, didactic tone is also unappealing** as it makes him appear a constantly negative critic rather than a neutral spectator. His **disapproval of everything**, rather than some particular things, **gives his overall message less weight** as he has been so offensive in making it. Larkin's comparison between old and new England is so *exaggerated* as to make his **point practically invalid**. His nostalgic fantasy of the England of times past, 'The shadows, the meadows, the lanes The guildhalls, the carved choirs', is far too idealistic, as it **fails** to recognize the bad sides of life at that time.

Although Philip Larkin may be making a point that some people agree with, he is not effective in expressing his idea in a way that most people can relate to, as his approach is so pessimistic and satirical. For me, it is this poem that best shows **Larkin as a 'grumpy old man'**, as he **fails to make the poem appeal** to the moral conscience of the nation because he insults them so much, calling them 'a cast of crooks and tarts.'

'Annus Mirabilis' is similar to 'Wires' in its approach. The tone is casual and rather comical, in fact. Rather than a long rambling fatalistic rant, 'Annus Mirabilis' is short and light hearted, with a message that allows us to see the dawning of the sexual revolution as both a good and bad thing. It was good, in that it made life more fun and enjoyable, but negative in that it meant people lost the sense of responsibility for their actions. In this poem, Larkin presents a **much more equal argument** – recognizing that 1963 was a year of enjoyment and promiscuity but also commenting that it was a gamble, as no game is completely 'unloseable'.

'Annus Mirabilis' is unlike 'Wires' or 'Going, Going' as it actually claims that things might have got better since the past in some ways! Larkin writes, 'Up until then there'd only been A sort of bargaining, A wrangle for a ring, A shame that started at sixteen.' He then contrasts this with 1963, when 'every life became A brilliant breaking of the bank, A quite unloseable game'.

In 'This Be The Verse', Larkin gives voice to a controversial concept. In his era, parents were to be respected and obeyed, not insulted. Although the title of the poem has religious connotations, the sentiments that he writes about are deeply irreligious: first, because of foul language ('They fuck you up'), second, because the Bible teaches that you must 'Honour your mother and father' and, third, because we are meant to 'Go forth and multiply' (instead Larkin suggests you 'don't have any kids yourself'). The irreverent tone of the poem makes it funny and catchy as well as being cynical and nihilistic. It is the fact that the poem **does not take itself too seriously that makes the message more appealing**.

'High Windows' reverts mildly back to the 'Going, Going' tone of emphasizing the transition made by every generation away from that of their parents. He shows the way that each new generation discards something that their parents valued – in the case of these 'kids', it is 'Bond and gestures pushes to one side Like an outdated combine harvester'. He also uses the word 'fucking' to imply that it is sex without emotion or bonds. It is strange that he uses the image of going '<u>down the long slide</u> to happiness' – an unusual way of putting it, as happiness is normally seen to be a journey upwards, and downwards as a decline in morality or values. Perhaps by this he is commenting that happiness comes when we forget traditions and manners, and succumb to hedonism: sex without responsibility, and life without imposed religion. By questioning whether the generation before him looked at him with disapproval, he is accepting the inevitability of change in society.

The last paragraph is in an entirely different tone to the colloquial familiarity of the first four stanzas. The lingering, transcendent image of 'high windows' is an ambiguous ending to the poem, perhaps suggesting that all we see is our own small sections of the world, like high windows from below, and that what we see is tiny compared with the whole picture. This could be saying that it is easy to be small minded but that instead we should be open to different ways of living. Alternatively it could be saying that our freedom should be framed with convention: our freedom being the 'deep blue air' beyond, and the bonds to it being like windows.

*So, in deciding whether Philip Larkin is really just a 'grumpy old man' or is our national conscience, we must look at how effective his poems are. I believe that he is usually extremely skilled in expressing his (often depressing) views, and it is these poems that really work. It is when his own sense of moral superiority overtakes that Larkin writes poems that elicit no empathy of agreement in the reader.*

**figure 5.1** sample article markup

From this highlighted piece, it should become more obvious to you that the main argument being put forward by the author of this piece is that Larkin's ideas carry more weight when he writes a poem with the right tone. The writer believes that, to be convincing, Larkin must suppress his tendency to act like a 'grumpy old man' and to write to gain the agreement of his reader.

The writer of this critique of Larkin's work backs up this argument with a consistent and logical review of how several of his poems work – or don't work – and why.

This essay was written by an unnamed student and as we do not know who the writer is or anything about his or her background, we are unable to evaluate whether there is any hidden agenda in the work. If, for example, we knew that it had been written by a competitor of Larkin's then we may assume a motive other than a straightforward critique with nothing to gain apart from marks for a college assignment. However, we can deduce that the argument was put together by someone who has studied and, in the main, enjoyed Larkin's work and is not imposing a political view on it.

The evidence that is produced in the essay is directly related to the work and, of course, anyone wishing to confirm any of the quotes and so on could simply look up the poems. However, even this straightforward evidence should not be taken at face value. Many of the assertions made are opinion and may not be fact. This is a good example of where it may be useful to read another view. Someone else might not find Larkin's tone in his poem 'Going, Going' 'aggressive and didactic'. They might find the tone forceful and instructive and, of course, the tone is an important part of the writer's view. It is the tone that the writer perceives that is central to the argument put forward.

Having noted that the arguments in this piece are often just the writer's opinions, they are, nonetheless, put forward logically and consistently.

# Evaluating arguments

Now that you've found the arguments, you have to evaluate them – weigh up the evidence for and against the idea that the author is putting across in the text. There are a number of decisions you have to make about the arguments and different ways to look at the material. Use this checklist to evaluate the arguments you found in the piece about Larkin's work:

- Who is making this argument? Would they have anything to gain by putting forward erroneous arguments?
- Where are they coming from? Is the author writing from a noticeable point of view – is he coming politically from the left or the right, for example?
- Is the argument relevant?
- Is it logical?
- Is the argument carried through logically?
- What evidence in support of the argument is included in the text?
- Is this evidence reliable? What sources have been used?
- Are the argument and its supporting evidence consistent?
- Do you know of any evidence against the argument?
- Have you heard this argument before? If so, where?
- Have you read an opposing view anywhere? If so, where?
- Does this argument support what you already knew?
- Is the reasoning sound – or flawed?
- If numerical data is used to make the case, has it been collected under fair conditions?
- Does the case that has been made fully support the conclusion reached by the author?

# Drawing conclusions

Do you agree with the author's conclusions? At this point, you should have evaluated the evidence and reached your own conclusion as to whether or not the author has made his or her case. Did the case convince you? If so, why and how?

The author's conclusions will normally come at the end of the piece and it is worthwhile to underline, highlight or jot down exactly what that conclusion is. You might like to do this on your first read-through of the text so that you can then check out whether the evidence supports it and whether the author makes a sufficiently strong case to convince you that his or her point of view is the right one. Reading in this way is reading critically or analytically and can be time consuming but is necessary when reading academic texts for a course of study. It is important that you do not merely accept an author's argument at face value. You must delve deeper and evaluate the evidence given (and the evidence not given) to prove or disprove the case.

# Using a critical approach in your writing

As you master the skill of thinking critically when you are reading, you will also be working on your writing skills and academic writing requires you to present arguments and then justify them with evidence in much the same way as the texts you have been reading. If you follow a step-by-step approach to this you will find that the standard of your academic essays, reports and dissertations will be substantially increased:

1 *Decide on your main argument* – your most important line of reasoning should run through your essay or other written work. Further arguments will be needed to add weight to your main one.

2 *Gather the evidence* – you will gather lots of evidence at the research stage of your essay writing but you must then be selective about which pieces of evidence you use. Too many will obscure your case and make the essay difficult to read and understand, so make sure that you choose the most convincing ones and that they clearly support your main line of reasoning.

3 *Consider other points of view* – how could someone argue against your case? If you have considered this as you write, your work will be much clearer and more convincing. You need to look at your arguments objectively so that you can consider not just the strengths but also the weaknesses in your case. If you can see a weakness and perhaps see that another writer could make a completely opposite case, you should try

to deal with this in your essay. Make the evidence for your main line of reasoning stronger and also bring the opposing view into your essay with evidence that you have found against it. Balance the weaknesses you find with strong evidence.

4 *Reach a clear conclusion* – this is most important. If your conclusion is not clear, your whole essay will lose its impact. From the very first words of your introductory paragraph and through all your arguments, the writing should be leading towards your conclusion. Your readers should be in no doubt as to what your conclusion is. It is a good idea to write down your conclusion as soon as you have decided what it will be – perhaps this will be early on in your research when you have just started to gather evidence – and you may need to refine it along the way, but knowing your conclusion will give you a better chance of producing a coherent piece of work.

5 *Review your work* – a quick read-through is not enough for critical writing and thinking. That may just find a few grammatical errors or maybe a bit of rewriting that is necessary but with critical thinking, a deeper evaluation is necessary. You will need to ask yourself questions such as:

- Is my main argument clear?
- Have I produced sufficient evidence to back it up? Have I got specifics – names, dates, numerical data, sources and so on?
- Have I put this argument in both the introduction and the conclusion?
- Is any of my reasoning flawed?
- What are the strengths and weaknesses of my case?
- Is the conclusion clear?

If you can follow these steps and answer these questions, you should be able to produce an essay – or other work – that will earn you good marks.

## Summary

In this chapter you have learned:

- That academic texts must not only be read and understood but also critically evaluated, deciding whether the evidence makes a reasonable and logical case.
- How to find and evaluate an argument by asking questions such as who is making the case, is it relevant and logical, is the evidence reliable, how does this argument fit in with what you already know, is the reasoning sound or flawed?

- That you must read critically – or analytically – rather than merely accepting at face value.
- How to write critically – by being clear about the main argument, presenting evidence to support this and heading for a clear conclusion.

## Quick revision test

1 Name three ways that an argument may appear in an academic text.
2 What will an author of an academic text use to convince you that his main line of reasoning is correct?
3 Where does a conclusion usually appear in an academic essay and what should you do when you find it?
4 Without which very important feature will an academic essay have less impact?
5 What are the five steps to the construction of a good critical essay?

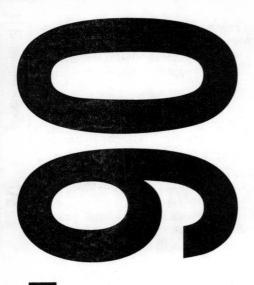

# 06

## research skills

**In this chapter you will learn:**
- how to develop your research skills
- how to explore two different resources for your research.

# Finding out what you need to research

If you're a fairly new student or if things have changed beyond recognition since you last studied seriously (after all, the Internet has only become widely used in the last few years) then you may be wondering exactly what you should be researching and how to go about it. But don't be worried by having to research. It is not some mysterious function of an academic, locked away somewhere in a dusty university library. It is simply about increasing your knowledge by reading and investigating and is a study skill that can be learned and improved.

Research information and its sources are often classified as either 'primary' or 'secondary'. To explain the difference, let's look at where you might find primary or secondary data, i.e. the sources.

Primary sources could include:

- Original documentation – treaties, birth, death and marriage certificates.
- Your own data – if you carry out an interview, experiment or questionnaire you will produce primary data.
- What you see for yourself – you might observe behaviour in animals or in people that you would use as primary data.
- Case studies – accounts of real-life scenarios.
- Original materials such as books, films and television programmes could be primary sources in the case of literature or media studies.

Secondary sources could include:

- Most of the academic texts, books and articles that you will use in your studies.
- Other people's data – observations, experiments and questionnaires carried out by someone else will be secondary data to you.

Having read the lists of primary and secondary sources, you will be able to see that the difference between the two is originality. If it is first hand to you it will be primary data, whereas if it is 'second hand', i.e. resulting from someone else's research, arguments and opinions and the criticism of original data, then it will be classed as being from a secondary source.

When you have to undertake research you will have a specific purpose. You will need to increase your knowledge in a particular area. For example, you may have an assignment to complete and need to find out more about the subject matter. In this case, don't rush to the library and get all the books remotely related to the assignment topic or go onto the Internet and search vaguely for hours for something relevant. You need to work smarter than that. You need to plan.

Your first step if you are researching for an assignment – say, an essay – should be to evaluate the assignment carefully. Ask yourself the following questions:

- What is the question? Analyse the question so that you know what is really being asked.
- How many words are required? This will help you to assess how deeply you need to research the topic. If you only have 250 words to write, then you will not be able to go into too much detail in your assignment. If, on the other hand, you are writing a dissertation of 25,000 words, then you will have to research the topic more thoroughly.
- Is the question a regular one? If the same question is asked every year on this course, then it is likely that you will already have studied what you need to put into the essay (maybe you've got a handout about it) and will only need to do a bit of research to find one or two pieces of evidence to back up the argument.
- Is the question pointing you to a particular article or book? If it's about a recent event or new research, then the area to research can be narrowed.
- How much time do you have? If the deadline for the assignment is imminent, you will have to tailor your research very carefully whereas if you have planned your timetable well and allowed yourself some time for the necessary research, you will be able to read around the subject.
- Can you find out how the assignment will be marked? If it's split into various parts, then you will be able to allocate your research time accordingly.

Right, now you have an idea how much research is needed and into what aspects of your subject. Your next step is to get on with the research. Will you do this in the library or on the Internet? Or a combination of the two? The next sections have tips on how to make the most of research facilities.

# Using the library

Do you know your library well? You should get to know what services are available and what research facilities are on offer. On your first few visits to a college library, this may seem daunting but, with a little effort, you will be able to find out just what is available and to familiarize yourself with the layout and the procedures to follow. This effort at the beginning of your course will pay big dividends as you go through your studies.

First, try wandering around noting what is there. Books, of course, but there will be plenty more. Some libraries have developed an advice sheet about what they can offer but if yours hasn't then it will be up to you to find out so that you can make the most of your library. The range of products and services may well include reference books, academic journals and research papers, computer equipment, photocopying facilities, binding and laminating machines (useful when you're putting a report or important assignment together), video or DVD players, audio- and videotapes, CDs and DVDs. During your wander around the library, you should also notice rules about how the loan system works (how many items can you take out at once, is there a charge for reservations, how long do books usually take to come if they are requested from the store, do you have to renew in person or can you do it by telephone or on the Internet?), joining instructions, opening times and so on. Note where the reference section of the library is and also the general lending section. If you're unfamiliar with libraries generally, you will need to know that books in the reference section (where the books that are generally only consulted for specific information and therefore not needed for loans for weeks at a time – directories, encyclopaedias etc. – are kept) cannot be taken out on loan. The general lending section, however, contains books that, if you are a member of the library, you will be able to take away to use for several weeks.

Second, following your initial 'familiarization tour', you can start to get more specific. Look for things that will be of particular use to you in your course of study. This will include noting the Dewey numbers (library references by subject area) for subjects of interest to you. Of course, the main thing you will want to be able to do in the library is find relevant books quickly and easily and there are several tips and tricks to help you to become proficient at this. Mastering the library system early on in your student career is definitely working smarter and will save you time and frustration. Try the following:

- Unlike fiction, non-fiction and reference books are not filed on the shelves in alphabetical order of the author's name. They are grouped together by subject area. Find your subject areas' numbers and keep a note of them.
- Learn how to use your library's computer catalogue. You can search this by various classifications and the most useful of these initially will be the keyword search. This can be a number of things. Try typing in your subject, e.g. politics or nuclear physics, and you'll be given a list of books on those subjects or try an element of your subject area, e.g. democracy or fission, and you'll get a more specific list. When you are more familiar with your course requirements you will be able to search for a particular author or book title. If you are in any doubt about how to use the system, ask for help. Most librarians are keen to help students to get the most out of the library and you will probably find, if you are using your college library, that one of the staff is an expert in your subject area and so will have an in-depth knowledge of the books and journals available that are relevant to your course.

---

**Top tip**

If you're researching for a specific assignment, try searching the catalogue using words from your assignment question. These will quickly point you in the right direction.

---

- Explore the academic journals that are available in your library. These will often be more up to date than books, which can take quite a few months to reach the library shelves. If you are using your college library and are expected to refer to specific articles in such journals then the appropriate journals will be available in your library. They will usually be stored in binders – one for each year – and these journals are indexed so that you can find relevant articles. Most academic journals supply abstracts (short summaries) of the articles so that you can either read the abstract (which might be enough for your purposes) or find out whether you need to read the full article.
- Check out what newspapers and magazines are available. You can quickly scan the broadsheet papers for relevant

articles for your studies and may find they lead you to further research for more academic articles and recently published books referred to in the newspapers.

Having familiarized yourself with what the library contains and where it is all situated, you will now be in a position to use the library for research.

# Using the Internet

The Internet is a relatively recent resource and it is enormous. A few words of warning before we look at how the Internet can help you in your studies; you must be aware that not everything that you will find on the Internet is true or even well researched. It should be treated with caution even if the website appears to be respectable or appears to have an academic base. There is no central ownership of the Internet, which is a set of networks that enables us to exchange information worldwide, and so there is no censorship or monitoring of any kind. For this reason you should always find at least two separate sources for information you find on the Internet.

The Internet is a bit like a library that is bigger than you could possibly imagine, so finding just the right piece of information when you need it can be difficult and time consuming. Just as you had to have a familiarization tour of the real library, so you will need to become familiar with this gigantic virtual library.

The World Wide Web is part of the Internet and is where you will find the information you need – if you search carefully. Search engines (such as **www.google.co.uk** or **www.lycos.co.uk**) will help you to find appropriate websites. Choose your favourite search engine and put in a search term related to what you are looking for. This is similar to the keyword search you used when looking in the library's catalogue but you will have to choose your search term carefully and refine it if you are to be successful in your searches. Although all the major search engines will search an enormous number of pages in the World Wide Web every time you carry out a search, none of them actually encompasses all pages, so if you are unsuccessful with one engine, it can be useful to try another one.

At this point in your studies it will be helpful for you to find the websites that are of particular interest to students of your subject or that are related to topics to be covered in your course.

You might even have been given a few example websites by your tutors or by other students who are 'web savvy'. Make a note of these sites (addresses start with www) as they may give you a shortcut to relevant and useful information for future assignments and research. If you are using your own computer to access the Internet (rather than using one in the library, for example) you will be able to 'bookmark' these sites using the computer's software. Even if you are able to use this facility, it is still worthwhile noting the correct website address – perhaps in a notebook you carry with you for just this purpose – so that you will be able to quote the correct source if you subsequently use information from the site in an assignment.

---

**Top tip**

Remember that a lot of the material to be found on the internet does actually belong to someone so you should be careful not to copy directly from it in large chunks.

---

During your initial familiarization with the Internet, you will find it useful to 'wander around' on the Web, noting what sort of information is out there and how the various sites work. Look at the address of the site, as there are some important clues there. You may be able – from the address suffix 'uk' – to ascertain that the site is maintained in the UK or be able to assess the trustworthiness of the research on the site by the suffix 'ac'. This means that the site is an academic one – usually maintained by an academic institution, so will contain reliable information. As you read the information contained in a website page, you will notice that some words on the sites are underlined and, as you hover over these words the cursor changes to a hand. This means that this is a link to another page or site. Click there and you will be taken to this other page.

Apart from the search engines, you will also find that specialized directories will help you to find the information you want. Check with your course tutor or a librarian whether an appropriate directory exists for your particular subject area. The more academic courses and subjects that are studied at higher levels will often be well served by a directory of this type.

Frequent use of the Internet will almost certainly mean that your efficacy improves but be aware that, unless you are very specific in your searches and have a very good idea of what you are looking for before you sit down at your computer, you may well end up with far too much information – much of which will be useless. Having too much information is almost as bad as not having enough as it will be time consuming and confusing to sift through it.

## Evaluating your research

When you've gathered together all the information that you think you will need on the subject you are researching, you will need to evaluate the results. You will need to check that the information you have obtained meets a number of criteria:

- Is it fit for your purpose? Does it answer the questions you set for yourself when you started your research?, i.e. did you find what you were looking for?
- Can you use it? Can you fully understand what the data you have collected proves? If not, maybe it does not belong in your work.
- Does it help to prove your case? The figures may be fascinating but if they are not relevant to your case, they do not belong in your essay.
- Do you know who wrote it or compiled it? The author's credentials are important to give weight to your case.
- When was it written? If the information is seriously out of date it may not help your case.

If you can follow these guidelines in evaluating your research your work should have authority and the information you use will help you to write critically to a much higher standard.

## Summary

In this chapter you have learned:

- That the difference between primary resources and secondary resources concerns originality. Primary resources are first hand while secondary resources are second hand.
- That the first step before researching for an assignment is to carefully evaluate that assignment.

- That there are a number of services – apart from reference books – available in a college library. These include academic journals and research papers, computer equipment, photocopying facilities, binding and laminating machines, video or DVD players, audio and video tapes, CDs and DVDs.
- How to conduct your initial searches on the Internet using search engines such as **www.google.co.uk** or **www.lycos.co.uk** and that you should exercise a degree of caution as there is no guarantee that the information you find will be correct unless from a known, reliable source.
- How to evaluate the information you have collected during your research by asking questions such as does it answer the questions you set for yourself when you started your research?, who wrote it?, is the information current? and does it help to prove your case?

## Quick revision test

1 Give one example of a primary resource and one of a secondary resource.
2 How does the reference section of a library differ from the general lending section?
3 What are 'Dewey' numbers?
4 What is an abstract of an academic article?
5 What suffix on a website address signifies an academic site?

# 07

# improving your writing skills

**In this chapter you will learn:**
- the different skills needed to accomplish various writing tasks
- how to plan your writing tasks
- ways of improving your writing.

# Why effective writing matters

Writing is a vital means of communication. Often it is the major means of proving to your tutors and examiners that you know your subject and have reached an acceptable level. If you are able to write clearly, getting your message across without confusion or doubt, then you will have a far greater chance of passing your course of study than if you are unable to write coherently even though you may know what you want to say. There has recently been a trend – especially in secondary schools – towards ignoring spelling and grammatical conventions, preferring instead to ensure that thoughts are put down in writing without worrying about such things. This theory can have its uses but you can be sure that you will always get better marks for an essay or report that is well-written with correct spellings and punctuation than one that is full of errors of this type. The reason for this is simple – pieces of good writing are far easier to understand. Spelling rules, grammatical conventions and punctuation have been developed simply to aid comprehension and being understood should be the first aim of any piece of writing – especially pieces done with the purpose of gaining marks to pass a course.

The type of writing that we will be dealing with in this book is, in the main, academic writing (rather than communication in business or with friends etc.) and the purpose of this is to present arguments and ideas effectively, provide evidence for these arguments and to reach conclusions that have been justified in the preceding text. For this reason, and also the fact that writing is a one-way method of communication (there is no immediate feedback, so you must try to judge what will be the reaction of your readers and alter your approach accordingly), academic writing must be planned, with a carefully thought-out structure that will guide the reader through the text.

As with all sorts of communication, academic texts should be written to be understood – there is little point in 'blinding with science' or using incomprehensible jargon. Keep it simple, straightforward but comprehensive.

# Types of writing task – and the different skills needed

The writing that you will do during your course may range from taking notes (when you will need to be brief and to the point) to writing essays or reports (when tight writing will be valued but points must be expanded) through to writing a dissertation (when a piece of work that demonstrates the depth of knowledge of your chosen subject will be essential). Let's look at the various writing tasks one by one to see the different skills that you will have to bring into play:

- *Note taking.* We've already covered this topic in detail in Chapter 04, but the essential skill for note taking is the ability to grasp the main ideas contained in a text and get them down on to paper in as useful (and short) a form as possible.

- *Essays.* These will be covered in more detail in Chapter 08, but to produce a competent essay you will need to be able to research your topic, devise a plan for the content of your essay and then write clearly so that you get your points across.

- *Reports.* Again, these will be covered in more detail in Chapter 08. The skills required to write reports include research and, as they usually present data from your own work, the ability to present and analyse numerical data in a clear way.

- *Work-based assignments.* If you are following a course closely connected with your job you may have to produce pieces of writing related to what actually happens at work. You may need to include examples from your working life and to demonstrate that what you are learning is useful in how you carry out your duties. We'll look at this type of writing task in a bit more detail in Chapter 08.

- *Projects.* As a project is based on research, then this will be an essential skill here. A project will also need to be carefully planned and managed and then written up clearly.

- *Numerical data.* This topic often gives people problems but there are tricks to learn to make it easier to help you to convey large amounts of information using numbers. We'll go into this in more detail later in this chapter.

- *Dissertations*. As a dissertation is an extended piece of writing involving independent study and lots of research, one of the major skills involved is that of staying power. You will need to be able to keep your interest in the topic going for some time and to manage both your schedule and your own motivation. Organizational skills are particularly important when dealing with such a major and lengthy piece of work and your research skills will be well tested. Pulling together the final version of the dissertation will need good presentation skills.

- *Presentations*. Clear communication skills are essential when giving an oral presentation but to get to the stage where you are ready to give the presentation you will have to have organized what you are going to say and the order in which you are going to say it, so some of the skills you would need to be able to write a competent essay or notes are needed too. If you decide to use a computer to assist you in your presentation, you will also need some competency with a software package such as PowerPoint ©.

- *Examinations*. In addition to the usual essay writing skills, exams demand that you can also think, plan and write at speed (and in longhand!). Writing essays specifically in exams is covered in more detail in Chapter 11.

All these writing tasks have different purposes and therefore require different combinations of skills but they have a lot in common too. The main skills that are required for any of the writing tasks that you will have to undertake are research skills and an organized approach. You will also need to ensure that your writing can be easily understood and a major part of this requirement can be achieved by using correct punctuation and grammar and we will deal with this – something that often worries new and returning students – in the next section.

## Grammar, punctuation and spelling

Following the rules of grammar, punctuation and spelling in all sorts of writing is extremely important. They make your essays, reports and projects easier to read and understand. If you make mistakes in any of these vital areas, your reader will have to pause to puzzle out what is being said:

- Poor grammar will make it difficult for your reader to work out the sense of what you are trying to say.

- A comma or full stop in the wrong place will interrupt the flow of your writing.
- An incorrect spelling will distract the reader while he works out what the mistake is.

It is not always easy to become perfect in these areas but awareness of the problems plus an extra effort to check your work will help to ensure that you communicate exactly what you mean to say.

## Grammar

Let's look at some of the more common grammatical errors:

- *Verb and subject agreement.* Mistakes in this area sound awful in conversation but may soon be forgotten, but if you make the same mistake in writing, it will be there for all to see and your work will give a poor impression. If a verb is singular then its subject must be singular too. Or both must be plural. For instance, we say 'He [the subject] is [the verb] clever and never 'He are clever' and 'They were late' rather than 'They was late.' This rule applies even if the subject is a word such as none, neither or either (all of which are singular) or collective nouns such as the committee, the government or the board – all of which are also singular. We would therefore say 'The committee has already given its decision on this.'
- *Double negatives.* If you use two negative words in a sentence, they will not express what you meant to say, as they will cancel each other out, e.g. 'I don't know nothing.' This can be corrected by taking out one of the negatives. So either 'I don't know anything' or 'I know nothing' would make sense.
- *Using 'I' or 'me'.* The trick to deciding whether to say 'you and I' or 'you and me' is to see if you can substitute 'we' or 'us'. If 'we' makes sense, then use 'you and I'. If the sentence makes sense using 'us', then it would be correct to say 'you and me'. For instance, we would never write 'The senior lecturer invited you and I to the meeting.' Using the rule of 'we or us', it would not make sense to say 'The senior lecturer invited we to the meeting.' so 'you and I' is also incorrect.
- *Split infinitives.* Infinitives are parts of verbs. For example, to go, to learn, to write. You should try not to put another word in the middle as this will result in a split infinitive. Examples of split infinitives include 'to boldly go' (as famously included in the opening line of *Star Trek*!), 'to quickly learn' and 'to

carefully write'. The way to avoid this is to change the order of the words. Say 'to go boldly', 'to learn quickly' and 'to write carefully'. This rule is being relaxed in common usage today. However, there is a school of thought that says you should at least know when you're making a mistake so that you will only make a mistake when it's acceptable.

* *Ambiguous sentences*. If what you write can mean two different things, then you are being ambiguous and that is never good in academic work. An example of this might be 'I need to leave badly.' This could mean that you need to make a poor exit or, more likely, you really need to leave. Confusion can also be caused by the careless use of pronouns. When you use a pronoun – he, she, they etc. – it should be absolutely clear to whom you are referring. If there is any doubt, it is safer to use the person's full name.

* *At the end of a sentence*. You should not use a preposition (words such as of, to, for, about) at the end of a sentence. They make your sentence sound clumsy. Examples of this type of error include 'The tutor is the one you will be reporting to.' To avoid this you could rephrase the sentence. In this case you might say 'You will be reporting to the tutor.' Often, with this type of error, you will need to use 'whom' instead of 'who'. For instance 'Who will you be reporting to?' could be replaced with 'To whom will you be reporting?'

To check your use of grammar, do the following quick test.

**Exercise**

Rewrite the following sentences using correct grammar:

1 The board of governors are going to meet tomorrow.
2 The first boy was the biggest of the two.
3 He could not make no contribution to the meeting.
4 You and me must attend the meeting together.
5 He was advised to quickly type the notes.

Everything clear? Now check your answers:

1 The board of governors **is** going to meet tomorrow. Remember a board, no matter how many members it may have, will always be singular so the verb must agree.
2 The first boy was the **bigger** of the two. Biggest would only be correct if there were more than two boys.
3 He could not make any contribution to the meeting, *or* He could **make no** contribution to the meeting. Both of these answers get rid of the double negative in the question.

4 You and I must attend the meeting together. Use the test for 'you and I' or 'you and me' – see if you can substitute 'we' or 'us'. As 'we' makes sense in this sentence ('we must attend this meeting together' rather than 'us must attend the meeting together'), you must use 'you and I'.

5 He was advised **to type the notes** quickly. Rearrange the words to eliminate the split infinitive 'to quickly type'.

## Punctuation

And now let's tackle punctuation.

Punctuation causes many problems for a lot of people but it is well worth making the effort to get it right as it will make your written communication much easier to understand. In spoken communication, we pause naturally to make our meaning clear and punctuation marks such as full stops, commas and semi-colons are designed to show the reader where the pauses come. Some people use a 'pepper-pot approach' to punctuation – sprinkling commas and full stops throughout their work. This does not help to raise the standard of the work any more than missing out the punctuation altogether, so it is worth learning a few basic rules to ensure that the punctuation you use makes your work easier to understand:

• Commas, semi-colons and full stops are *not interchangeable*. Each has its correct place in a sentence and can be used to create pauses of differing lengths.

*Full stops* come at the end of sentences and represent the longest pause. It is used to show the end of the thought contained in that sentence. The next sentence will then begin with a capital letter.

*Commas and semi-colons*, by way of contrast, come in the middle of sentences and denote pauses of shorter length. Commas are used as follows:

1 To separate an introductory word or phrase, e.g. However, the essay was well received.

2 To separate a phrase within a sentence, e.g. The letter, which arrived yesterday, contained details of the manager's proposals.

3 To separate single words in a series, e.g. The file contained copies of reports, notes, essays and articles.

Semi-colons give a shorter pause than a full stop but a longer one than a comma. Use them for the following purposes:

1 To separate two sentences that are closely connected (in meaning). For example, 'The lecture was a long one; it covered many different subjects.' The semi-colon can be tricky in these circumstances and it is often safer to write two sentences separated by a full stop.

2 To separate a series of phrases (instead of using commas) where there are already commas in the phrases themselves.

- Apostrophes probably cause more problems than any other punctuation mark. There are just two uses for an apostrophe:

1 To show possession. For example the apostrophe in the phrase 'the tutor's office' shows that the office belongs to the tutor. It can often be difficult to decide where to put the apostrophe, especially when a plural is involved. To help with this decision you should ask yourself who owns the object. If the answer is singular, then the apostrophe should be placed between the last letter of the singular word and the 's' that shows ownership. If the object is owned by more than one person, then the apostrophe must be placed after the 's' that denotes that it is plural. So, with only one lecturer for example, we would write 'the lecturer's books' but with several lecturers we would write 'the lecturers' books'.

2 To show where letters are missing. e.g. don't for do not, it's for it is, can't for cannot, we're for we are.

Here's a quick exercise to check that you've understood how to use apostrophes correctly.

### Exercise

Put apostrophes in the right places in these sentences:

1 The girls hat was blue.
2 'That isnt true,' she said.
3 All the students bags were full of books.
4 The company met all its targets this year.
5 'Dont touch the paint! Its wet!' he shouted.

And here are the answers:

1 The girl's hat was blue. The hat belonged to the girl so the apostrophe signifies possession in this case. There's only one girl – it's not plural – so the apostrophe must go before the 's'.

2 'That isn't true,' she said. Put an apostrophe in isnt to show there's a letter missing.

3 All the students' bags were full of books. Here we've got a possessive plural so the apostrophe must go after the 's'.

4 The school met all its targets this year. This is a common error – don't be tempted to put an apostrophe in 'its' unless it is used in place of 'it is'.

5 Don't touch the paint! It's wet!' he shouted. There were two missing apostrophes in this question. One in 'don't' and the other in 'it's' – both to show missing letters.

## Spelling

And finally in this section, we'll try to improve your spelling if you have problems in this area.

A lot of people lack confidence in their ability to spell. English spelling is not easy but some people find it more difficult than others and it is not possible just to 'learn a few rules' to solve the problem completely – but it can help. A complete guide to English spelling is way beyond the scope of this book, of course, but just a few tips could make a difference.

Many words just have to be learned but some difficulties can be overcome by paying attention to some rules such as:

• Using 'i' before 'e' except after 'c' – when the sound is long ee. This will help you with words such as 'belief' and 'receive'.

• Adding 'ise', 'ize' or 'yse' to the end of words. Many words can be spelled in more than one way but most can be spelled using 'ise'. Some notable exceptions are capsize, analyse and paralyse.

• Use 'c' if it's a noun and 's' if it's a verb. Some words sound the same but are spelled differently according to whether they are nouns or verbs. So, for example, use advise, practise and prophesy if you need a verb (a 'doing' word) but use advice, practice and prophecy when a noun (the name of a thing) would be correct.

Check your spelling of some commonly mistaken words by completing the following quick test.

**Exercise**

Which is the correct spelling in each pair of words:

1  Seperate or separate?
2  Desperate or desparate?
3  Receive or recieve?
4  Accommodate or acommodate?
5  Sincerley or sincerely?

The correct answers are:

1  Separate
2  Desperate
3  Receive
4  Accommodate
5  Sincerely

If there are words that you know you are doubtful about, get into the habit of looking the word up in a dictionary. Frequent use of a dictionary can make an enormous difference to your spelling ability and will help to make your work look more competent.

With attention to detail – especially punctuation, spelling and grammar – your assignments will make a much better impression, could gain better marks and make you feel much more confident. And, of course, if you can improve the standard of your writing now, it will stand you in good stead for the rest of your life.

# Organization – a beginning, a middle and an end

While all different writing tasks have different requirements because of their different purposes, they will all be improved by an organized approach. They all need to be planned before they are written and they all need a beginning, a middle and an end. It will help if you follow a logical approach to your writing tasks and get into a routine of how you tackle a writing project early on in your studies. If you develop a plan now, you will be able to follow the steps to produce work more easily for years to come. Whatever the writing task, these steps will help you to get organized with it:

1 Rewrite the question – the aim of this is to make sure that you understand what you are being asked to do. It is vital that you keep to the subject. Do not rewrite the question so that it asks what you wish it had asked or asks something entirely different from the reality. The purpose of rewriting the question at this stage is not to invent something else but to put it into your own words and, in the process, increase your understanding and start to organize your thoughts on it. The main fault that tutors marking questions find is that students simply haven't answered the question. If there are any words in the question that you're not sure of, look them up in a dictionary or find them in your set books. It is impossible to write a good essay, dissertation, project or report if you are not absolutely clear what is required. You need to know where you are going and how you are going to get there. So, your first step should be to rewrite the question so that it clarifies for you exactly what you are going to do. In the process you will be analysing the question to see what is required. Let's look at an example of how you might do this:

*Original question*: Argue the case against the banning of capital punishment with reference to recent legal cases.

First you could underline the crucial bits of the original question:

<u>Argue the case</u> <u>against</u> the <u>banning</u> of <u>capital punishment</u> with reference to <u>recent legal cases</u>.

Think about how you could reword these bits: 'Argue the case' refers to arguments so it could become 'What are the arguments for' while you could turn around the next section. Change it from 'against the banning of capital punishment' to 'for retaining capital punishment'. When you read the next part 'with reference to recent legal cases' you can start to think about what recent cases involving capital punishment you have read or heard about and change this part to 'examples from recent cases'.

The final rewritten question reads:

*Rewritten question*: What are the arguments for retaining capital punishment? Support these arguments with examples from recent cases.

Now that you have gained an understanding of the question, you need to start to think what is needed to come up with an answer. Here are some suggestions for the sort of the questions you should be asking yourself as you analyse the question you have to answer:

- What is the focus of the question?
- Why are they asking this question?
- What do I already know about this?
- What else do I need to find out?
- Where will I find this information?
- Is there some important research that I should refer to in my answer?
- Is this a topical issue?
- How many different sources of information should I use?

2 Gather your information – this is where you get all your ideas and information together and then try to make sense of them. Note the last question in our last list, 'How many different sources of information should I use?' The extent of your research will mainly depend on how many words the finished essay or report is to be. A 500-word essay on a major topic will have to be very carefully focused and will probably only need the information and ideas you already have in your head – perhaps clarified or confirmed by a quick look at your notes, whereas a 5,000-word essay or report will require some in-depth research and may involve several sources of information such as articles, books, the Internet, your notes, your course books, handouts from your tutor and so on. There will be more about researching information for a writing task in the next chapter.

3 Outline – this is where the real planning and organization comes in. You've got a proper understanding of the question and you've gathered the necessary information so now you need to put it into an order that will produce a good piece of writing. Remember that you need a beginning, a middle and an end, so you should organize your information along those lines, ensuring that you are answering the question that was set and discarding information that does not help you to answer the question. Details of how you can use the information you have found to produce a competent essay will be given in the next chapter.

4 Write – this is the final stage of your writing task. Do not be tempted to start writing as soon as you see the question. That would be a disorganized – and ultimately unsuccessful – approach. Use the previous three stages of the writing process to ensure that you understand what is being asked of you,

have all the necessary information to hand and have put that information into a logical order. Writing without planning is like setting off on a long car journey without a map or a plan of how you are going to get to your destination – you will get lost and waste time finding your way. It will take you much longer to reach your destination.

The next section will give you a few ideas as to how you can improve the readability and quality of your writing – after you have done the planning!

# Signposting and other ways to improve

There are plenty of easy ways to improve the 'flow' and readability of your writing. Let's look at a few of these now:

- Signposting – this can be a very effective way of letting your reader know where you are going with your writing. It can help them to follow the argument you are making. You know where you are going with your essay or other written work but, unless you use signpost words carefully, your reader may lose the thread of your argument. If you allow your reader to get lost, you will have squandered your chance of a good mark. There are various words and phrases that you can use to remind your reader where you have been and to point them in the direction of where the argument is going. Remember that what will be obvious to you in your argument is rarely as obvious to the reader so use a few signposts to show them the way. Here are some examples of words and phrases that can be used to 'signpost':

Now that we have …
Having considered X, we can now look at Y.
In short …
As we have seen, …
Despite X, there still remains …
But before we can deal with X, we must first look at Y.

- Using link words – these can be a bit like the signposting words just discussed in that they can give the reader a small clue as to where things are going in your writing but they can also be used to make the connection between parts of your argument and to make the words flow. To make your argument more accessible, you must link the ideas and each new paragraph together so that the reader can see how they relate to one another. For example, you might use 'On the other hand' when you give an opposing view. This will link two ideas together. Here are some more ideas for linking words that will help the flow of your writing:

Of course, …
However …
Conversely, …
It is a fact that …
At the same time, …
Despite this, …

But first we must …
To be able to understand …
Nevertheless, …
It could also be said that …
But we should also consider …

Using link words and phrases well will ensure that your ideas are tied together so that the reader can see the relationship between them. It will avoid your ideas floating around in the midst of your writing without a connection to the other ideas and arguments that are there.

- Using paragraphs – you should use a new paragraph for every new idea in your piece of writing. If you start a new argument, start a new paragraph. For this reason the best time to decide where new paragraphs start is during the planning stage. When you are deciding on the running order of your essay or report, you will be able to see where the new ideas and arguments are introduced and this is where new paragraphs will be started.

It is a good idea to number them on your rough plan as you go along. It will then be a simple matter to start with 'Para 1' – your introductory paragraph – and include the ideas that you have decided go in there before you move on to 'Para 2' – your first argument in the body of your piece of work. Paragraphs are a useful tool in making a piece of writing easier to read in that each new paragraph will immediately tell your readers that a new idea is coming up. Use a new paragraph for each new theme or idea and do not allow them to be too long as paragraphs are a way of showing how the argument is developing – keep your readers in the picture.

- Sentence length – this can be varied to keep the writing interesting. Generally speaking, shorter sentences are best.

Long, convoluted sentences will do more to lose your reader than any other element of your writing, as it can be difficult to understand the central meaning in a sentence that tackles a variety of issues. If you split it up into two, three or even more sentences you will find that the sense will be improved. However, not all sentences should be very short. This would give the writing a boring aspect and, of course, this is another way of losing your reader. So, the best way is to vary your sentence length. Very short, punchy sentences can be used to draw attention to simple statements of fact while longer sentences can be used to explain more complicated ideas and can also be more analytical and useful when you are explaining and developing your argument. It is therefore important that you are conscious of sentence length as different lengths have different uses and will give your writing texture and interest.

- Summarizing – this should be done at regular intervals during a long piece of work as this will help your reader to keep up with your arguments without having to look back. Of course, you may summarize your topic and the purpose of the piece of writing at the start of your essay or report and will always have some element of summing up in the last paragraph but it is also useful to sum up as you go along too.

It will keep your readers at ease in that they will know that they have understood what has gone before and are prepared for what is to come. To introduce a summary you may write 'Having looked at X and Y and found that Z is usually the case, we can now examine ....' or 'Despite the failure of X, Y is still in existence so ...' or 'To build upon our case that ....'. Use these summary ideas but also think of some of your own and put one or two extra summaries in every assignment that you have to complete and you will find that your work becomes much more easily understandable.

If an essay or report is well-signposted, with a new paragraph for each new theme, varying sentence lengths, plenty of link words and summaries to show the reader where they have been and where they are going, you will keep the reader's interest and get your points across much more effectively.

Having written your assignment or project, there are several checks you can carry out (apart, of course, from the essential proofreading to eliminate any typing errors and so on). Go through the text carefully looking at the overall structure and ask yourself:

- Is the introduction clear? Can the reader immediately see what the theme of the piece will be?
- Is there a separate paragraph for each of the main points?
- Are these paragraphs in a logical order?
- Does it 'flow'? Signposting words can help with this.
- Have you made a convincing case? Make sure you have sufficient evidence for points you have made and for your conclusion.
- Does your conclusion draw the whole argument together succinctly and logically?

## Presenting numerical data

The last section in this chapter is slightly different in that it will not need too many words or require advanced skills in punctuation or grammar but it is a skill that you will often need when completing assignments. A well-thought-out and presented set of figures can improve a piece of writing. The analysis and/or presentation of numerical data will be used in most subjects – not just maths or scientific subjects. For instance, if you do a survey or questionnaire in a social sciences project you will need to present and analyse the data you collect.

Numbers, presented in the right way, can give you access to an enormous amount of information in a very short time. Of course, you will have to invest some time to learn how to interpret and present the information but that will be well worth while as it will save you time in the long run. A lot of the knowledge we need to have to be able to interpret numerical information is learned in everyday life. Most of us in our society, for example, know that percentage is represented by the sign % or that a mile is further than a kilometre but, unless we've had some tuition or plenty of practice, we may not be able to correctly read and use the information contained in a table, chart or graph. This is where the investment of time is required.

Figures can add weight to many aspects of academic study. It is not sufficient to say that 'most' people are in favour of a change or that 'very few' families take holidays in a particular country. Far better to be able to present data efficiently and inform your readers that '93 per cent' of the people surveyed (and to be able to be specific about the numbers surveyed) were in favour of a specific change in society or that only 200 families took their holidays in Serbia in 2004 compared with 2 million families taking their holidays in Spain in the same period. These figures are all made up – but you get the picture.

There is a variety of ways in which numbers can be presented and if you want to include them in an assignment, you must choose the most appropriate way. There are tables and many types of charts and graphs that all display information in different ways. The aim is to show the figures in a way that makes them clear and accessible. They must tell the story that you want them to tell and choosing the type of chart etc. and making informed decisions about how you show the data is a skill you can learn.

There are a few basic rules about using tables, charts and graphs that will help to make your data clear for your readers:

- Don't just drop the table etc. into your essay or project without explaining first what the data shows. Without this explanation your readers will be lost and the impact of the data will be lessened. Give a short introduction to the table or chart, giving brief details of how the data was collected and what the numbers show. Do not try to explain everything that the chart or table is there to say, simply give a short summary by way of introduction and orientation for your readers.
- If you have copied the data, i.e. it is not your own original work, then you must note the source. Usually you would credit the source at the bottom of the chart with a brief note. See the example in Table 7.1.
- Give your table or chart a clear title.
- Use labels so that every aspect of your table or chart is clear. This includes units of measurement (is it £000s or tonnes or percentages?) – don't leave your readers to guess.
- Put the table or chart in the right place. This should be as close as possible in the text to the point that the data illustrates.

Let's look at tables first. Tables are an easy way to present numerical information in an organized and easy-to-understand format. They can be used to arrange numerical data so that it is possible to see the relationships between different parts of the information and to look up specific details. For example, in the following table you could easily see the best performing product group or find out which year was most profitable.

| SALES FIGURES – YEARS 1 TO 3 | | | |
|---|---|---|---|
| Sales (£1,000s) | | | |
| Product group | Year 1 | Year 2 | Year 3 |
| A | 1,420 | 1,560 | 1,610 |
| B | 2,670 | 2,940 | 2,880 |
| C | 4,100 | 3,690 | 3,140 |
| D | 2,360 | 2,830 | 3,120 |
| E | 930 | 1,040 | 860 |

**Source:** *Succeed at Psychometric Testing – Numerical Reasoning Advanced Level*, Hodder & Stoughton, Bernice Walmsley (2004)

**table 7.1** sample table showing presentation of data

Can you spot the product group with the highest sales in Year 3? In a table, information such as that is easy to pick out – we can immediately see that the answer is Group C and this demonstrates the value of using tables.

Take another look at Table 7.1. Note the title, the fact that the figures represent thousands of pounds and cover the sales of five product groups over three years. From this example, you can see that tables are a good way to present numerical data in a compact, understandable and efficient way. Here are a few tips to help you to interpret and present information in this way:

- Do not be tempted to skip tables when you come across them in a text. And do not rush them – give yourself time to fully understand them. With practice you will get quicker and better at using numerical data.
- Familiarize yourself with the main idea of the table as a first priority – check out the title and also any other information in the text immediately before and after the table.

- Look next at the headings – across the top of the columns and down the side of the table.
- Make sure you've noted the scale – is the table telling you about product sales in thousands of pounds as in our example or production of tonnes of product or percentages of people in a survey?
- Then check the highs and lows. The highest figures in a column and the lowest will tell you the limits of the information. From our example table, for example, this would tell you that the most profitable product was product C in Year 1 and the least profitable was product E in Year 3. If you were a production or sales manager trying to decide which product to make more of or which to discontinue, this information would be invaluable.
- Don't forget to check when the information was gathered. If it represents the results of a survey of computer ownership 10 years ago, then the figures won't tell you much about current trends in technology.
- Try summarizing in words just one aspect of the data presented. This will not only check that you have understood it but will also show you just how much information can be fitted into a small space.
- Finally, treat numerical data with a healthy degree of suspicion. Ask yourself who has presented the information and what case are they trying to put forward. Could they have presented the statistics in such a way that you are given an incorrect picture? This is not usually the case but it does no harm to ask yourself the question.

Let's look next at some of the various types of graphs and charts you could use. They introduce a more graphic element to the presentation of data and are therefore visually stimulating and will make it easier to understand. Charts and graphs are therefore very useful in text-heavy reports, projects and dissertations as they help to break up huge chunks of text.

First up, the line diagram, shown in Figure 7.1.

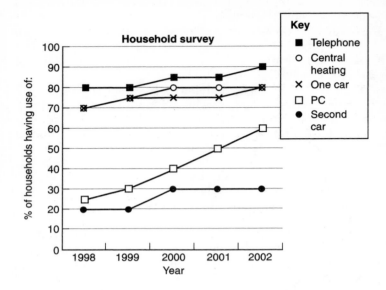

Number of households surveyed = 1,000

**Source:** *Succeed at Psychometric Testing – Numerical Reasoning Advanced Level*, Hodder & Stoughton, Bernice Walmsley (2004)

**figure 7.1** sample line diagram

This sort of graph is an ideal choice to represent data with a limited number of categories. There are five lines (representing PCs, telephones etc.) in this figure and this is probably the optimum number. Any more and the diagram would appear cluttered and confusing and with fewer categories, say two or three, the graph would not be as informative.

Check out the information shown in the graph. You can see the dramatic increase in ownership of PCs between 1998 and 2002 and the steadier progress of the other products. Note that the figures down the left-hand side of the graph are in percentages rather than actual numbers of households. To work out the number of households in the survey that had, for example, a second car in 1999, you would need to take into account the additional information shown below the graph – the number of households surveyed = 1,000. You could then calculate 20% of 1,000 = 200 households. Taking account of each of the products and each of the years, you can see that there is an enormous amount of information incorporated in this graph and, if you add that to the ability to see trends (e.g. the rising ownership of PCs) then you will appreciate just how useful a graph can be.

Another way of displaying data is shown in Figure 7.2.

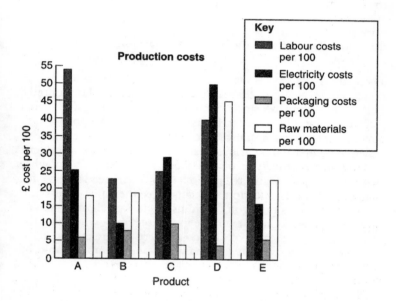

**Source:** *Succeed at Psychometric Testing – Numerical Reasoning Advanced Level*, Hodder & Stoughton, Bernice Walmsley (2004)

**figure 7.2** sample column chart

This is called a column chart because, as you can see, the data are represented by columns. These columns can be grouped together as they are here or placed singly. With groups like those in the figure, there must be a very limited number of categories to make the information shown in this way manageable. If you used single columns, then a greater number of categories could be displayed. Look at the information shown around the outside of the figure. On the left, we are told that the cost per 100 items of each of the products is shown in pounds. Along the bottom axis, we can see that each group of columns in the chart gives information for one of five different products. On the right of the chart is a 'legend' or 'key' that tells us that each of the columns represents a different type of cost (again per 100) and how you can distinguish between the different columns. Finally, don't forget the title, at the top of the chart, which tells us quite simply that the chart tells us about 'Production costs'.

There are many variations of a column chart. The columns can be placed vertically as they are in our example or horizontally. The columns can be stacked rather than the categories being placed side by side. This can be useful to display proportions. In our example, with a stacked column it would have made it easier to compare the various cost components of the products. Your choice of the type of chart or graph depends on what information you want to get over to your reader. So, for example, if the proportion of costs was the most important point to get across then you would use a stacked chart or maybe a pie chart – see the next example in this section – whereas if the actual figures for each of the costs were the relevant bit of information to convey, then a chart like our example would be a good choice.

Finally, we'll look at Figure 7.3, which shows a very popular way of displaying numerical data – the pie chart, so called because it is made up of slices, or wedges, just like a pie!

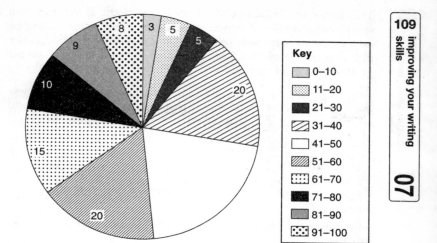

Figures around the outside of the pie chart show actual number of exam entrants. The key shows scores achieved

**Source:** *Succeed at Psychometric Testing – Numerical Reasoning Advanced Level*, Hodder & Stoughton, Bernice Walmsley (2004)

**figure 7.3** sample pie chart

Our pie chart deals with a type of data that will be very close to your heart – examination results. The figures in a pie chart are displayed as part of the 360° whole. The data for each category is converted to a slice of the 360° that represents the correct proportion of the whole data. Pie charts are usually produced using computer packages rather than manually, as it can be difficult to work out the relative proportions of sets of data in relation to the 'pie' and therefore to be accurate about the size of the wedge.

Nevertheless, once produced, pie charts are very useful and easy to read. As a quick check on how much information you can get from a chart like this, work out how many people failed the exam if a mark of 41 or more was needed to pass. The answer is, of course, 33 and you should arrive at this figure by adding together the numbers represented by four of the wedges.

Two items are of particular note on this chart. First, that each wedge represents the actual number of exam entrants falling into that category and, second, that the key or legend on the right-hand side shows how you can distinguish each of the grouping of marks gained.

Pie charts can make a good visual impact in a report or project but take care when using them. They can be a bit simplistic and also should not be used when more than 10 categories are involved as the slices become too thin to have the desired effect. It is also not easy to compare two sets of data so you should stick to using them to display proportions, for which they are ideal. Another useful way of displaying the data is to 'explode' the pie chart, i.e. separate the wedges so that you can see the distinct pieces.

A variation of the pie chart is a 'doughnut' chart – so called because it is like a pie chart but with a hole in the middle. This type of chart would be more useful to display data about a very limited number of categories as the 'doughnut' tends to look a bit messy divided into too many 'pieces' – four or five would probably be the most you would use.

Many of the tips for reading tables would also apply to reading any other sort of presentation of data (and remember that a table and a chart or graph could all be used to present exactly the same data) but there are a few extra ones that are relevant to graphs and charts:

- Initially, try to ignore the different colours and all the lines and concentrate on the words around the edges.
- Make sure you understand the 'key' or 'legend'. This will tell you what each colour or shading pattern represents.
- Find out what the axes represent. The horizontal axis (the bottom edge, also called the X-axis) and the vertical axis (the left-hand edge, also called the Y-axis) will both have been given a scale so you should be sure to examine these in detail.
- Graphs and charts are often the best way of presenting information as they give us a pictorial representation that often makes the information easier to remember and can be used to present extensive information in a concise form.

Choosing a method of displaying numerical data will be, to some extent, a matter of trial and error. You will need to try to visualize how the information and categories of data you want to show will look using the various types of tables, graphs and charts available to you and you must also be very clear about the point you are trying to get across. Statistics can be manipulated to push anything to the fore, so make sure that your tables, charts and graphs present your information fairly but with the 'slant' or focus you require.

If you are proficient with the spreadsheet function on your computer, you will find that producing charts and graphs will be a relatively quick and simple matter so that you can easily see which type best makes your case. You will also need to take into account the type of document you are considering putting the information into and the audience at which it is aimed.

## Summary

In this chapter you have learned:

- That different writing tasks require different skills. These may include, depending on the type of writing, research skills, organizational ability, thinking, writing and planning at speed (for exams), motivational skills (especially for dissertations and other lengthy projects), clear presentation and the ability to grasp ideas and get them down on paper (for note taking).
- How to avoid many common grammatical errors such as verb and subject disagreement, double negatives, using 'I' or 'me' inappropriately, split infinitives and ambiguity.
- How to use common punctuation marks correctly. Full stops, commas, colons and semi-colons are used to denote pauses of varying lengths. Apostrophes have two uses – possession and to substitute for missing letters.
- A few spelling rules – 'i' before 'e' except after 'c', where you should use 'ise', 'ize' or 'yse' at the end of words and the use of 'c' or 's' in similar sounding words with different meanings ('c' for a noun and 's' if it's a verb).
- How a logical approach – giving all pieces of work a beginning, a middle and an end – will help with all writing tasks.
- Some tips and tricks to improve your writing such as signposting, using link words, using paragraphs, varying your sentence lengths and summarizing at intervals to help your reader.
- Some basic rules about using tables, charts and graphs to help make your numerical data clear and to add weight to your essays and reports.

# Quick revision test

1 Why have spelling rules, grammatical conventions and punctuation been developed?
2 Why is use of a double negative considered incorrect?
3 Give the two uses of an apostrophe.
4 Name the four steps of an organized approach to writing tasks.
5 Would a line diagram be more effective to display data with a small or a large number of categories?

# 08

## writing essays and reports

**In this chapter you will learn:**
- the difference between the various types of assignment
- how to plan your writing tasks
- how to get on with the writing.

# What is an essay?

Most students will have to produce an essay at some point in their studies as it is a way of demonstrating that they have understood, and can use, the information that they have been trying to absorb as part of their course. You can read any number of set books or recommended articles, spend hours researching in the college library and make notes on every lecture you attend but until you have attempted to convey some of that information to your tutor or examiners, you will not have proved that you have learned anything at all. Submitting an essay will give you that proof. So what is an essay? It is a short piece of writing on a particular topic that usually takes the form of an argument leading from a question asked at the beginning (this question can take the form of a statement or title that can then be argued with), going through the evidence in the main body of the essay and leading to a conclusion at the end.

Although an essay's main purposes are to display knowledge and to put forward arguments, it is also a useful learning tool in itself. The work that you have to do to write an essay – thinking about the topic, understanding the question, researching the subject, organizing the material into a coherent argument, planning the writing, drawing conclusions and then writing up the material – means that you will end up with a far deeper understanding of the topic of the essay than you would if you had merely read about it. While you are writing your essay it is also worthwhile thinking about how this can help with your exam preparation. Keep your planning notes – the outline and so on – as these may help you see how you arrived at the structure of a successful essay (or, alternatively, if your essay receives a poor mark, will help you to see what went wrong and show you how you can improve in the future) and will be useful during your revision period.

A good essay, like any other type of academic writing, will be well planned and will 'flow' so that the reader finds the argument easy to understand and to follow as it is developed in the body of the essay. There will be a clear introduction at the start of the essay, setting out what the writer intends to do (what the essay is about, its title, the main points to be covered and so on) and will end with a summary and a well-reasoned, intelligible conclusion at the end. It is useful to recall the old description of an effective essay:

- Tell'em what you're going to tell 'em (this is your 'beginning' or introduction).
- Tell'em (this is the 'middle' or body of your essay).
- Tell'em what you've told'em (this is your 'end' or conclusion).

Although this simplifies effective structure perhaps a bit too much, it still gives a broad outline for an essay. We'll look in more detail at essay planning later in this chapter.

# Writing reports

Reports differ from essays in that they are a far more structured form of communication. Whereas essays are almost exclusively used for academic purposes, the original use of reports is set in business and the world of work. Reports are therefore thought to be more related to 'real life'. They will contain more numerical data presented in tables, charts and graphs than an average essay. There are some similarities between an essay and a report – they both require careful planning and research.

Many courses – both academic and work based – will require the production of reports. Where a report is a work-based assignment on a professional development course, for example, it will usually be very closely linked to the student's working life. She may be required, for instance, to investigate a possible cost-saving measure that could be taken in her department and then to produce a report about it, evaluating the viability of the measure and making recommendations as to how to proceed. These assignments are therefore not just academic exercises but have a real purpose and relation to real life.

The accepted format for a report to be used for either business or academic purposes is as follows:

- *Contents page.* This simply lists all the elements that are included in the report and their page numbers. A contents page would be included in all reports apart from very short ones.
- *A summary.* As you would expect, the summary at the beginning of a report sums up the contents of the report including the conclusions and recommendations and its purpose is to make it easy for the reader, in a work situation, to find out quickly and easily what the report is about.

- *Introduction.* The first two sections are then followed by a brief introduction of the report's purpose and why it is being written. The purpose here is to outline the key issues that are dealt with in the report.
- *Research methodology.* This is where the report details how the information contained in it has been obtained. You will need to describe how you have conducted your investigation, what sort of information you have used and how you have collected it.
- *Findings.* This is where you will develop the main body of your report. This part of the report will be divided into several sections. You will include the results of your research and will develop the case that the report puts forward. You can display the data you have gathered in tables, graphs and charts according to the method that will get your point across to best effect. When using data in this way, ensure that it is neatly presented, properly labelled and that sources are clearly shown. You will usually intersperse this numerical data with descriptive writing to explain what the tables and charts show and to lead the reader towards your conclusion. It is important that you follow a logical order and include sufficient detail to justify the conclusions and recommendations that will follow.
- *Conclusions.* Here you will give your verdict on the data you have gathered. You must link this in to the introductory section and show exactly how what you have found proves your case.
- *Recommendations.* Here you will draw all the threads together to make viable recommendations as to action to be taken to solve the problem set in the introduction. Always try to show the effect of your recommendations. For example, if following your recommendations would reduce costs then say so and quantify this as far as possible.
- *Appendices.* This is where you will put all the very detailed information that you have gathered to back up your case. For example, you may have taken a few relevant figures from a very detailed survey and used them in a different format to explain your case in the findings section and then this is where you can include the longer version of the data. Or you may have conducted a survey and this is where you can include a full copy of the survey questions. While the appendices will usually contain many data, you should select important numerical information to include at the correct point in the findings section to help your readers to

understand the points you are making rather than relying on them to search for them in the appendices and interpret them for themselves.

- *Bibliography.* All the sources you have used should be detailed here. Include all books, articles and other research.

# Presentations and other types of assignment

## Presentations

Making a verbal presentation can be a daunting task. Apart from wondering about the content of the presentation, most people will feel nervous and self-conscious about delivering the presentation. But planning and preparation will help to make delivering a verbal presentation a satisfying and successful experience. Not only will good organization result in a more competent presentation but the preparation will increase your confidence and will in turn help to reduce the anxiety you may feel. As always, there are a number of steps you should follow:

- Set aims and objectives – what do you want your presentation to achieve? What information or arguments do you want to put across? You might simply want to impart information or your objective might be more ambitious – to change attitudes, for example. Decide on your goals before you start and also decide how you will know whether you have been successful or not. You could give out a feedback sheet after your presentation to check your audience's response so that you can monitor your goals.

- Take care not to try to include absolutely everything you know on the topic in your presentation. If you have more detail than you can easily present, then make a simple case, including a few relevant figures and then include the unabridged data in a handout. You should aim at being easy to understand, straightforward and developing a strong case.

- Check out your audience. You must consider the level of your audience and tailor the way in which you present your facts and information. Take into account the age range, how formal they will expect you to be, their current level of knowledge of the subject of your presentation and their possible attitudes. You will need to adjust your presentation content and delivery style if you find out, for instance, that your audience has been forced to attend and will be resistant to your viewpoint or that your audience will be made up of people well-qualified in your subject.

- Plan the presentation with a beginning, a middle and an end – as always the structure of your work is of paramount importance. Ensure you have an introduction that clearly sets out your case and tells your audience exactly what you are trying to do. Then go on to develop your points one by one – perhaps with a slide or other visual aid for each point you are making. Finish with a well thought out conclusion. At this point don't be worried if you think you are repeating yourself. Your conclusion should link back to your introduction and also tie in all the points you have made in the main body of your presentation.

- As with written work, you should make life easier for your audience by using signposts. In your introduction, you should let them know where you intend the presentation to lead and then, along the way, sum up where you've been and make it clear where you are going next. Check out the chapter on improving your writing skills if you are in any doubt as to how to do this.

- Include handouts and visual aids – these will help your audience to understand the information you are presenting. Think carefully about when you hand out your written information. There is a case for keeping the handouts to yourself until the end of the presentation as it can be distracting to have people flicking through sheets of paper while you are trying to present. Visual aids such as slides or a PowerPoint © presentation should be carefully designed to enhance the information you are including in your presentation. It will usually summarize the points you are making and you can then develop them in your verbal presentation. Whichever type of visual aid you are using, it will be possible to reveal the points one by one as you get to them rather than having the audience read them all instead of listening to you. You will find more help on using visual aids in the next section.

- Rehearse – this is when you will be able to get your timing right. You will be able to reduce or expand your material at this stage to ensure that your presentation is the required length (but don't forget to allow a little time for questions at the end). Take particular note at the rehearsal of any annoying little habits you may have that are creeping into your presentation. Things such as jiggling coins in your pocket or tapping your pen on the table will distract and irritate your audience and will not add anything to your presentation. Lots of 'erms' and 'aahs' will have a similar effect. Try not to read all of your presentation. You will have written out your presentation in its entirety and will almost certainly have to have some notes to prompt you, but do try not to simply read them out. This results in a very dry, boring presentation – and that is not what you are aiming for.

- Double-check everything – make sure that your equipment works, that you've got a plug point nearby, take a spare bulb with you if you're using a projector and also a hard copy of your presentation even if you're using a computer and so on. If something goes wrong you want to be able to cope and give a competent presentation rather than letting just one problem ruin things for you. Check that the venue is set up as you require. This means checking the number of seats laid out and also that everyone will be able to see you. Actually go and see where your audience will sit and see whether the layout is right. There are lots of things that can be wrong and the point when your audience is coming into the room is not the time to find out that you don't have enough chairs for them or that the plug point is too far from where you were planning to place your computer.

- Go for it! – dress appropriately (you should feel comfortable but, above all, smart and suitably dressed for the occasion), stand up straight, face your audience, speak clearly so that everyone can hear you (you should have sorted out the pitch of your voice at rehearsals) and smile. Show plenty of enthusiasm for your subject – that always goes down well and, as they say, it is catching. With plenty of practice and knowledge of your subject you should feel confident and comfortable so that you can enjoy the experience.

- Decide when you will deal with questions. Unless you are very confident and/or experienced, you should probably opt to ask your audience to save their questions until the end of your presentation. It is not really possible to predict what questions you will be asked but knowing your subject is your best preparation. If you are asked a question to which you do not know the answer, then say so and offer to find out the answer. Try not to let one member of your audience dominate the question period – move on.

**Tips for using visual aids for a presentation**

For a presentation to look polished and professional, it is usually necessary to use visual aids. This may include a computer linked to a screen, using a PowerPoint © presentation, an overhead projector and transparencies, flip/charts, slides, videos, objects related to the subject of the presentation or even music. It has been proved that people remember far more information (approximately three times as much) when they can both see and hear the information than when they are merely listening. Used in the right way and at the right time, visual aids can help to make sense of difficult concepts and can reinforce ideas.

Laptop presentations are particularly popular now and, if you are confident of your ability to use the equipment, they can be very effective. However, a common equipment malfunction is that the remote control for changing the slides has a slight delay and it can be difficult to recover composure after making a mess of the slide changes. You will need to decide on an overall theme (including colours and fonts to be used) for the appearance of your slides so that your presentation will have a pleasing, uniform look but make sure that your theme does not use too many colours. You want to end up with an easily visible, unfussy image on the screen. When you're putting your presentation together limit yourself to just one main point per slide and use charts and graphs to demonstrate points and to present statistical information. They will be far easier to understand than using figures in tables. Finally, don't forget that you can – and should – print out your notes from the PowerPoint © presentation for use during the session.

Flipcharts are readily available but, despite its apparent simplicity, it can be daunting to write on a flipchart in front of a roomful of delegates. Getting the size of your writing just right, keeping it straight rather than writing diagonally across the page, and making sure that everyone can read what you have written – even at the back of the room – can be surprisingly difficult. So, unless you are very confident, practise a lot beforehand or prepare written sheets for the flipchart in advance. If you know in advance what points you want to make (you do, don't you?) and also how you want to illustrate them, then pre-prepared flipcharts will save you time, potential pitfalls, and possible embarrassment during your presentation. Use letters at least 2.5 cms high to make them possible to read. Obviously, the further away the delegates are from the chart, the bigger the writing needs to be. A last piece of advice for using flipcharts – try not to turn your back on the delegates for too long while you are writing.

Overhead projectors (OHPs) are still popular and produce a large, clear image without the need for putting out the lights in the room. During your rehearsal, position the OHP carefully so that it does not obscure the delegates' view of you. Keep your audience's attention by only displaying the transparencies when you want them to be the focus of attention. When you've dealt with the topic on a transparency take it away and move on. Leaving it displayed will distract your audience.

Professionally made videos or DVD presentations can be extremely effective but they must, of course, be genuinely relevant to your presentation and not be too long. It might be that you will not be able to use a video or DVD in your presentation as it will not be considered your own work so check this before you make this part of your plans. Used correctly, a video can break up a long presentation and provide light relief for both the presenter and the delegates while imparting useful knowledge and illustrating points you have made.

Physical objects – again, so long as they are relevant to your presentation – can be a very useful and effective way of getting an idea across and can also brighten up a dull presentation. It can give a feeling of reality to an abstract idea.

Presentations can be a time-consuming and daunting type of assignment but they are also an ideal way to learn a number of skills that will be invaluable in employment. The following skills and aptitudes will all be involved in a presentation:

- Oral communication.
- Adapting communication styles.
- Public speaking.
- Planning.
- Use of visual aids.

- Influencing your audience's behaviour.
- Control of an audience.
- Non-verbal communication.
- Increasing confidence and self-esteem.
- Timing and time management.
- Research.
- Goal setting.
- Dealing with questions and interruptions.
- Personal effectiveness.

Use the power of positive thinking (say to yourself 'I am well-prepared and competent') to get through a presentation and you will be able to look back on the experience as rewarding and ultimately valuable in career terms. Don't forget to add details of a presentation to your CV.

## Work-based assignments

Many courses are closely linked to specific professions and occupations and will often be studied at the same time as working full time. The main reason for studying this type of course is to improve employment prospects. National Vocational Qualifications (NVQs) are an example of this type of qualification but there are also examples to be found in the wide variety of management courses studied at local colleges or independently by distance learning, and in the professions such as accountancy and nursing.

Although much of the advice that applies to writing essays also applies to writing work-based assignments – planning, structure, research and so on – there are particular things to take note of when tackling a work-based assignment. First, these assignments are often shorter than the average essay (although they may consist of several distinct parts so the total word count and effort required will be similar), so keeping explanations concise and to the point is especially important. Second, these assignments usually require you to base them on examples taken from your workplace. This means that you must choose your examples carefully to ensure success, and also to make the assignment easier to write. This is similar to the need to make sure that you answer the question when writing an essay. The example you select must allow you to demonstrate your understanding of the principles involved. Let's look at part of an assignment of this type to see the possible pitfalls:

*Question*: Describe a significant change that has recently been carried out in your workplace and explain how it has affected you and the people you work with. Identify two barriers to change and two forces for change that existed in this situation.

The most difficult part of this will be choosing the *example of change* to discuss in your answer. Read the question carefully – it specifies a significant change, so a minor change such as someone leaving and being replaced would probably not be a good example to choose. A major reorganization of the department, a change in working practices or a programme of redundancies would be more appropriate examples. You are also asked to explain how the change affected you and your colleagues so choosing a major change that only affected another department would not be right.

Your next step should be to identify the *principles* you are learning about on your course that are the subject of the question. In our example, you would need to bring in something about managing change so you would look through your notes for relevant topics. When you've found them you need to work out how you can apply these general principles to the specific example you have chosen. If you really cannot see how this would be possible, then perhaps you have not chosen an appropriate example.

Another thing to be aware of with assignments of this type is that the *word count* is often very restricted. You would therefore have to be extra careful about making your answer concise and may want to consider using tables to bring in principles such as, in this example, *barriers to change*, as this is an economical way to give a large amount of information. You could use a table that lists barriers to and forces for change and then, following the table, identify which of these were present in the chosen work situation.

Courses that you could take that are closely connected to work situations and will have assignments that require you to produce writing that deals with real-life examples rather than the more academic essay questions usually found in college or university courses include:

• Professional nursing exams – you may have to produce a care management programme.

- Certificate of Professional Competence – a qualification in the transport industry that tests your knowledge of vehicles and regulations.
- Taxation exams – where you may have to work through actual examples of tax returns.
- Accountancy qualifications – you may have to develop balance sheets and profit and loss accounts for actual companies and to explain some of the anomalies found.
- NVQ in healthcare – you will have to develop case studies based on real-life examples of the care people in your work environment need.

## Dissertations

Dissertations are quite a common type of assignment in higher education. They are a type of research project and will often be quite lengthy pieces of work culminating in a report-style document and sometimes a presentation too, so look back at some of the tips for those types of work as well as these specifically about dissertations.

If you have to do a dissertation as part of your course, you will usually find that you have a lot of freedom about how you tackle it and about your choice of topic. It will not be directed by your tutors in the same way as, say, an essay would be. This lack of guidance and focus can make dissertations quite daunting. You will have to manage the project yourself so there are additional skills to be learned. You will have to carry out extensive research, decide for yourself the questions to be answered and decide on the appropriate research sources without too much guidance from your tutors. To do this successfully you will have to develop a high level of personal commitment to the project and to manage your time very carefully. There are a number of strategies that can help you with this type of independent work:

- *Start early.* There is a lot of work involved in a dissertation so it is especially important that you do not leave things until the last minute.
- *Choose a topic carefully.* It must really appeal to you and also must have plenty of scope for research. Don't choose something that you think will impress the assessors but will bore you rigid within days or that you will be unable to find much research material about. Try brainstorming a few subjects that would interest you and then check out the

resources in your library and on the Internet. Finding that there has been extensive research in the area you are considering is vital but you should also be trying to give the topic your own individual twist.

Perhaps you will be able to apply the central question to your local area or to a group of people that you have knowledge of and personalize the research in this way. Topic choice for a major project or dissertation is particularly important in that you only get one chance – unlike in exams where there is a number of questions for you to prove yourself, you can only display your knowledge and research capabilities on one major project.

Spending some time looking carefully at possible subjects at this early stage will save time later, as it will ensure that your choice is right for you and will help you to avoid a false start or, worse still, the pain of having to carry on with a project that is not right for you.

- *Plan every step of the way.* With a lengthy piece of work like a dissertation, it is doubly important that you carefully schedule your time. Consider all the small steps that will lead you to a successful dissertation, list them and then make a detailed schedule of exactly how long each will take and when you plan to do them. Although dissertations are essentially pieces of work that you are required to carry out independently, you will still get guidelines from your tutor as to the approximate number of words required, how they expect it to be presented and when, and may also give you some pointers as to source materials. Use all the information they are able to give you to ensure that your plan is as comprehensive as possible.

- *Keep in touch with your tutors.* If you have regular meetings scheduled, make sure that you are punctual and well-prepared for them. At different stages of the project they will be able to give you valuable advice and help. They will be unlikely to tell you directly what you should be doing and when but they will certainly be able to point you in the right direction for appropriate source materials and to let you know if the scope of your dissertation is right. They will let you know if you have chosen a topic that is too wide or too ambitious or, just as importantly, a topic that is not big enough. A good dissertation topic will be challenging but not overwhelming.

- *Collect sufficient data.* You will need enough to get reliable results and to enable you to make a convincing case but it is not helpful to collect too much information because then you will have difficulty presenting it and, of course, data is time consuming to collect. Look for trends in the data you have collected – you can then draw conclusions from it that will add to your case. See the following section on designing questionnaires that will help you to collect data.

- *Keep motivated.* A long piece of work like this will demand a lot of you and you must keep your focus on the end result. Use any trick in the book to keep your motivation high – such as ticking off items on your schedule as soon as you have completed them or rewarding yourself when you reach each milestone.

- *Summarize your research.* Use different ways of presenting your data – tables, graphs, and different types of chart so that not only do you make the dissertation appear more interesting but you can also compare the different methods and the effect they have on your data. Do not be tempted to draw any conclusions that you are unable to support with competently gathered data.

- *Present impeccably.* Make sure that you have checked and double-checked your dissertation, including all the data presented and that it is bound and presented so that it gives the impression of being an important document – which it is!

## Questionnaires and surveys

Questionnaires and surveys can help you to find effective data for use in reports or dissertations but the questions you use will have to be carefully written if they are to result in easy to use data that will prove your case.

In designing a questionnaire you should aim at a small number of well-worded questions that you can put to a large number of people. Take note of the following to make sure that you get questions that will produce answers that you can use effectively:

- Keep the questions short and easy to understand.
- Make sure ambiguity doesn't creep into your questions. If the questions can be taken in any way differently to how you intend them – rewrite them.
- Only a few questions should be necessary.
- Make sure that the responses you get will be clear – yes/no answers are best but make sure you can obtain, and count, clear responses.

- Check out the questions on a test group first – this can be a few friends and family – to make sure there is no ambiguity.
- Do not ask leading questions simply to get the responses you want. That will downgrade your research.
- Keep the time it takes to complete the questionnaire as short as possible while still obtaining meaningful data.
- Make sure that the responses are easy to record and to analyse.
- Keep accurate records and organize your results into tables.
- Compare your own findings with current research literature.
- Look for patterns and trends when you analyse the data so that you can draw meaningful conclusions.

## Group work

From time to time you may be required to work as part of a group and to submit work done as a group that will count towards your final result for the course or year. Group work is often used on courses, as it mimics a real-life work situation where people almost always work as part of a team. Of course, working as part of a group can be very different to working alone as the various personalities and requirements of the team's members affect how the work is done. Some members will work slowly and methodically while others will want to work more quickly. Or some may be perceived as 'not pulling their weight'. Frustration can then build up and the end result – a report or other piece of work – may be less effective as a result.

As working in groups can be an important feature of college life and is almost inevitably something that you will have to master in a work situation outside college, it is well worth understanding how groups work and how you can use them to their best advantage.

Let's look first at some of the advantages of working as a group. A major plus of being part of a group working on any large project is that you will get support from fellow team members. Being a student can be a lonely and uncertain occupation so working closely with others can provide support, reinforcement, social contact and a feeling of camaraderie – 'we're all in the same boat'. In addition, the large volume of work will, of course, be shared and ideas and skills from a variety of people will be brought to bear on the project, making it, in theory, easier to complete.

There are also, however, disadvantages to group working. These include differences of opinion and personality clashes that may arise among the members.

A number of skills can be gained as a result of working in groups and many of these are highly valued by employers so they are well worth working on. These include:

- Using resources effectively.
- Listening to others and taking their views into account.
- Being able to convey information to others and, in turn, to gain information from them.
- The ability to evaluate ideas and to weigh up all the possible options that may be on offer in a group situation.
- Being aware of how your behaviour can affect others.
- Offering constructive criticism to others and accepting it from others in the group.
- Inclusive behaviour – being able to ensure that everyone is included in discussions.
- Taking on a variety of roles.
- Working with others to reach decisions or solve problems.

Now we can consider the four main roles that will almost always be present in group-working situations:

- A coordinator – the person who takes on this role will bring together the efforts of the group.
- An ideas person – this team member will generate ideas and new ways of working.
- An information person – this person might be the best researcher in the group and will provide data and other information to help with the task.
- An evaluator – this team member will evaluate the information obtained by the group and will often monitor the progress being made towards the group's objectives.

Note that each of these roles could be carried out by more than one person within a large team.

Although there are disadvantages to working on a project in a group, these can usually be overcome if a few simple rules are followed that will ease the way around personality clashes and problems of communication:

- Clarify goals right at the start and agree who will do what – and how success will be measured.

- Agree that you will all express feelings freely – but with consideration for each other.
- All ideas must be given a fair hearing.
- Decisions must be taken by a consensus.
- Conflicts must be resolved before moving on.
- Criticism should be constructive and delivered one-to-one – and will be listened to.

Being an enthusiastic and effective team member is vital if you are to get the most out of working in a group. Not only will you be making a significant contribution to the efforts of the group as a whole but you will also be paving the way for an excellent learning experience for yourself. You cannot expect to get anything out of the group if you are not prepared to put anything in – so help the group, and yourself, by making the effort to:

- *Listen.* Pay attention to what others are saying and you will learn from their experience and perhaps cut down the amount of time you need to spend on your own studies.
- *Be encouraging.* By the things you say and the body language you use, you can make everyone feel appreciated and you will encourage them to add even more to the group. You can nod in agreement with someone or speak to them to show your approval of what they have said or done.
- *Do your share.* Volunteer to take on a task – and then do it. A group member who does not do what she says she will do will never be a valued or effective member of the team.
- *Move things along.* If you think things are stuck and the group is getting nowhere, try summarizing what you've achieved so far and asking for (or making) suggestions as to how you can build on this.
- *Only offer criticism if you are sure you can help someone by giving it.* Make sure it is constructive and that it is balanced by also stating what has been done correctly or what is good about someone's behaviour. Don't suggest changes that are impossible to make and, whatever you do, don't get personal.
- *Accept criticism positively.* Listen carefully and make sure that you ask questions if there is something you don't understand. Don't react immediately – take the comments away with you to reflect on later.

Remember that every team is a mixture of every member's skills and that everyone has something to contribute. With this – and clear goals – in mind, working on a group project can be a rewarding experience.

An important way of working with others and of improving our study skills is to form a study group. These support networks can be formal, where you meet at a certain time and place every week or month and have a formal agenda that you work through each time, or they can be informal and be almost nothing more than a group of like-minded students who keep in touch via telephone or e-mail. Here are some suggestions for study activities that such a group might get involved in and gain from:

- Keep in touch by telephone – this might be informal calls when you have a problem or want the benefit of someone else's opinion on a study issue or you might want to arrange a schedule so that every Monday evening, for example, you take turns to call each member of your group (this would only work with relatively small groups, for obvious reasons). Even the occasional phone call can help to alleviate the feelings of isolation that often accompany the more independent study that is expected today, and chatting informally about your studies with someone else can often provide a solution to a particular problem.

- Review activities – you could, for example, meet in a room at the college after a particular lecture each week and review the learning outcomes of that lecture. You will often find it beneficial to hear someone else's 'take' on what has been taught, and putting your own thoughts into words will be constructive too. Try to keep this sort of support group meeting more formal by giving each member of the group a few minutes to go through one of the main points, while others listen.

- Be supportive – everyone needs support and encouragement from time to time and if you are all doing a dissertation or difficult assignment, for example, getting together and discussing problems can be just what is needed.

- Help with problems – this can be as unstructured as simply a sympathetic ear at a difficult time. More formally, it can be an arrangement whereby each person is given a few minutes to tell the others about a current problem – for example, difficulty choosing a dissertation topic or finding arguments for an essay. The others then brainstorm a solution. Seeing how others view, and solve, the problem is informative in itself. The person with the problem must then choose his or her solution and talk about how he will proceed.

- Share ideas – here you might agree that you will all read different articles or texts then meet up and share your findings with the group. The discussion that takes place after you have summarized the text you have read for the group is especially useful.

- Share resources – it might not be necessary for everyone to buy a copy of a set book. If you can agree a fair schedule for use of the books the members of a group buy in this way, then it should be possible to save money but still have access to all the books you need. Another resource you can share is website addresses. If one member of the group finds a valuable new resource on the Internet, it makes sense to share it with his fellow support group members.

## Analysing the task

Writing an essay or other type of assignment is about much, much more than the writing. It is about researching, planning, analysing, organizing as well as about writing down your considered thoughts so that they are clear. Long before you get to actually writing an assignment, you will need to be totally clear what is required of you. An analysis of the task is therefore essential.

Start this analysis by dissecting the question. Try to sum it up in your own words. With a long, involved question it can be helpful to split it into its different parts and make sure that you understand these individually before you attempt to answer the whole question. You should, at this stage, make sure that you understand how the question relates to your course – why are you being asked this particular question? You should also check that you know the general requirements – how many words are required, what deadline you have to meet and the required format (if any) that you must follow. If you are in any doubt about any of this, ask for help from your tutor as soon as you can.

The majority of academic questions will follow an accepted format and will often use words such as:

- Discuss – here you will be required to examine the topic in detail so that you can debate the arguments involved.
- Compare and contrast – as you can see, there are two parts to this type of question. First, you will need to find similarities and differences between the two topics in the question and, second, you will need to examine the differences and provide reasons for these differences.

- Consider – weigh up the different aspects/arguments in the question.
- Criticize – put forward your assessment of the opinion or argument involved in the question, giving evidence in support of your reasoning.
- Describe – provide a detailed account.
- Assess – weigh up the importance and value of a statement or argument.
- Account for – provide reasons with supporting evidence.
- State – give a brief account of the main points.
- Interpret – explain the meaning of a statement and provide evidence in support.
- Evaluate – examine different aspects of a statement, giving your own judgement and using evidence in support.
- Examine – investigate evidence available on a topic.
- Differentiate – explain the differences between two statements or aspects of a topic.
- Relate – demonstrate the differences and similarities of two or more aspects, showing how they are connected.
- Justify – substantiate conclusions or statements, providing evidence for your case and defending it against the probable main objections.
- Distinguish between – detail the main points of two arguments or statements, showing the differences between two things.
- Review – examine a topic in detail.
- Summarize – give a short, clear account of a topic, including just the main information.
- Refute – here you must argue against and disprove an argument or statement.
- Illustrate – this type of question requires you to give plenty of examples from different sources to explain the point made in the question.

The key to using this list of words successfully is to read your question carefully and note what type of instruction you are being given. Each of these instructional words will require a slightly different approach to the question and you must tailor your answer accordingly.

The next stage in analysing the question is deciding what you already know about the topic. The best way to do this is to do a brainstorming exercise. Jot down the key words in the question and examine what you know about these topics in the context of the question. As ideas come to you, write them down.

Figure 8.1 is an example of how this might be done using an essay question, from a politics course, of 'To what extent are there divisions within New Right ideology?':

> To what <u>extent</u> are there divisions within <u>New Right ideology?</u>
>
> [Note the underlinings – the beginning of an analysis of the question. These are the key words in the question that you should be concentrating on to start your brainstorming session.]
>
> New Right – blend of neo liberalism plus neo conservatism – formed 2nd half of 20th C (reaction against Keynesian welfarist economics, a weakening of authority and start of permissiveness)
>
> New Right economic policy – Adam Smith, Hayek, Friedman. 'Invisible hand' 'giant nervous system'
>
> Different views on:
>
> **The state**
>
> Neo liberalism rejects government intervention e.g. Margaret Thatcher privatization. Roll back the state. Rely on market. Less government, more freedom e.g. not state religion
>
> but
>
> Neo conservatism supports established values, hierarchy and order, state authoritarianism, powerful state, law and order e.g. prison sentencing
>
> **Society**
>
> Neo liberalism – self-interest, individuals rather than groups
>
> but
>
> Neo conservatism – believe society is one collective organism (tradition, authority)

### Human nature

*Neo liberalism – rational, reasonable, self reliant therefore less state control necessary*

*but*

*Neo conservatism – individuals are frail, immoral, corrupt therefore need state authority, order, discipline*

### International affairs

*Neo liberalism – support internationalism, globalization, more power in foreign hands e.g. IMF, market forces*

*but*

*Neo conservatism – value national identity and autonomy from Europe*

*Above = ideological discrepancies/contradictions*

**figure 8.1** sample brainstorming exercise on an essay question

As you will see from this brainstorming session on the subject of divisions within the New Right, there is sufficient material for the basis of an essay with just a bit of research (about the examples used, for instance) needed then the student will be ready to tackle an outline for the essay. We'll go back to this example later in this chapter when we look at drawing up a map for writing your essay.

If you find this technique difficult to get started on and you sit with a blank sheet of paper, thinking 'I don't know much about this topic', then you need to ask yourself a few questions to get the ideas flowing. For example:

- Where does this fit into my course? Check your course notes.
- Why am I being asked this particular question? What knowledge are you expected to display?
- What experience do I have of this subject?
- Do I agree with the statement, opinion or argument in the question?
- How would I argue against it?
- What evidence do I have for or against this?

At this point, you should have sufficient understanding of the question to enable you to make a preliminary plan as to how you will tackle the question. Do you understand what you are being asked to do? Have you decided on your central theme or argument? Jot it down and keep it by you.

When you feel you've exhausted all the ideas you already have about the question, and decided on your approach to the question, you will need to decide what other information you will need to find out to enable you to write your essay. For this you will need to plan your research so let's look at that task in the next section.

## Research

When you're starting to research an answer to an assignment question, you will need to:

- Decide on the case you want to make.
- Find the separate arguments that go towards making your case.
- Search for evidence – find things that other people have written that are for or against your arguments.

If you follow these steps, when you start to research – perhaps in the library or on the Internet – you will have an idea of what you are looking for. Look at the notes you've made on what you already know on the topic and then quickly review your course notes on it. This should direct you to what extra research you need to carry out. By now you will have decided on a central argument or theme for your essay but need some extra evidence to prove your case or evidence against your case so that you can present a balanced case and some respected sources to quote. Or maybe you need some additional arguments and ideas to support your central argument. It can be very useful at this stage to write yourself a list of the information that you still need. Then you can get busy with the research. Go to the library or on to the Internet or to the set books you have handy to consult.

It is vital that you do not get carried away while doing your research for a specific essay. You will come across lots of information that, while it may be fascinating, is not relevant to the question you are trying to answer. Keep your mind focused on the task in hand by asking yourself 'How am I going to use this information?'.

When you've got your information down on paper in this way, you're ready to start planning your essay. Let's look at how you might proceed.

# Drawing up a map

At this point, you will be planning how you can get from this collection of information and ideas to a completed, coherent essay and you will need to be selective. You cannot include everything you know or have found out about the topic in the question. When you have drawn up an outline that will take you from the introduction to the conclusion via all the arguments you have decided to include in your essay, you should be able to see how much of the essay can be devoted to particular points that you want to make. Your aim is a balanced, coherent essay so it is important that you do not write too much on one aspect of what you know about a topic, leaving you insufficient space to devote to other, equally important, arguments and points. Another problem that a plan will highlight at this stage is where you do not have enough material for the assignment. Making an outline of your essay will ensure that you know what you are putting where, what points you intend to make, that you have evidence for each argument and that all the arguments can be brought to a successful conclusion. Do not skimp on this aspect of your preparation. The better your outline, the easier your essay will be to write.

Your first step is to work out the order in which you will introduce and develop your arguments. Your plan, using the example brainstorming session as shown earlier, might follow the guidelines as shown in Figure 8.2.

*To what extent are there divisions within New Right ideology?*

**Introduction** *New Right is a blend of neo liberalism plus neo conservatism – formed 2nd half of 20th C as a reaction against Keynesian welfarist economics, weakening of authority and start of permissiveness in 1960s*

*New Right economic policy – broad range of ideas including those of Adam Smith (18th C), Friedrich Hayek and Milton Friedman (20th C). Friedman saw economy regulated by 'invisible hand' and Hayek saw it as a 'giant nervous system'. Laissez faire*

**1st argument** *– The state*

*Neo liberalism rejects government intervention e.g. Margaret Thatcher privatization. Roll back the state. Rely on market. Less government, more freedom e.g. not state religion but neo conservatism supports established values, hierarchy and order, state authoritarianism, powerful state, harsh law and order e.g. prison sentencing*

**2nd argument** *– Society*

*Neo liberalism believes society made up of self-interested individuals rather than formation of groups but neo conservatism believes society is one collective organism (tradition, authority)*

**3rd argument** *– Human nature*

*Neo liberalism – rational, reasonable, self-reliant therefore less state control necessary but neo conservatism believe Individuals are frail, immoral, corrupt therefore need state authority, order, discipline*

**4th argument** *– International affairs*

*Neo liberalism – support internationalism, globalization, more power in foreign hands e.g. IMF, market forces but neo conservatism value national identity and autonomy from Europe*

**Conclusion** *Examples of ideological discrepancies/ contradictions given show that there are deep divisions within the New Right*

**figure 8.2** sample plan, using the brainstorming exercise

Having taken the results of the brainstorming session and a little extra research that it became obvious was necessary when writing down the initial ideas for the essay, the student has formed an outline – a plan – for writing the actual essay. She has set up her views for the introduction, defining and explaining some of the key terms and then marshalled the arguments in favour of her conclusion that there are deep divisions within the New Right.

Note that she has numbered these arguments so that she will know what order to put them into the essay. Note also that this essay plan clearly sets out the beginning, the middle and the end. Figure 8.3 shows, to bring this set of exercises to a satisfactory conclusion, the final essay that resulted from the brainstorming session and the outline.

### 'To what extent are there divisions within New Right ideology?'

*With the acceptance of social democracy in the UK after 1945, a set of more radical ideas was slowly developing within the Conservative ideology during the second half of the century. These were primarily a reaction against the culture of dependency that Keynesian welfarist economics encouraged (also seen as the cause of the early 1970s' recession), the weakening of authority in society and the permissiveness of the 1960s and 70s. This broad range of ideas was termed the 'New Right', and was an amalgamation of two key theories: neo-liberalism and neo-conservatism. There has been lengthy debate, however, over how compatible these two are with each other. In this essay I will try to support my view that there are significant divisions within New Right ideology.*

*Neo-liberalism is the economic policy that the New Right advocates. It is often seen as a return to the classical liberal ideology, where the economy is held to be at its healthiest when left to itself, hence a 'laissez-faire' approach. Although the original liberal theorist was Adam Smith in the 18th century, neo-liberalism was heavily influenced by 20th century theorists Friedrich Hayek and Milton Friedman, who reiterate Smith's conception of the economy as regulated by 'an invisible hand' – Hayek* likened it to a giant nervous system. Neo-liberalism completely rejects government intervention, seeing it as a threat to individual liberty, and focuses instead on fewer restrictions on business and economic development. This stance has been summarized as 'private good, public bad'. During the New Right era of Margaret Thatcher, this manifested itself in the widespread privatization of many public services, for example, British Rail services. This move was criticized by some as 'selling off the family silver', but supported by others as necessary for healthy economic competition. Neo-conservatism would suggest a very different economic policy. The importance that they place on the established values of a strong and cohesive society, hierarchy and order are directly jeopardized by the neo-liberal free market, which is dynamic and unregulated (except by the supposed 'invisible hand'). The fact that the two stances run counter to each other, even harming each other, raises questions as to how compatible economic liberalism and social conservatism are in the context of the New Right.

The goal of the New Right was often described as having a strong but minimal state. However, neither neo-liberalism nor neo-conservatism seems to support this aim. Neo-conservatives subscribe to a form of state authoritarianism, with strong emphasis on the maintenance of authority, 'tough' law and order, and heavy-handed punishment, shown for example in the increase of prison sentence lengths in the 1980s. Neo-conservative views would, on the one hand, suggest support for a powerful and extensive state as the only method for tackling the problems of law and order, and public morality. Neo-liberalism, on the other hand, is an anti-statist doctrine. Margaret Thatcher seems to support this doctrine through her phrase 'Roll back the state'. Neo-liberals aim to reverse the trend towards a large and powerful government that had been emerging in the 20th century. It is the market that is seen to be more important than the government, and individuals ideally have negative freedom, which is freedom of choice without the constraints the state might impose. Historically, for *example, this would have meant absence of a state religion, allowing people free choice of faith. So, it seems that the New Right policy of 'strong but minimal' state does not cohere to either of the two stances.*

*The two also differ significantly over their view of human nature. For both of them, their policies concerning almost everything, for example, the state or the economy, originates from their view of human nature. Like in classical liberalism, the foundation of neo-liberal ideology is in the belief that humans are reasonable, rational and self-reliant. This influences a number of their policies, for example, the conception that the state should allow the sensible human being to take full control of his individual private matters. According to neo-conservatives, however, humans are frail, insecure, and essentially limited. This low opinion explains their view that humans should be provided with authority, discipline and order by the state. New Right campaigns such as a return to 'family values', as important in providing structure and hierarchy, have clearly been influenced by these neo-conservative tenets. Furthermore, neo-conservatives view humans as innately immoral and corrupt, resulting in the belief that delinquency illustrates corruption of the human soul rather than social injustice, therefore harsh sentencing is popular. The fact that neo-conservatives and neo-liberals disagree so widely about human nature suggests deep divisions within the New Right, considering how profoundly their attitude can affect the ideology.*

*On the subject of 'society', neo-liberals and neo-conservatives hold quite different opinions as well. The former hold that society is primarily atomistic: it is made up of a collection of self-interested individuals, rather than social groups ( we can see how this view stems from the liberal view of human nature too). The latter refute this, claiming that society is one collective organism, held together by the bonds of tradition and authority. The new right combines the two into what they call liberal atomism.*

*Neo-liberalism inherently supports the concepts of globalization and internationalism, seeing as neo-liberal priorities rest with the interests of the economy, which is not confined to national borders. The fact that globalization gives large amounts of power into the hands of multinational corporation bosses means that corporations such as IMF have unprecedented power over our democratically elected British government, decreasing its importance. This seems to go against the ideology of the neo-conservatives, who value concepts such as national identity and pride highly, and generally try to maintain as much autonomy as possible from Europe. This is illustrated in the current Euro-sceptic Conservative party stance. Neo-conservatives also try to keep immigrant levels low, and oppose multi-culturalism as weakening the bonds of nationhood. These opposing values must be reconciled within the term New Right.*

*Not all those who subscribe to New Right ideas support both neo-liberalism and neo-conservatism. However, though there have been those who reject the idea of a free market, or who disagree with conservative social theory, it is the fusion between neo-liberalism and neo-conservatism that make the New Right distinctive. I believe, nevertheless, that it does not present a fully coherent political ideology. Although the two may manage to work together in practice, as shown by both Thatcher's and Reagan's administrations, the ideological discrepancies and contradictions between neo-liberalism and neo-conservatism lead me to the conclusion that there definitely are deep divisions within the New Right.*

**figure 8.3** sample final essay resulting from the plan and brainstorming exercise

Look carefully at the three exercises carried out with this essay question. You should be able to see a clear progression from the brainstorming session in Figure 8.1 through the outline shown in Figure 8.2 and culminating in the finished essay shown in Figure 8.3.

Let's look now at how you might apportion the words allowed for an essay among all the elements that you want – and need – to include. With a word limit of, say, 1,500 words, you could proceed with your plan as follows:

*Introduction*: Allow about 200 words to tell your reader what the essay is about and where you are going with the topic.

*Main body*: Use approximately 1,000 words to bring in all your main points and arguments.

*Conclusion*: Use your remaining 300 words to draw your conclusion and to bring together the main points.

The end result of making a plan along all these lines will be a well-structured essay that has a beginning, a middle and an end. As you decide where to put all the points that you want to make, you will be able to see any shortfalls in your research and any inconsistencies in your case. As you allocate an approximate number of words to each of the main sections, you will be keeping yourself on track and avoiding using up too much or too little of the word total on a specific section. Is there anything you will need to leave out? If so, what? Do you need to fill out some of your arguments with more evidence? When you're confident that you have the right amount of material and that your arguments are balanced and all are relevant, then you can start on your first draft.

As you can see, there is a lot of planning involved in writing even a straightforward essay but it is a vital part of the writing. On no account should you be tempted to just start writing without following these planning stages. That will almost always result in a poor-quality essay that could miss out vital elements or seriously under or overrun the word limit.

## Getting to the first draft stage and editing

Now, finally, we've got to the stage where you start writing the essay. At this point you're just working on the first draft. Don't worry too much about anything other than following your outline at this stage – you will be able to improve the essay in later drafts. It can be easier to transfer the sub-headings from your outline and use these as the basis of your essay but you will need to delete these headings before you finish the piece of work as essays, unlike reports and so on, do not usually include them as they interrupt the flow of the prose. You don't have to start by writing the introduction, although this can sometimes help to focus your thoughts and, as you're telling your reader where you are going with the essay, you will be reminding yourself too. You can go through the sub-headings 'filling in the gaps' until you have used up your material and made your case. You will now have the basis of an essay down on paper and will be able to refine your work.

## Fine tuning

Read through your first draft (you might find that it helps to have left it on one side for at least a few hours or even a day or two before you do this as you will come back to it with a fresher, more objective point of view) and note where there are problems. This checklist will show you what you're looking for:

- Does the essay answer the question? This can't be said often enough. The most common cause of poor marks for essays is that the student didn't answer the question.
- Lack of clarity – is any of it difficult to understand or seem a bit confused?
- Flow – does each paragraph lead on in a logical order from the last one? Have you used signposts to help your reader? (See Chapter 07.)
- Order – connected information should all be together, not scattered throughout the essay.
- Paragraphs or sentences that are too long. One point per sentence (if there are two or more points, then split the sentence into two or more) and one argument or topic per paragraph (again, split them up if necessary).
- Are any points made that are not backed up with evidence?
- Inconsistencies.
- Incorrect spelling – run a spellcheck but also check it yourself.

In addition to making sure that your arguments are made succinctly and are backed up by evidence, you must also have a strong beginning and a convincing end, so read through your introduction and conclusion again. Does your introduction state clearly the purpose of the essay? Does your conclusion show exactly what your judgements are and how you arrived at them? Ideally, the introduction and the conclusion should echo each other so that you tell your reader where you are going and then tell them where you have got to.

When you have read through and corrected your essay a few times (as many as necessary), your next task is to compile a bibliography or list of references.

---

**Top tip**

When you think you've polished your essay as much as you can, read it out loud – you may be surprised by the mistakes you will find in this way.

---

Your final task is to ensure that your work is presented perfectly. This task is made easier with the use of a computer and we will look at the use of information technology in studying in the next chapter.

## Summary

In this chapter you have learned:

- That an essential ingredient of an essay is a well-reasoned argument. This should have evidence to support it, leading to a clear conclusion.
- That verbal presentations should be organized and structured, geared to your audience, and include handouts and the use of visual aids to good effect.
- Brief details of how to use visual aids such as OHPs, flipcharts, PowerPoint © presentations and videos to enhance a presentation.
- Some tips about completing a dissertation, including starting early, choosing a subject with sufficient potential material and that will maintain your interest over a period of time, the value of planning and keeping in touch with your tutors, using numerical data in a variety of ways and high-quality presentation.
- Some tips for producing a questionnaire.
- The advantages and disadvantages of working in a group. The advantages include increased support, social contact and the sharing of a workload. The disadvantages include differences of opinion and personality clashes.

- Some of the key instructional words used in essay questions.
- How to plan the distribution of words in an essay so that it is well-structured and balanced.
- How to fine tune and check an essay – ensuring you've answered the question and produced a clear piece of writing that flows.

## Quick revision test

1 List the elements of a report.
2 When is it recommended to deal with questions when you give a presentation?
3 Why would you use pre-prepared flipcharts for a presentation?
4 Give two ways to keep yourself motivated during preparation of a dissertation?
5 What are the three steps to take when starting to research a topic?

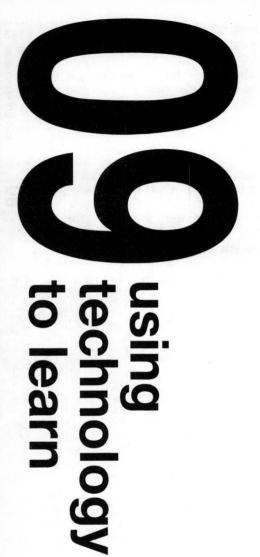

# 09

## using technology to learn

**In this chapter you will learn:**
- how to develop your computer skills
- how technology can help you in your studies
- about uses of the Internet in studying.

# Effective computer skills

There are lots of ways in which using a computer can help you with your studies. These include:

- *Word processing.* This is the most obvious and popular use of a personal computer as a study aid. Proficient use of a computer when writing essays, reports and dissertations can make your work look impressively competent. So long as you don't go too far with fancy fonts, different colours and complicated layouts, work that is word processed will always make a better impression than handwritten work. Writing using a word-processing package also gives you the advantage of being able to edit without too much trouble. You can move words around, delete them and add them without all the rewriting and crossings out that come with these tasks if you are handwriting a piece of work. Here are some other things that a word processing package will give you:

  1 Word count – useful when you're trying to stick to a word limit.
  2 Spellcheck – but always carry out your own proofreading check too.
  3 Storage of your work so that you can always reproduce it if the original gets lost.
  4 Writing many drafts of an essay and saving them all. It avoids the rewriting that comes with handwritten drafts.

- *Handling data.* Spreadsheet and database packages allow you to manipulate large quantities of information. You can use these packages to sort information into lists or groups, to make long, involved calculations and to perform statistical analysis very quickly.

- *Charts.* Very professional looking charts, tables and graphs can be produced with the help of word-processing and spreadsheet packages. Most packages give a choice of the type of chart or graph to be produced with a set of data that you have typed in and then take you step by step through creating these illustrations for your work.

- *Presentations.* Microsoft PowerPoint © will help you to make a slide show style presentation with ease, bringing in information already stored on your computer and adding special effects to keep your audience's interest.

- *Library searches*. You will inevitably have to use a computer database in college libraries to carry out searches for the book or article that you need.

So, in view of these important uses, it is obvious that it can be well worth investing some time in becoming proficient with a computer. Most programs include some sort of tutorial to guide you through the basics and you can quickly become confident in using a computer to help you in your studies and to make your work look more professional. There is even software designed to teach you to type. You don't have to be an expert typist to produce an impressive looking essay on your computer (computers are far more forgiving than old-style typewriters used to be) but learning to touch type can make life a lot easier. You don't even have to have an in-depth understanding of how the computer works – just learn enough to be able to use it. If you lack confidence and/or skills in this area, there is lots of help available. Local colleges and training providers will offer courses to suit everyone from the beginner to the advanced learner.

If you are fairly proficient at using your computer to produce essays and reports but don't really understand how things are stored on it and are therefore frequently troubled by lost files, you will find it useful to know a little about your computer's system. An easy way to understand file storage on your computer is to see it as a version of a 'real' filing system with filing cabinets, drawers and paper files. Each of these has an equivalent on your computer:

- Your computer's hard disk (its main memory) is like a filing cabinet.
- Within this filing cabinet – or hard drive – are drawers. Each drawer is represented by a folder. For example, you might have a folder (or drawer) that contains everything connected with one of the subjects you're studying and another folder for a different subject.
- Within each of these folders are sub-folders that relate to the paper folders you would keep in drawers. You might have a paper folder – or sub-folder – for assignments and another for notes.
- Within the sub-folder you would then keep all the files. A file – or document – would relate to the paper files on which you've done your assignments and so on.

Apart from acquiring the technical skills, you will have to take an organized approach to information technology if you are to use your computer successfully while you study.

And finally, just a few shortcuts and tips to help you save time:

- Use your mouse – there are plenty of shortcuts you can master using your mouse. Try a single click in the left-hand margin to select a line, double-click to select a whole paragraph, or triple-click to select the entire document. Or try using your mouse to select and drag words, phrases or paragraphs instead of using the menus to cut and paste. Another shortcut is to right-click the mouse to give you a drop-down menu.

- Keyboard shortcuts – using Windows, if you want to close a program key Alt + F4. Press F7 to perform a spellcheck and don't forget the useful keys marked 'Home' and 'End' that will help you to move easily through your document.

- More keyboard shortcuts – this time using Word. Just by pressing the Control key and another key, a number of actions can be carried out:

| | |
|---|---|
| Ctrl + C | copy |
| Ctrl + X | cut |
| Ctrl + V | paste |
| Ctrl + N | create a new document |
| Ctrl + S | save |
| Ctrl + P | print screen |

- Find function – a valuable function if you're coming back to a piece of work and want to start in a particular place. Just think of a word or two near the spot you're looking for, type them into the 'Find' function and it will take you to the place you're looking for, ready to start work again.

- Find and replace – this takes the 'Find' function a step further and is useful if you want to change something that occurs a number of times in a piece of work. For instance, you might want to change the spelling of a place name. To do this you can use the 'Find and Replace All' function and all will be replaced by the correct word – as if by magic.

- Styles – if you can master this function, you will be able to carry out a number of tasks relating to the way your work is presented. For example, you will be able to change the style of all the headings in a document with just a few clicks.

- AutoText – with this facility you can store frequently used text (your name and address, for instance), and insert the phrase or words into any document with just a couple of key strokes.
- Chart wizard – guides you through a choice of charts and graphs to present numerical data in a way that looks very impressive.
- Table wizard – helps to lay out your table perfectly.
- Change case – with this facility – available in the format menu – you can change text that you have typed in upper case into text in lower case and vice versa. This is useful if you've been typing with the Caps Lock key on by mistake, for example.
- Word count – useful when you're writing an assignment to a specific length. You can check your progress as you write so that you don't write too much in any one section of your work.

These few functions and shortcuts are well worth learning as they will save time and help to make your writing tasks and presentation of your work easier. Do not, however, spend so much time fiddling with the computer that you have no time to produce any work!

## Getting organized

If you don't get organized when you're using a computer to produce essays and other written work for your course, you will soon begin to experience frustration and, if disaster happens and the computer crashes, sheer desperation if you lose valuable work that you haven't been organized enough to copy. There are therefore two ways in which you simply must get organized with your computer working:

- Know where all your files are stored and what is in them.
- Keep backup copies of all your work.

Both tasks can be achieved easily if you develop routines that will ensure you work in a way that will minimize the frustration and time wasting that can accompany a disorganized approach. The solution to this problem is quite straightforward:

- Create folders that will segregate your various types of files. Maybe you will have a folder for each subject and within each of these folders you may have a sub-folder for assignments and one for notes. The way you set up your files and folders is up to you – you are the only one who can decide what will suit you and your way of working.

- Name your files creatively. Don't fall into the trap of just dating them or, even worse numbering them – that will not give you any clue about the contents of the file and when you're looking for an essay you've written or need a copy of some notes on a particular topic, you could open an untold number of badly named files before you find the one you want. The file name should describe what's in the file. You could then, if it suits you, incorporate the date in a file name – just so long as it's obvious what the file contains.

- Name your file as soon as you start working on it. It is easy to become involved in your writing, forget to save your work where you can find it, and then lose it.

- Keep track of the different drafts you produce by saving each draft with a number at the end of the document title that indicates the version. For example, the first draft of this book on my computer is entitled TY Study Skills 1 and the next draft will be TY Study Skills 2. In that way you will always know which is the latest version but can refer back to earlier versions.

- Use the headers and footers facility. You can put the title of the document in the header plus the version number and your name and date (sometimes just use the month if work on it will be spread over quite a few days or weeks) and/or the assignment number in the footer. In this way, you will have these details printed on every page of your work.

- Back up your files regularly. You should save your work (and any other files you have on your computer – household accounts, letters etc.) to CDs or floppy disks then keep them in a safe place. Make sure that you label your disks so that you know what files are saved on them and will be able to lay your hands on them easily when needed.

- After you have backed up your work, delete any files on your computer that you are not currently working on. This will reduce the files that you have to sift through and will, if you have deleted large quantities of information (especially graphics), free up space on your computer, helping it to run faster resulting in more time saved. Delete all old files that are out of date or no longer needed. For example, last year's assignments can be stored on a CD or floppy disk so that they are available for reference but are not taking up valuable hard disk space on your computer.

This brings us to the subject of computer crash problems. Having too much 'stuff' on your computer is one of the things that is likely to make your computer sluggish and, ultimately, could cause it to crash – losing your precious work and taking up time in getting it to work again. If it is running badly, it will run slowly causing frustration and wasted time. There are simple ways to clear out your computer:

- Remember to empty the bin. When you delete files and put them in your recycle bin they will stay there – taking up space on your hard drive – until you empty it.
- If you use the Internet, you will be storing lots of temporary files that are no longer needed. These are 'cookies' that websites you have accessed will have deposited on your computer. You can delete them by opening 'Temporary Internet Files' in the Windows folder or, for Mac users, access the Cache folder in the Preferences folder.
- Clear out old programs. If you've lost interest in a hobby or now have the super-duper more up-to-date version of your favourite game, then ditch the programs you no longer use. Make sure that you delete the entire program rather than just deleting the desktop shortcut or the directory for a program.

Using your computer and taking care of it in this way will help to avoid problems and takes much less time than sorting out a disaster caused by neglect or lack of organization.

Time management is another issue of which you should be aware when using a computer to help you with your studies. Unless you are exceptionally skilled at sorting out computer glitches, crashes and problems, you should expect to have to build a bit of time into your schedule to keep things running. As we saw earlier, you can do some basic 'tidying up' of your hard disk and this will help to head off some of the problems that are sometimes caused by a computer that is running low on memory. You will need to allow time for regular clearing out of unused files and programs plus learning how to deal with common problems. You will manage your time better if, when facing a deadline for an assignment, you do not ignore the problems that can occur.

---

**Top tip**

Get to know how to escape a computer crash – the most common way is press Ctrl, Alt, Del. If all else fails, switch your computer off for a few seconds and then back on again.

As we saw earlier, a computer can be used for so much more than the production of professional looking assignments. If you have an Internet connection (or go to the library to use their facilities), you will be able to do a lot of your research online. You will also be able to use electronic mail facilities to keep in touch with your tutor and other members of your study group. In fact, if you are studying a distance-learning course, it can be the very best way of sending your assignments for marking, and sending queries about the course material to your tutor. It is quick and easy and will mean that you have a record of what has been sent and when. Yet again, you will have to take an organized approach to using your computer. E-mail software has facilities to store different types of sent or received items of mail in different folders and will date and time the transmission and in this way you can keep track of your work.

# What is e-learning?

E-learning could be defined as any learning that is supported or made easier by the use of information and communications technology. It can be anything from a part of your course materials being made available to you via a computer or assignments being marked via computer right through to a whole course being provided – and assessed – online. Let's look at some of the ways that aspects of your course can be supported by electronic means:

- Networked information – this is the most straightforward use of e-learning. Many colleges and university libraries have linked their computers and made available through this network CD-ROMs that contain some of the more popular and useful journals. It is often easier to access articles and information in this way than to use paper-based texts because of the extensive and rapid search facilities. Not only will you be able to go straight to the relevant piece of work in a journal but also many students can access the same piece at the same time because of the networked facility.

- Other reading materials may be provided electronically including items such as course handouts, lecture notes, up-to-date information on your course and its schedule and revision notes.

- Communication – online communication can help in all sorts of ways to support your learning. It may give you greater access to your tutors or it may foster online support groups for your course. Without the use of e-mail, a student could feel isolated but it is now possible to keep in touch online and to have access to a tremendous level of support from fellow students or your tutors. You may also have assignments delivered to you electronically and then be able to submit them online – saving time and paper.

- Online assessment – some or all of your assignments may be assessed via computer. This might take the form of a set of multiple-choice questions for you to answer that will be automatically marked and the result – and possible comments – immediately transmitted to you so that you will be able to take remedial action if problems are uncovered.

- Design software – programs are available that will help you to design surveys or questionnaires and also to help you to analyse the data that you collect.

- Interactive programs – this type of material is becoming more common, although it is expensive to produce. With an interactive element, learning materials on computer can individualize the direction the learning takes and the speed at which it is delivered according to the responses received from each learner. This type of program can be used, for example, to develop technical skills or to take part in simulated exercises or case studies.

- Complete courses – a whole course can be studied via a computer. This may be by using a CD-ROM where the advances in technology in recent years mean that the courses and tutorials provided in this format include sophisticated graphics, interactive aspects and marking systems to give an ideal learning environment without having to leave your home. Or it may be by logging on to a learning provider's website. We will look at these online courses in more detail in the next section.

With all these choices available, it would be easy to sign up for everything available online. Before you know it you could find all your time taken up chatting online, e-mailing fellow students, searching complicated databases of information and dealing with the computer problems that will inevitably occur. As with any other learning medium, you must be selective. Find the ways you can use a computer that will enhance your learning and make life easier for you.

More and more universities and colleges are embracing the technology available to help their students and are setting up virtual learning environments (VLEs). When a student logs on to the website from their home or using the college's facilities, they can work independently using the learning materials made available via the VLE. Logging on will also bring up features such as details of the individual student's progress against targets. In this way, students must take responsibility for their own progress and have all the details they need continually available. VLEs can also incorporate the following:

- Bulletin boards.
- A course overview and outline – useful when trying to get to grips with what you are aiming at, as we saw in Chapter 02.
- Conferencing facilities.
- A calendar.
- Automatic reminders about assignment deadlines, exam dates etc. tailored to individual students.
- Course materials, notes and handouts.
- Assessment materials.
- Tracking tools – to be used either by students to monitor their own targets and deadlines or by tutors to monitor levels of activity.
- An online chat room for students of the university as a whole or one restricted to a particular course.

As these types of facility become more widely available, the amount of information readily obtainable by students will, of course, increase and their studies will be made easier – and hopefully more successful – as a result.

## Online courses

An enormous variety of courses are available to buy and complete online. They range from degree and MBA courses, to languages, to literature to practical skills courses.

The main advantage of online courses is their flexibility. As courses offered in this way can be studied in 'bite-sized chunks', they can be accessible to many more learners than conventional full-time courses. A conventional degree student would usually need to attend college or university every day and would not be able to carry out any other occupation than perhaps a part-time job. This obviously has financial implications and therefore excludes many people from further and higher education. The flexibility of online courses makes high-level courses accessible to many people – especially mature students who may have jobs and family responsibilities to consider. In addition, as online courses can be made available to a far greater audience, they become much more affordable. The materials for these courses are usually very expensive to produce but economies of scale ensure that their costs compare favourably with conventional university education.

When studying a course online, a great amount of self-discipline is necessary. If you are the sort of person who doesn't complete an assignment unless reminded several times by your tutor of the consequences of not handing it in, then using e-learning in this way is unlikely to be for you. If, on the other hand, you are a well-motivated person who has little problem in working independently, then online courses might be an ideal way to improve your qualifications. It is possible to complete these courses in your own time, fitting them in to your existing work patterns or around family commitments – and maybe a social life too. Online courses can be completed at home, in your workplace (if it is a work-based course or your employer is encouraging you to study) or in a specially established learning centre. Training providers may offer the use of these centres as well as offering a package of support and guidance.

## Online debating

Online debating is part of the increase in e-moderated learning that has taken place over recent years. The moderator of the online debating forum will often ask questions to stimulate debate in appropriate areas and this can be a very worthwhile learning experience. It provides an opportunity to learn from others while organizing and expressing your own thoughts and knowledge of the subject. Debating face to face can be a daunting experience but if done online, the intimidation of taking part in a discussion is lessened and will lead to more participation. If this facility is offered in your college or university, it is worthwhile to take advantage as, properly moderated and targeted, online debating can reinforce learning.

# Summary

In this chapter you have learned:

- Various ways in which using a computer can be useful in your studies including word processing, handling data, using charts, graphs and tables, producing presentations and for research.
- How the computer's storage systems work and how you can get your computer organized so that you are not troubled by lost files. Advice includes backing up files regularly, naming files creatively and using folders to segregate different subjects.
- Some simple shortcuts using your keyboard or your mouse that will make life easier.
- How to avoid your computer becoming overloaded – by emptying the recycle bin, deleting cookies and clearing out old programs.
- About ways of e-learning, i.e. supporting your studies by electronic means, including using networked information provided by your college, communicating online with your tutors or as a member of an online support group, online assessment or even taking an entire course online.

# Quick revision test

1 What shortcut would you be using if you pressed Ctrl + N?
2 What facility would you use to include the assignment number at the top or bottom of every page in a document?
3 How can e-learning help to overcome problems of isolation for a student?
4 What is a virtual learning environment?
5 Give one advantage and one disadvantage of an online course.

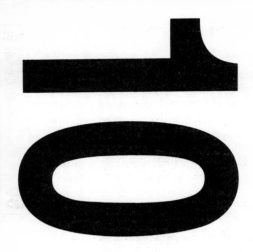

# 10

# revision skills

**In this chapter you will learn:**
- about the purpose of revision
- how to organize your revision
- some revision techniques.

# Revision – not the time to learn something new

The purpose of revision is to go through materials that you have already studied, in preparation for an examination. An examination gives you the chance to pull the entire course together and to look at the bigger picture. Rather than concentrating on just one aspect, as assignments usually do, revising for exams should cover the whole of your course. Revision does not normally mean that you will be learning something new. Instead it allows you to re-examine materials and commit them to memory so that your tutors or external examiners can see that you have understood the material for your course and can use the knowledge you have gained.

There are many effective ways of revising and there are just as many ways of wasting time in the name of revision. Let's look at some of the pitfalls involved in revising for examinations:

- *Reading through notes and other materials repeatedly.* This is not likely to be very effective (you may learn a little as a result of the repetition but not as much as you could learn by other methods) and it will be boring. Being bored while you're revising is something you should avoid, so putting a little extra effort into finding the revision techniques that are right for you will pay dividends.

- *Writing out essays that you've done as part of your coursework.* Although this could be viewed as active learning, this wastes time because it is highly unlikely that exactly the same question will come up in the exam. The questions you have been answering as part of your coursework have different aims from those you will encounter in the examination. You would be working far more effectively if you devised new exam-type essay questions and practised writing essays under exam conditions – more of this later in this chapter.

- *Thinking that you must sit for hours studying a troublesome topic.* You can learn a lot in very short – but intensive – spells, so make the most of the 10 or 15 minutes you have available before lunch, the time you spend travelling by bus, train or while someone else is driving and while you're having a quick coffee. Be prepared for these short bursts of revision activity by always carrying some work with you.

- *Getting bored.* Find different techniques for your revision, use active learning techniques, shorter periods of study and more variety (perhaps switching from subject to subject) to stave off boredom.
- *Procrastination.* Make a timetable for your revision time and plan in all the other things that you absolutely must do so that you do not use them as an excuse not to start revising. Plan to give yourself the occasional reward too – perhaps an evening out with friends or watching a bit of television.
- *Extreme stress.* Remember that stress can be a positive force as it should push you into an intense period of revision. You should also acknowledge that everyone wants you to pass. There is no trickery or mystique – exams are a straightforward way of you showing the knowledge you have gained during your course.

There are ways to avoid all of these common pitfalls and, as always, getting organized is vital. Arranging your materials before you start (but don't let this take you too long or use it as an excuse not to start the actual revision!) can not only help you to see more clearly what lies ahead but also will help to put you in the right frame of mind. You should also plan the revision strategies you are going to use at this stage – more on these topics follows.

## Making a plan

Scheduling your revision – and sticking to it as much as you possibly can – is really important. Many people wonder when they should start revising and the only answer to that is 'as soon as possible'. It is a good idea to keep revision in mind when you are first producing and collecting the course materials – right from the very beginning of your course. You can do this in a number of ways:

- Go quickly through your work on a regular basis – this will not only help you to become really familiar with the material but will also allow you to see the inconsistencies and problem areas that will inevitably creep in.
- Make revision cards as you go along. When you finish studying a topic, summarize the main points on an index card and file it away – ready for revision time.
- Plan your studying timetable to leave you plenty of time for revision at the end of studying new topics. If you are the sort

of person who leaves all their assignments until the last minute, you will find that this will encroach on time that could have been used for revision.

- Make your notes as clear and brief as possible. Muddled notes that ramble on without making the key points clear will be boring and time consuming to produce and will be of little use when it comes to revision time. Produce your notes with revision in mind.

Having said that revision should be considered – and carried out – alongside the rest of the work on your course, the reality is that many students leave serious revision almost until the last minute. Even if you have managed to be conscious throughout the course of the forthcoming examination, you will no doubt find that your revision will become much more intense immediately before the exam. For this period you will need a plan. You will become more organized and probably much calmer if you draw up a detailed timetable covering this period of revision. There are a number of activities that you must fit into this plan:

- Sorting out your course materials – see the next section.
- Summarizing your notes and handouts – this is an important revision technique. We go into more detail later in this chapter.
- Looking at past examination papers. This is an invaluable revision technique that will point you in the right direction of what to revise – more detail later in this chapter.
- Practising answering exam questions. This revision technique works on two levels. First, it gives you confidence as you become familiar with both the exam format and the subject matter of your course and, second, active revision like this will deepen your understanding of your course materials.
- Normal life – if you have a job as well as being a student, you will need to plan that into your schedule before you start to allocate time to revision. You'll also need to plan in travelling, food preparation and eating, sleep and time for family responsibilities – all the things that are necessary to keep life going.
- Relaxation – of course, examinations will be important to you but they are not life threatening. So, treat them sensibly and allow yourself a life outside your course and exam revision. With an appropriate and moderate amount of free time planned into your schedule immediately prior to the exam, you will find that you will enter the exam room in a

calmer frame of mind and will cope with the revision period much better than if you tried to spend every spare minute revising.

You may have noticed that there are one or two activities not included in this list – trying to memorize all your course notes is not advisable, neither is spending your every waking hour frantically revising everything you can lay your hands on. An exam is *not a test of your memory*. They are not designed to see just how big a proportion of your course notes you can regurgitate. Rather you are being tested on how much of your course you have understood and can now use. Your revision plan should therefore be geared towards active revision that will help you to deepen your understanding of the work you have covered. It should not involve endless, mind numbing rereading of your notes or set books.

Now that you have seen what should – and should not – be included in your revision timetable, you can begin to pull it together. Draw a schedule of the 168 hours in each week of your revision period. First, block out time for sleep plus work and family commitments, add in a few hours of relaxation and then you will be able to see how many hours are left that you can realistically devote to your revision activities. Before you start to add revision activities to your timetable, make sure that you have a good understanding of the proportions of your course. Reviewing the course – knowing exactly what the course has involved – will help you to see how you should be allocating your revision time.

Plan to organize your notes and other materials early on in your revision schedule and then make your next task condensing all your materials to make revision easier. We'll cover this in the section on revision techniques. After these two tasks have been accomplished, you will be able to plan in all the other activities that will help you to pass the examinations. Make sure that the time you allow for each subject area is proportionate and that the revision activities you are planning in are relevant, effective and varied. If you simply plan in revision time – without specifying an activity – you may find yourself reading aimlessly and this will be a waste of your valuable time. Be more specific by planning in, for example, a period of time to condense notes on a particular topic or write a practice essay under exam conditions. Think carefully about what areas you want to revise and what activities would be appropriate to these areas and to you. You may find that you find writing essays under examination conditions very stimulating and productive but don't enjoy working on revision with other students. In this case, plan in more of what helps and less of what doesn't.

Of course, you will probably not stick to your revision schedule completely but the act of drawing it up and thinking about what works for you and what doesn't and analysing the different subject areas, deciding their importance in terms of the examination, will be productive in itself. Try to keep to the schedule as far as you can, as it will keep your mind focused on the exam.

*Focus* is a vital asset when exams are approaching and most people who find settling down to revision difficult will lack this ability to home in on what really matters. Let's look at a typical example of an unfocused student. She knows she should revise, as the exam date is approaching fast. In fact, she meant to start a few weeks ago but she had a problem at work and then it was her boyfriend's birthday and then she was a bit short of money so she couldn't afford to buy some extra paper, index cards and files so that she could get organized. Now she's starting to panic. Getting more and more anxious as the days pass, she comes home from work one Friday evening and resolves to get down to some real work that very night – after she's watched her favourite television programme. At 9.30 p.m. she gets her books out and feels so tired that she takes nothing in before going to bed at 11. The following morning she's up bright and early and intends to spend the whole day studying. She stares at her books, thinking she should read through this passage four or five times because it's obviously very important. She's bored and her mind wanders, thinking about all the things she could be doing around the house.

She realizes she's not concentrating very well and makes herself a cup of coffee and returns to her books with new determination. Now it's nearly lunchtime so she has a break and reconsiders her plans. All day with the books would drive her into a stupor so she goes out for a walk and spends a couple more hours with those same books when she returns. On Sunday morning, she gets up having realized overnight that she's wasted the whole of Saturday and that her real problem is not a lack of ability to study or concentrate – or even a lack of time – but that she is not organized. She has finally realized that she will get nowhere with her revision if she doesn't work out a strategy. Sitting staring at books is time consuming and ineffective. With some clean sheets of paper, she works out how much time she can realistically spare in the next few weeks before the exam and, allowing herself some time for phoning friends or watching a bit of television, she decides on the revision techniques that will help her and assesses just what she needs to do to pass the exam. Ultimate result – success and satisfaction!

Don't be the disorganized student – make a plan. *Now.*

If you're still resisting making a structured plan for your revision period, maybe because you are trying to avoid working harder –after all, you already work hard enough, don't you? – then you must take on board the fact that you are not being asked to work harder but to work *smarter*. With a timetable you will not work more hours than without one (think of our student who sat for hours staring at her books but absorbing nothing, making no progress) and you will not have to perform feats of stamina or superhuman concentration. With a plan you will work at relevant tasks, for predetermined times and with your own aims and aptitudes taken into account.

One final piece of advice about working to a timetable – be prepared to modify it. If, for example, you had planned to work on writing essays under exam conditions for two hours first thing on Monday morning but find it difficult to concentrate and think you would be better doing a few shorter tasks to get you into the swing of things and get your brain going, then change your plan. It's your plan and it should work for you and bring you closer to your goals. So long as you're making changes that will help you to get through the revision and help you to pass the exam, then tweak the plan as much as you like.

---

**Top tip**

The last item in your revision schedule – after all the examinations – should be a treat for you. Plan to reward yourself when all the revision is over with a social event or shopping trip.

---

## Organizing notes and other materials

First, a word of warning – although getting organized is essential, do not let this task become just another way of putting off the start of your revision proper. If you let sorting out all the junk in your drawers and all the piles of notes on your desk take too long, it will be counterproductive. Plan it into the start of your revision timetable and do the minimum that is needed to get your notes and other materials into a state where you're ready to do other revision tasks.

Sorting out your course materials at this stage is part of the task of getting organized in preparation for a period of revision. Of course, it would have been better to have kept the notes and so on in an organized state throughout your course, but if you're looking an exam date in the face, then it's too late for regrets. So, how should you tackle the task of organizing notes? Your first job is to get all your piles of paperwork together. Gather up all the loose papers that are scattered on your desk, all the bulging files on your shelves, your course overview (you did produce an overview of your course right at the beginning of your studies, didn't you? – see Chapter 02 for more details), any past examination papers you have collected, your course books, copies of articles that you thought were essential and all the other bits and pieces that relate to your course including the loose papers in your bag or under your bed! Put like with like, i.e. everything related to each individual subject in one pile per subject and an extra pile for general items such as your course overview or exam papers. Just this small act will probably make you feel more organized.

While you're sifting through paperwork, use the time to also get a picture of what you have and how you will be able to use it to do the necessary revision. In fact, this should help you on to the path of deciding what revision you should do. Take particular note of the overview and learning outcomes for your course. These are important because they will guide you as to what you should be aiming at with your revision plan. Topics that are specifically mentioned in the learning outcomes will be likely to figure somewhere in the examination. Note the balance of different topics in each of the subject areas you are studying and be honest about how much of the course you have already mastered. If there are areas that you feel comfortable with and you are fairly confident that you will be able to answer almost any question on that topic, then you may be able to skim through those areas and spend more of your revision time on areas you are less confident about.

Having organized your materials and got a realistic view of what you need to do to pass the exam, you are now in a position to start your revision in earnest.

# Revision techniques

Revision is not easy. When you see the mounds of notes and piles of books and realize that the examination is a very short time away, it can be extremely daunting. The key to keeping your interest and making the time and effort that you put into your revision worthwhile is to make sure that you use active revision methods rather than passive ones. Passive methods such as rereading your notes or copying out chunks of books or articles may be covering the right material but the chances of your retaining and understanding much of it are slim. You need to engage with the material to ensure that you are using your time to best effect. So, active methods such as condensing your notes or practising essay questions will be the more effective way to learn. In addition, using a variety of techniques will help to keep you interested in your revision and will make sure that you cover different angles too.

Remember that exams are an opportunity to display your understanding of the subjects you have studied. You should not view them as a test of memory. If you tried to memorize the whole of your course you would not only be guaranteeing boredom for the whole period of your revision but also be planning to fail. You will already, of course, have an understanding of your course materials and your revision should further that understanding. You will need to remember the basic points of any topic but other than that it is not your memory but your understanding that will ensure success. Try a combination of these revision techniques (they are all active methods) to improve your understanding of your course materials:

- *Condense your notes – then condense them again.* Take a topic and aim to write everything you need to know about it on one A4 sheet of paper. Note that I did not say write everything you know – but everything you *need* to know. This means that as you write you should be deciding what are the most important bits of information. Write these down and discard all the extraneous detail. At this point you are trying to integrate all the different sources of information that you have collected on the topic. If you can develop a set of these sheets of paper covering your whole course, you will have a valuable asset. You could then refer to these sheets frequently in the run up to the exams – it won't take long to read an A4 sheet of paper. But you can take this a step or two further. Take one of these sheets of important facts and condense it even more until you can get the really important information about that topic on to an index card (usually 10 cm × 15 cm). This will take an even shorter amount of time to read and will be handy to carry about with you as you approach the exam period. You could then try to distil this information into just a few key words and phrases – maybe 10–15 – that will encapsulate the topic and act as triggers. When you recall these words under exam conditions, they will spark off your understanding and memory of sufficient detail of the whole of the topic – or at least the part of that topic that you need to use in answering the question. If you can get to the index card stage for all the major subject areas in which you are sitting exams, you will be able to carry the cards about with you in the period immediately prior to the exams and use the odd bits of time that you have (while you're waiting for a bus, having a coffee or before you go out in the mornings) to quickly run through the whole of your course. If you do this frequently, you will find that you retain most of the key points.

The aim with this revision technique is not only to provide you with some quick and easy notes to revise at the last minute but also to ensure that you work actively with your materials. While you are condensing your notes, you are engaging with the material, understanding it and manipulating it. This will mean that you are far more likely to be able to use the information under exam conditions.

- *Selecting topics to revise.* Take care with this technique. Just revising the bits you've enjoyed during the course or the sections you find easy will not necessarily help you to pass the exam. You should be finding out – if you don't know already – what the most important topics are in each subject and revising these thoroughly. You will probably need to do a bit of detective work to decide what to revise. You can look at exam papers from previous years (more of this later), check your course outline and overview to see what topics are given prominence and you can ask your tutors. They may be able to give you some guidance on what to revise but they may feel unable to be too specific. In any event, pay particular attention to the topics they concentrate on in the last few lectures or tutorials. Although it can help to try to reduce the amount you must revise, do not take this method too far or use it as an excuse not to revise sufficiently. Most exams cover a representative sample of the course.

- *Use past exam papers.* These are often available in your college library or your tutors will tell you how you can obtain copies. It is useful to examine as many as possible so that you understand the type of questions that will be asked – the structure of the exam, the format of the questions, how long is allowed for each question and so on. This revision technique will ensure that you don't turn over the exam paper in the exam and get a shock, realizing that your revision has not been geared to the type of questions you see in front of you.

  Do some analysis of the papers by checking which questions or topics come up regularly. If a version of a particular question is asked every year, then it is obviously considered an important part of the subject and you should ensure that you are competent in answering that type of question.

- *Practise answering essay questions.* This technique follows on from the last one. With a good supply of past examination papers you can use the questions as practice. This will ensure that not only do you get a deeper understanding of the topics you are covering, but also you will be gaining vital practice in putting together answers to suit the exam.

  Your first task (after you have analysed the papers as just discussed) is to take note of the way the questions are worded. Look back to Chapter 08 where we discussed the key words used in essay questions. Do you need to 'compare and contrast' or to 'discuss with examples'? Work out your approach to each of the different types of question. Try to develop an essay outline for each question on all the papers you have. Brainstorming the question and producing an outline will show you how much you know – and don't know – about the topic. It will also give you valuable practice in essay planning for an examination. If you do enough of this type of revision, you are unlikely to be too worried about doing it under exam conditions.

  You should then take these outlines and produce essays from some of them – as many as you have time for. Time yourself and if you have difficulty producing an essay in the time that would be allowed in the exam, ask yourself – and perhaps your tutors too – if you are writing essays that are too long or too detailed. Consider what is required by the examiners. If you only have 40 minutes to write an essay in an exam, you will not be expected to produce something that tells all you know about a topic in 5,000 words! Focus on the question – what is being asked, what part of the topic should you concentrate on, what should you leave out – and then try again.

Practice and focus will ensure that you are capable of producing competent, succinct answers under exam conditions. While you're doing this, don't forget that in the actual exam you will have to write your answers longhand. If you're used to producing all your course assignments using a computer, you may find that you need some practice now to increase your handwriting speed and legibility. It is vital that you attempt some practice at producing essays from exam questions like this so that you can iron out any problems before the day of the exam.

- *Record yourself.* If you find that you are spending a lot of time when you are unable to sit down with a pen and paper – when you are travelling, for instance – you may find it useful to record yourself reading some of your condensed notes so that you can play them over and over again. If you get distracted by things happening around you, don't worry. If you listen to the same tape enough times, you will be distracted at a different point each time and will eventually have covered the topic in its entirety. This is a good technique to allow you to use otherwise 'dead' time.

- *Work with others.* Discussing topics with fellow students will further your understanding as it will give you exposure to a wider variety of views and ideas. Vocalizing your take on a topic will also be helpful. As you speak and try to formulate your thoughts on something, you realize where the gaps in your knowledge are and also put things into a logical order in your mind. Working with others is also a good discipline in that if someone else is working hard, you will probably follow suit. Just make sure that you don't just casually meet up with friends for a coffee with the vague notion of doing some work. Here again, structure is important. If you plan what you are going to study as a group, you are far more likely to be successful. It is a good idea to go over past examination papers with a group of fellow students. Hearing how they would answer questions is often illuminating. Do not automatically assume that others will be right but consider their ideas alongside your own.

- *Keep attending tutorials.* This will keep you in touch with your tutor and with other students. You will find out what other students are up to and will also gather many useful tips from your tutor.

# Memory

Many students panic about exams not because they don't know their subject but because they are afraid that their memory will fail them. They fear that, under exam conditions and with the limited amount of time available, they will simply not be able to recall what they know. There are a number of tricks and tips you can use to overcome this fear and to improve your memory. Understanding how you learn will help to direct your revision more effectively so look back at the section on learning styles in Chapter 02. Help your memory along by trying the following:

- Planning – it can't be said often enough, organized study is far more effective than a haphazard, untidy approach.
- Keep what you have to commit to memory to a minimum – condense your notes as much as possible.
- Learn actively – interact with your notes.
- Understand what you're learning – it is far easier to memorize something you understand than to learn by rote. If there are important parts of your course that you do not yet understand you will be able to obtain help from your tutor if you do not leave it too late.
- Use repetition – go through the same subject matter in a number of different ways to help you to remember them. You might use different sources for the same information – notes, articles, your condensed notes and so on.
- Use colour and illustration – the more visual the material, the easier it is to remember it, so use different coloured highlighters and pens, add little drawings if you're artistic and underline or highlight the particularly important points in your condensed notes. You may find during the exam that a particular revision card or sheet of notes comes back to you because of the colour – you will visualize how it was written.
- Make connections – find links between the different parts of the subject that you are studying. Spider diagrams are useful for this – look back at the various ways to take notes discussed in Chapter 04. This is part of active learning and will help you to recall a lot of information at once.
- Discuss the material with fellow students – this will clarify your thoughts and help you to organize your knowledge. It may also show where you need to put in some further work.
- Test yourself – use previous exam papers or exam-type questions you have made up for yourself to give you useful practice in recalling what you know.

- Try mnemonics. These are devices used to help you remember important facts and some people find them really useful. A common mnemonic is using the first letters of a number of keywords to make another word. This new word will then remind you of the original concept. If your tutors or fellow students have suggested any mnemonics, make a note of them and see if they are helpful to you.

- Consider what memory tricks you already use – you might arrange words in a particular order, link words with mental images or use colour to help you remember – and use them to full effect during your revision period.

---

**Top tip**

The signs in the *Highway Code* have to be memorized in order to pass the theory test. This task can be made appreciably easier if you have practical experience of using these signs – so get out and about and take special note of the signs you see.

---

## Summary

In this chapter you have learned:

- How revision gives you the chance to pull the entire course together and to look at the bigger picture.

- Some of the pitfalls of revision such as reading through notes repeatedly and being bored by it, writing out essays you've already completed, procrastination and extreme stress.

- How you can start your revision early by reviewing your work regularly, making revision cards, planning revision periods into your study timetable and by making brief, clear notes from the start.

- How to draw up a study timetable and what to include in it – organizing course materials, summarizing notes and handouts, practising with exam questions as well as 'normal life' activities like sleep, work and family commitments plus some time for relaxation.

- About some active learning revision techniques – condensing notes, using past exam papers, recording yourself and working with others.

# Quick revision test

1 How can you be prepared for making the most of short periods of time becoming available during your revision period?

2 Give two ways in which practising answering exam questions is a useful revision technique.

3 Name three things you should get together when you are organizing your study materials at the start of your intensive revision period.

4 Name two passive methods of revision and two active methods.

5 How can you use index cards to good effect in your revision?

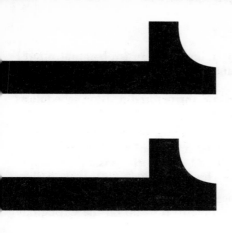

# exam
# preparation

**In this chapter you will learn:**
- how to plan to pass your examinations
- how to write essays in exams
- about techniques that will be useful on the day.

# Plan to pass

Have you heard the saying 'failing to plan is planning to fail'? Good preparation and planning will help you just as much in passing examinations as in any other area of your life. In the case of exams, you must follow a structured revision schedule as discussed in the previous chapter and also plan the strategy that you will follow on the day.

As the exam day approaches and you are well into your revision, you should have found out all the basic information concerned with your exam. This will include:

- The exact dates and times of each exam. Double-check these – it's not unknown for people to turn up on the wrong day for an exam.

- Where the exams will be held. Do you know how to get there? And how long it will take you? Note that the time your journey takes could vary according to the day of the week and the time of day. Allow yourself plenty of time. Arriving late can be disastrous – you could arrive stressed and not give your best performance or, worse still, you could be so late that you're refused entry.

- The instructions you will be given. These vary little from year to year so check out previous years' papers and make sure you understand them. They usually cover where to write your name and your identification number if you have one, how many questions you will have to answer, how long you're allowed, whether you can use rough paper for workings out and if you have to hand these rough notes in.

  Another aspect that might be covered here (and if it isn't then you need to find out the information for yourself, well ahead of the exam) is just what you are allowed to take with you into the exam room. Most exams ban books apart, perhaps, from a dictionary but your exam may be different. You may be allowed to take a calculator into the room plus a supply of pens and pencils. You may have to leave any bags and briefcases outside the exam room. Exam rules and conventions can vary widely so make sure that you know exactly what instructions you must follow.

- The structure of the exam paper. How many questions? Are they all allocated equal marks? Are they all essay questions? Or multiple-choice?

- Exactly how you will be assessed. Find out whether the exams will be marked internally or externally, will all the questions have equal marks allocated or are some questions more valuable than others?

Another important part of your preparations should include staying positive. You must plan to pass and be convinced that you are perfectly capable of being successful. Of course, a small amount of worry about your result is normal and can even be helpful if it makes you work more effectively to ensure success but too much worry and negativity can be a definite drawback. Try not to build up the exam out of all proportion. As we've said before, it is not a life-threatening event. However, you definitely do want to pass this exam that you've put so much effort into, so you need to give it your best shot. As we said way back in Chapter 01, the essence of positive thinking is that you can achieve more if your thoughts are positive ones than if they are negative ones and this is especially appropriate in exam preparation and performance. If you continually catch yourself saying 'If I fail...' consciously change it to 'When I pass...'.

Use visualization techniques. Picturing yourself with that certificate or receiving your results envelope – with good pass marks, of course – will help to build your confidence. Visualization can also be used to make taking the exam more comfortable and worry free for you. Picture yourself walking into the exam room, seeing how it is set up and the invigilators waiting, then sitting down at a desk and listening carefully to the instructions you will be given. In your mind's eye, turn over the question paper. Now, do you know what you will do next? If not, this is where some planning has to be done. Make sure you know the following:

- How long you will allow for each question.
- Will you start writing straight away or read through the paper and plan which questions you will answer? Some people need to find a question they like the look of and get writing immediately to settle their nerves, whereas others prefer to allocate a few minutes of their time to working out the questions to tackle.
- What sort of outlining technique will you use? Will it be in list form or a spider diagram or simply notes quickly jotted down? You should have practised this as part of your revision schedule.

Visualizing this sort of scenario in this amount of detail can be very helpful in settling your nerves as it will feel familiar when you actually do it. It will also help to highlight where the deficiencies in your revision are.

## Writing essays in exams

Writing essays in exams is different from writing them for coursework – but there are many similarities too. Let's look first at the similarities:

- You should start by analysing the question – check out the details of this in Chapter 08.
- They still need planning – look back to the section about essay outlines in Chapter 08.
- They should have a beginning, a middle and an end.
- You must stick to the point. Do not attempt to write everything you know about the subject of the question. Adding irrelevant detail will not win you any marks. The examiner will have a schedule of marks to allocate. If you mention something that is not on this schedule, you will not get any extra marks for it.
- Most importantly – you should ensure that the *essay answers the question*.

Now we can move on to the differences. These are important because they can make your task easier. Many of the areas of difference are caused by the fact that time is limited in exams. The examiners know that you can only produce a restricted amount of detail in the time allowed and that in the stressed circumstances of an exam most people will not be able to recall everything they know or to present the work in the way in which they would like under normal circumstances. Here are the main differences:

- You will have far less time available. How many hours do you usually spend producing an essay as a course assignment? Two, three, five or even 10 hours? No matter what sort of examination you're sitting, if you have to produce more than one essay you will not have anywhere near that amount of time. You may well have less than one hour. You will need to reduce all the processes that you usually go through when producing an essay – the planning, searching (in your mind) for material, producing an outline and writing – down into the 40 minutes or whatever time you're allowed. Although there's so little time available, do not be tempted to abandon the planning stage. Brainstorming and preparing an outline will be time well spent because it will make the writing easier – you won't run out of things to write and you'll know just where you're going with your answer.

- You will write fewer words. There just isn't time to produce a major work.
- You won't be able to include all the detail that you would use if you were able to research the topic thoroughly and spend more time on it.
- Your presentation is less important. As long as your writing is legible, it will be OK – even if it does look a bit scruffy or spidery!
- Minor errors in spelling and grammar are not usually penalized.
- You won't be able to include a bibliography.
- They will be far less polished than essays you've produced for coursework – but that's fine; it's normal.

Despite the constraints, you will be surprised by just how much you can cram into the time you're allowed. Producing a winning essay in an exam is as much about taking an organized approach as it is about the actual writing. Later in this chapter we will look at the practicalities of writing an essay under exam conditions.

# The day before

It's certainly tempting to try to cram in as much revision as possible on the day before your exam. You might get up early and go over all your revision notes and cards and keep going, fuelled by plenty of strong coffee and some junk food, until you can hardly keep your eyes open, finally falling into bed in the early hours and then tossing and turning until the alarm goes off on the day of the exam. Don't. A far better approach is to do very little – even take the day off from studying if you possibly can. Most people, however, will need the reassurance of at least running quickly through their notes and checking a few final details. It's unlikely at this stage that very much will sink in so don't spend the whole day and evening revising. This will just result in your feeling tired and confused. Your time would be better spent relaxing. Check your details for tomorrow – exam location and time, getting your things together (pens, pencils etc. plus the clothes you're going to wear) – so that on the day you will have as little as possible to worry about.

Try to relax the evening before and do not let that relaxation involve too much alcohol – that will just put you in danger of feeling groggy in the morning and that's no way to be on an exam day. Far better to get some fresh air and exercise or to do any activity that takes your mind off the forthcoming exam. Get to bed reasonably early the night before – have a relaxing bath before you go.

# On the day

Even before you arrive at the examination centre there is plenty you can do to help yourself to pass the exam. Your aim should be to arrive in the peak of condition, in a calm state of mind, in plenty of time and fully equipped. Here's a checklist of what you can do:

- *Eat breakfast.* A hungry body does not function at its peak so make sure you have a healthy breakfast before you leave home (and lunch, of course, if the exam is in the afternoon).
- *Relax.* If you find yourself with a bit of time before you have to leave home, you could perhaps meditate a little or listen to some soothing music.
- *Breathe deeply.* Practising a breathing exercise will only take a minute or two but will calm you down if you're starting to feel in a panic. Sit quietly and breathe in through your nose. Count the length of your in-breath (Just breathe naturally. You might breathe in for a count of three, four, five or more – that's not important). Then simply breathe out through your nose for the same count. Continue for five more breaths. Equalizing your breath in this way will mean that you're not thinking about anything else and you will very quickly relax.
- *Set off in plenty of time.* Rushing into the exam room at the last minute is not conducive to a calm start to the exam so allow time for traffic problems and so on. If you arrive early, try not to stand with friends indulging in mutual panic. Find a corner for yourself so that you can keep calm, or go off for a walk on your own.

When you're finally in the exam room, seated at your desk, make sure you listen. The invigilator will probably read out some instructions – what you should do in the case of a fire (and yes, this does happen; it happened to me once!), what warning, if any, he will give when the exam is nearing its end, what you should do if you need anything such as extra writing paper, when you can start and what you should do if there are problems. He may also give you specific instructions about your question paper. Ignoring such instructions could mean the difference between pass and fail.

When you first turn over the question paper, you will probably feel nervous and not quite able to take in any detail so it's a good idea to give the paper a quick skim through, noting questions that you think you might be able to do a good job on. As we said earlier, the structure of the exam should not be a surprise to you if you've done your research and checked out plenty of previous exam papers in advance. When you've settled down a bit – just a couple of minutes into the exam as there's no time to waste – it's a good idea to make a time plan so that you know what you should be doing and when. You need to make the very best use of the limited time you have in an exam and a timetable is the best way to keep track of time. With an exam time plan you will schedule in all the tasks you have to accomplish in the time allotted – reading the paper, choosing the questions, deciding the order in which you will answer them, the outlining and the writing. Let's take an example based on a common exam format – with four essay-type questions to answer in three hours. You cannot just divide the three hours by four and then spend 45 minutes on each question as this will not allow you time to plan, to think and to check your answers at the end. So, how might your plan look?

| | |
|---|---|
| 2.00 p.m. | Read quickly through the paper, noting which questions you might attempt – a simple tick or asterisk on the exam paper next to the relevant questions will be sufficient |
| 2.10 p.m. | Brainstorm and outline the answer to the first question you have decided to attempt |
| 2.15 p.m. | Write your answer to the first question you are answering |
| 2.50 p.m. | Plan your answer to your second question |
| 2.55 p.m. | Write your answer to the second question you are answering |
| 3.30 p.m. | Plan your answer to your third question |
| 3.35 p.m. | Write your answer to the third question you are answering |

| 4.10 p.m. | Plan your answer to your fourth question |
| 4.15 p.m. | Write your answer to the fourth question you are answering |
| 4.50 p.m. | Check through your answers |
| 5.00 p.m. | Hand in your paper |

Of course, this is a *very* rough plan – it is highly unlikely that you will be able to keep to it precisely but it should guide you as to how much time you can spend on each task and prevent you from going seriously over on one question to the detriment of others. That is almost certainly the route to failure.

Next make your decision which question you're going to answer first. The sooner you can start writing, having given proper consideration to your question choice of course, the sooner you will lose your nerves a bit and start to gain marks. So, how do you make your question choice? Remember that the whole point of your being in the exam room is to pass and that the first marks you get for each question you attempt are the easiest to gain. You will – hopefully – cover the important basics in each of your answers and gain the bulk of your marks relatively easily. The extra detail in each topic will provide the additional marks that you need to get a good pass and these marks are harder to come by.

What you're looking for in making your question choice is a number of topics that you have revised and therefore are confident of the basic, but important information to include. Choose questions where you can get the easy marks. Do not let the wording of the questions put you off. You're looking for the topics you've revised so try to get to the nub of the question straight away. If it's about a topic you know little about – discard it. If, by the same token, it's about a topic that you know well, which figured prominently in your revision plans – perhaps some of the detail from your revision cards immediately springs to mind – then that is definitely a question you should attempt. The wording may be a little complicated but you can sort that out when you're analysing the question and brainstorming your answer.

You're now sitting in the exam room, question paper in front of you, your rough plan completed and you've found a question that you want to attempt. Let's look at your next moves – before you start writing:

- *Look carefully at the question.* What is it actually asking you to do? It is often helpful to underline key words in the question. For example:

'Freedom of speech is a right that we must all defend.' Discuss.

You may underline as follows:

'<u>Freedom of speech</u> is a <u>right</u> that we must <u>all defend</u>.' <u>Discuss</u>

Remember that when the question says 'discuss' it means that you must examine the topic in detail and then debate the argument (refer back to Chapter 08 for other important words you'll find in essay questions) so you'll need to know what is meant by 'freedom of speech' and 'right'. As we discussed earlier, it is sometimes helpful to rewrite the question for yourself – or at least to paraphrase it. This will help you to understand what the question requires.

- *Brainstorm what you know about the topic that will help you to answer the question.* Write down everything that is relevant and don't worry about writing it down in order or making it neat. Just get your ideas and the things you need to remember to include in your answer down on the rough paper without delay.
- Now, take the results of your brainstorming session and use them to *write an outline of your answer.* Remember the all-important beginning, middle and end. Decide how you will start your essay, then decide the order for the main points that you've jotted down that will form the main body. You may like to write a number next to each point indicating the order in which you will use them. Plan how you will end your answer by drawing all the important points together and reaching a conclusion.
- *Make sure you're going to answer the question.* Does your outline look like it's covered what will be needed in the answer? It's easy to go off at a tangent and write down all sorts of irrelevancies but you will know by now that you will get no marks if your answer does not answer the question. You might have misread or misinterpreted the question, so read it again now that you've got an outline – just as a last check.
- *Keep calm, stay confident* – and *then start writing.*

But what if you think you can't answer any of the questions? This might be just as a result of stress. Take a deep breath and read through the questions again. If you've revised well you should now find that some ideas are springing into your mind. You will be recalling a few points that you can put into some of your answers. Jot them down. If you're still in a panic, choose just one question that you at least understand the general gist of and start an outline for it. Brainstorm *everything* you know about it as detailed above. This will trigger off some ideas and by this time you will be on your way.

# Some common exam mistakes

As you plan and write your answers, make sure that you are not making one of the following common exam mistakes:

- Not answering the question – this is one that examiners always mention as being a reason for failure.
- Not keeping to the point – don't go off at a tangent. The things you're writing may be perfectly correct but if you've strayed from the point you won't get *any* marks for them.
- Poor presentation – while you won't get too many marks for a perfectly presented answer paper unless you've answered the questions properly, you should make things as easy for the marker as possible. This includes making sure that your writing is legible and using correct spelling, punctuation and starting paragraphs in the right places.
- Giving a biased answer – you are expected to present a balanced case, including arguments and evidence to support both sides of a case, especially if the question says 'discuss' or 'compare and contrast' so do not concentrate on only one view.
- Not giving enough evidence to prove a point – you should not simply state a point and expect your reader to believe it, but must provide sufficient relevant evidence.
- Lack of time management – if you spend too much time on one question it will probably be to the detriment of other questions so you must have a rough time plan in mind and stick to it as much as you can. An even worse thing to do is to produce a perfect – but time-consuming – answer to one question and then miss the answer to another one altogether because you've run out of time.

# And finally, checking

What are you checking for? Do you think 'Well, I've done my best I don't know any more about this subject. I just want to hand in this paper and get away. I never find any mistakes anyway'? You've allowed 10 minutes in your plan for this task and this is what you should be checking for:

- Have you answered the question? This is the single most common reason for exam failure. Read again each question that you've answered and make sure the answer you've given matches up and does the job. If you find, at the last minute, that you've missed out some important pieces of information or argument, write them down at the end of your answer paper, making it clear which question they refer to.

- Is the whole answer legible? If there are any bits where you've rushed too much and your writing is unclear, cross it out and correct it.

- Have you followed the instructions about numbering your questions and so on? If not, this should be easy to put right.

- Have you answered the correct number of questions? This is a particularly easy mistake to make if you have to choose a certain number of questions from each of two or more sections of the exam paper.

- Spelling mistakes – they're easy to make when we're under pressure.

- Punctuation – a missed comma or full stop makes things more difficult to read and we don't want to make life difficult for the examiner, do we?

- Does any more information spring to mind while you're reading through? If so, add it to the end of your answer paper, again making it clear which question it refers to.

When you get to this point you should feel that you've done all you possibly can to pass this exam. Follow the instructions for handing in your answers and leaving the exam room, breathe a sigh of relief and then start celebrating!

# A different exam – the driving theory test

Since 1996 everyone who wants to obtain a driving licence must sit an exam to prove they have knowledge of the *Highway Code* and the right attitude to safe driving. The driving theory test, which must be successfully negotiated before the practical test can be taken, can be just as nerve wracking for the entrants as any other exam and is especially stressful because many of the people sitting it are not used to being in an exam situation.

The most commonly failed sections of the theory test regard documents and the rules of the road and the main reason for these failures – as with any other type of exam – is insufficient or ineffective preparation. There is plenty of material available to help with this preparation – some material, in the form of a CD ROM explaining the process of taking the theory test is sent to entrants along with their first theory test-booking confirmation letter. Becoming familiar with this is obviously essential and is the equivalent of entrants of other types of exam becoming familiar with the instructions and format of past examination papers.

The driving theory test is split into two distinct parts:

- A multiple choice test of 35 questions.
- A hazard perception test of 14 video clips in which you have to identify 15 developing hazards.

For the multiple-choice questions there are three books that form the source material:

- The *Highway Code*.
- *Know Your Traffic Signs*.
- The *Driving Skills* series.

Demonstration of complete familiarity with these source materials is necessary to obtain a pass. Other material can also be a tremendous help in the revision period prior to taking the test and this includes many books that are readily available or the complete set of theory test questions and answers can also be obtained in book format or on CD ROM. Studying for the multiple-choice section of the theory test is mainly down to hard work and developing a memory bank of the road signs etc. but taking driving lessons (and also taking notice when being driven about by other people) at the same time as studying for the theory test will be extremely helpful as the signs will become more meaningful and therefore easier to recall.

The hazard perception test requires just as much preparation and this can be helped by working with specially prepared materials supplied by the Driving Standards Agency (the DSA). A DVD or video can be obtained entitled 'The Official Guide to Hazard Perception' that is designed for use with the guidance of a professional trainer. It adopts a modular, structured approach to identifying hazards and includes:

• Looking for clues.
• Scanning and planning.
• Prioritizing.
• Responding to hazards.
• Risk reduction.
• Use of the 'mirror, signal, manoeuvre' routine.
• Example video clips of hazards.

Again, hazard perception can be learned using the recommended materials but will be made easier with practical driving experience.

As with any other learning task, preparing for the driving theory test takes plenty of effort and will be greatly helped by actively engaging with the topic. Although the temptation is to simply learn the traffic signs and so on by rote, make sure that you do not take an exclusively passive approach. Get out there and see the signs you're trying to learn. See them in use and think about what they mean to drivers, what action you are expected to take when you see it and whether it is a command or simply there for your guidance. Think about the signs and their meanings and actively use them and this will ensure that you remember them in that all-important test.

## Summary

In this chapter you have learned:

• And reviewed the basic information you must check as your exam approaches – exact times and dates of the exam, the venue, the exam instructions and structure and how it will be assessed.

- About visualization techniques and positive thinking and how they can help you to pass the exam and to cope with exam stress.
- The differences between essays in exams and those written for assignments and found that, because less time is available, far less is expected of an exam essay.
- That you should take it easy the day before an exam.
- To prepare a checklist of what you need to do on the day of the exam.
- The value of planning a rough timetable to use during the exam and looked at an example.
- About some common exam mistakes such as not answering the question, going off at a tangent, not giving sufficient evidence, poor presentation, giving an unbalanced answer and a lack of time management.
- Things you should check your answer paper for.
- Why many people fail the driving theory test and what you can do to improve your chances of success.

## Quick revision test

1 Give three similarities and two differences between writing essays under exam conditions and writing them as assignments.
2 Name three things (apart from turning up!) that you need to do on the day of the exam.
3 When planning your timetable for an exam, why shouldn't you just divide the time allowed by the number of questions to be answered?
4 List three things that you should check your answer paper for at the end of an exam.
5 What are the two distinct parts of the driving theory test?

# 12

# where to next?

**In this chapter you will learn:**
- what to do and what not to do when the exams are over
- about the choices and decisions to be made
- where to look for help and advice.

# Introduction

When you have finished taking your exams, you may feel a bit lost. This can happen to people who pass as well as those who fail. Sometimes it is not about your future plans but about coming to the end of a difficult and intense period of your life. The sudden cessation of what has become a major part of your life – revising for exams – can cause you to wonder what to do with yourself. There will be a big gap in your life. But life will go on and you will need to make some decisions about your future at this stage regardless of whether you have passed or failed your exams.

# Pass or fail?

However you feel after the exam has finished – elated, confident, disappointed, fearful, hopeful – try not to worry. The exam is over now and you cannot affect the result – it is all now in the hands of the examiners. You can do no more.

One scenario that almost always follows an exam is the post mortem. This is where you meet up with fellow students and go through the paper question by question. Try not to get involved in this. As we've said, the exam is over now so it's too late to do anything about it but inevitably the post-exam discussion will throw up some people saying how easy they found it (putting fear into you that you've done it all wrong) or other people saying it was impossible and that nobody could have passed such an exam. Taking notice of either of these viewpoints will do you no good. Neither will make you feel better and, of course, other people's views of the paper are irrelevant.

All that's left for you to do now is to celebrate the end of a difficult, intense period, take it easy and wait for the results to drop through your letterbox. In the meantime, do not panic. It is impossible to be 100 per cent sure of your result so patience is required now.

If the results arrive and you've obtained a good pass, congratulations! You will need to plan your next move carefully, so look at the later section in this chapter entitled 'Moving on'.

If, on the other hand, you get results that are not satisfactory, you will need to consider whether you will be able to do a resit, to repeat the year or even if you will be able to appeal against the marking decisions. Incorrect marks are very occasionally given but it is unusual because marking goes through a number of checking procedures to ensure fairness and accuracy. Mistakes do happen, however, so you should consult your tutor immediately if you think you may be the victim of a marking error. He will, if he is in agreement, arrange for an official complaint to be sent to the examiners.

It is far more likely that, in the event of a failed exam, you will need to resit the exam or even repeat the whole year. Remember that there is no compulsion about this and what you do at this stage should be a decision you will take with the help of your tutors and possibly counsellors from your college. There may also be financial implications of your failure – will you be able to afford to repeat the year? Again, consulting the experts will help. Your college tutors and counsellors will be the best people to help you with this dilemma.

Above all, try to keep things in perspective. It is only a failed exam and there are always choices that can be made and solutions to be found.

## Sources of information and support

If you have questions following the receipt of your exam results – whether you've passed or failed – the first people to approach are almost always those concerned with running your course. This may be your tutor or a counsellor depending on the situation you find yourself in. They will probably have dealt with questions similar to yours many, many times and will usually have the information you need readily available or will be able to point you in the right direction. There may also be a careers counsellor in your college who will be able to advise you as to what your choices are at this point. Do not ignore this sort of assistance. It is there because students always have questions and need help to find the best solutions to their problems and to find the best sources of information.

If the exam you have just passed was the end of your course, you may be wondering just where you go next (although deciding this is usually a process best carried out alongside studying in your final year rather than leaving it until the very end of your course). Most colleges and universities have specialists who can help you to plan your personal development and you should take full advantage of this. In the next section we will look at how you can plan your future career.

Don't forget also that you may get help and support from your family and friends. Just talking about a problem can sometimes help you to see the way through it.

There are also lots of sources of support online – check out the useful website section at the end of this chapter.

## Moving on

The majority of people who study and sit exams do so to further their career prospects. If this is you, then you will need to continue your career planning following your exam results. As with any other sort of plan, a career plan will need to set out your goals and give you strategies for making progress towards them. After a major milestone such as finishing a set of exams – and perhaps achieving an important qualification – your career plan will need to be reviewed and brought up to date. Perhaps, if you have passed your exam you will simply go on to the next phase of your plan but it is still worthwhile to review that your goals continue to be right for you and to remind yourself of where you are heading. If, however, you have failed your exam you will definitely need to review your plans for the future. It may be that you will simply need to delay your plans while you take a resit or repeat the year.

More seriously, your exam result may mean that you have to shift direction. Of course, career planning does not just involve passing exams and moving on to the next course of study. There are many elements to a comprehensive plan that will lead to the well-rounded, well-qualified and experienced individual to impress prospective employers. Your plan should cover things such as employment experience, skills that you have, or will acquire, volunteer work and evidence that you can take responsibility in addition to your qualifications. In short, you need to build up a portfolio of evidence of skills and attributes that an employer will value. You must start looking at how you will appear to an employer and then make a plan that will improve you as a whole. Most employers will be looking for:

- *Good exam results* in appropriate subjects.
- *Work experience*. While any work experience is better than none (even bar or shop work shows that you are capable of turning up regularly for work) you should try to get some work that will show other skills. Maybe you can get some holiday work in the area in which you aim to work when you

have finished studying. In this case, you will not only get the chance to see if it is for you but also it will be a valuable addition to your CV and may impress prospective employers.

- *Volunteer experience.* This is always valued by employers and can be a unique experience for anyone, with a lot to be learned.
- *Evidence of skills acquisition.* To decide what skills you need to acquire and to demonstrate on a CV you need to think like an employer. You're looking for things that will make you stand out from other applicants. Perhaps you've funded your own studies (good money-management skills, resourcefulness) or have been involved in a project that took up a lot of your time and helped people less fortunate than yourself (commitment, selflessness, altruism) or have nursed a member of your family through illness (caring skills, commitment).

If you feel that you have shortfalls in any of these areas, then your career plan will need to address them. You may need to improve the quality of your work experience and plan to apply for some interesting holiday work for your next break or to check out the volunteer opportunities that are available to you.

The careers advisory services attached to your college will have enormous resources available about careers and how to prepare for them. They will be able to advise the details of prospective employers and the training programmes that may be on offer. But more than this, they will be able to talk to you to discover your aims and ambitions and then help you to match these to what you can achieve and how to go about it. They can advise on subject options, know what the competition is like for the more popular job areas and will have close connections with many of the larger employers. In short, they can help you to make a career plan or, if you already have one, to refine it so that you continue to make progress towards your goals.

If you are preparing or updating your career plan, you can now see that if you concentrate solely on obtaining qualifications you will not have sufficient to interest an employer and to set yourself apart from other applicants. Your plan should include writing a CV and keeping it up to date. Imagine yourself discussing this CV with potential employers. This might highlight your shortfalls if you realize that you have very little to discuss. While updating (or starting to write) your CV, don't forget to include the study skills you will have learned while working your way through this book and your course. If at first you think 'Well, there won't be much call for exam revision skills in the business world!' then think again. What about the analytical skills you've developed (reading to learn), the ability to express yourself succinctly (note taking), coping under pressure (sitting an exam) or goal setting and planning (organizing your study schedule)?

There are always opportunities to develop yourself and you should take advantage of as many of these as you possibly can. It will not be wasted time.

If you are now coming to the end of a course of study you will probably have realized that it is just the end of one phase of your life and, if your career plan is up to date you will now be moving on to another phase with your goals in mind. You will also have realized that learning never ends. To keep progressing in your career, your education and in life in general, you will need to continue to develop in all sorts of ways and the study skills you have learned by working through this book will stand you in good stead.

## Getting help if you have problems

As we all know, things do not always go smoothly. If you have been suffering high levels of stress during your course of study you may need to get help to deal with it so that it does not affect you seriously in the future. Counsellors will be available to you at your college and you should take full advantage of the services they offer. They will be able to give you in-depth advice about how to deal with stress in all areas of your life, with a particular emphasis on how it affects your studies. If you are a mature student, perhaps studying independently, then your GP should be your first port of call if you feel that you are suffering unduly from stress. A certain amount of stress is, of course, normal, especially when studying and dealing with the additional strain of exams. But if the stress affects your sleep patterns or makes you feel unable to cope with normal life then you must get help.

It may be that you need to completely reorganize your plans and you will find that, immediately following exams, there will be plenty of help available. Colleges are usually geared up to help students – whether they have passed or failed – to decide on their next move.

Being a student can be a lonely experience and your problems will not get better if you hide away and ignore them. Whether you have study-related problems, stress, financial or health problems, you can be sure that the counsellors in your college will have seen and dealt with your problem before. They will know what resources are available to you and will point you in the right direction.

Financial problems are very common among students. Again, counsellors will be able to help and you could also approach the Citizens' Advice Bureau for assistance in managing your debt. As with other problems, getting help early is really important so don't delay – things will only get worse while you sit worrying about debt and not really tackling the problem.

When you're seeking help with a problem, no matter what the nature of the difficulty you are having, and regardless of who you are approaching for help, whether it be your tutor, a counsellor, a careers advisor, your GP or someone from an outside body such as the Citizens' Advice Bureau, you will help yourself to get a better result if you prepare for the meeting. As in any other area, you should plan ahead. Try to accumulate evidence and background to your problem such as:

- A note of what you think your problem is.
- What you've already tried.
- Details of your exam results if these are part of the problem – solid information, rather than just stating 'I've failed', will be an invaluable aid to the person helping you.
- Up-to-date figures of all your incomings and outgoings if your problem is about your finances.

Whatever sort of problem you encounter during your studies, you should try to work through it but if it starts to affect your everyday life then you should get help – it will always be available and you just need to have the confidence to seek it out.

## Special problems

If you find that things that you've had to cope with throughout your life are getting in the way of your studies – maybe you have dyslexia, a physical challenge or difficulties with reading, writing or numbers – there will be help available. There are lots of examples of people who have achieved greatness despite their drawbacks or disadvantages, so don't let anything stand in your way. It is often the case that people who have experienced difficulties during their school years return to education later and need a bit of help. They may have been judged harshly at school and then ignored and their problems not explored and resolved or their disadvantages may have caused a lack of continuity in their education. Sometimes it is not possible to catch up at the time but then, many years later, lots of people come back to education with a new determination. For these people there is plenty of help and support.

If you have basic literacy or numeracy difficulties, the sooner you get some assistance the better. Many local colleges offer free classes to help to improve basic skills that will enhance not just your exam chances or career prospects but will help in many other areas of your life. If you're employed, try asking your employer for help with literacy and numeracy skills as there are plenty of programmes available that they can give you information about.

Up to 10% of the UK population have dyslexia, with around 2 million people in the UK severely affected, but in years gone by the problem was not as well recognized as it is today so a lot of children had dyslexia that affected their educational development but were not given any help. Things have now, thankfully, changed and help is available from various sources. Try getting in touch with the British Dyslexia Association or the Dyslexia Institute (full details at the end of the chapter).

Likewise there is specialist help available for other barriers to education such as physical challenges, lack of childcare facilities or being a single parent – you just have to go out and find the help and use it, together with your determination, to improve your circumstances. Check out the following section.

# Useful websites and organizations

**British Dyslexia Association (BDA)** – www.bdadyslexia.org.uk; 98 London Road, Reading RG1 5AU; Helpline 0118 966 8271; Tel 0118 966 2677

**Citizens' Advice Bureau** – www.citizensadvice.org.uk

**General advice for students** – www.studentuk.uk.com Plenty of information to help you during your studies – www.support4learning.org.uk

**Learn Direct** – www.learndirect.co.uk; Tel 0800 101 901. Careers advice and advice about courses.

**National Association of Volunteer Bureaux** – www.navb.org.uk

**National Literacy Trust** – www.literacytrust.org.uk

**The Dyslexia Institute** – www.dyslexia-inst.org.uk

**The Lone Parent Support Group** – www.lone-parents.org.uk

**The Open University** – www.open.ac.uk

**UCAS** – www.ucas.com. Website for the University and Colleges Admissions Service.

**UK Government** – www.direct.gov.uk. Contains many useful links and contacts.

**UK Volunteer Opportunities** – www.do-it.org.uk. Find one near you by simply entering your postcode.

# Further reading

Bavister, S. and Vickers, A. (2004) *Teach Yourself Neuro-Linguistic Programming*, Hodder & Stoughton

McKenna, P. (2004) *Change Your Life in Seven Days*, Bantam

Wilding C. and Palmer, S. (2005) *Moody to Mellow*, Hodder Arnold

Wilkinson, G. (1997) *Understanding Stress*, British Medical Association

## Chapter 01

1 Note taking, reading, writing essays and reports, planning, revising for examinations, sitting examinations.
2 Expected learning outcomes.
3 You can achieve more if your thoughts are positive ones than if they are negative ones.
4 Facing the fear.
5 To make them easier to deal with.

## Chapter 02

1 A writing surface, a bookshelf, room for a computer, suitable lighting and a chair at the correct height.
2 Back up your files.
3 Never rewrite notes, stay focused, keep notes brief and tidy and develop an effective filing system.
4 Visual, auditory and kinaesthetic.
5 Irritability, insomnia, eating, smoking or drinking too much, spending all your time studying, thinking that everyone is doing better than you, clumsiness, feeling sick at the thought of an assignment.

# Chapter 03

1 Gaining a general understanding of the subject and some background knowledge.

2 Ignore them.

3 Your finger or a sheet of paper.

4 No. Some things, such as detailed instructions or texts that you have to closely analyse will require slower, more concentrated reading.

5 The contents page and the back cover blurb.

# Chapter 04

1 To aid memory, to help to assimilate and understand information.

2 To gain information to write an essay, for exam revision, to help to understand a complicated piece of text.

3 Whether there are any handouts, your own way of working, whether you 'wander off' during lectures.

4 In the centre – like the spider's body.

5 Passive – reading them. Active – condensing them, recording the key words, using for another purpose such as writing mock exam answers.

# Chapter 05

1 A line of reasoning, a case being made, a point of view and a position being taken.

2 Evidence and examples.

3 At the end of the essay. You should highlight it or underline it and then decide if it is valid.

4 A clear conclusion.

5 Decide on your main argument, gather evidence, consider other points of view, reach a clear conclusion and review thoroughly.

# Chapter 06

1 Primary resources – original documentation, your own data and observation, case studies, and original materials. Secondary resources – academic texts, books and articles and other people's data.
2 You are not allowed to take books from the reference section out on loan.
3 Library references by subject area.
4 A short summary.
5 'ac'.

# Chapter 07

1 To aid comprehension.
2 Two negative words in a sentence will not express what is meant, as they will cancel one another out.
3 To show possession and to show where letters are missing.
4 Rewrite the question, gather information, outline the essay or report etc, and then write.
5 A small number of categories would be better for using a line diagram.

# Chapter 08

1 Contents page, summary, introduction, details of the research methodology, the report's findings, the conclusion, recommendations and appendices.
2 At the end.
3 They will save you time, potential pitfalls, and possible embarrassment during your presentation if your writing is not straight.
4 Tick off items on your schedule and reward yourself when you reach each milestone.
5 Decide your case, find arguments and search for evidence for and against these arguments.

# Chapter 09

1 Creating a new document.
2 Headers and footers.
3 By facilitating online support groups and regular communication with tutors and fellow students.
4 A VLE is a system provided by a college that enables students to use learning materials and also to access details and facilities such as individual progress, bulletin boards, reminders, tracking tools and conferencing facilities.
5 Advantage – flexibility; disadvantage – discipline needed.

# Chapter 10

1 Always carry some work around with you.
2 First, it gives confidence as you become familiar with both the exam format and the subject matter of the course and, second, active revision deepens understanding of course materials.
3 Your course overview, past exam papers, course books and articles, your notes, handouts plus all your files and loose papers.
4 Passive – rereading notes and copying out material. Active – condensing notes and practising essay questions.
5 From prepared A4 sheets of important facts you can condense the material until you can get the really important information about that topic on to an index card (usually 10 cm × 15 cm) to carry about with you and use when you have a few minutes to spare during the day.

# Chapter 11

1 Similarities – you analyse the question in the same way, plan your answer by doing an outline, they both have a beginning, a middle and an end, you have to stick to the point and you must answer the question. Differences – in an exam there is less time available, you write fewer words, use less detail, do less research and presentation is not as important.

2 Eat, relax and set off in plenty of time.

3 This will not allow you time to plan, to think and to check your answers at the end.

4 That you have answered the question, the whole answer is legible, you have followed the instructions and answered the correct number of questions. Also check for spelling mistakes, punctuation errors. Finally, does any more information spring to mind while you're reading through?

5 A multiple-choice test and a hazard perception test.

# index

# correct english
b. a. phythian & albert rowe

- Do you need help with writing English?
- Do you want a guide to the rules of grammar, punctuation and spelling?
- Do you worry that you sometimes make mistakes?

**Correct English** is a practical guide and reference book which will help you to improve your command of both spoken and written English, whether you are preparing for an English examination or simply want to improve your language skills. Learn how to avoid the commonest mistakes and pitfalls and increase your confidence to write letters, summaries, reports and essays.

**B A Phythian's** classic has been extensively simplified and updated by **Albert Rowe**, an experienced English teacher of many years.

# letter writing skills

david james with anthony masters

- Do you want to write clear, persuasive letters?
- Do you want to communicate more confidently?
- Do you need to update your letter-writing style?

**Letter Writing Skills** is an invaluable guide to writing letters
which say exactly what you want to say – and bring the desired
response. It offers practical advice on layout, style and tone
and examines different types of letter, from personal to
business correspondence. A section on electronic
communication helps you to make the most of email.

**Anthony Masters** is a writer of both adult and children's fiction
and non-fiction books. He also runs writing workshops for
adults and children.

teach yourself

# speed reading
tina konstant

- Do you need to read quickly at work, college or home?
- Are you frustrated by your reading speed?
- Do you want to read and analyse text more efficiently?

**Speed Reading** is a practical guide to effective speed reading. It includes tools and information for a variety of reading and memort techniques which you can use and practise as you read. It teaches you to read effectively under pressure and helps you to concentrate in noisy or distracting environments.

**Tina Konstant** is a coach, researcher and professional speaker on human potential and learning skills. She has produced and presented a TV series on effective learning.

**teach yourself**

**time management**
polly bird

- Do you need to maximize your time?
- Do you want to maximize your clutter and chaos at work?
- Do your days need restructuring?

**Time Management** shows you how to declutter your life by recording, monitoring and improving your use of time – and helps you to cut down on stress, achieve your goals, improve your performance at work and free up more time for your personal needs. It contains practical advice on prioritizing, planning your time, reducing paperwork, handling phone calls, delegating, training staff… and learning to day "no"!

**Polly Bird** is a professional writer of business and training books.

# winning at job interviews
## igor popovich

- Are you new to the job market?
- Are you contemplating a return to work?
- Do you want to boost your confidence at interviews?

**Winning at Job Interviews** shows you how to be the best applicant for the job you want. Its clear, step-by-step format covers both basic and advanced strategies for winning in the job market, with sample questions and model answers to help you recognize your strengths and weaknesses, evaluate interview situations and deal with difficult questions.

**Igor S. Popovich** is the director of a career-help consultancy which offers training courses on interviewing, job hunting and career management.

LUTHER'S RHETORIC

# CONCORDIA ACADEMIC PRESS

# LUTHER'S RHETORIC

## STRATEGIES AND STYLE
## FROM THE INVOCAVIT SERMONS

NEIL R. LEROUX

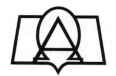

**Concordia Academic Press**
A Division of
Concordia Publishing House
Saint Louis, Missouri

The Invocavit Sermons printed as the Appendix are reprinted from LUTHER'S WORKS, VOL. 51, edited by John W. Doberstein, copyright © 1959, Fortress Press. Used by permission of Augsburg Fortress.

All Scripture quotations, unless otherwise indicated, are taken from the King James or Authorized Version of the Bible.

Scripture quotations marked RSV are taken from the Revised Standard Version of the Bible, copyright © 1952 [2nd edition, 1971] by the Division of Christian Education of the National Council of the Churches of Christ of the U.S. of A. Used by permission. All rights reserved.

---

Library of Congress Cataloging-in-Publication Data

Leroux, Neil R.
   Luther's rhetoric : strategies and style from the Invocavit sermons / Neil R. Leroux.
    p. cm.
   ISBN 0-7586-0002-X
   1. Luther, Martin, 1483-1546. 2. Lenten sermons—History and criticism. 3. Lutheran Church—Sermons—History and criticism. 4. Rhetoric—Religious aspects—Lutheran Church—History. 5. Preaching—Germany—History. I. Title.
   BR332.S75 .L47 2002
   251'.0092—dc21                          2001007671

---

1  2  3  4  5  6  7  8  9  10        11  10  09  08  07  06  05  04  03  02

# CONTENTS

# PREFACE

This is a book about Martin Luther. It is also a book about rhetoric, style, Scripture, and preaching. Those are five reasons why, in part, this work took so long to complete. I found myself nearly overwhelmed with the breadth of the task. And I struggled for a long while trying to determine whether this would be a book about Luther or a book about rhetorical style. When I thought I had resolved the dilemma in favor of Luther, Ross Wolin suggested that perhaps the book can do justice both to style and to Luther. My readers will ultimately decide whether Ross was right.

My interest in Luther began 15 years ago during a course in Renaissance rhetoric with Tom Conley. As a fairly new pastor to a small congregation in central Illinois, I had begun graduate studies in Speech Communication at the University of Illinois at Urbana-Champaign, only 22 miles away. Tom's courses were stimulating because the range of his expertise goes far beyond understanding the history of rhetoric. During his seminar on style, I first acquired a taste for, and I hope some ability in, the careful reading of a text. I learned some fundamental principles for examining the intricacies of arguments and the language in which they are expressed. When Celeste Condit suggested to me that my experience in biblical exegesis produced important insight into Frederick Douglass's speeches, I began to feel more at home in rhetorical criticism. Once I realized that Luther's discourse was virtually untouched by rhetorical critics, at least in America, I began planning a dissertation on the Invocavit Sermons. I wanted to discover why Luther's sermons interested me so much—how they were so clear and yet so powerful. My focus was on Luther's style, which Conley agreed was a fruitful area to explore. The dissertation was a delightful experience, and much of that enjoyment can be credited to Tom's support and standards of excellence. Joe Wenzel and Jack Bateman helped shepherd the project to completion, and Jack was one of the first to encourage me to bring the work to publication as a monograph. During the 1990s, both Jack Bateman and Heiko Oberman simply expected the book to be finished, even when I had plenty of doubts. I am grateful I was able to meet Professor Oberman before he died.

Yet the task of converting the manuscript into a book was daunting, so much so that the more I contemplated it, the more I was convinced the job should wait until after I had tenure. One of the most difficult areas was my lack of personal experience with liturgical churches. After spending my entire life, in both pew and pulpit, in what we in the United States call "evangelical" churches (Christian churches, Baptist, Evangelical Free, Nazarene, and some independent churches), I had little idea what it felt like to be surrounded by Christian images in cloth, paint, and sculpture; neither did I understand the liturgies—Protestant or

Catholic. Most of the historical conflicts regarding images, the Lord's Supper, Baptism, and confession were only vaguely familiar to me. I was unfamiliar with canon law, the church councils, and the sacraments. So becoming conversant with these topics meant considerable research. I suppose the "outsider" perspective can be something of an advantage, though. As some historians of Luther observe, confessional loyalties can cloud one's perspective. As a non-Lutheran who studies Luther, I formed great admiration for Doctor Martin, not only for the prodigious writings and sermons he gave to the world, but also for his expertise with language, his vast knowledge of Scripture, and the passion with which he preached, wrote, and shepherded his flock, beginning with his own family, colleagues, and students.

Moreover, the issues of the Wittenberg Movement of 1521–1522 were perplexing for those involved, and they required both passion and prudent leadership to resolve. On the side of the more zealous reformers in Wittenberg during Luther's stay at the Wartburg, Andreas Karlstadt and Gabriel Zwilling were equally passionate about what should be done with their newly discovered Gospel and its implications for society. After studying several of Karlstadt's writings, and being fortunate to work with Ulrich Bubenheimer, I have acquired an appreciation for the "radical" side of the controversy. It was important to research the views Luther came to oppose in the Invocavit Sermons, not only to better understand Luther's positions and strategies, but also because historical and rhetorical research demanded it, if such research is to be truly scholarly. Furthermore, to investigate vigorously a matter so the truth can be exposed (if truth is possible in controversies such as these) and to humbly acknowledge one's debt to others is, I believe, pleasing to God, who alone is the source of all truth. Augustine reminds us that for a Christian, "wherever he may find truth it is his Lord's" (*On Christian Doctrine* 2.18.28; cf. prologue 8). In my work with Bubenheimer, I became more familiar with the current resurgence of scholarly research on Karlstadt. My project was additionally blessed by the opportunity to work on the Wolfenbüttel Manuscript, which Prof. Bubenheimer discovered in the mid-1980s. Once published, this manuscript (from an unknown hand that recorded Luther's preaching) will foster additional research into the Invocavit Sermons. It may even advance our understanding of how Luther preached because we have so little evidence beyond published sermons.

The debts acquired for this project are huge. The "Notes" and "Further Reading" sections acknowledge the sources I have consulted. Additionally, so many people have assisted me during the past 10 years that trying to mention them all is risky. I owe much to my students at the University of Minnesota, Morris, many of whom have produced striking insights into texts of all kinds in their papers. My student assistants—Julie Brotzler, Sylvia Anderson, Matthew Kauffmann, and Cindy Norberg—have made enormous contributions. My colleagues at UMM in Speech Communication—Mary Elizabeth Bezanson and Barbara Burke—have continued to support and encourage me. UMM colleagues from other humanities disciplines—Dwight Purdy and Laird Barber in English, Ray Lammers (emeritus) in Speech Communication, and Fred Peterson in Art History—read the entire manuscript in a version much longer than the present one. Librarians Margaret Swanson, Maggie Larson-Dylla, Ardath Larson, and Leann Dean processed hundreds of requests for books and articles through inter-library loan and via the simply wonderful Minitex system we have in Minnesota. In short, it is a blessing beyond words to be able to work here at UMM. I have also benefitted from the assistance of nearby libraries: St. John's University, Collegeville, Minn., and Luther Seminary in St. Paul. Financial assistance for research and travel came to me from many sources: in-state travel grants, out-of-state travel funds, and a single-quarter leave from the University of Minnesota, Morris; international travel funds from the International Studies Program at the University of Minnesota; graduate school summer fellowships from the University of Minnesota; and McKnight summer fellowships from the McKnight Foundation. My thanks for personal encouragement and scholarly assistance is also due to: Ted Underwood, Fred Farrell, Jenny Nellis, Cindy Poppe, Jayne Hacker, Tom Mahoney, Dieter Fauth, Erika Schulz, Tom Benson, Craig Kallendorf, Heiko Oberman, Robert Bast, Carter Lindberg, Carol Jablonski, Ernst Wendland, Andries Snyman, Bruce Shields, Ronald Heine, Bruce Parmenter, Hans Hillerbrand, Gerhard Krodel, Linda Mitchell, Jameela Lares, Tom Duncanson, Gary Selby, Pete Verkruyse, Tap Payne, Jim Aanerud, Mike Sager, and Cindy Winter. I am grateful to colleagues of the Rhetoric Society of America, the International Society for the History of Rhetoric, the National Communication Association, and the Sixteenth Century Studies Conference for opportunities to present my work. A huge thanks to Ken Wagener and Dawn Weinstock of CAP/CPH (along with their readers) for believing that this book is a worthwhile endeavor and, especially, for their untiring and cheerful suggestions. Lastly, to my family—Joyce, Shelly, Mandy, and Brian (1967–1984)—to you I am the most grateful because you never gave up on me. All praise be to God!

# INTRODUCTION

For Martin Luther, the man about whom more has been written than any other Western mortal of the modern era, there still is a scholarly frontier that is only beginning to be charted—Doctor Luther's preaching.[1] So far, Luther scholarship of the past 60 years has but minimally responded to James Mackinnon's lament in 1930 of a lack of scholarly work on Luther's preaching.[2] Elmer Kiessling's 1935 monograph[3] on the early sermons remains one of the few detailed studies we have in English that investigates some portion of the vast amount of extant preaching material (homilies, sermons, and postils) from one of the European tradition's most influential orators. However, contemporary scholars such as Birgit Stolt,[4] Klaus Dockhorn,[5] Ulrich Nembach,[6] John W. O'Malley,[7] and Knut Alfsvag[8] have recently begun to investigate the rhetorical practice of Luther (and also Calvin), which, when compared to the rhetorical theories of Erasmus or Melanchthon, has previously been much neglected. It now has been convincingly shown that not only was Luther thoroughly trained in the art of rhetoric and dialectic, but that most of his writings cannot be fully appreciated or even understood without taking into account the rhetorical intent and context in which they were composed. To be sure, a failure systematically to investigate Luther's preaching for its contributions to our understanding of how rhetoric works represents an opportunity missed because it is in the engagement of audiences that Luther excelled. Indeed, enemies and followers alike—in different ways and toward opposite ends—attested to the rhetorical skills of this "German Cicero."[9] Preaching in the Reformation was not only popular, but central, and the reformers articulated the theory for the prominence of preaching.[10] One Reformation historian has stated:

> The religious reform was first and foremost a powerful preaching revival. The first act of any community which developed an interest in the new ideas was to request a preacher to proclaim the "pure Word of God." It was not held to be sufficient to read printed tracts or even the Bible: the desire was to *hear* the word. Indeed, for Protestants "hearing the Word" became virtually a third Sacrament alongside Baptism and the Lord's Supper. Communities cared enough about this to pay out of their own pockets to support a preacher if no benefice was vacant, and to put considerable pressure on magistrates who were reluctant to provide or permit such a preacher.[11]

Others have already shown Luther's knowledge of—and regard for—rhetoric.[12] I will demonstrate Luther's adeptness at rhetorical skills, regardless of how, when, or where he acquired them. I will show that Luther, who preached weekly for 34 years at the *Stadtkirche*—daily during Lent, and on many of those days he preached three or four times—was skilled with argument and rhetorical devices and that he knew how to draw listeners—his congregation—into his messages.[13]

Furthermore, because not only Luther's preaching, but also his written commentaries on Scripture have been said to display the same kind of *oratorical* style,[14] Luther was a skilled rhetorician who was intensely committed to the interpretation and proclamation of God's Word from both lecture desk and pulpit [*Katheder und Kanzel*]. In Bubenheimer's words, Luther was "Word possessed."[15] In addition, an essential component behind Luther's messages consisted in the fact that he believed listeners should embrace the Gospel and that faith entailed that one could do so. One of the most well known Reformation paintings is on the predella of the Wittenberg city church altar (1547); indeed, the entire altarpiece still captivates the attention of visitors to the *Stadtkirche*.[16] The painting is Lucas Cranach the Elder's depiction of Luther in his *Kanzel*, pointing the congregation to the crucified Christ. The audience consists not only of Luther's own family, but also of Wittenberg leaders. Moreover, the cross and crucified Jesus seem to stand on that very church floor! To preach meant to preach Christ to people; preaching is the Word enacted. In short, Luther's concept of faith was deeply indebted to rhetoric, faith being an affectively present phenomenon, one that derives from the Holy Spirit's own role as rhetor.[17] Thus, scholars ought to be keenly interested in Luther's sermons.

A study of Luther's preaching surely can contribute to the exploration of intriguing questions homileticians have asked: What sorts of sermon structure did Luther employ in his career? Did he—and in what period of his preaching career—continue, modify, or abandon the so-called "thematic" or "university" sermon with which we are so familiar? To what extent did he adopt the "homily" or "expository" sermon format? What commitments might have brought this about? However, I prefer to venture directly to a question of potentially far greater general interest not only to homileticians, but to all scholars who care about how words work: the question of what I call Luther's style.[18] Precisely what I mean by style—how I examine it and what we learn from it—is addressed in chapter 1. While my approach is somewhat nontraditional, this perspective on style is not without precedent in American rhetorical criticism.[19] The argument in the case study is that careful rhetorical analysis of sermons, through an innovative approach to rhetorical style, opens up Luther's discourse to reveal a preacher (rhetor) engaging an audience. The reader (critic) will begin to appreciate the audience-orientation for its crucial role in the persuasive choices the speaker has made, and the critic can rightfully speculate with a measure of confidence upon the kinds of effects certain language choices may have on their actual and potential listeners. The analysis will attempt to show readers how better to read—to learn to be more sensitive to the strategies, style, arguments, and potential effects upon readers or listeners—by attending first to their own responses.

Unlike Luther's correspondence, theological tracts, Bible translations, and postils, the sermon texts found in collections of Luther's works are questioned by many scholars who doubt that the texts authentically preserve his pulpit speech. One reason for these doubts is a belief that Luther normally spoke extemporaneously, while the sermon texts seem carefully crafted.[20] Another reason is that many extant texts come from the hands of note takers, not from Luther himself. Although the scribes were sympathetic to his agenda (most had been Luther's students), there are inherent transmission problems in note taking. For example, note takers used shorthand dictation—often inserting Latin phrases as abbreviations—to which they later added missing words as they were able to recall them (or words they think Luther should have said or had said on similar occasions). Hence, many of the sermon texts are macronic—mixtures of Latin and German.

Nevertheless, the problem of textual authenticity is nothing new for rhetorical scholars who analyze speech texts. We often work with artifacts of the rhetorical act, texts that do not issue directly from the hands of the rhetor. Indeed, rhetorical critics must often work with "nonofficial" texts, those not released for publication by the author. Moreover, for most ancient texts there are no extant autographs, and still we vigorously investigate those texts for what they can suggest about what is said, how it is put, why the given language choices might have been made, and what plausible effects might have resulted (and can result) from hearing and reading the piece.[21] Undeniably, crafting a tract or sermon are in many ways similar rhetorical tasks. For those who were literate, Luther's vernacular tracts were readily available for devouring. For the many more who could not read, the same engaging style made his ideas available to all who cared to attend to the messages—whether directly from his pulpit, his pamphlets, or those many people who shared the oral transmission of those messages. As the *salutatio* to Luther's "A Sincere Admonition" (1521) announces, "To all Christians who read this pamphlet or hear it read [*Allen Christen die dissen brieff leszen odder horenn . . .*]."[22]

A particular instance of this challenge is the case of the so-called Invocavit Sermons of 1522 (LW 51:70–100). These were eight sermons that Luther preached—one each day during the first week of Lent (March 9–16)—in Wittenberg, sermons that helped end the turmoil surrounding controversial church reforms that had occurred during the 11 months Luther was away at Wartburg castle. These were the early days of theological and educational reform—affecting church, monastery, university, and city in Wittenberg and Electoral Saxony. Hence, this was a pivotal period in the German Reformation. In addition, this Wittenberg Movement was the first serious threat to emerge from *within* the evangelical camp because it provoked occasional violence and strong repercussions by rulers. Therefore, what Luther had to say in these sermons was of keen interest.[23]

The Invocavit Sermons are still the most famous of all sermons preached by Luther. Familiar lines from them are ubiquitously quoted;[24] their historical situation is discussed in every comprehensive Reformation history; and the texts are preserved in many important collections of Luther discourse in English.[25] These sermons and the situation that surrounded them continue to be crucial not only for understanding Luther's rhetoric, but also for appreciating the positions and strategies of Luther's opponents. Contemporary scholarship on the so-called radical reformation, for example, commonly refers to Karlstadt's role in the Wittenberg Movement because he was chiefly responsible for many of the church reforms that Luther opposed in the sermons. Thus, Karlstadt—Luther's senior colleague on the theological faculty of the university and initially a strong supporter—became Luther's chief opponent in the sermons. Karlstadt is considered by some as a chief forerunner of Anabaptist and Pietist traditions, and his participation in the Wittenberg Movement, as well as all his writings, have been under intensive reassessment for the past two decades.[26]

What is disconcerting, however, is that historians and theologians have conducted no detailed analysis of the organization, strategies, and style of the Invocavit Sermons. Discussions assess the historical situation, summarize the arguments, and comment that the sermons were effective, but these discussions do not carefully explore how Luther's arguments function logically and psychologically. Birgit Stolt of Stockholm has provided careful rhetorical analysis of other selected Luther sermons based on classical rhetorical categories; Sergiusz Michalski has recently reemphasized the important substance of Luther's arguments about images in the Invocavit Sermons.[27] The English-speaking world also needs case-study analysis of Luther's rhetoric, and such analysis is stronger when it considers not only ancient rhetorical categories, but also contemporary rhetorical theories and critical methods.

Two examples will show how my rhetorical analysis will challenge or bolster existing studies. First, James Preus argues that in the Invocavit Sermons Luther's differences with Karlstadt were over pace not purpose, policy not theology. In other words, the two reformers differed about tactics and timing but were united in theology.[28] My analysis shows that the "tactical" differences also reveal divergent theological perspectives. Second, historians often acknowledge Luther's concern in the Invocavit Sermons for "love" and for the "weaker brother," leaving the implication that these were new themes for Luther. However, it is not the case that these were new themes, and my analysis will demonstrate that fact. Moreover, the analysis also reveals how Luther embodies these themes in his style.[29] In addition, the major issue of iconoclasm—whether artwork in the church should be permitted, removed, or destroyed—continues to occupy art historians; the theological and pragmatic arguments of Luther and Karlstadt in 1522 provide important sources of scholarly debate.

A particularly challenging feature of the Invocavit Sermons is the state of the texts. The modern German texts derive from early printed editions of 1523 and 1526, which most scholars agree came from the hands of people other than Luther. The only manuscripts that exist are fragmentary texts: (1) A Latin manuscript contains approximately 125 words: 10 *propositiones*—followed by two brief explanatory paragraphs—that summarize the major positions that Luther maintained in the eight sermons. (2) One handwritten German text (and three other prints) contains approximately 1,500 words, which parallels some of the material in sermons 1 and 2.[30] (3) A recently discovered German manuscript, what I call the Wolfenbüttel manuscript, consisting of approximately 2,000 words is believed to be a stenographic record of one of the sermons.[31] However, in April 1522 (only a few weeks after the Invocavit Sermons were preached) Luther published a pamphlet that addresses many of the same topics as the sermons but in different order, arguments, and evidence: "Receiving Both Kinds in the Sacrament" (LW 36:231–67). Which documents, then, constitute what Luther "said" during those eight days in the pulpit? The answer is, of course, we may never know. But the printed texts are the best we have.

While the present study can only begin to plumb the depths of Luther's preaching, I hope that the background material provided in chapter 1 sufficiently orients and intrigues readers to better understand how rhetoric, rhetorical style, and rhetorical criticism are important tools for learning how Luther's discourse—how any discourse—works. In chapter 1, I explain the important concepts of rhetorical form (Kenneth Burke), how an argument advances (Chaim Perelman and Lucy Olbrechts-Tyteca), and some important rhetorical devices used to advance an argument. The chapter will prepare readers to follow the careful exposition and analysis of the Invocavit Sermons by sharpening their critical "eyes and ears" and by giving them a critical vocabulary with which to articulate their observations.

In chapter 2, I provide important historical and theological background for understanding the Invocavit Sermons. Included in the background material is a discussion of the historical and theological issues that provoked the sermons. The explanation covers not only what Luther did and wrote about prior to his exile in Wartburg, but also discusses the people and events surrounding the Wittenberg Movement. The chapter covers both the preacher Luther and his audience members, their concerns and vested interests.

In chapters 3 through 6, I describe in detail the flow of arguments and exhortation Luther pursues in the Invocavit Sermons. I explain how the sermons are organized, specifically what arguments, appeals, evidence, and exhortation are present. Without knowing this "substance," one cannot understand the "form." Conversely, it is only the form (or style) through which and in which the substance of Luther's preaching can possibly be appreciated because no idea comes without form.

In chapter 7, I present a brief discussion of Luther's "Receiving Both Kinds in the Sacrament" (April 1522), which is a revision and summary of the Invocavit Sermons for reception by towns surrounding Wittenberg that were facing the same issues she faced upon Luther's return from Wartburg. I also offer some observations about how the Luther documents analyzed in this book—the eight Invocavit Sermons and "Receiving Both Kinds"—can be understood to represent differing points in the rhetorical situation. I also draw some concluding summary remarks about key features of Luther's rhetorical style. Although the thrust of the study differs from other analyses of Luther's discourse, my arguments participate in a wider scholarly dialogue about Luther as preacher.

# CHAPTER 1

# RHETORICAL CRITICISM
# AND STYLE

To appreciate Luther's skill as a preacher, a brief discussion of the processes of understanding any sermon can be helpful. Because preaching and sermon construction draw heavily upon the principles of rhetoric, a review of the key concepts and aims of rhetoric and its subfield, rhetorical criticism, may prove helpful. Rhetorical criticism that closely monitors not only some skeletal outline, but the very language (diction, rhythm, strategy, etc.) of the discourse can help listeners open up the discourse they are reading or hearing because it can train listeners to hear and see—to understand—what had formerly been missed.

Rhetorical criticism is the attempt to describe, analyze, and evaluate discourse, much of which can be called "functional communication,"[1] which is oral and written speech designed for—and which should thus be judged as—"influencing men in some concrete situation."[2] The preponderance of contemporary criticism draws upon traditional Western rhetoric, which consists in five parts, or "canons," that represent the stages of planning, composing, and delivering a speech: invention, arrangement (*dispositio*), style (*elocutio*), memory, and delivery.

Speeches in the Greco-Roman world were of three types, distinguished according to whether or not the audience acted as "judge." When they did act as judge, the decision audiences were to make was often about what had happened in the past. In such cases the species was forensic (judicial), and the audience ultimately decided the guilt or innocence of a defendant. When the decision considered the future, the species was deliberative, and the audience's judgment ruled on a course of action. If the audience did not act as judge and did not have to render a specific action decision—about past or future—the species was epideictic (ceremonial). The nature of this last species has raised many questions throughout the generations not only because its occasions seem less uniform than the other two, but also because the role of the audience may arguably still be seen as judging something. One suggestion about what that "something" is holds that the audience's role is to judge the quality of the speech and the speaker. Others argue that the values at stake in the praise and blame appeals of the speech are what are ultimately judged (hence, what constructs and deconstructs the culture).

In the ensuing centuries, Western rhetoric has influenced all discourse in many ways, not the least of which is that all human communication can be appreciated for its effort to influence people. It is this broader sense that I bring as a domain for rhetoric and which I have in view for an analysis of Luther's Invocavit

17

Sermons. I want to attempt to discover how the discourse functions, beginning with how it functioned in its own concrete situation.

The context, or "situation," can be studied with help from the rhetorical tradition. Bitzer's theory of "rhetorical situation" (and subsequent critiques), which I address in chapter 2, can help us consider what the speaker and audience are up against prior to the speech. In addition, other resources speakers have at their disposal are (1) the facts and evidence pertinent to the issue—what Aristotle calls inartistic proofs—and (2) the three forms of artistic (manipulable) proof in traditional rhetoric, which are interlocked and dynamic throughout the speaking occasion. These forms are *ethos*—the proof residing in the character of the speaker (as ascertained by the audience); *logos*—the proof deriving from the arguments of the message; and *pathos*—the proof consisting in the audience's disposition (feelings) toward the speaker and the speech. Hence, the speaker (*rhetor* in Greek; *orator* in Latin) will attempt to design a discourse that presents a compelling case. Accordingly, rhetorical criticism tries to ask how the discourse functions. To do that, one must know what the rhetor is trying to accomplish with the audience. But how shall a critic begin? What features should be examined?

Rhetorical criticism, as it has developed over approximately the past five decades, has taken on many agendas—for example, neo-Aristotelian criticism, movement studies, dramatistic criticism, genre criticism. All have been attempts to apply, reconstruct, or improve on a long tradition. What is striking about this body of critical literature is that none of it takes very seriously one of the paramount concerns of that tradition—namely, style. Indeed, a survey of some periodical literature in communication journals shows that there persists a fundamental neglect of style in both the theory and the practice of criticism.[3] While various theoretical and critical practices represented in this body of literature suggest that style is a frustratingly amorphous creature, eluding easy definition, most of the material does not venture much beyond theory and is, for the critic, consequently inadequate. It falls short of a level of analysis that would reveal *how* discourse works. As a result, such criticism often fails to provide a useful critical approach to reading a discursive text. What has happened in some applications of rhetorical criticism is instructive. For example, in biblical studies (particularly of the New Testament) much criticism in the past two decades has been preoccupied with scrutinizing a piece of discourse—say, a Pauline epistle—according to the prescriptions found in Greco-Roman rhetorical handbooks. These prescriptions have, to a great extent, applied the requirements of *dispositio* that were thought pertinent to the appropriate genre (species) to which the epistle is judged to belong. Most of the subsequent critical analysis, then, follows (and flows from) a diagnosis of what type of discourse the epistle is characterized as. Features of style are taken to be incidental to this critical process; that is, the invention and arrangement dictate the style.[4]

In one respect, this line of thought shows that some incisive remarks about the importance of style in criticism made more than 40 years ago have been either forgotten or disregarded.[5] While style may follow invention and arrangement in the natural transpiration of events in the speech planning process, the opposite occurs in the speech listening (or speech criticism) process. Style is apprehended first; arrangement of the arguments, the "parts of the speech," and the strategy of the speaker usually must be inferred by both audience and critic. Moreover, those inferences generally reconfigure the speech's own idiom, translating it into the critical vocabulary of the analyst, which often results in abridgment of the speech into only its motives, content, strategies, and arguments. Consequently, the language that actually affected the hearers, and which the speaker took such pains to develop, is often overlooked.[6]

Style, then, is of primary, paramount concern to the critic, especially if that critic wants to know how the audience might be receiving the message (a crucial factor in attempting to determine the function of discourse, which I argue ought to be the *modus operandi* of the critic). Moreover, both the interpretation of discourse (literary and rhetorical criticism) and the production of discourse (composition, preaching) can profit from careful attention to style. If, as Donald Bryant has suggested, "style is the final elaboration of meaning,"[7] then surely style is the initial encounter through which auditors (listeners, readers) *apprehend* meaning. Does it not seem reasonable that style ought to play a major role in the critical act of analyzing discourse?

However, granting that scrutinizing style in criticism has been neglected, what do I mean by style? To begin, we should not regard style as the mere "department" of *elocutio*, but in it *dispositio*, and even *inventio*, participate:

> It is difficult at best to consider the functioning language of discourse without becoming involved at once with the ordering of the discourse. Furthermore, if we go beyond the static idea of disposition as arrangement, to the potentially dynamic idea of disposition as *disposing*, as Wagner thought necessary, we may conclude that for the critic the two names signify the two lenses for a stereopticon view of a single factor in discourse. This factor is best conceived as style because that name suggests the foundation of discourse in language.[8]

Such a conception of style may seem radical, particularly in view of narrow (and tainted) conceptions of style—as decoration, eccentricity, fashion, or falsehood. Yet construing style as a phenomenon worthy of a critic's concern is not new—not for Bryant or Comte de DeBuffon[9] or others.[10] Style, then, is functional, not only ornamental; rhetorical, not merely literary. Style "*does*, and the real question is always 'How well does it *do*?' So we judge style according to the demands of a particular move; we judge style move by move."[11] Reaching back into disposition and invention, style becomes the "order and movement we give to our thought."[12] Moreover, style is a crucial factor in traditional rhetorical criticism, even revealing insights of which the speaker might possibly be unaware. C. Joachim Classen argues:

For there is no good reason to assume that a text could and should be examined only according to categories known (or possibly known) to the author concerned. For rhetoric provides a system for the interpretation of all texts (as well as of oral utterances and even of other forms of communication), irrespective of time and circumstances (except, of course, for the fact that some rules of rhetoric immediately concern the external circumstances).[13]

In fact, then, there is no reason why our critical repertoire need be limited to classical categories. Luther's Wittenberg colleague Philipp Melanchthon made an enormous contribution to the development of rhetorical criticism, introducing new categories and new terms. By implication, he encouraged any reader or scholar to apply rhetoric in its most advanced form or even to develop it further when and where needed.[14]

In what follows, I sketch an outline of a coherent conception of style for use as a critical approach. Then, to develop some procedure or approach for perceiving style, I offer an analysis of the rhetorical process—three operations that occur when a rhetor sets out to secure (or to strengthen) an audience's adherence to an idea, for which I develop a lexicon of critical tools. I hope that what I show will serve as a framework for use by the critic who would understand the function of a discourse for its audience.

## A Coherent Conception of Style for the Critic

One of the first setbacks in casting about for a starting point with style is the pedagogy of style. The handbooks are largely prescriptive. If we resist the aesthetic standards of stylistic prescriptions discussed in the handbooks—clarity and appropriateness (Aristotle); clarity, brevity, sincerity (Richard Lanham)—to what will we turn?[15] I suggest we put aside the handbooks until *after* we have more fully clarified the nature of discursive style, that business of manipulating language for the purpose of executing the rhetorical function, "adjusting ideas to people and people to ideas."[16] In describing what he calls "textual criticism" (a term somewhat misleading, especially to scholars familiar with classical and biblical studies), Stephen Lucas argues that "meaning and effect are produced, not by the text as a static entity, but by the progressive interaction of the audience with the temporal flow of the ideational, dispositional, stylistic, and syntactical elements in the discourse. Each word, each phrase, each sentence *conditions the response of the audience* to each succeeding word, phrase, and sentence."[17]

While his project of close analysis of texts is on the right track, Lucas fails to provide an effective anchor for an encompassing theory of style. To be able to apprehend the "progressive interaction of the audience with the . . . elements in the discourse," the critic must have a way to engage the discourse as she encounters it in the text. To do that, I have found extremely helpful an approach that provides framework and tools for analyzing a discourse, one that incorporates some fundamental, but overlooked, notions of Chaim Perelman and Lucy Olbrechts-

Tyteca and of Kenneth Burke. Using the ideas of these scholars, I have devised a set of principles that helps organize a practical, critical vocabulary.[18] My approach consists of two lenses, two foundational ways of thinking: (1) a formal, structural, or dramatistic lens; and (2) a stylistic, argumentative, rhetorical lens.

The first lens derives not from Burke's later work on motives, but from his concept of *form*, which he offered most accessibly in his 1931 collection of essays, *Counter-Statement*.[19] The second lens derives from Perelman and Olbrechts-Tyteca, who characterize argumentation as the attempt to secure audience *adherence* to theses and who present their analysis of figures according to their argumentative, not aesthetic, function.[20] Both of these lenses together allow the critic to analyze discourse in much the same way one holds a prism to the sunlight. The prism does not *impose* colors upon the white light; rather, it *enables* one to discern what is already there by enhancing one's observational (and analytical) capabilities.[21]

## BURKE'S *FORM* AS RHETORICAL ACTION

Burke offered a compelling case for understanding how artistic discourse works in social interaction. Instead of insisting that interpreters continue trying to get inside the mind or world of the artist, he maintained that we should be asking what the audience is thinking and feeling as they encounter the work of art. The key to understanding what makes discourse persuasive is *form*: "an arousing and fulfillment of desires."[22] Burke's project in the 1920s was to challenge a dominant elitist aesthetic wherein a work of art is primarily the avenue by which an artist may *express* something—most often an idea or emotion the artist experiences. Against this consensus was Burke's "counter-statement," in which he insisted that the essence or goal of an artistic work is to *evoke* something in others, that is, in audiences. Consequently, Burke saw discourse as communication, as rhetorical action, with *identification* between artist (speaker/poet, etc.) because identification (not "persuasion") is the artist's goal.[23] The audience is then able to participate in the action because the artist has deliberately chosen "forms" in which to instantiate ("individuate") her or his emotion or idea via an argument, plot, story, etc. Hence, an author fashions (*inventio*) a work in which an audience can participate not only through the information presented, but also through the forms into which the information is organized. Information can bring satisfaction through its newness, but form has the capability repeatedly to satisfy because of its power to elicit our recognition of its rightness or fittingness. Furthermore, this rightness— our cooperation with and ability to apprehend, appreciate, and participate in form (whether by agreeing with it, rejoicing at it, mourning over it, being terrified by it, etc.)—is the work's *psychology*, the explanation behind its function. What makes audience identification happen is usually not information, but form, "the creation of an appetite in the mind of the auditor, and the adequate satisfying of that appetite."[24] Therefore, to dichotomize form and content—making content primary, form merely something later selected (as shape, container, or format)—is misguided. Rather than being irrelevant or in opposition to content, form and content are inseparable; form becomes part of, is the "body" of, the (dis- or pre-embodied) content.[25]

It may seem that, rather than having a new concept of form, Burke is simply insisting the interpreter gives greater priority to form. In arguing that form, not information, is what "hooks and holds" audiences, has not Burke merely taken the notion of shape and/or arrangement of information and given it greater importance than the information itself? Somewhat to the contrary, I believe when Burke says that literary works of art normally should strive for some balance between form and information and that those works violating this principle are either bad or highly specialized art, Burke appears to have muted the objection. Moreover, if "everything that gets communicated does so through form,"[26] we need to ask, How complex is form and whence does it come?

Form is a natural ability to function in a certain way. Just as we possess heartbeats, we humans possess forms. Thus, we can respond to or be aroused by (though we may not always know what to call) form when it appears in artistic works. "An ability to function in a certain way implies gratification in so functioning. A capacity is not something which lies dormant until used—a capacity is a command to act in a certain way."[27] While Burke seems to describe form in psycho-physical terms, such as "muscular imagination" (and many others), he really is interested only in form's employment through our language systems.[28]

Two fundamental "aspects" of form, or patterns of order through which it seems to operate, are the most common in discourse.[29] Indeed, unless we understand these aspects, most rhetorical figures remain mere decoration—apparent stylistic novelties. First, *progressive* form occurs in its most straightforward manner (syllogistic progression) as linear or temporal advance. This form occurs whenever one element leads to another element of a different kind, such as when A leads to (suggests, requires, permits, causes) B, an argument advances step by step, a plot moves along scene by scene, premises force a conclusion, a cause results in effects, or effects cry out for causes. For instance, when a theatrical audience learns of the discovery of a murder, they anticipate (desire) the apprehension of the villain. This "requirement" for the apprehension exists because similar phenomena already have been experienced by persons alert to their own empirical and artistic worlds. We "expect" certain outcomes, whether we call them logic, justice, "just desserts," or "the breaks." Because we have previously experienced it, forward movement of some pace and magnitude is something we have come to expect, recognize, and desire (or dread). Consequently, an artist sensitive to these existential recurrences can play on our human psychological expectations, installing syllogistically linked episodes within the work. The fascinating introduction to Burke's essay "Psychology and Form" is itself a demonstration of how syllogistic progression works. It describes how the audience has long expected the ghost's arrival in the fourth scene of the first act of *Hamlet*: "This ghost . . . is the rich fulfilment of a promise. Yet this satisfaction in turn becomes an allurement, an itch for further developments."[30]

So this development illustrates first of all form itself. Then, because the satisfaction provided, despite its expectedness (which has been cleverly enhanced by delay and diversion), is a desired outcome—a payoff—the version or aspect of form is syllogistic progression. To be sure, this progressive form is behind the "logic" of story, and we are all well aware of some contributions that narrative insights have brought to interpretation and preaching. Stories seem to "move" and succeed in their ability to address both "itch" and "scratch."[31] Hence, we now realize that the ordering of sequences in a story—what Latin handbooks call arrangement [*dispositio*]—"works" because of progressive form. It works for us primarily because we encounter progression in the natural world (for example, the progressive cycle of the seasons; the sense, during an oppressive hot spell, of an impending storm; a disobedient child's dread of "Just you wait until your father gets home!") even before we experience it in artistic creations (for example, expecting happy endings or anticipating a character's being startled when the camera lets us watch her or him gradually retreat backward on stage). Before these became established literary or cinematic codes and stereotypes (conventions), our experiences allowed these patterns to ring true. So at the level of larger units— parts sequenced to fit into a whole—progressive form is at work when an artistic "tale" advances in an acceptable fashion for us. It possesses *narrative probability*— the story coheres—and *narrative fidelity*—the story is somehow congruent with lived experience.[32] Even when fidelity is in question and still we willingly suspend belief, we are consenting to the continued telling of the story because the progressive essence of the endeavor has us in its grip.[33]

Furthermore, it is a simple matter to perceive progression at more minute linguistic levels. For example, even the syntax of a verbal language (subject, verb, complement) reflects this progression.[34] "A naming must be completed by a doing, either explicit or implicit. The subject demands a predicate as resolutely as the antecedent of a musical phrase in Mozart calls for its consequent."[35] Yet in a matter as small as a single sentence, the formal satisfaction may go unappreciated, except where lacking, because we are "spoiled," we are accustomed to satisfaction. It can be "better revealed by our dissatisfaction with an uncompleted thought than by our satisfaction with a completed one."[36] So when, in our act of critical reflection, we "turn aside to see this thing which has come to pass," forcing form and content to "go to their separate corners," we are better able to detect form at work. All other times, however, content cannot be experienced apart from its form.

An alternate variation of progressive form is *qualitative progression*, something far less clear and not nearly as easy to understand as syllogistic progression. Nonetheless, the link between episodes is still one of before/after; however, the *after* episode is not expected (demanded, desired, dreaded, etc.). It is still *fitting*, though in less predictable ways, because the presence of a quality or mood prepares the audience for the introduction of another, different mood. This mood "prepares" because the audience is oblivious to the outcome (and its fittingness) until later, often much later than would be the case with syllogistic progression. One scholar argues that qualitative progression is distinguished from syllogistic progression precisely because subsequent developments are unexpected rather than demanded.[37] Another scholar finds qualitative progression in the Gospel of Mark to be those "unexpected developments" or "reversals of expectations," primarily when some occurrence (for example, the disciples' reaction to Jesus' pronouncements) is different than the one expected by the reader, yet one the reader eventually accepts as having been prepared for because the proper state of mind for it was created.[38] So syllogistic progression always looks forward, and qualitative progression reflects back; the latter is surprising and discernible only in retrospect, while the former is expected, desired, and immediately recognizable. For both types of progressive form, however, there is audience satisfaction at finding a contrast, a difference in-kind, between subsequent developments as they are encountered in a work of art.[39]

The second fundamental aspect of form reveals that even as audience expectations respond to linear movement among contrasting, complementary episodes, they also respond to discursive developments that continue the *same* unit (topic, claim, attribute, theme, or characteristic). Indeed, were it not for *repetitive* form, all would be in flux, a perpetual grasping for change. Of necessity, then, there must be some continuity, which is seen especially in examples from music and drama. Repetitive form develops through the consistent maintenance of a principle under new guises, the restatement of the same thing in different ways. Sometimes the repetition is sustained and immediate, or it may be scattered throughout a piece. Beethoven's Fifth Symphony clearly develops many rich variations of its thematic paean; a dramatic villain manifests many behaviors and characteristics consonant with what we have come to expect from such a person. Surely the idea of thematic and verbal repetition/variation needs little explication or defense. Or does it?

In the discursive arts, we have come to recognize, laud, and practice *good* repetition while trying to avoid, even loathe, *mere* repetition. Wherein lies the difference? Is it in some magic number of repeatings and no more (few or many?) or in their nature (verbatim or variation)? Each of us has our preferences. Surely more votes would be cast for variety and the number three. Mark's gospel, for example, prefers verbatim patterns (particularly threes), while Greco-Roman manuals advocate minor variations.[40] The author of the *Rhetorica ad Herennium* advises, "We shall not repeat the same thing precisely—for that, to be sure, would weary the hearer and not elaborate the idea—but with changes."[41] Moreover, the difference between instances of bad and good—that is, the difference between *repetitious* and *repetitive*—is not in their design, but in their reception, which is what the rhetorical manuals also sought:

> *Repetitious*: when a word, percept, or experience is repeated with less impact at each recurrence; repeated to no particular end, out of a failure of invention

or sloppiness of thought. *Repetitive*: when a word, percept, or experience is repeated with equal or greater force at each occurrence. Successful repetition depends both on the inherent interest of the recurring unit and on its context.[42]

Repetition, then, is an attempt to make manifest an experience for the purpose of evoking audience response to that experience. If the experience is inherently interesting and intense, an author may, in places, resort to repetition to inculcate—even to enact—those qualities. The reader, whose own experience coalesces to some degree with the experience being described, will have no trouble feeling the intensity; the repetition will not be repetitious. Bruce Kawin says: "[N]or do I scold Lear that he has made his point, [or that] the last four *nevers* are unnecessary. On the contrary, Lear's cries attain an intensity possible only in unremitting repetition; it is the power of his howl that is under discussion here, and its tendency . . . to open on areas of experience generally considered inaccessible to language."[43] Accordingly, parents who encounter King David's repetitive "my son" (five times in one verse), cried out as he reels from hearing about the death of Absalom (2 Sam 18:33), come to *feel* the "stammer of anguish."[44] As Luther put it, "Troubled hearts are fond of repetitions."[45] Should parents ever themselves have to endure that kind of pain (and there are few things worse), they can lend their testimony to what other readers, spared the actual experience, have perceived in the text as virtual experience. Hence, as the "key to our experience," repetitions (one's heartbeat, a ticking watch, a horse's hoofbeats, a flashing semaphore, a daily habit) become the "key to our *expression of* experience."[46] Whereas Plato said the forms derive from the heavens, Burke is interested only in their omnipresence in nature and particularly in our human capacity, as unique among the natural creatures, to know and use them. David Buttrick would have us consider the uniqueness of Jesus' resurrection—its lack of both precedent and repetition—as an important dimension of our difficulty in believing it: "Repeated events are credible—what does happen is likely to have happened [before]—and singular events are incredible."[47] Repetitive form is, therefore, basic to any work of art or any kind of orientation; it is "our only method of talking on the subject."[48] Buttrick's own compositional style reveals a mastery of alliteration (rhyme through initial consonantal repetition), which is consistent with his commitment to careful selection of "appropriate" poetic language to convey the Good News. But using rhyme well, not with "superficial arbitrariness," is certainly a challenge for one who employs it.[49]

Both repetitive and progressive form can (and often do) work in combination. For example, in the two repetitive series in Rom 8:35 and Rom 8:38–39, we may notice one formal device—*polysyndeton*. We also intuitively sense these series working on our emotions. The former series ("shall tribulation, or distress, or persecution . . . ?") builds expectation and anxiety through carefully contemplating—via the conjunctions—manifestations of trouble; the latter series ("neither death nor life nor angels . . .") matches in-kind the anxiety by providing its solution—

thus, we have progression.[50] Moreover, uncomplicated instances of form are easy to locate in literature (especially poetry) and in music, and they can also be found quickly and accurately in drama and prose. Most people can easily grasp the progression and repetition of nursery rhymes, especially when demonstrated orally (in song) and/or visually (in print).

1 Three blind mice,
2 Three blind mice.
3 See how they run,
4 See how they run.

5 They all ran after the farmer's wife,
6 She cut off their tails with a carving knife,
7 Did you ever see such a sight in your life
8 As three blind mice.

Without recounting the most obvious repetitive elements both of sight and sound (including musical pitch), the progression is also manifest in moving from cause in the first quatrain to effect in the second. Children are thus invited to follow these patterns as they psychologically initiate and agitate their expectations through repeating words, images, and rhymes ("any chiming of the sounds of words").[51] They are drawn along in a delightful, easily followed narrative. Although here a satisfaction felt mostly by the resolution of tension produced by the sustained, repetitively generated crescendo of lines 5 through 7, *assent* seems granted by virtue of a collaboration by audience and author, who in this case is not even needed but would be in situations where we are not so willing to suspend disbelief or judgment. Despite how the decades have dimmed my memory, I was able to reconstruct this verse by recollection simply by singing it to myself. By next adding punctuation, I managed to document more of the cognitive sense of the narrative flow, or progression, which I had already felt as my recitation transpired. Recitation and song, therefore, have always been powerful pedagogical devices.

We can now legitimately attest to the power of these two types of form, in such simple states as they are here demonstrated, to promote consideration of discourse by participants. As would-be reflection of raw emotion (the case of David and Absalom) and as playful deployment of progression/repetition in children's literature, form directs audience thought-feelings. In addition, these strategies even reflect upon their maker (author). Philo of Alexandria's repetitive "lists" employ a logic that accounts for participation of his readers' emotions: "Chains of epithets and lists of persons and things . . . tend to generate expectations of consistency and direction. By the time Philo has accumulated half a dozen epithets for the wicked man . . . his audience anticipates consistency as he adds more . . . ." The effect is that the auditor "must begin to marvel both at the profundity of wickedness *and* at the resourcefulness of anyone who can so thoroughly exhaust the available vocabulary of wickedness."[52] James Muilenburg has convincingly shown all three of the above results of repetitive form. What is less convincing is Muilenburg's claim that the repetitive tendencies found in the Hebrew Bible give us an "open avenue to the character of biblical thinking."[53] Such a view of style—as if it were a "window to the soul," whether of an individual artist or of a culture—was long a prevalent concept.[54] My argument here, however, is more interested in the *fact* that form is present (to what extent, of what type, to what ends) than with precise processes *by which* form gets into the text.

Both progressive (syllogistic and qualitative types) and repetitive form are patterns of order and, as arranged by the author, often work their wonders without audience awareness of their nature. Another aspect of form is a phenomenon quite different from these: When auditors *expect* a work to acquiesce to some prior notion of appropriateness, they display a categorical expectancy wherein form that *appeals as form* occurs. For example, we insist that a work start with a sense of beginning and end with a sense of closure; we follow the word order and inflections of a particular language; we adhere to the constraints of a 14-line sonnet. These conventions are not requirements learned but regularities experienced in works of art. Moreover, intricacies of convention may ultimately become fitted for occasions and fixed by consensus. Conventions are pliable and evolving, and artists have always toyed with them; jurisdiction over conventions is negotiable. Yet this does not negate the power of conventional form; indeed, the fact that conventions are "noticed" with such vigor, even controversy, attests to their potency to involve and satisfy audiences. Conventions can be seen as "tacit contracts" authors have worked out with their contemporary audiences.[55] But the matter of whether or when to "violate" them is difficult:

> [H]is expectancy [that is, a reader's] may be so imperious that he will condemn the slighting of this form even in an author who is aiming at different effects. Yet in violating a convention, an author is undeniably violating a major tenet of form. For he is disappointing the expectations of his audience; and form, by our definition, resides in the fulfilment of an audience's expectations. The only justification which an author may have for thus breaking faith with his audience is the fact that categorical expectations are very unstable and that the artist can, if his use of the repetitive and progressive principles is authoritative enough, succeed in bringing his audience to a sufficient acceptance of his methods. And as the history of art fully testifies, if the changes in conventional form are introduced to obtain a new stressing, to produce a kind of effect which the violated convention was not well able to produce, but which happens to be more apropos to the contemporary scene, the changes may very rapidly become "canonized" in popular acceptance and the earlier convention may seem the violator of categorical expectancy.[56]

Finally, small, individual instantiations of form within a work can be more or less present in a work as *minor forms*. Such forms contribute to the development of the whole—by repetition, progression, or convention—but they also have their own "episodic distinctness" worthy of consideration apart from their context.

Examples of these forms are metaphor, paradox, disclosure, reversal, contraction, expansion, bathos, apostrophe, series, and chiasmus. Form crafted by an artist helps an audience to "dream" the dream that led to the creation of the artistic work. "It is, rather, the audience which dreams, while the artist oversees the conditions which determine the dream."[57] However, just as art is not simply the weak representation of some actual experience, neither is the arousing of emotion *per se* the goal of art. The goal, the essence, of art is eloquence, and the emotions that we experience in life are the material on which eloquence feeds: "Eloquence is not showiness; it is, rather the result of that desire in the artist to make a work perfect by adapting it in every minute detail to the racial appetites."[58] Considering, then, the long-standing struggle between wisdom and eloquence, should we not investigate form and come to critically assess the *eloquent truth* of biblical passages or preaching, "God's Word in *man's language*"?[59]

## PERELMAN AND OLBRECHTS-TYTECA'S *NEW RHETORIC*

The perspective on argumentation as the attempt to gain "adherence to theses" (or to strengthen adherence) is an important concept, one that focuses on the communicational goal of discourse. Such a perspective emphasizes the relationship between audience and message. And this perspective is particularly significant and fundamental to my approach because, as with the concept of form, the audience-thesis connection properly maintains a strongly functional objective to the analysis of discourse.[60] In short, style is not the traces of an author; style is the workings of a rhetor's discursive intentions toward audience adherence.

Accordingly, the manner in which Perelman and Olbrechts-Tyteca proceed with their consideration of rhetorical figures proves instructive for this approach because they discuss figures according to their argumentative function: "We refuse to separate the form of a discourse from its substance, to study stylistic structures and figures independently of the purpose they must achieve in the argumentation."[61] Of course, here the authors do not use "form" in the sense that Burke does, nor do they indicate that they understand "substance" in the sense of act.[62] Yet Perelman and Olbrechts-Tyteca are sensitive to the function of argumentation as inextricably bound up in the way ideas are expressed, that is, how those familiar elements of style—chosen, arranged, presented—become the "means whereby a particular presentation of the data establishes agreement at a certain level, impresses it on the consciousness with a certain intensity and emphasizes certain aspects of it."[63] Put another way, simply identifying and classifying figures according to their manner of deviation from the norm only labels the obvious and describes the surface. Stylistic criticism needs to delve into the reasons behind, the objectives in view, and the effects that might plausibly be achieved by figures employed.

One further note concerning the functional approach to discourse is the discussion of selected grammatical features related to their application in argumentation. Here Perelman and Olbrechts-Tyteca do not allow themselves to be guided by grammatical rules; rather, they analyze the effective tendencies that these features are capable of producing. Many of the features they discuss present stimulating suggestions, some of which I have found nowhere else. Philological reference works (for example, lexicons and grammars) tend to document and classify tendencies or prescribe rules, but they do not raise questions about argumentative function.[64] Some brief examples of helpful discussions in the *New Rhetoric* are the sections on Modalities in Expression of Thought,[65] Tense,[66] Pronouns,[67] Singulars and Plurals,[68] and Demonstratives.[69] Through their rhetorical approach to argumentation, Perelman and Olbrechts-Tyteca show how persuasive force obtains in discursive style: "What is required is not so much the exactness of specific logical modalities attributed to what is asserted, as the *means of obtaining the adherence of the audience* through variations in the way of expressing thought."[70]

One of the most quickly noticed features of situated oral discourse—once a critic has been sensitized to notice it—is pronoun usage, particularly a shift in tendency (for example, from "I" to "you") or a preponderance or paucity of similar personal pronouns. A speaker or author can do many things with pronouns:

1. Hold a subject at a distance by using a predominantly *third-person* prevalence. When a discussion addressed to an audience is dominated by "he/she/it/they/them/those," the sense conveyed is that of detachment. The audience feels a disconnection from what is being discussed. Knowing they are not part of the subject, the audience is free to examine it, to feel frightened by it, to think themselves superior to it, etc. The particular mood or disposition felt depends on how that subject is being characterized. The third-person pronoun is helpful for casting blame elsewhere, for vilifying an enemy. Moreover, not unlike the third-person pronoun is the demonstrative, which can be used to dramatically call special attention to a nearby subject already contemplated ("this/these") or to cast light on a far removed subject ("that/them").

2. Create a strong sense of speaker *ethos*—one of authority and experience, one of fearful self-disclosure, one of bravado or rage, etc. The *first-person singular* ("I/me/mine") draws attention to the speaker; the more it continues, the greater the presence of the speaker from the perspective of the listeners. When speakers want to assert difference and distance between themselves and their audience, they can turn to first-person singular.[71] Accordingly, even when not intending that effect, a feeling of distance is produced when speakers heavily use first singular. Audience members feel unlike/removed from the speaker. Of course, without context we cannot predict whether the audience will desire or loath to be like/near the speaker.

3. Cultivate a sense of inclusiveness by using *first-person plural*. Of course, it is possible to use "we/us/ours" in an exclusive way (apostolic authors occasionally do that to call attention to their own authority as a special group), but one can just as easily be perceived as attempting to incorporate the audience into one's world. Erasmus's use of the editorial "we" and the fraternal "we" is an

example.[72] When a speaker tries to draw her audience close, she may relinquish some of the authority and control over them in exchange. But the rhetor's strategy is often to accept such losses in pursuit of greater gain: sharing a stake in the issue; appearing to understand, to see things as audience members do; or appearing to risk being involved in the problem (its cause, its blame, its solution). Such gains in speaker-audience communion would not be necessary if *ethos* and *pathos* did not enter into the mix of proofs, if *logos* alone mattered.

4. Address listeners in the most direct and intimate way through the use of *second-person pronouns*. Normally the plural is used when addressing an audience, but a singular pronoun can draw attention to an individual, perhaps when a rhetor wants to develop a typical scenario for one person that can be contemplated by all. The speaker can single out a special (nontypical) individual—with or without naming the person—whereby others then are spared the intimacy (and its attendant comfort or discomfort) and can listen in on and benefit from what is said. Second-person pronouns abound when speakers are confronting, challenging, blaming, exhorting, or pleading with their listeners.

Overall, pronoun watching can be most productive for the critic not merely for attaching a label such as "confrontational style," but for compiling observations, along with other evidence, and for asking how the speaker's stylistic tendencies with this audience are presently functioning to advance a thesis—whether to celebrate a cause, to blame an enemy, to charge with a fault, etc.

## THREE OPERATIONS FOR SECURING ADHERENCE

The traditional lines for classifying dispositional and stylistic devices are "figures of thought" and "figures of speech," or schemes and tropes. Schemes have to do with expression, tropes with content.[73] However, I resist dichotomies of that sort and choose instead to develop a critical vocabulary for perceiving and analyzing style that employs three broad categories of rhetorical function, categories that subsume "expression and content" or "speech and thought." My primary rubrics for discussing style are three categories of intended effects—*focus*, *presence*, and *communion*. In other words, besides examining how devices are constructed, we shall ask what need they were conceived to meet.

*Focus* is that which the speaker seeks to achieve by directing the audience's attention to specific aspects of subject matter. Focus is one of the first means of controlling the perceptions and expectations of the audience, an issue that a rhetor cannot afford to ignore.[74] While the rhetorical situation in many ways constrains what ought to be said, the speaker still controls the agenda through which the discourse addressing the situation proceeds. *Presence* is that element of proof that is created when a speaker makes a focused-upon subject more impressive, significant, and real to the audience. Although presence is an important concept in *The*

*New Rhetoric*, I am simply interested in what a speaker does with the topic before the audience.[75] Presence is unquestionably explained largely in sensual, especially visual, terms by Perelman and Olbrechts-Tyteca and their critics.[76] It is not at all misleading to consider presence the "fine-tuning" or "zooming in" or development of focus not only as to function, but also in the temporal progression of the adherence-gaining process. As the proverbial blind person is led to the elephant (and not to the giraffe) before examining (by feeling) its parts, so focus precedes presence. However, it would be foolhardy to attempt to rigidly separate focus and presence.

Through focus and presence, the audience's disposition toward topic and speaker contributes to proof—*pathos* and *ethos*. However, because a relational dynamic between the two human participants in the discursive transaction also plays a role, *communion* is crucial. *Communion* refers to the bond that exists between the rhetor and the audience, while "stance" or "persona" denotes only the speaker. Many strategies for achieving communion elude easy description under the rubric of "stance."[77] Moreover, persona seems to be a conclusion that a critic draws late in the process of apprehending a speaker, a puzzle constructed with many pieces. Communion, on the other hand, can be scrutinized in much clearer disclosure at almost any point in the discourse.

In summary, these three functional categories constitute a systematic attempt to unwrap the discourse. They provide a means for linking descriptive taxonomies to strategy, function, and effect. In the next section, I explore some ways that focus, presence, and communion are created in discourse, drawing on examples from Luther and from the English Bible.[78]

## LEXICON OF CRITICAL TOOLS FOR USE IN ANALYSIS

### FOCUS

Many of the stylistic devices and rhetorical strategies that are intended to focus attention are argumentative in nature because they aid in getting at the issue or cause of the situation. In other words, they are in service of *inventio*. Directing and controlling an audience's attention to a subject is often accomplished by the specific stylistic device of *distributio*, traditionally the division of a concept and the apportioning of its parts.[79] This can be done more or less explicitly; sometimes a single thematic statement provides a map for what follows. Consider, for example, Exod 23:14–16: "Three times thou shalt keep a feast unto me in the year. Thou shalt keep the feast of unleavened bread . . . . And the feast of the harvest . . . and the feast of ingathering . . . ." Occasionally a speaker wishes to direct the audience's attention to one of the parts, particularly when considering choices or alternatives rather than parts. By eliminating all but one choice, the speaker employs *expeditio*, preserving attention to the selected choice. Such a process of elimination, of course, goes beyond mere selection; the surviving option consequently has achieved greater stature by virtue of appearing not equal with, but superior to, the others.[80] Genesis uses *expeditio* in 2:18–25, having the LORD God first bring Adam "every living creature" (among which there was still no "help meet for him"). Only the woman—made special and brought last—was found to be the answer to the man's aloneness, the only condition that the LORD God had deemed "not good," having previously declared all others "good" or "very good." John 1:13 displays *expedito* within a sentence, incorporating *polysyndeton* (discussed below) for greater effect: "Which were born, not of blood, nor of the will of the flesh, nor of the will of man, but of God." If a speaker wants to clarify the focus of attention by entertaining objections, the device of *prolepsis* is available.[81] The objections can be serious or trivial, actual or hypothetical, anticipated or responded to, and they can come from within or outside the audience, from a single skeptic or a large group of concerned people.

In 1 Cor 15:12–14, Paul takes up the challenge to his argument: "Now if Christ be preached that he rose from the dead, how say some among you that there is no resurrection of the dead? But if there be no resurrection of the dead, then is Christ not risen: And if Christ be not risen, then is our preaching vain, and your faith is also vain." There are, of course, degrees to how seriously the objection is to be taken, with corresponding variations in the effect upon the audience. The objections also can be introduced through rhetorical questions. These are but a peek at the variety of means that are at a speaker's disposal for selecting, contextualizing, apportioning, and weighing a topic and its constituent elements.

## PRESENCE

A multitude of language variations and tactics can enlarge or vivify a subject. Some grammatical constructions do this by directing attention in particular ways. *Asyndeton*, the rapid listing of expressions (words, phrases, clauses) without connectors, is most commonly used for lists of terms (items) that are short: single words or terse phrases. This device allows speedy enumeration, sometimes indicating high energy, as if under duress or as if being driven by the idea in view. Perhaps a reason for suspecting such a motivation is the fact that we expected conjunctions and heard none.[82] One need not rush through the list, though, because instead of verbalizing connectors, a speaker can and must pause, thereby taking in more breath at each successive item, thus adding emphasis, as if raising the hammer for another blow. "By their invitation to survey a whole, the hearer may readily secure something for himself: an end may be swiftly attained by grasping many as one. It is in the pleasurable perception of easily intelligible wholes that hearers attain a binding conviction."[83] Asyndeton is seen when Luther frequently mentions the "devil, sin, death, and hell" (probably reeled off rapidly). Conversely, the scene Jesus depicts in Luke 17:27–28 is more serene: "They did eat, they drank, they married wives, they were given in marriage . . . . Likewise also as it was in the days of Lot; they did eat, they drank, they bought, they sold, they planted, they builded."

In comparison, *polysyndeton* generates presence by using an abundance of coordinating conjunctions. Choosing to have too many conjunctions can sometimes "give the sense of an ever-lengthening catalogue of roughly equal members."[84] *Polysyndeton* is to string out the elaboration instead of rushing it—to build, rather than blast. The speaker would have the audience consider a list more carefully and deliberately, more a sense of contemplation than compulsion. Consider Paul's use in Rom 8:35, 38–39: "Who shall separate us from the love of Christ? shall tribulation, or distress, or persecution, or famine, or nakedness, or peril, or sword? . . . For I am persuaded, that neither death, nor life, nor angels, nor principalities, nor powers, nor things present, nor things to come, Nor height, nor depth, nor any other creature . . ." Indeed, that passage may well have inspired the famous creed of the U. S. Postal Service ("Neither rain nor snow nor sleet . . ."). An even more astonishing display occurs in the genealogy of Christ in Matthew 1:

> Abraham begat Isaac; and Isaac begat Jacob; and Jacob begat Judas and his brethren; And Judas begat Phares and Zara of Thamar; and Phares begat Esrom; and Esrom begat Aram; And Aram begat Aminadab; and Aminadab begat Naasson; and Naasson begat Salmon; And Salmon begat Booz of Rachab; and Booz begat Obed of Ruth; and Obed begat Jesse; And Jesse begat David the king . . .

Not only are the polysyndetic connectors important for suggesting continuity, but in this example we also have the stronger, chaining effect of *anadiplosis*—the repetition of the last word of one line or clause to begin the next. This effect results in climax because the connected chain is linear, heading to a destination.[85]

When one wants to convey progression, polysyndeton is the better choice, especially when the author wants to show a smooth, natural connection or progression. The connectors draw the items together, lessening the emphasis on each term and making the parts into more of a whole. Thus, the author draws attention to the movement and flow, rather than the stasis. Moreover, the abundant connectors allow the author to continue amplifying the claim, allowing the elaboration to play itself out, as if the thought—once brought into view—simply defies abandonment until fully explicated. Paul's prayer in Eph 3:18 ("May be able to comprehend with all saints what is the breadth, and length, and depth, and height"), when read in its fuller context (vv. 14–21), clearly shows that the author simply found himself unable to stop the contemplation of God's goodness and resources. The connectors—while scarcely noticed—bridge the descriptors together, and the passage ends (v. 21) with doxology. With disjunctive connectors, however (as in Romans 8 previously), the repeated "no/not/nor/or/neither" obviously calls attention not only to the terms in the list, but especially to the negations, the breaks, the absence. In Luke 9:3, Jesus' travel instruction to the twelve disciples stresses how they should take *nothing*: "neither staves, nor scrip, neither bread, neither money; neither have two coats apiece." Thus, the repetition establishes the connector itself as a theme, a *Leitwort* [key word] or motif.[86] For a circumscribed, complete description, asyndeton will do: "north, east, west, and south"; "up, down, all around." These lists also are driven by requirements of rhyme, meter, and melody—constraining influences not as prominent in oration or essay.

One of the most widely used rhetorical devices, especially in poetry, is *hyperbaton*, the syntactic alteration (usually inversion) of normal word order. This can be done to effect a slowing of action or a directing of attention to particular terms of a sentence, as when Luther puts his verbs in first position to develop stress on the verbs: "I will preach it, teach it, write it"[87] [*predigen wil ichs / sage(n) wil ichs / schreybe(n) wil ichs*].[88] In Luke's final statement in Acts (28:31), the terminal word is an adverb [ἀκωλύτως] that is translated "unhindered" (RSV) or "no man forbidding him" (KJV). Yet the main verb, a present participle, is "preaching" [κηρύσσων], which is the *first* word of the verse. The "modifying" adverb comes 15 words after its verb. The reason is simple: Luke wants to leave his readers with the thought of the Gospel's catalytic freedom, its liberation from constraint. He can best do that by positioning the adverb in its second strongest possible position: last in the sentence (and for the Book of Acts, last in the work!).[89] Another grammatical device, *paraphrasis*, promotes scrutiny of a topic by choosing longer, more elaborate, more indirect wording than usual. It is a way of fleshing out the ellipses that are bound up in more abbreviated language. For example, when Luther speaks of his category "free," he may on occasion stretch out the wording for a particular emphasis, as in "what God has made free." God as agent creating the freedom is brought to consciousness in a way untouched in the solitary term "free."[90]

A second range of devices for presence illustrates the variety of ways in which repetition and variation around a single theme are effected. When the repetition or variation forms a progression rather than a singularity of thought, I call it *gradatio*—a *crescendo* if the progression employs vocal qualities to evoke progressive thoughts or feelings.[91] Geoffrey Leech speaks of repetition's purpose and potential effect:

> By underlining rather than elaborating the message, it presents a simple emotion with force. It may further suggest a suppressed intensity of feeling—an imprisoned feeling, as it were, for which there is no outlet but a repeated hammering at the confining walls of language. In a way, saying the same thing over and over is a reflection of the inadequacy of language to express what you have to express "in one go."[92]

The inclusive term *repetitio* can suffice, though the precise way in which it underlines an idea ranges from "free verbal repetition" to "verbal parallelism." Geoffrey Leech distinguishes these two categories, the former being exact copying (whether immediate or intermittent) of some previous part of a text, the latter being more particular ways of ritually introducing the same thought. As with free repetition, there is physical sensibility to *repetitio*, audible to the hearer, visible to the reader.

Such verbal parallelism sets up a "special relation between expression and content: the outer form of the message not only expresses underlying meaning but imitates its structure," so we can actually see and hear the "shape of the ideas expressed."[93] In language reminiscent of Portia's description of mercy as heaven's gentle rain, "twice blessed,"[94] sound can have a potent *expressive* relationship to sense: "In this sense, verbal parallelism says the same thing twice over: the expression hammers home the content. To this quality of 'sound imitating sense' it owes its declamatory force, the power of emphasis which makes it a stock device of political oratory and of emotionally heightened language generally."[95] Moreover, the particular position in the sentence, or the idea employed, can vary, producing a bewildering assortment of terms in the handbooks. Verbal parallelism occurs commonly by strategically positioning a key term—signaled for listeners by its position in the clause and/or its vocal stress—at the beginning of successive clauses (*anaphora*, as in Hebrews 11, where the writer uses "by faith" [πίστει; 18 times] or at the end of each clause [*epistrophe*]). Using sound itself (*rhyme*)—*as* in alliteration, the repetition of the initial sound, or the internal and terminal repetitions of vowels (*assonance*) or consonants (*consonance*)—the same theme (mood, characteristic, dilemma, etc.) can be developed, heightened, sustained, or tapered off.

Would Luther be averse to using the vocal power of his own language in service to the Gospel, the "good shouting" about Christ? Martin Brecht is now convinced of Luther's power as a craftsman of language: "Reading Luther, one is repeatedly surprised by the selection of individual words or even the creation of words, the combination of words, the modulation of sound by the use of specific words or their combinations, and even the flow of sound in sentences."[96] Moreover, Luther's theology not only permitted, but welcomed, such a perspective. Speaking and hearing were more important even than seeing because the essence of the *imago dei* in a human is that he "utters words like God"; God is a *deus dicens*, to whom a *homo audiens* corresponds.[97]

A small, brief example of Luther's use of repetitive sounds to underline a single theme is "*klaren, starken spruch*" [a "clear, strong text"].[98] The "r" and "k/ch" sounds of the two adjectives are what linguists call phonemes; those sounds alone make no reference.[99] Yet when enlarged with vowels, these morpheme[s]—a joint semantic-phonetic unit that is shared by both words—do make reference, whereby each word has something in common in both meaning and sound.[100] Take away the shared meaning and all that remains is *homonymy*—like sounds; without the rhyme, one might have only what we call *synonymy*—like meanings. Luther uses synonymy to expand a theme by appearing to exhaust it ("all our works, intentions, thoughts").[101] But when our two morphemic sounds [*klaren, starken*] are also present in the noun they modify [*spruch*], we have to ask what this might mean. The similarity of sound makes us think of their possible connections, so I suggest that the shared sounds poetically and rhetorically construct a phonemic bridge among the three terms—they comingle—and we need not concern ourselves at all whether there is any "natural" connection between the sound and the things signified. Unless the listener either knows nothing about the ideas or is vehemently opposed to the claim, he or she may be drawn along by the artistry. Supposing, then, that some stronger connection between sound and sense already obtains, even before the rhetor constructs a repetitive bond, what about the potential for "phonetic symbolism," a leading representative of which is *ono-matopoieia*?

The notion that speech sounds have symbolic values at the phonological, as well as morphological, level has been much debated and tested. Some evidence suggests that particular sounds—especially vowels—are associated by the brain with our perceptions of the world that depend on elemental contrasts, such as light/dark, high/low, big/small, warm/cold. However, tribal experience and/or simple chance seem to exert clear influence on which sounds become associated with which feelings. The following are some guidelines for hypothesizing about phonetic symbolism.

First, certain sounds—the voiceless /s/, for example—possess a range of potential suggestibility rather than a fixed or single capability. Thus a prominence of /s/s is capable of suggesting certain classes of sounds (rustling, hissing, sighing, whispering) but not other classes (booing, humming, hammering, or groaning). Second, this power of suggesting natural sounds or other qualities is relatively weak—too weak to operate unsupported by meaning—and because of its range, this power is only latent. The semantic content of words has to activate and focus this imitative potential. If the semantic content does not do this, then the collo-cations of sounds are in most cases neutral.[102]

Thus, one needs to proceed with caution when suggesting how sound aids sense. It is physically accurate to note that "like /s/ and /z/, the sighing of the wind is a fricative sound, produced by the passage of air through gaps or past obstruc-tions."[103] However, it is quite another—and requires meaningful, relevant, sup-porting context—to conjecture that the sibilant /s/ must mean a "soft" or "soothing" sense. Winds blow for good *and* ill; a sleeping baby may indeed breathe gently, while a terminally ill patient may struggle for each breath; the mythical "hissing" snake is anything but soothing (except to herpetologists); the gas leak is not at all comforting. However, when a pattern (of sound or rhythm or theme) can be detected, that pattern is indeed an inextricable element in the meaning, force, or impact of an argument. If repetitive associations do not "work," then product advertisers and songwriters are only fooling themselves (and us). David Buttrick's advice on "making language 'come alive' through imitation" is helpful. Note carefully that his first two statements "practice what they preach":

> Quick things can be said quickly. Labored activity can be expressed with a labored syntax. Syntactical imitation will also employ the sounds of words, vowel-sound repetitions, and other rhetorical devices. Of course, many of the so-called tropes, such as antithesis, or anticlimax, and the like, are best under-stood as imitations. While many ministers are apt to overdo some devices, notably, alliteration and onomatopoetic systems, the notion of imitation is

helpful. A mere striving for effect is, of course, pernicious, but imitative language can assist a congregation in grasping meaning.[104]

Presence can be achieved by more than language choices and placement, however. It develops, for instance, through the use of supporting ideas, often through employment of *topoi*—lines of reasoning that tap premises held by the audience. One such strategy is to offer evidence such as an *exemplum*, a concrete instance that shows presence through elaboration on a lower level of abstraction. Examples can clarify a principle or elicit audience identification. Luther pursues the former when he suggests an historical instance in which an action or principle he is recommending to his audience had already been carried out by someone (say, a biblical heroine) of exemplary stature. The exemplary person's behavior suggests what the action is and that it is possible. Of course, if a preacher wants his audience members to envision themselves through an example, he must choose the material carefully. A contemporary preacher knows that scarcely anyone thinks herself "rich" (or poor, either). Therefore, the listener may think she can escape culpability when hearing of the rich man in Luke 16:19–31 or when reminded that "the love of money is the root of all evil" (1 Tim 6:10) because who thinks she *loves* money? Still, evidence of the correctness, appropriateness, or clarity of a thesis (subject) can also be brought through analogy or contrary examples. An instance of this *contrarium* for presence is when Luther argues that coercing people to do even "necessary" tasks is wrong, thus his audience can conclude that it is even more likely that coercion is inappropriate in the "free" or "unnecessary" matter. Simplistically, if we do not execute all murderers, we surely should not execute all petty thieves!

Speakers often dramatize a subject to enliven it in the minds of the audience. A character can be introduced as one who is the source (creator, discoverer, interpreter) of the evidence. Supporting evidence can then be put into some character's mouth as a statement or a question—hence, we have speaking in character (*prosopopeia*). Further, the character can enter into dialogue with the speaker or another character—hence, we have dialogism (*sermocinatio*).[105] Stephen's defense speech in Acts 7 is an extended narrative employing these devices. He utters words from the mouths of God, Moses, a Hebrew slave, and the children in the Sinai desert—all as part of a dramatic story. Luther did, on occasion, incorporate additional voices into his sermon in such a way as to bewilder the audience, as if they were witnessing a debate, one not at all easy to resolve. For the reputed dogmatist Luther to do this seems unusual—until one realizes that the situation required it. The idea of scriptural complexity and the corresponding attitudes of humility and patience necessitated a dramatic presence or enactment.[106] Finally, the speaker can evoke feelings and evaluations about a subject by the use of *epithet*. The use of "fool" not only suggests an evaluative characterization for Luther's audience to consider (or endure), but it clearly reveals the speaker's feelings about the subject (or the audience).

## COMMUNION

While a speaker effects choice and presentation of particular features of the topic, and through strategies generates presence of that topic, *communion* between speaker and audience is constantly in flux. Many of the devices already discussed, particularly those for presence, work toward building communion. For example, (1) rhetorical questions that seek no explicit answer but give plenty to think about often carry obvious, implied answers; and (2) dialogue in which simulated exchange occurs allows interaction between speaker and audience, involvement that the speaker hopes will dispose the audience more kindly toward the message through their heightened exchange with the messenger. In 1 Cor 12:29–30, Paul uses seven successive rhetorical questions in rapid, asyndetic succession, every one beginning with the Greek μὴ.[107] Each one carries an obvious "No!" response: "Are all apostles? are all prophets? are all teachers? are all workers of miracles? Have all the gifts of healing? do all speak with tongues? do all interpret?" The use of epithets, carefully chosen examples, and *contraria* facilitate the bonding through shared perspectives of authority, judgment, and value. Direct address to an outside character (*apostrophe*) can have the effect of the speaker acting out his or her subject, thus creating presence, but it also is a way of acting on behalf of the audience.[108] Direct address to the audience, such as Luther's frequent use of what I call "endearment" ("Dear friends"), is an obvious use of a strategy for communion because Luther's need in the Invocavit Sermons was, more than anything else, to restore his credibility and leadership in the minds of the Wittenbergers who had seen others assume leadership in the movement and had heard rumors of Luther's death.[109] The first Johannine epistle is an example of strategic use of direct address to the audience. Its five short chapters, consisting of 105 verses, contain 20 instances of direct address. Usually the vocative[110] comes at the beginning of the sentence, but 1 John 2:12–14 is different, both in syntax and dictional variety. Unmistakably, it becomes a *song*:

> I write unto you, *little children*, because your sins are forgiven you for his name's sake. I write unto you, *fathers*, because ye have known him that is from the beginning. I write unto you, *young men*, because ye have overcome the wicked one. I write unto you, *little children*, because ye have known the Father. I have written unto you, *fathers*, because ye have known him that is from the beginning. I have written unto you, *young men*, because ye are strong, and the word of God abideth in you, and ye have overcome the wicked one. (*my emphasis*)

The song is *not* a gratuitous display of what has been learned from a handbook; rather, it becomes a formal enactment, an incarnation, of the content it seeks to convey: that genuine knowledge of the "word of life" creates and maintains meaningful relationships between God and people in their familial roles.

The invoking of authority and values through Bible stories, proof texts, and revered characters is an unmistakable means of working with (and most likely within) the belief structures of audiences holding those values. The citing of *sententiae* (maxims, proverbs, aphorisms) not only demonstrates familiarity and shared cultural circumstances, but it has the benefit of apparent command of a subject, an aura of wisdom and common sense, that speakers inherit as their own credibility before their audiences.[111] Humor and hyperbole of varying degrees can be ways of delighting an audience; alarm and puzzlement, too, can aid a speaker if these expectations are successfully fulfilled or channeled. The "feet of them that preach the gospel of peace" (or protect from the bad or solve a mystery or relieve an anxiety) are deemed "beautiful," along with the adherence to the good news itself.[112] *Exclamatio*, the ejaculation of utterance of feeling, is another display employed for consideration, approval, or rejection by the audience.

While these features can be found everywhere, they are especially prevalent in epideictic rhetoric, where praise and blame are most prolific. The stance of the speaker toward the subject and toward the audience (and vice versa) are inextricably intertwined and extremely crucial to persuasive outcomes. There is, in short, no end to the amount of detail style offers for critical analysis; however, that has never been a problem. But we must be careful to guard against several dangers:

1. Considering the task of our stylistic criticism to be finished once we have identified and classified the devices. Although to name is to claim a certain power over something, taxonomic power is limited to describing only one portion of a stylistic phenomenon. In the case of a locution having several possible names, what are we to call it? Shall we hyphenetically link all the candidate designees together—if so, in what order? Besides that, the names are only descriptors of a phenomenon as observed from a particular angle or bias—usually, that of deviation from some norm.[113]

2. Thinking that we simply *know* what the intended result, or plausible effect, of the stylistic figures is or was. The "figures" are not that precise, nor do they occur in discrete order; they overlap and may contradict. Even if we knew the probable outcome, actual effects would be subject to a host of other variables, particularly that of audience premises and values.

3. Believing we have determined the ineluctable emotive "cause" behind each figure. Gérard Genette cautions us:

> Of all the French rhetoricians, the Cartesian Lamy no doubt carried the psychological (affective) interpretation of figures farthest, to the point of seeking in each of them the "character," that is to say, the mark of a particular impression: a figure for every symptom. *Ellipsis*: a violent passion speaks more quickly than words can follow it. *Repetition*: the impassioned man likes to repeat himself, just as the angry man delivers several blows. *Hypotyposis*: the obsessive presence of the loved object. *Epanorthosis*: the impassioned man constantly corrects his discourse in order to increase its force. *Hyperbaton* (inversion): emotion disturbs the order of things, and therefore the order of words. *Distribution*: one enumerates the parts

of the object of one's passion. *Apostrophe*: the impassioned man turns in
all directions, seeking everywhere help, etc.[114]

What Genette is problematizing is, of course, not the manifested effects upon the language of figures because that is open for all to observe. Rather, what he objects to—rightly, I believe—is a preoccupation with fingering the presumptive, discrete, psychological cause of a figure. If we allow Burke to temper our critical analysis, however, we can examine discourse for what phenomena are there for apprehension. And if those phenomena are perceptible to us, they are plausibly perceptible to other audiences because style "cuts across all levels of language: phonology, vocabulary, syntax, and discourse."[115] If we can fit a knowledge of the style—the rhetor's crafted effort to identify with an audience—with some information about the context (the rhetor's background, the rhetorical situation, and the audience), then we are on the way toward an informed criticism, and we have a reliable means of accessing Luther's discourse.

# CHAPTER 2

# LUTHER'S RHETORICAL SITUATION IN THE INVOCAVIT SERMONS

To understand the style of Luther's Invocavit Sermons, we must be familiar with their context—the persons, events, issues, and concerns that surround and inform the discourse. The notion of rhetorical situation can be a useful starting point.[1] Only traces of the constituents of rhetorical situation find their way into the sermons (or any other discourse) because the discourse reflects primarily the perspective of one person—the rhetor. So when we analyze the sermons, we are, in a sense, penetrating the preacher's perspective on the rhetorical situation.[2] Accordingly, a reader-listener or critic cannot analyze a text that seems alien, that speaks her "language" but does not connect with that critic's world. One has to be familiar enough to follow the discourse; one must know the context. For Bitzer, rhetorical context includes <u>exigence, audience, and constraints</u>. In other words, we have to know what problem(s) a speaker and others faced, who had a stake in those problems (including those responsible for rectifying them), and what limitations and possibilities are open to speaker and audience. Neither speaker nor audience can know or use what was unknowable or unavailable at the time. Similarly, neither speaker nor audience is likely to develop solutions—starting with agreement on the problems—until a functioning relationship between them can be established. Only in understanding this milieu of persons, problems, and relationships can we follow the arguments—how they are organized (disposed of) in the transpiration of each sermon, what Luther is claiming, how he supports his claims, and in what manner he approaches his audience. To be prepared for the discourse, then, we must "catch up with" the participants so we can recognize and discern the places, names, and ideas in the sermons.

The following is a brief sketch of the relevant details so we can better assess the arguments of the sermons. The tangle of theological, political, social, and personal concerns embedded in the Invocavit Sermons can be approached from the perspectives of Luther and his audience. First, we will look at the relevant details from Luther's career at Wittenberg from 1518 to 1521, which will show Luther's training, his early lectures and writings, and the other players around him. While we cannot be certain who heard his Invocavit Sermons, Luther's colleagues and competitors influenced the problems he dealt with and the manner/means with which he addressed them. Second, we will trace some of the more important institutions that had a stake in the reforms at Wittenberg from 1521 to 1522. This suggests some of the ways in which power and authority were complications for implementing church reforms. These complications help us understand not only the events preceding the sermons, but also how Luther viewed the legitimacy and impact of reform actions undertaken during his absence and which he largely opposed in the sermons. Third, we will address a chronological discussion of the events that led up to the preaching of the Invocavit Sermons, what is commonly called the Wittenberg Movement. This discussion reveals that the events that occurred prior to Luther's return from the Wartburg in March 1522 are, for the most part, undisputed by scholars. It is far less clear, however, precisely who was responsible for some of the unrest, and it was anything but consensual about what to do next. Following this discussion of the context, we will analyze two important pieces of discourse that preceded Luther's sermons: Karlstadt's Christmas Day 1521 Sermon and his "On the Removal of Images," which was published in late January 1522. These addresses of Karlstadt provide important glimpses into the problems Luther addressed in the Invocavit Sermons because they present the arguments supporting reforms Luther sought to challenge: evangelical reforms to Sacrament observance and the hasty removal of images from churches.

## LUTHER: MONASTERY TO WARTBURG

The events following the "Ninety-five Theses"[3] in 1517 and the "Explanations of the Ninety-five Theses"[4] in 1518—both documents written and published in Latin—propelled Luther to a leadership position in the reform movement in Wittenberg. Born in 1483 to a middle-class family at Eisleben—and educated at Mansfeld, Magdeburg, Eisenach, and at the university in Erfurt (originally, to study law)—Luther entered the Erfurt monastery of the Observant Hermits of St. Augustine in 1505. In the Black Cloister—so called because the monks wore black robes—the Augustinian Hermits were a strict order, but they were generally spared the public criticism of corruption leveled at other monastic orders. In the order where monastic reforms began, Luther completed a bachelor's and a master's degree at the university.[5] The order also had a monastery in Wittenberg, where Luther was transferred in 1511 upon his return from Rome. Now he was not only a member of the Augustinian monastery, but also the newest member (complete with his doctorate, which was obtained in 1512) of the theological faculty at Wittenberg University, where he lectured on the Bible from 1513 until his death in 1546. Luther's counselor and mentor, Johann von Staupitz (c. 1469–1524), the prior general who also chaired the theology faculty at Wittenberg from 1502–12, selected Martin as his successor to the chair of biblical theology at Wittenberg.[6] Furthermore, Staupitz also appointed Martin preacher at the monastery [*Augustinerkloster*], and Luther soon became preacher of the City Church [*Stadtkirche*], of which he once said in 1536: "I've preached here for twenty-four years. I've walked to church so often that it wouldn't be at all surprising if I had not only worn out my shoes on the pavement but even my feet. I've done my part. I discipline myself."[7]

Luther's original concern over clergy corruption, especially fostered by a newly commissioned sale of indulgences brokered by Johann Tetzel, was only the beginning. By 1518 Luther had already lectured on Psalms (1513–15), Romans (1515–16), Galatians (1516–17), and Hebrews (1517).[8] Despite being released from his vow of obedience in 1518 by Staupitz, Luther continued his monastic life, wearing his habit for 15 years.[9] (Not until at the Wartburg in 1521 did Luther himself renounce his monastic vows.)[10] He led an overhaul of the theology curricula at Wittenberg, which was greatly assisted by a turn to humanistic studies, especially given impetus when the Elector brought the brilliant young classical scholar Philipp Melanchthon (1497–1560) from Tübingen to Wittenberg. Luther and his theological colleagues Andreas Bodenstein von Karlstadt (1486–1541) and Nikolaus von Amsdorf (1483–1565) soon saw their new "Wittenberg Theology" become entrenched at the Leucorea (University).

In 1520 Luther's three great reform tracts appeared in the German language. The *Address to the Christian Nobility of the German Nation*[11] attacks "three walls" of the papacy, which maintained that (1) spiritual authority is superior to secular authority, (2) the pope is sole interpreter of Scripture, and (3) the pope is the only lawful convener of a church council.[12] Luther contended that all Christians, not only clergy, are spiritual; that all Christians may interpret the Bible; and that magistrates have a right to call a council. In the *Babylonian Captivity of the Church*,[13] Luther denies the scriptural legitimacy of some of the sacraments, reducing the number from seven to three; he retains only Baptism, penance, and the Eucharist. Further, Luther states the cup should not be withheld from the laity; the Mass (as a sacrifice) should be abolished; externals such as vestments and ornaments should be done away with in the worship service; vows and holy orders are unscriptural. *The Freedom of a Christian*[14] teaches that salvation is by faith, not through works. Faith in Christ justifies a person in God's sight, releasing the individual from the penalty for sin; thus, one need not be enslaved to the Law. Faith results in love and good works to others as free expressions of gratitude, not as means of making one righteous. These three inflammatory writings hastened Luther's excommunication by papal bull in 1520—which he publicly burned on the final day of the 60 he had been given in which to recant—and eventual criminalization by the Edict of Worms.

These early years also saw Luther become immensely popular among the German laity, as evidenced by the fact that his practical devotional tracts—about marriage, how to pray, how to face death, etc.—were strong sellers. This monk, whose own life had been fundamentally changed by the Gospel, who wanted to be taken seriously by his readers (he continued until 1520 to sign his writings, "Martin Luther, Augustinian"), had found a way to appeal to the spiritual concerns of daily life, as well as to stir great controversy at higher theological levels.[15] While modern scholars still debate the extent to which the Luther Reformation in Germany was caused by theological influence from the top down, clearly—at least in Saxony—Luther's name was a household word. Indeed, Luther wanted others to benefit from Christian teaching that had helped him. Luther's 1518 edition of one of his favorite books, the 14th-century, anonymously authored *Theologia German-ica*, shows that he valued God's teaching made plain, as we find in the preface:

> We read that Saint Paul, in spite of his lowly and despised status, wrote mighty and fearless letters and testified that his speech was not embellished with ornate and flowery words yet it proved to be full of treasures of knowl-edge and wisdom. This is the manner of God's wonders. Look at these won-ders and you will find that pompous and vainglorious preachers are never chosen to proclaim God's words. Rather, as it is written, *ex ore infantium*, that is to say, out of the mouths of babes You have most fittingly brought forth Your praise. Again, God's wisdom loosens the tongues of the slow of speech so that they speak most eloquently. . . . For this noble little book, poor and unadorned as it is as far as wording and purely human wisdom are concerned, is all the richer and abundantly precious in true knowledge and divine wis-dom. And, if I may speak with biblical foolishness: Next to the Bible and Saint Augustine no other book has come to my attention from which I have learned—and desired to learn—more concerning God, Christ, man, and what all things are.[16]

Moreover, Luther had strong political support in Germany, especially in Electoral Saxony—with its capital at Wittenberg—and at its university, where control of the faculty and curriculum was wrested from the scholastics and where Luther enjoyed protection under Frederick the Wise (1480–1525).[17] For his own safety, and to allow the Luther-led Reformation to continue unmolested by Rome or the emperor, Frederick had Luther covertly kidnapped in the spring of 1521 and taken to his Wartburg fortress in the Thuringian hills above Eisenach. Luther remained at the Wartburg for almost a year, busily writing and translating. He labored first on his postils—careful expositions of Scripture intended to be sermon models for pastors. Later he worked to complete his German translation of the New Testament. Both of these efforts were prodigious scholarly efforts on their own, aside from the matters of correspondence with leaders in Wittenberg and elsewhere. Moreover, both translation of Scripture and practical exposition of it rep-resent a preoccupation with equipping the people, especially pastors, to engage the Word of God directly—to return to the sources, *ad fontes*, as the humanists put it.

Meanwhile, however, Wittenberg was left to adjust to Luther's absence and even his rumored death. Wittenbergers struggled to know what to do with the message of Luther: "At the very moment when the time seemed ripe for the change from words to deeds, from mere criticism to the practical work of reform, it [Luther's disappearance] robbed the Evangelical party of the life-giving pres-ence and aid of its born leader."[18] Up to the summer of 1521, few changes in church practice had taken place. Now, however,

> What was to be done? How should the radical rhetoric of the new Gospel of Wittenberg be translated into action? To what extent did the message imply creation of radically new institutions; or might the old ones suffice, slightly

altered? What would be left when the first-generation leaders were dead and gone? At what pace should the movement be implemented, and under whose direction and leadership?[19]

While Luther was away, his senior theological colleague Karlstadt emerged as a major leader of the reform movement.[20] Together with other members of the theological faculty (Justus Jonas [1493–1555] and Amsdorf [1483–1565]) and Gabriel Zwilling (1487–1558) of the Wittenberg Augustinian cloister, Karlstadt sought to implement reforms.[21] As they worked for changes in public religious observance, these men were essentially supported and encouraged by Melanchthon, who remained a member of the arts faculty despite Luther's efforts to recruit him to lecture on the Bible. Melanchthon also escaped Luther's attempt to have him appointed to fill his vacancy at the pulpit of the *Stadtkirche* because the city council rejected the application.[22] Thus, Melanchthon had no administrative authority in the churches of the city. Innovations were opposed by the conservatives of the All Saints' Chapter. This struggle continued to evolve, and as the Wittenberg population—indirectly through the city council—became involved, the instability distressed the Elector, who was patron of both the University and the All Saints' Chapter and who was concerned about possible political repercussions in other cities.

In addition to his university faculty position, Karlstadt was a priest and archdeacon of the *Schloßkirche* (Castle Church, which was dedicated to All Saints), where he had license to preach. After undergoing a virtual conversion from scholasticism to a more Augustinian theological stance, Karlstadt shared much with Luther. He had presided over the awarding of Luther's doctorate, shared the distinction of participating in the 1519 debate with Johann Eck at Leipzig, and was even named with Luther in the papal bull *Exsurge Domine* of 1520. Karlstadt's theological theses and tracts during Luther's absence show an impatience with what he saw as the harmful effects of church rites and practices on spiritual life. Chief among the grievances Karlstadt addressed were images, the Mass, clergy vows, the withholding of Communion in both kinds, and confession. Some of Karlstadt's positions exceeded Luther's; the arguments on celibacy and its implications for priests and nuns provoked response from Luther at the Wartburg.[23] For the most part, however, until June 1521 Luther and Karlstadt maintained positions that were compatible, though not always alike. However, there was never, from what we can tell, any real friendship between the two. But the compatibility began to change as autumn approached and Luther was kept informed of events in Wittenberg, both by close associates in the city and by the Elector.[24]

## LUTHER'S AUDIENCE

The city of Wittenberg is on the Elbe River in the northern lowlands of Germany. In the early 16th century, it was the capital and cultural center of the Saxon Electorate and a free electoral city of roughly 2,500 people. Despite its small size, the city was the headwaters of Reformation activity in central and northern Germany because Luther taught there from 1511 until his death in 1546. We will now trace the institutions comprising the religio-political situation of Saxon Wittenberg during the period 1521–22. Six groups of people were involved in some way in the events preceding the Invocavit Sermons.[25]

The two seats of secular authority were the Saxon Elector, Frederick the Wise, and the Wittenberg City Council. Frederick ruled from 1484 until his death in 1525 and, of course, wanted to maintain civil order; he did not want to have to contend with the emperor. Although he was delighted with the humanistic reforms at the university, Frederick had to balance his nervousness and impatience with theological reforms in Wittenberg with his strong commitment to Saxon independence and, consequently, to protecting Luther. The city council was a ruling body of 24 prominent citizens, which had extensive administrative, legislative, and jurisdictional powers. The population at large also had some voice in the affairs of the city through the more broadly based Assembly of The Forty. The city council, together with the assembly, often intruded into areas that the church considered its bailiwick. Especially in the wake of Luther's condemnation of church domination, the people of Wittenberg—who cherished their freedom— turned to their secular authorities for religious, as well as social, matters.[26] Both the Elector's right to govern his cities and the council's authority to call Luther back to the city are crucial matters for the Invocavit Sermons. The Elector felt the enormous weight of broader responsibilities, including the repercussions from unrest in Wittenberg that could spread to other cities. The council, however, considered its responsibilities to the city—especially to the City Church, where Luther was the preacher.[27]

In addition to the secular institutions of Elector and council, the Elector's influence and concerns are manifest in three other institutions that he established or patronized: the university, the Castle Church, and the Augustinian cloister. This is especially important because reform activities and disturbances occurred at these sites, as well as at the City Church.[28] Frederick founded the university in 1502. When Luther arrived, scholasticism and humanism were vying for dominance, but Luther's new theology won several of the faculty, among them Melanchthon of the arts faculty and Amsdorf and Karlstadt of the theological faculty. Karlstadt had converted from a conservative scholastic to a strong reformer alongside Luther. It was Karlstadt who emerged as the most radical and most threatening leader during Luther's Wartburg confinement.[29] The university's welfare was of great concern to Frederick, and the faculty's support was highly regarded in matters of reform. Frederick asked, at one point, for a ruling from the theological faculty on reform measures, but they were too divided to make a definitive decision. The Castle Church had been rebuilt by Frederick at the turn of the century, and it was the home of his prized collection of relics. The center of conservative reaction to reforms in Wittenberg came from this collegiate church. Struggles between the University and the All Saints' clergy—the majority of the

60 canons were conservative—tended to hamper Frederick's ability to deal with the situation.[30] Frederick had great economic concerns regarding the potential loss of endowments from private masses—should they be abolished—and for the safety of his relic collection. Karlstadt was also archdeacon on the Castle Church clergy. He eventually used that position to implement reforms, announcing that he would celebrate an evangelical Mass at the Castle Church on New Year's Day 1522 (he later moved up his timetable to Christmas Day). The final group of interest is the Augustinian Hermits, Luther's monastic brethren. The cloister had been rebuilt by Frederick in 1503, and it housed university professors as well. The leader of the Augustinians was Gabriel Zwilling, who became a zealous reformer. As Zwilling preached against private masses, Communion in one kind, and monastic vows, he encouraged brothers to leave the monastery. It was virtually shut down by the time of Luther's return. Zwilling and Karlstadt were the two most aggressive leaders in the reform movement.[31]

However complex and unpredictable were the sociopolitical dynamics of Wittenberg during the reform movement of 1521–22, the theological issues propelling (and emerging from) the reform activities are readily identified.

1.  The Mass. Luther had particularly condemned private masses, at which no congregation is in attendance and the Mass is said on behalf of the dead or to generate income, but he also condemned the sacrificial nature of the Mass in general. He charged that the character of the ceremony wrongly consisted in a human work of merit, not an act of faith.[32] Within the broad context of the corporate worship assembly, then, several other specific theological issues arose from practices and circumstances within the Mass.

2.  The role of the clergy—priests, monks, and nuns—particularly their separation from the rest of society by means of monastic vows, especially of celibacy (monks and nuns took mandatory vows while priests took voluntary vows of celibacy).[33] Because he had previously written that celibacy was evil, Karlstadt proposed an academic disputation on celibacy in June 1521.[34] Turmoil over celibacy led to the dismantling of the Augustinian cloister.

3.  The function of the clergy in celebration of the Eucharist.[35] The matter of clergy withholding the cup from the laity became particularly important in Wittenberg. The issue, as Luther manages it in the Invocavit Sermons, widens to encompass the attitudes and practices of communicants in sacramental observance. The matter of "both kinds" shifted from the cup being withheld (unavailable to laity) to virtually required by Scripture, as Karlstadt was teaching and as Zwilling was preaching.[36]

4.  The presence of images in the church. From Luther's early condemnation of indulgences and relics, the question soon centered on the legitimate place and function of all images within the churches—whether their mere physical presence or actual worship of them constitutes sin (or at least an impediment to spiritual development). The main impetus to this issue were some acts of

renegade destruction of images and Karlstadt's teaching, especially in "On the Abolition of Images."

5. The place of auricular confession—its legitimacy and purpose. Could it be rightfully required, by whom, and for what purpose? It had been mandated by the pope that all Christians must confess, then partake of the Sacrament annually at Easter. According to Ronald Sider, "In his Christmas sermon . . . Karlstadt went well beyond Luther. Whereas Luther had continued to insist that confession is useful although not necessary, Karlstadt condemned the practice not only because of the abuses and absence of 'divine institution', but also because he felt it detracted from the Eucharist."[37]

Although many other problems and questions abound,[38] these specific issues of theology and practice underlay the reform efforts and Luther's response to them. Planned reform efforts, and apparently unplanned disturbances at Wittenberg, occurred on and off between November 1521 and February 1522 until what seemed to be the final straw: The city council passed the Wittenberg Ordinance of January 24, 1522, which promulgated 17 reform orders, of which Luther had no qualms with 15. It was those orders pertaining to the issues of Mass, images, and Sacrament (which are detailed below) against which Luther spoke in the Invocavit Sermons on March 9–16. The following is a synopsis of the events preceding Luther's return. This chronology will enable us to understand how the new theology came to be influential in ways not completely to Luther's (or everyone else's) satisfaction, and it will provide a more specific situational context for the sermons.

## CHRONOLOGY AND SUMMARY
## OF THE WITTENBERG MOVEMENT

*Spring through autumn 1521:* There is a spate of reform activities in Wittenberg. The reformers abandon private masses, question vows of celibacy, and experiment with reforms to the Mass—especially Communion in both kinds. Priests begin leaving the cloister. These reforms culminate in Karlstadt's public evangelical Mass on Christmas Day. Luther is kept apprised of most activities. In general he is satisfied with things in Wittenberg. We have virtually no response from him, however, to Karlstadt's Mass.

*May 3, 1521:* Luther is taken to Wartburg castle.

*June 1, 1521:* Luther's "On Confession, Whether the Pope Has the Power to Require It" is released. It is published in Wittenberg in September.[39]

*Aug. 1, 1521:* Commenting in response to Karlstadt's theses of June 21 and July 19 on celibacy, Luther writes to Melanchthon that he is not yet convinced that monks and priests are in the same category when it comes to vows of celibacy (priests were established by God to be a free order; with monks, this is not the case). Luther also says that he will never celebrate a private mass again, referring favorably to experiments with an "evangelical" form of Communion taking place in small groups in cloister and university in Wittenberg. Luther disagrees with Karlstadt, who says that those who receive only one kind of Communion (bread only) sin because Christ does not require Communion when circumstances (the world or a tyrant) forbid it.[40]

*Sept. 19, 1521:* Luther writes to Georg Spalatin, Elector Frederick's chaplain, urging that Melanchthon be appointed to preach in Wittenberg through the calling of the city council.[41] *September 29:* On St. Michael's Day, Melanchthon and students take Communion in both kinds (bread and wine), without reference to sacrifice, and speaking in German. Although there is historical uncertainty whether the celebration occurred in a private residence[42] or in the City Church,[43] it is generally agreed that the ceremony was not open to the public.

*Oct. 5, 1521:* Antonians from Lichtenburg on the Elbe, who had come as usual to preach and collect offerings, are insulted and harassed by students.[44] *October 6:* Augustinians, under the influence of Zwilling's preaching, begin quitting private masses and abandoning their vows.[45] *October 9:* In a letter to Wenceslaus Linck at Nuremberg, Melanchthon confirms that they now celebrate Communion in both kinds commonly in Wittenberg.[46] *October 10:* Frederick appoints a commission of members of the university faculty and of the All Saints' Chapter to investigate the actions of the Augustinians. *October 13:* Zwilling again preaches against the adoration of the host and against private masses, demanding Communion in both kinds and announcing that he would no longer say Mass.[47] *October 17:* Karlstadt presides over a disputation on the Mass, questioning its legitimacy but recommending that the magistrates and full congregation be consulted. Melanchthon advocates certain reforms, despite any objections by brethren of weak conscience. *October 20:* The university members of Frederick's commission submit their majority report, urging the Elector to institute major reforms in the Mass. The Catholic canons warn that changes should await a church council, and they blame Zwilling for modifying the Sacrament observance. Two of Luther's tracts appear; both are written and published in German: *On Monastic Vows*[48] and *Concerning the Abuse of the Mass*.[49] The latter urges abolition of the Mass but cautions that faith and love are needed. *October 25:* Frederick asks for caution and order and clarification of the reforms discussed by the commission.

*Nov. 1, 1521:* Communion in both kinds is made available on All Saints' Day, a report made in an anonymous letter of early December announces. It also spoke of the preaching and Communion in the Augustinian monastery that, the writer says, brought tears to the eyes of many parishioners.[50] *November 11:* Luther writes to Spalatin that he is forwarding his book on the abolition of the masses.[51] *November 21:* Luther dedicates his *On Monastic Vows* to his father, Hans Luther, indicating that he now realizes that his youthful decision to take a monk's vows was against his father's knowledge and will. Luther voluntarily continues to live as a monk for another four years, however.[52]

*Dec. 3, 1521:* A mob of students and townspeople disrupt services in the parish church, intimidating priests of the Franciscan order.[53] The Elector demands apprehension and punishment of the guilty. (Pope Leo X had died on December 1, but news of his death had perhaps not reached Wittenberg yet. Whether this news did/could have played a role in the riots is an open question.)[54] *December 4:* Disguised as "Knight George" [*Jünker Jorg*], Luther makes a secret three-day visit to Wittenberg. He subsequently writes to Spalatin in praise of the reforms at Wittenberg, while also stating that he intends to address the matter of violence, which occurred in his subsequent "A Sincere Admonition by Martin Luther to All Christians to Guard against Insurrection and Rebellion."[55] Frederick presses his commission to come up with a unanimous policy before changes are instituted. The commission members cannot agree and submit separate reports. Karlstadt, Melanchthon, Amsdorf, and Schurff demand abrogation of private masses and the institution of Communion in both kinds. *December 4–7:* Citizens of Wittenberg demand amnesty for those arrested for the disturbances, presenting six demands to the city council that call for evangelical preaching and specific social measures.[56]

*Mid-December 1521:* Luther's tract "A Sincere Admonition by Martin Luther to All Christians to Guard against Insurrection and Rebellion" appears in German. It argues that only secular authority can force changes; others can only teach, preach, speak, and write.[57] Although no major disturbance had occurred before the night of December 3, Luther's response is somewhat surprising, indicating perhaps that he underestimated the situation. Undoubtedly, he was generally pleased with the reforms and possibly less concerned with the disruptions.[58] However, we must note that the first thing Luther did upon his return to Wartburg was write a tract about the wrongness of rebellion! *December 15:* Frederick asks that all complaints and demands be referred to him as prince. Four days later, realizing that agreement is not likely, he orders a return to customary practices, the halting of further innovations, and the continuation of discussion and consultation. *December 18:* Luther writes to Johannes Lang (of the Augustinian monastery in Erfurt) that he is unhappy with the disorderly departure from the monastery, adding that he plans to remain at Wartburg until Easter.[59] *December 21:* Albert of Mainz writes to Luther, claiming he will remove the idol at Halle that Luther had written to him about. (This is one of the three or four extant letters written to Luther at Wartburg.)[60] *December 22:* Karlstadt announces that he will celebrate a simplified Mass on New Year's Day in the Castle Church, offering Communion in both kinds. Frederick responds to this news by urging Karlstadt to postpone the plan.[61] *December 24:* Bands of townspeople roam the streets, disrupting Christmas Eve services. *December 25:* Karlstadt enters the City Church in a layman's clothes, preaches a sermon ("On Receiving the Holy Sacrament"[62]), offers Communion in both kinds to all who desire—whether or not they have confessed—making no reference to sacrifice, eliminates the elevation of the host, and conducts the liturgy entirely in German.[63]

From Christmas to early February, things change dramatically. Events in Wittenberg in late January include, despite Luther's warning about rebellion in "A Sincere Admonition," the beginnings of iconoclasm and the institution of mandatory reforms to the Mass and to poor relief, which were passed by the city council. Again, from the correspondence record, there is virtual silence from Luther about the Wittenberg Ordinance or Karlstadt's "On the Removal of Images." Luther realizes that he cannot remain at the Wartburg until Easter, as he had planned.

*Dec. 26, 1521:* Karlstadt announces his intention to marry Anna von Mochau, who was approximately 15 years old.[64] The wedding itself occurs on January 19; Melanchthon and Jonas make the trip to Sagrena with Karlstadt for the betrothal. A week before the marriage (January 13), Luther reports in a letter to Amsdorf that he is pleased about the prospect of Karlstadt's marriage.[65] *December 27:* The Zwickau Prophets arrive in Wittenberg.[66] One of these three laymen, Marcus Thomae (called Stübner because his father owned a bathhouse [*Badestube*] at Elsterberg), was a former student at Wittenberg. The other two, Nicholas Storch and Thomas Drechsel, were illiterate weavers. Zwickau—about 80 miles from Wittenberg in Electoral Saxony—had a thriving cloth industry and is said to be the second city in Europe, after Wittenberg, to become Protestant.[67] The Zwickau Prophets' claims of direct revelations from the Holy Spirit—apart from the Word of God—and their apparent command of Scripture highly impress Melanchthon, who writes both Luther and Frederick that he cannot refute the prophets. Melanchhon urges that Luther be recalled to Wittenberg.[68] Frederick sends Melanchthon to meet with Spalatin and the counselor, Haugold von Einsiedel, who persuade him to forget about the prophets.

*Jan. 6, 1522:* Reforms are now spreading to other towns at the instigation of Zwilling.[69] The Augustinian General Chapter, following Luther's advice, releases each monk to make his own decision about leaving the cloister or staying—under more evangelical conditions.[70] *January 11:* Augustinians, led by Zwilling, remove and destroy altars and images in the cloister chapel, ripping pictures and burning them.[71] *January 13:* In letters to both Melanchthon and Amsdorf, Luther tells them not to worry about the Zwickau Prophets and that he intends to remain at Wartburg until Easter.[72] The letter to Melanchthon is a richly argued, carefully organized response, laden with Scripture passages designed to show how to test the spirits. The letter is intended to stabilize Melanchthon, who is told he is "more richly endowed with the Spirit and with learning than I am" (a remark Luther later uses in the Invocavit Sermons).[73] *January 17:* Luther expresses concern to Spalatin regarding events in Eilenberg, stories that he says are either false rumors or indications that the people are being forced to engage in new sacramental practices (for example, both-kinds Communion). Luther says it was similar rumors of forceful reforms that made him journey to Wittenberg on December 3. He adds, "Lord willing, I shall definitely return in a short time; if I don't stay in Wittenberg I shall certainly stay somewhere else, or wander around.

The cause itself demands it."[74] No further word from Luther until February 22 is extant.

*Jan. 20, 1522:* The Imperial Council of Regency [*Reichsregiment*], convened at Nuremberg, issues a mandate aimed especially at Electoral Saxony—probably Wittenberg, in particular—forbidding all innovations and demanding return to the *status quo ante.* This mandate would be implemented through an official visitation in Saxon territory by responsible bishops. Considerable pressure now moves Frederick toward more forceful intervention in the Wittenberg situation. *January 24:* The city council issues the Wittenberg Ordinance, sanctioning and regulating evangelical reforms in public worship, providing for removal of images, and giving further elaboration to establishment of a common chest for poor relief and low-interest loans for workers and artisans, which will be financed by income from discontinued religious endowments. Karlstadt is instrumental in this action and was undoubtedly involved in the authorship of the ordinance itself. *January 27:* Out of concern that the Wittenberg Ordinance might not be implemented, Karlstadt publishes—together in the same binding—"On the Removal of Images" and "That There Be No Beggars Among Christians." It includes the phrase "in the Christian City of Wittenberg" in the preface.[75] *Late January:* Other neighboring princes are worried about the Wittenberg situation, and some order their students to leave the university.[76]

*Feb. 1, 1522:* Altars, images, and pictures are destroyed in the parish church by townspeople. *February 3:* Haugold Einsiedel, the electoral counselor, instructs Karlstadt and Zwilling (through Melanchthon) to moderate and limit their preaching.[77] Karlstadt denies responsibility for the disruptions.[78] *February 13:* Negotiations take place between Einsiedel and representatives of the university, the All Saints' Chapter, and the city council, resulting in a compromise, semireformed order for public worship.[79] *February 17:* Frederick objects strenuously to his counselor's sanction of the establishment of an order for public worship in face of the demand of the imperial government for restitution of customary usages.[80] *February 22:* Luther, after previously announcing his desire to return to Wittenberg by Easter, alludes to an earlier return in his letter to the Elector.[81]

*March 5, 1522:* Luther announces in his letter to the Elector his return to Wittenberg, claiming his return has been requested by the Wittenberg congregation. The Elector sends a message attempting to discourage Luther from returning.[82]

In summary, of its 17 total articles, the Wittenberg Ordinance of Jan. 24, 1522, included the following two provisions that were highly controversial:

> (13). Likewise, the images and altars in the churches shall be done away with in order to avoid idolatry, for three altars without images are enough. (14). Likewise, the Mass shall not be held other than as Christ instituted it at the Last Supper. For the sake of the weak in the faith, however, singing is allowed. Only the first part of the Missal containing the *missae de tempore* shall be used, not the second part of the Mass of the saints, and the *introit, kyrie,*

*gloria in excelsis et in terra*, the collect or *preces*, epistle, gradual, without the sequence, the gospel, creed, offertory, prefact, *sanctus* without the major and minor canons (i. e., *Canon Missae* and offertory prayer) so long as they are not out of accord with the Scriptures. After this begins the evangelical mass; if there are communicants the priest consecrates and summarizes it with prayers for that purpose. Thereafter he concludes with the collect without the *Ite missa est*. Also the communicant may take the consecrated host in the hand and himself put it in his mouth; the same may be done with the cup, hence drinking from it.[83]

What had earlier pleased Luther as desirable reform activities eventually brought him out of hiding to return to Wittenberg. The confusion that must have been the lot of Melanchthon and many of the townspeople, Karlstadt's consternation at having his plans questioned, and the tension between the council and the Elector were results of violent episodes, disrupted services, and reformed institutions. All this comprised the rhetorical situation of the Invocavit Sermons, the situation Luther felt he now had to return and deal with personally.

# CHAPTER 3

# THE FIRST AND SECOND INVOCAVIT SERMONS

The Invocavit Sermons do not follow a traditional Lenten lectionary agenda; they are, instead, messages directed to current problems at a particular location. The following are the topics (issues) of controversy in Luther's sermons, representing—as I have construed Luther's strategy—the manner in which the sermons proceed. In the First and Second Sermons, Luther addresses the "musts," what one is required to do, for example, about the Mass. In the Third through Eighth Sermons, he focuses on the "frees," what it is best to do, that is, the remaining topics. The last six sermons present the following themes: Third Sermon—how one should handle vows/images; Fourth Sermon—how one should handle images/foods; Fifth Sermon —how one should handle the Sacrament (Eucharist); Sixth Sermon—how one should handle the Sacrament, continued; Seventh Sermon—how one should handle love, an "issue" for Luther in particular; Eighth Sermon—how one should handle confession. In modern printed editions,[1] the sermons are arranged as follows:

- First Sermon (Invocavit Sunday, March 9; LStA 2:530–34): Introduction—the crucial difference between what Christians "must do" and are "free to do" (which governs how each divisive issue of the *Aufruhr* ought to be approached by Wittenbergers).
- Second Sermon (Monday after Invocavit, March 10; LStA 2:534–38): Abolishing private masses in the proper way—through preaching.
- Third Sermon (Tuesday after Invocavit, March 11; LStA 2:538–43): Handling clerical vows and what to do about images.
- Fourth Sermon (Wednesday after Invocavit, March 12; LStA 2:543–47): Images and the eating of meats.
- Fifth Sermon (Thursday after Invocavit, March 13; LStA 2:547–51): The blessed Sacrament.
- Sixth Sermon (Friday after Invocavit, March 14; LStA 2:551–54): The blessed Sacrament.
- Seventh Sermon (Saturday before Reminiscere, March 15; LStA 2:554–55): Love, the fruit of the Sacrament.
- Eighth Sermon (Reminiscere Sunday, March 16; LStA 2:555–58): On confession.

## THE FIRST SERMON (LW 51:70–75; LStA 2:530–34)

We can expect Luther to provide in this sermon some sort of guide so the audience can know what to expect from this and the remaining sermons. Surely his hearers anticipate that he will address the issues in dispute, and they probably are curious about how he will proceed in the interpersonal struggle between himself and Karlstadt—whether agreement is even possible in the Wittenberg situation.[2] But "they" does not identify a unified audience of dispassionate observers; the audience is a heterogeneous group of participants in the struggle. So Luther must not presume consensus, nor does he rush to confront. Instead, he begins by speaking to the individual responsibilities of every Christian, seeking to defuse the autonomy that groups might feel, should the preacher attempt to mediate among them. This strategy summons every listener as one addressed, one accountable. If this strategy succeeds, there will be communion even among the listeners because they will share the experience as those addressed by the preaching. The sermon's structure moves from broad points of agreement (praise) to disagreement (blame) in the following manner:

- Introduction (530.3–9):[3] Luther clarifies his relationship with the audience and establishes his theme. He then elaborates the theme, the "chief things [*hauptstück*] of a Christian," in four sections.
- Section I: All are sinners (530.10–15).
- Section II: Faith in Christ frees sinners (530.16–25). Luther praises his audience for their enlightenment on both points 1 and 2.
- Section III: Love is product and proof of faith (530.26–531.15), a condition Luther confronts, claiming a wide gap between what *is* in Wittenberg and what *ought* to be.
- Section IV: Patience with one's neighbor is needed (531.16–534.25). This section takes up the remainder of the sermon because here is a greater gap between *is* and *ought*.

In Section IV Luther addresses the issues of controversy. First, he envisions the ideal of "patience" (531.16–24). Next, he distinguishes between what is legal and what is helpful (531.25–532.3), a distinction continued and broadened in the following ways: (1) the "mother" analogy and exhortation (532.4–15); (2) the "sun" illustration and exhortation (532.15–29); (3) the militant exhortation—(do this, not this) (532.29–533.3); (4) a counterexample that shows what not to do, which introduces the Mass (533.4–28); (5) an exhortation and teaching on the distinction between "must" and "free" (533.29–534.12); and (6) a closing exhortation (534.12–25). By not explicitly mentioning any Wittenberg controversy until past the midpoint, Luther keeps the sermon in conformity to a fairly standard pattern for him—Christian proclamation and exhortation from Scripture. He is not treating the situation as a theological disputation or a quarrel; to do so would be to violate what he claims is the power of preaching to change hearts.

## INTRODUCTION (530.3–9)

The opening premise suggests a motivation for the sermon (death), a possibility on Luther's mind as he left the Wartburg to return to Wittenberg.[4] To whatever extent death is a shared concern among the audience, the opening is somber. Further, Luther may have introduced the notion of death in his earlier remarks on the Gospel pericope.[5] His objective is twofold: (1) to frame an argumentative context that discloses a general purpose and topic, namely, death's demands require everyone to be sufficiently prepared with the "chief things" of a Christian; and (2) to clarify and construct a relational context of audience and speaker within the argumentative context.

We observe the speaker establish a relational context in three ways: implicitly through the death motif, explicitly through antithesis and negation, and clarified through direct address. In setting the death theme, Luther fashions a *definitio* of death by amplifying death's predicates: It has "battle" characteristics (verbs) that, paradoxically, are shared by all, yet the *definitio* presents individual challenges to the person. The handling of pronouns bears this out because twice Luther makes a "we"/"all":"each"/"every one" distinction.[6] He makes this distinction explicit in the antithetical negative of 530.6f., where he soberly warns his audience that, when facing death, "I cannot be with you nor you with me." Although he frames this in the mode of possibility, Luther establishes an affective expectation, nonetheless. His use of singular pronouns points to a dominant concern for establishing communion between speaker and audience.[7] He brings the context to fruition with the endearment "you, my beloved," which is also singular and brings out the intimacy of affection and possession. Luther implies intimacy in the rest of the clause as well, invoking his past stable relationship with the audience. So we see an arc of emotions in the opening whereby a benevolent mysteriousness draws the hearers to keep listening to this friend whom they know, trust, respect, and perhaps fear. We see the psychology of form as the preacher responds to and shapes audience expectations. The first things he says provide emotional appeal—that is, reasons to listen.

This relational context is evident in the way Luther begins his argument. The argumentative context of the "chief things" is set up by the relational context. He begins by laying down the theme of *Hauptstück*. The word itself implies choices (important/unimportant, greater/lesser, etc.) that, in the absence of a prescribed lection for the day (or despite one), become the text, the basis for the material focus of discussion. Luther's choice may appear arbitrary, and there is as yet little hint of any other pragmatic purpose for the sermon in which eventually he will discuss reforms applied to the Mass. The predicates he attaches to "chief things" ("know"/"be armed") are not merely synonyms, but they suggest more. Indeed, at 530.10, Luther proposes a *distributio* of the "chief things," enumerating four parts. The parts are not clearly linked to his two activities of "know"/"be armed," but they preserve the tension between the general position of salvation by faith and

Luther's present insistence that Wittenbergers must maintain an appropriate, consistent connection between doctrine and practice.

We can see how Luther works to secure adherence to his propositions in each of the four parts by observing even the modalities of his verbs. The "assertive" (indicative) is the standard modality of argumentation, and in Sections I and II we find strong propositional assertions fulfilling the expectation of "heard from me" (530.9).[8] By contrast, Sections III and IV are new ground—that is, they are not grammatically linked to Sections I and II because Luther shifts to a new modality, "injunctive" (imperative).[9] Section III is in the imperative ("we must have love"); Section IV is a mild imperative ("we need patience"). The assertives, then, are statements that require slight support. Injunctives require considerable development because one must do more to obtain adherence of an audience not predisposed to grant the speaker his claims. Notice that Luther dispatches the early parts enumerated by the *distributio*; it operates as an *expeditio*, establishing a repetitive form wherein we can see in each of the first three sections a similar pattern: (1) claim; (2) scriptural backing; and (3) illustration or manifestation from experience, mediated through Luther's relational strategies—the use of pronouns, especially.

## SECTION I: ALL ARE SINNERS (530.10–15)

The first assertion is a positive, universal proposition ("we are all children of wrath"), concluding with a virtually universal negation ("are nothing at all"). The strength of the claim is evident in what immediately follows: Luther admits a need for strong supporting evidence, so he cites a Scripture text. This section, then, develops a focus on the validity and strength of the assertion. Luther generates presence primarily through synonymy and amplification: "we" becomes "our works, intentions, thoughts." Confessing a need for a supporting text is itself an implicit claim—that a text can indeed be sufficient evidence—that is made more vividly present (made more effective) through asyndeton, blended with internal assonance [*klaren, starcken spruch*].

This will become a frequent pattern for Luther in these sermons. He often, though not always, authoritatively cites Scripture texts as unassailable proof. Having made his assertion and promising textual support, the audience is better prepared to accept it. So the speaker identifies the text and its author, shifting briefly from assertive to imperative ("Note this well"), thus slowing the action[10] and directing audience attention to the Scriptures and not to himself as authority. The focus on Scripture as authoritative is given presence by *synecdoche* ("there are many such [texts] in the Bible") and *reprehensio* ("I don't wish to overwhelm you"). Luther's strategy is to confront firmly but gently the audience in such a way that the speaker shares with his audience the same force of the earlier confrontation ("we are all children of wrath"). The section, then, shapes shared convictions of the audience, blending what they all agree is true and clear, without exception.

## SECTION II: FAITH IN CHRIST FREES SINNERS (530.16–25)

Luther continues using first plural assertive, recalling for the audience the Gospel's positive response to the previous negative. The current premise (that God has freed us from wrath through Christ), as with Section I, is supported by a New Testament proof text, and the audience begins to sense the pattern we observed of claim-plus-text, which may become for them an *ad hoc* convention. Luther insinuates that the single text all believers need to be familiar with is representative of others, as he stated for the first section. He introduces the devil as the personified enemy, rather than death. He has reminded the audience that confronting the devil successfully requires Scripture.[11]

## SECTION III: LOVE IS PRODUCT AND PROOF OF FAITH (530.16–531.15)

Luther resumes the first plural, beginning with the injunctive "we must." Significantly, this section is a confrontation and an exhortation toward a goal fallen short of—something to strive toward, not celebrate in. Luther mentions biblical Capernaum, forewarning the audience that unpleasant confrontation can be expected; obviously Luther expects his audience to recognize Capernaum.[12] He presses the doctrine/deeds gap further, acknowledging to his audience that they speak about but do not practice love as part of their faith. In fact, he delivers a stinging rebuke when—through a rhetorical question—he contrasts the audience with an ass [*esell*]. The audience feels the devastating effect because their person, actions, and pride are chastised. So obvious and humiliating is that rhetorical question that Luther again resorts to direct address ("dear friends") to retain audience communion, beginning a brief declaration on genuine faith and love. His argument summarizes the dichotomy he has been creating. Notice how the dissociation constructs a *definitio*:

> Dear friends, the kingdom of God,—and we are that kingdom—does not consist in talk or words [1 Cor. 4:20], but in activity, in deeds, in works and exercises. God does not want hearers and repeaters of words [Jas. 1:22], but followers and doers, and this occurs in faith through love. (51:71) [*Also lieben freündt / das reich gottes / das wir sein / steet nit in der rede oder worte(n) / sonder in der tha(e)ttigkeit / das ist in der that / in den wercken vnd vbunge(n). Got wil nit zuho(e)rer oder nachreder haben / sonder nachuo(e)lger / vnd vber das in dem glaube(n) durch die liebe.*] (531.9–12)

The language of the dissociation is rich in scriptural allusion, picking up on the passage in 1 Corinthians, without any explicit reference to Scripture. Even the analogy of the mirror "reflects" Scripture (1 Cor 13:12), yet it does not cite Scripture as proof. Luther's intention is to appeal to audience concerns and values without alienating his hearers. Dissociating genuine from counterfeit, then, Luther bonds faith and love so the audience cannot take refuge in an allegedly secure faith, should their love be condemned. The analogy of the mirror affords a chance to soften his direct confrontation, injecting an additional focal point. While not hesitating to assert his authority (based on God's Word) through confrontation, Luther is careful to follow attack with exhortation and teaching from Scripture.

## SECTION IV: PATIENCE WITH ONE'S NEIGHBOR IS NEEDED (531.16–534.25)

Luther briefly introduces "patience" [*die gedult*] with a first plural injunctive, then shifts to third singular assertive for the next eight lines! These brief "we" statements are used to repeatedly remind the audience of speaker-audience communion, and they serve as preludes to and retreats from longer assertive sections. The preacher offers a *definitio* of patience, pictured as faith and love in operation toward one's neighbor [*nechsten*], a term of significance for the remainder of the sermon.[13] Thus far, attention has been on the beliefs and actions of the audience, but now Luther shifts attention to the recipients of the actions—neighbor (531.17) and brethren [*bru(o)der*] (531.24). He introduces the devil as catalytic agent, so patience has an opportunity to express itself and so regenerate the heart. The remainder of the sermon amplifies the developing theme, that is, the four sections of the *distributio* of *hauptstück*.

Luther focuses on brother and neighbor through an argument grounded in Paul's writings (1 Cor 6:12) and quoted in both Latin and German.[14] The Scripture is prefaced by Luther's premise that one's rights [*recht*] should yield to a brother's needs (531.26f.). The *Septemberbibel* translation of 1 Cor 6:12 uses *furderlich* for "helpful," so the quotation seems apt, especially because Luther has prescribed the context of brother already. The fact that the scriptural context of 1 Corinthians 6 has more to do with individual care for self (sex, food, etc.) causes little difficulty because it is the *principle* of choice or deference being invoked, a principle with both scriptural authority and the *ethos* of a maxim. Note the balance of clauses (51:72): "[A]s Paul says, '*Omnia mihi licent, sed non omnia expediunt*, All things are lawful for me, but not all things are helpful' " [*Alle ding mo(e)gen mir wol thu(o)n, aber alle ding sind nit fürderlich*] (531.27f.).[15] However, the logic of the principle needs developing, and Luther does this in first plural by appealing to an earlier premise: individual differences in people's faith (530.21–25). Not only does this support the principle, it again strengthens communion between speaker and audience (in addition to hinting at Wittenberger culpability).

This sermon so far shows little evidence of a crucial confrontation among leaders in an intense struggle. Luther establishes his beginning by developing communion with his audience through his personal aggressiveness and his concern for the audience, by their sharing with him the values of scriptural authority and the bonds of faith and love. For one of these qualities, especially "faith," Luther praised them; for the other, particularly "love," he found them lacking and exhorted them to persevere. In both cases, however, the values of each quality are sources of agreement. We have seen Luther recognize and shape audience expectations, and much of the minute stylistic detail showed expectation and fulfillment at the sentence level. Preacher and the Scriptures have gained presence repetitively, while gaps between doctrine/practice, "lawful"/"helpful," and "strong"/"weak" have been focal points. Especially important are these dichotomies in the remainder of this sermon because they prove occasions for exploitation by the devil.

## The Introduction of the Mass

A turning point of the sermon comes at 533.4, and it is quite subtle. Indeed, none of the editors makes a paragraph break at this point. Using a strong conjunction [*derhalben*] to alert attention, Luther unfolds a charge that turns the sermon's focus toward a specific issue. He makes a blanket accusation, partitions its elements, names the specific locus of the error, then repeats (from 532.13) the general nature of the problem: "Therefore all those have erred who have helped and consented to abolish the mass . . ." (51:73) [*derhalben habe(n) alle die gejrrt / die darzu(o) geholffen vnd verwilliget haben / die Messe abzethu(o)n . . .*] (533.3–5). We can reasonably assume no full stop at *abzethu(o)n* but merely a pause, dissociating good cause from bad result. But Luther makes a crucial distinction between ends and means. Observe the balanced clauses of the *interpretatio* at 533.5f.: "[N]ot that it was not a good thing, but that it was not done in an orderly way" (51:73) [*nicht das es nit gu(o)t wa(e)r gewesen / sonder das es nit ordenlich gethan ist*]. Substituting the correct standard for the offense committed is neither synonymy nor tautology, but it introduces further problems: Wittenbergers have failed to cooperate and communicate with authorities, ignoring the possibility for a solution. The solution, however, must wait until Luther develops a case against Wittenberger reforms of the Mass. This is something essential because the charge he makes requires support because it comes both abruptly and in a challenging manner. So we see the narrated outline of the problem, one delaying specific development of the case until later. Hence, Luther orchestrates audience expectation.

Luther anticipates and engages an audience objection: that a good cause warranted by Scripture (and by implication, at least, by Luther's own teachings elsewhere) is *ipso facto* unassailable. The *prolepsis* is blunt and clear, cast as a dialogue between a hypothetical-typical speaker and Luther: "You say it was right according to the Scriptures. I agree, but what becomes of order?" (51:73) [*Du sprichst / es ist recht auß der schriefft / jch beken(n) es auch / aber wo bleybt die ordenu(n)g?*] (533.6f.). We realize the preacher is sure of himself, the objection bothering others and not him. Luther then magnifies the seriousness of the error by considering what could have been done (and obviously was not); by his personal confession of what *he* would have done; and as *correctio*, stating that he would reverse the reform! Because this issue of the Mass may be the one reformers in Wittenberg thought the least objectionable to Luther, they must have been stunned to hear this. Yet his subjunctive conditional allows the reformers some satisfaction that they had good ends in mind.

At 533.12 Luther's chastisement explores just how defensible might the reform of the Mass be to others. Luther puts increasingly more psychological distance between himself and the audience—45 lines (533.3–534.12) without first plural pronouns! He forces them to watch as he tries to defend their action against the lightweights ("papists and blockheads"), but this is expressed in subjunctive ("could"), so the inescapable impression is that "he will not." Further, the defense is weak because it merely asks a question of, rather than making an assertion to, those who could not know the answer. By dramatizing in this way, Luther plants the impression that "papists and blockheads" represent anyone who hides behind Scripture to conceal or overlook intentions. At 533.13f. he admits defeat before the real enemy, the devil. He has had his audience watch him struggle; they did not have to face the devil themselves; they should feel relieved their despair is not greater. So using the devil works as a floodlight to reveal fully the extent of his listeners' error: They have failed to know their enemy and have grievously misjudged how serious is the fallout of these reforms upon the weak!

Luther next reveals the basis for such despair, maintaining the psychological distance, continuing to use mostly third-person assertives. Using paraphrasis to heighten the isolation and futility of the venture ("those who began this affair"), two Scripture passages are quoted in Latin. Notice how, when transferred to the present context, the third-person mysteriousness of the passages rings ominously: "Every plant . . . will be rooted up" (Matt 15:13).[16] "They ran and [*et*] did not send them I" (Jer 23:21, literal translation). The purpose of citing Scripture in Latin is probably for authoritativeness and because some Latin phrases had become commonplaces. The syntax of the tight-lipped, paratactic *et* implies, but does not assert, the connection between "ran . . . send" and "they . . . I"[17] Luther shows the action of unsanctioned reforms as without authority or support; the implication, of course, is that God is the one who issued no orders.

To the crescendo establishing audience helplessness the preacher responds with his own aid: The situation is far from hopeless, and Luther immediately initiates another series of "I" clauses, though they do not progress much beyond the condemning mode. Instead, they move right back into a condeming mode, yet only by implication: "But I will" (533.20); "I know" (533.21f.); "I was called" (533.22); "I was willing" (533.23). In a few lines, then, Luther has moved back and forth—from looking forward in confident, future hope to looking to the current situation with scolding. For Luther, hope is to be realized only in rallying the listeners to himself. The basis for the scolding is the relationship between Luther and the Wittenbergers; it is about trust and communication more than anything else. His claim of being "called [back] by the council to preach" (533.22) stands in sharp contrast to the lack of authentic authority implied in the earlier-quoted Scripture passages. Luther argues, in a manner especially heightened by his use of *reprehensio*, that the Wittenbergers listening to him had improperly undertaken reforming initiatives and then wanted him to be responsible, an obviously cowardly act (533.26f.).

For the first time, then, the speaker clearly tells his audience they can forget about getting off easy. He is committed to *them*, not their actions, and they are involved with him (the last endearment was "dear brother, follow me," [532.25]). The present rebuke—for failure to consult authorities—runs all the way from 533.9 to 533.27, where it concludes with Luther's stinging observation: "Here one can see you don't have the Spirit [*Geyst*] . . . ." This is the only time *Geyst* is uttered in this sermon, and Luther rebukes his audience. He thus drives a wedge between "Spirit" and "Scripture."[18]

Luther's rhetorically constructed dichotomy, developed earlier around the scriptural notion of "all things lawful/not all things helpful" (531.26f.), now becomes a focal point through a *distributio*, which begins at 533.28: "Take note of these two things, 'must' and 'free' " (51:74) [*mercket die beyden stück müssen sein / vnd frey sein*]. The two categories are major distinctions for the remaining sermons. At 534.1 Luther applies the rationale represented in the two categories in a confrontation that accuses the audience (in second plural) of making a "free" into a "must" by leading others astray. The confrontation, though, is a warning that implies possible escape rather than an accusation of irreversible damage. Thus, Luther exhorts his audience as well as blames.

Luther (at 534.6) shifts to an explanatory amplification of the harm done. The result is empathy for the audience, winning back their confidence so they will be more amenable to agreement with his thesis: how the well-intentioned (but poorly conducted) action would turn out. Using the battle motif again, Luther claims the people leading the reform of the Mass would themselves retreat under pressure (534.6–9). This is an alarming idea—that innovations might collapse and the pioneers flee. He then draws upon his own credibility to show that if *he* proved such a coward, the results to poor people would be disastrous. This draws the contrast between the cowardly leaders of Wittenberger reform of the Mass and Luther's authoritative leadership. The unacceptability of considering Luther's own plausible cowardice, then, is clear: It means disgrace for those who lead, dismay and deception for those who follow.

To speak to the devastated audience, Luther now brings his sermon to a conclusion. Beginning at 534.12, he applies a motif used earlier (nurture with mother's milk) with an explicit goal that others' faith might grow. He makes present the likelihood that the proper means of reform is teaching, not hasty action. Another first plural exhortation ("Therefore let us" [51:74] [*Darumb last uns . . .*] [534.16]) draws together the "patience" idea as the key to showing love to one's neighbor, thus incorporating those three significant elements introduced earlier: "patience," "love," "neighbor."[19] Whereas the psychology of an earlier exhortation stressed looking at one's neighbor and his need, this second exhortation appeals more to the audience's self-interest (51:74f.): "If we do not do this, our work will not endure," (534.17); "if we do not . . . all the misery . . . will come upon us" (534.20–23). The third exhortation in the conclusion drops the future orientation, making one last appeal concerning the present situation—Luther's return to Wittenberg. He reasserts his legitimacy and determination (note the modals) and his personal concern (note the pronoun): "Therefore I could no longer remain away, but was compelled to come and say these things to you" (51:75) [*Hierumb han ich lenger nit künden außbleybe(n) / sonder habe müssen komen, sollichs euch zusagen*] (534.23f.).

The interesting feature of the later portion of this sermon is the way in which, once the Mass is in focus, vehemence and affect emerge first, then teaching takes over. Not that they are disconnected strategies because affective confrontation and teaching are, in the final analysis, intermingled; but Luther seems to vent his frustrations over the Mass first, then to teach and exhort through themes he has earlier developed (patience and neighbor). Through it all, he has tried not to alienate his audience, carefully returning to communion with them by standing together with them in the face of their mutual adversaries, the papists.

## THE SECOND SERMON (LW 51:75–78; LSTA 2:534–38)

At the close of the First Sermon, Luther had promised to talk about "images" (534.25), but he does not get to it in this Second Sermon, other than to further prepare for that theme with his categories of "faith" and "love," "must" and "free." Indeed, the strategy in the first two sermons delays direct discussion of the Wittenberg controversial issues until Luther has established both communion with the audience and an argumentative context, the "chief things." Thus, he first assures the audience of his pastoral authority over them, his feelings for them, his close relationship with them, and his responsibility to them. Once he has established a theological framework that consists in constructed realities (faith/love/patience) and principles of action (love and patience toward one's neighbor and brother), the audience is adequately prepared to engage new, and often threatening, perspectives on specific, volatile issues of practice. A simple strategy, then, in the opening sermons: (1) "theory," then practice (theory explained with practical examples); and (2) agreements, then differences (agreements explained with innoculations against future problematic issues).[20]

How much did Luther adjust his overall plan after preaching the First Sermon? We can only speculate that he decided to reinforce the argumentative context by bolstering his distinctions between must/free, preach/force. These are oppositions that inform each issue he will address. He may also have felt that he discussed the Mass too briefly. Whatever the motives, we observe Luther returning to the issue of the Mass in this sermon, extending the authority of Scripture and those who obey it through his use of Paul and himself as examples. In this Second Sermon, then, Luther extends the argumentation of the First Sermon without introducing new issues.

I have divided the sermon as follows, though Luther does not signal his structural movements as clearly as he did in the First Sermon.

- Introductory remarks (534.28–535.5): A review and clarification of the distinctions between "must" and "free," those things through which faith toward God and love for fellow human beings are expressed; even in the "must" area, force is wrong.
- Section I (535.5–24): The speaker clarifies his contention that private masses should be abolished, yet not by force. Instead, one must preach, leaving results to God, otherwise one interferes with God's work.
- Section II (535.24–536.27): Luther explores and makes present the distinction between force and preaching. First, he offers a rather quick condemnation of force (535.24–536.6); next, a more extended display of preaching (536.6–19); finally, a comprehensive exhortation (536.19–26), using the antithetical distinction between force and preaching, adding threats and pleadings.
- Section III (536.26–537.2): Luther explains the "preach"/"force" distinction with an example from Scripture (Paul's specific action with respect to idols), then applies it to the broader issue of the Mass.
- Section IV (537.2–538.11): Luther recounts his own past practices as examples of the *preach, don't force* credo in action. He also traces a brief history (Paul, Jerome, Augustine) of the church's interpretations of the principle, portraying the "must" (force) interpretation—Jerome—as wrongly reversing Paul and Augustine.
- Concluding remarks (538.12f.): Luther ends the sermon as he did the previous day, repeating the warning against making laws. Then he closes succinctly.

## INTRODUCTION (534.28–535.5)

Luther gives a longer introduction than usual. Because the First Sermon had to reestablish credibility and set a proper tone, at the start of the Second Sermon, the speaker needs to review what has gone before, much as he would review the context of a scriptural pericope. Furthermore, Luther continues what he began in the First Sermon, so the introduction to the Second Sermon reviews and clarifies. He establishes his stance warmly, yet firmly ("Dear friends, you heard yesterday . . ." [51:75]). Nevertheless, this is the only endearing (or any other kind of) direct address in the sermon! Instead, Luther uses the first plural in assertives, continuing a communion already established. The third-person assertives here give these lines a straightforward, neutral tone, one without much sign of changing the emphasis on either the ideational or relational elements. A couple of tactical moves, however, are subtle and noteworthy.

First, Luther's simple, almost reductive, *distributio* ("Faith is directed toward God, love toward man and one's neighbor . . ." [51:75]) is not as simple as it looks. He appears to apportion *all* faith to God and *all* love toward man, but at 535.1 he tightens the relationship between faith and love, summarizing their boundaries (51:75). Besides, he needs to cast love as faith's response—a flexible faith. Luther tries to show that the free, "of choice and not of necessity" [*das da frey ist vnd vnno(e)tig*] (534.33), can be flexible ("may be kept or not"), but it is still subjected to some restrictions. The "free" need not jeopardize one's faith and judgment, yet it is still constrained. Luther's style personifies the abstract "love" ("love must deal ... love never uses . . . it must walk") in a manner reminiscent of 1 Corinthians 13. This tightening of faith and love is important because the categories of "must" and "free" could be drastically misunderstood, should they be too simplistically assimilated—as in, for example, faith necessarily belongs in the "must" category and love belongs in the "free" category.

Second, Luther has tried to head off the above misconception with two statements (51:75) that repeat the same principle—that the love one gives should itself be measured out by (1) "as we have received from God without our work and merit" [*Wie wir entpfangen haben von got on vnnsern verdienst vnd werck*] (534.31); and (2) "as God has dealt with us" [*wie vns von got geschehen*] (535.1). The first plural pronouns in these statements encourage communion, but they also clarify ideas. Luther prescribes the notion of love not only as flexible and free—especially in the lines quoted—but also as constrained and defined by faith, which includes the character of God, as expressed by the love of God, characteristics of consistency and tolerance. Luther has to develop this notion of love considerably more in this sermon because love is related to the *haste* and *lack of order* themes of the First Sermon. The *force-coercion* theme will be condemned largely because it is human effort, not God's. As we noted, Luther inserted within the first four lines the phrase "without our work and merit," and in this sermon he will seek to dissociate God's Word from human work. In this introduction, then, he offers a review of the principles and categories of faith and love, must and free, first by dividing and explaining, then by compressing and constraining. The constraint theme is what he will now expand.

## SECTION I (535.5–24)

In this section Luther begins at the "must" category, represented by an unassailable example ("believing in Christ"), and proceeds to argue that even here the use of force is wrong. The argument focuses on the Mass, which functions as "a sacrifice and work of merit" [*ein opffer vnd verdienstlich werck*] (535.6); therefore, it belongs in the category of "musts." Luther argues that the Mass is evil and must, therefore, be abolished; that much he concedes. Yet if he can show that even "musts" do not justify using force, then surely neither do "frees." This is the argumentative device of *contrarium*, which introduces the more/less certain. If it is likely that force is wrong for the Mass, it is more likely to be wrong for other, less "necessary," issues. The argument has a strong connection between use of force and notion of work-merit, showing that force can only affect the body (represented by "ears") and not human "hearts." Therefore, human work is not only futile, but it interferes with God's Word. This section, then, begins in the "must" realm, establishing that the Mass belongs in that realm. But Luther argues that, regardless, force must not be used. He is obviously taking pains to advance the previous day's argument. The Mass *is* evil—he wants that realized, and his style throughout the section is didactic and assertive rather than confrontational. "You" scarcely appears at all, and the "I" eventually functions to show a contrast between human works, which the preacher makes present through the generic "I," and God's Word.

## SECTION II (535.24–536.27)

Luther expands the antithesis already initiated (that is, *preach, don't force*), broadening his impersonal assertives as he explores in more personal language and more lively style the anticipated outcomes, first of force, then of preaching. He culminates the section in a strongly confrontational stance, capitalizing on his credibility and relationship with the audience by refusing to support Wittenberger reforms. First, Luther shows "force" by a hypothetical example—though not contrary to belief—to demonstrate the claim made earlier that one can compel only outward behavior but not the heart. He posits evidence (he suggests that there are people who might indeed submit to force yet be ignorant of the reason). Then Luther makes this notion more present by having the characters who were compelled speak (*prosopopeia*). What his characters say in chorus is the same as what Luther himself had said, but it now has greater effect, especially because it is uttered in reverse order, forming a chiasmus that can be paraphrased as follows:

> A (Made to follow), B (Don't know right from wrong): B (I don't know right from wrong), A (I was made to follow). [*so seind jr vil die das müssen eingeen / vnd wissen nit wie sie darjnnen sein / ob es recht oder vnrecht sey / sprechende. Jch weyß nicht ob es recht oder vnrecht ist / weyß nicht wie ich daran sey. Ich habe der gemeyne vn(d) gewalt volgen müssen.*] (535.25–536.3)

The emotional effect of hearing this stems from the fact that the chorus becomes mere puppets, thus incarnating the confusion Luther predicted, and the audience hears this. Indirect discourse becomes direct discourse. The other effect is argumentative because, as chiasmus implies, Luther has taken the discussion right back (to "force," or compulsion) where it was but now with heightened presence.[21]

Next, at 536.6, the preacher turns to the preferred goal: to win the hearts. Luther does something similar to what he did previously, though he elaborates the action to be taken, using speaking in character again. This time, however, he does not use the compelled, confused character, but his own character, one who rightly preaches. Whether Luther means himself personally or representatively is not important. The voice gives a synopsis of what would be said. He resumes his discussion, qualifying the voice's remarks with what would not be done. Then, at 536.9, Luther returns to third singular, developing the scenario of what results might occur. This is all in subjunctive, constituting a narrative designed to make preaching seem a plausible option. He envisions results that are two-sided only to the extent that not all change in hearts would be instantaneous or unanimous. The speaker's stance at this stage is not prominent because he has been spinning a *gra-*

*datio*, which concludes with both speaker and hearer (both singular) deferring to the superior, inexorable power of God. We see this because both speaker and hearers are attuned to another object, as seen through the absence of first- or second-person pronouns in 536.6–10.

The argument on the Mass has now substantially been made. In the remaining sections of the sermon, Luther seeks to support his argument with examples, evidence, and the testimony of other witnesses. Thus far he has shown that (1) the Mass is within the category of faith, yet even here force must not be used; and (2) using force is futile, even to the extent that what is done is done—the Mass should now remain abandoned because coercive ordinances that forbid or demand are all bindings instituted by men.

## SECTION III (536.26–537.2)

Luther returns to the theme from the First Sermon of the demands of love and compassion for the weak. This is motivation for implementing what has already been argued. He makes two appeals: (1) from apostolic precedent and (2) from personal authority. Both appeals are complementary. Beginning with the confrontational "you" singular, Luther implies—through the scriptural account of Paul in Athens—that the audience can and should do the same as Paul did. That is, they should preach about idols, not smash them (536.27–34).[22] Then Luther immediately places himself back in the dilemma in which the Wittenbergers found themselves while he was at the Wartburg: what to do about reforming the Mass! He tells what he would have done, concluding with a "we" exhortation in an assertive mode. Thus, overall, the section is a nonthreatening, didactic encouragement, one fulfilling the expectations implied at 536.26f.: "What harm can it [the Mass] do you? You still have your faith in God, pure and strong so that this thing cannot hurt you" (51:77). That kind of reassurance requires positive support, the kind that comes from a strong example. Luther has reassured those fearing what hurt might result if force is abandoned by showing courageous action that worked and that is exemplary (by Paul, by Luther, and, presumably, by the Wittenbergers), so, indeed, those who will share this kind of faith will find it pure and strong and effective.

A few interesting features of particular stylistic details further inform our summary of this section. First, the scriptural story is clearly intended as an example of action to be followed, not resisted. Luther prefaces the story with these words: "Love demands . . . that you [singular and familiar] . . . as all the apostles had" (536.27f., *my translation*). Second, both the story and the speaker's own invented example of himself use vivid, exaggerated images of force, images which earlier had been used to describe Wittenberger actions (51:77): "he did not kick down a single one of them with his foot" [*aber er ru(o)rt keinen mit keym fu(o)ß an*] (536.30f.); "I would nevertheless not have torn them from it by the hair" [*so hett ich sie dannocht nit mit den haren*] (536.36f.). The Scripture story is connected to Luther's own account by "likewise" [*also*]. Clearly, then, both examples work together, making a similar, unmistakable point, and the preacher cannot but absorb apostolic credibility. Third, despite the way this section is directed at the present hearers, the story from Scripture (cited by Luther and clearly an *exemplum* invoking recognized authority) and the scriptural quotation ("the Word created heaven and earth and all things" [537.1f.]) plainly shift attention to the Word and away from the speaker. Hence, the audience will have to answer to the Word, not to the pulpit. (This was, in fact, always Luther's goal in preaching.) Luther accomplishes this by (1) *repetitio* of *Wort*—twice in 536.37f., *es* in 537.2); and (2) a positive *contrarium* that follows the enthymeme, so Scripture documents the more certain premise ("the Word created all things"). Thus hearers are more assured that the Word operates in the less certain ("the Word will create this"—changed hearts) matter of admonition and prayer.

## SECTION IV (537.2–538.11)

This portion, as it brings the sermon toward its conclusion, continues to reinforce presence in the antithesis Luther established in Section I—*don't force, but do preach and teach*. He draws upon values and persons significant to the audience, as well as reconstructs history for his hearers. Once they see the two alternatives in their full presence and as applied to the immediate controversy, the speaker will leave the audience in an uneasy state, warning, as he did the previous day, of what might happen if his exhortations are not heeded. First, Luther summarizes the antithesis in strong terms. Blending asyndeton, hyperbaton, and internal rhyme, he crafts an expression worthy of its initial, alliterative word-pair:

> In short, I will preach it, teach it, write it, but I will constrain no man by force, for faith must come freely without compulsion. (51:77) [*Su(m)ma sum-maru(m) predigen wil ichs / sage(n) wil ichs / schreybe(n) wil ichs. Aber zwinge(n) / dringen mit d(er) gewalt wil ichs nyemants / dan(n) der glaube wil willig vngeno(e)tigt / angezogen werden.*] (537.2–5)[23]

Using that strong attention-grabbing start, Luther bids his audience to take him as example [*Nempt ein exempel von mir*] (537.5). That this is thus far the clearest instance of the speaker's reference to himself is unmistakable (1) from the syntax (note the emphatic *von mir*) and (2) from the very next word—*Ich*—which Luther uses several more times. Earlier we heard him align himself with Paul in Athens, yet that was hypothetical; this rendition is concretely assertive [*Jch bin . . . jch hab . . . hab ich*] (537.5–7). Moreover, Luther had himself applied the present principle (*preach, leaving the results to God*) throughout the indulgence controversy. He is calling upon convictions most of the audience share with him about the rightness and success of prior reforms (51:77): "I simply taught, preached, and wrote God's Word; otherwise I did nothing." He mentions friendly colleagues[24] (1) by name (Melanchthon and Amsdorf, who drank with him and were doubtless in the audience) and (2) by title (emperor, prince, and pope, who are seen as powerful but hapless before the action of the Word). This is a celebration of common values and goals, a uniting in the face of enemies. The strategy should gain audience adherence to the thesis in question.

Thus far Luther has directed his audience to two "witnesses"—himself and the Word. In 537.16–21 a third witness is called—the devil. Luther mentioned the devil three times during the First Sermon (530.20; 531.34; 533.16), but this is the only reference to the devil in the Second Sermon. For the first time, the devil speaks, or, rather, the preacher speaks the devil's thoughts, introducing them with a rhetorical question. The speaking in character is vivid, allowing the audience to visualize the devil as he thinks about them: "He sits back in hell and thinks . . ." [*er sitzt hinder der helle(n) vnd gedendckt*] (530.17f.). But the character's presence is held in check by Luther's rapid intervention, resuming talk about the Word almost as if to interrupt the devil. The speaker carefully qualifies that one must allow the Word alone to operate. The result—the "work" (537.21), also called "thing" at 537.17—"will fall of itself." That prediction has been given presence through evidence accumulated in Sections II, III, IV, and it has been developing a repetitive form of its own.

Luther has now supported the *preach, don't force* option from his own authority and from scriptural authority. Yet the audience knows Scripture requires interpreters and that listening to interpreters can often be confusing. So Luther moves to respond to that need, citing at 537.22 another "example" that is intended to be analogous to the problem of the Mass. The example he uses shows differing positions on an issue, thereby allowing the preacher to cast his vote and shape interpretive guidance where he wishes. Luther invokes Paul again as the (by now, familiar) authority who demonstrates proper action (*preach* rather than make a *must* of it). Luther's "example," however, has the additional feature of putting the audience in a more favorable light than the former Pauline example on Athenian idols did. There, only Paul's role showed a favorable object for comparison, implying *do as Paul did*. Here, *all* the participants in the scriptural issue are Christians—Jews and Gentiles; now the audience can gain a second perspective. After already viewing Paul's exemplary actions in Athens, the audience can now view themselves as innocent parties in a controversy.

That Paul's actions were correct is strongly implied by a single *sententia* of aphoristic quality. Luther casts Jerome, who introduced "force," as villain. Enter, on the other side, Augustine, who sided with Paul.[25] Now Jerome seems more an interlocutor than a villain as Luther depicts the two as opponents in debate. In brief, the *grob exempel* turns into a dramatic story told for the audience's instruction and pleasure. All three characters are saints; Paul and Augustine agree with Luther, but Jerome's position won out. Subsequent history ("popes") brought disaster. The story has a narrative, dramatic power of developing an expectation of dread, that caving in to force could return all that mess again. The speaker has shown through his narrative how the law [*gesetz*] of Moses crept back into the church—through the forceful interference of Jerome's ordinance-making and again with the popes and their laws [*gesetz*]. This narrative, with its repetitive *gesetz*, brings a strong sense of dread to the audience, tainting the Wittenberg Ordinance they have passed.

## THE CLOSING (538.12F.)

In this terse section, Luther again leaves the impression that perhaps the next sermon might move on to new things. Yet lest the audience relax too much, Luther employs in his final warning the first plural ("let us beware . . . lest we . . ."), allowing the dread to linger. In summary, we have found Luther to be much more a teaching pastor than a confronting preacher in this Second Sermon. While personal credibility was an important prerequisite to establishing authority and communion in the First Sermon, here the preacher clarifies the *preach, don't force* position on the Mass. Then Luther supplies evidence to support the case for preaching and against force. Specifically, in Section I he argues for the genius of preaching and the limits of human responsibility for bringing change. In Section II Luther shows vividly through dialogue that force is a poor choice, and he exhorts his audience to renounce force (or he will renounce them). In Section III scriptural evidence shows that preaching can be used effectively and that exemplary leaders (such as Paul and Luther) avoided force. In Section IV an additional piece of scriptural evidence, a second analogous issue (the first was idols; the second was circumcision) shows a precedent for tolerance on "free" matters (even troublesome matters). It also reveals a sorry tale of woe resulting from the application of force. In short, Luther has begun to practice what he preaches, allowing preaching from Scripture—in all its interpretive richness and persuasive power—to do more of the communicative work than forceful confrontation.

# CHAPTER 4

# THE THIRD AND FOURTH INVOCAVIT SERMONS

## THE THIRD SERMON (LW 51:79–83; LStA 2:538–43)

In our observations on Luther's sermons, we have noted his bold, self-conscious beginning, especially evident in the abundance of confrontations of the "I" and "you," including many "you" singulars. At the same time, we have noted how he deliberately cultivated audience communion, as seen in the several "we" and "let us" clauses. Having thus asserted and clarified his credibility, authority, and relationship with his audience, Luther took a moderate tone in the Second Sermon, using few first- and second-person pronouns and almost no endearing terms of direct address. Instead, he used assertive statements in the third person to convey and clarify a lesson.

We see these strategies of stance even more clearly when we observe their function within the argumentative context, that is, the issues or topics Luther wanted to address and the inventional strategy he uses in dealing with them. The First Sermon did not foreshadow all the topics specifically, but it initiated an inventional schematic for eventually understanding them. Luther established the "chief things," consisting in faith, love, and patience, as behavioral responses to God's providence in a world where these responses must accomodate neighbor and brother. He instantiated the categories of "must" and "free" as a means for more specifically sorting out the appropriate Christian response. Luther established these structures with scriptural citations and interpretations, which subsequently became his source for confrontive exhortations to the audience. Luther had to develop his own agenda and demonstrate an urgency that would necessitate such an agenda. The good of others and the present unrest in Wittenberg provided that necessity.[1]

In the Second Sermon, Luther directly focused on the abolition of the Mass, speaking precisely about what category the Mass belongs in—that of "musts"—speaking clearly, authoritatively, and emphatically about how the Mass is to be handled. Because the Mass is one topic the preacher assigns to "musts," he is conciliatory in agreeing that the goal of abolishing the Mass is a worthy one while asserting a more proper means for attaining this goal: preaching rather than force. Coercive action Luther shows to be always improper because it becomes a human work, thus futile when compared with the power of God's Word. In the First Sermon, Luther emphasizes the harm that coercion brings to others; there he is a bold, prominent speaker. In the Second Sermon, he shows how the futility of force quickly pales before the power of the Word; there he is a calm, informed speaker. In both sermons, antithesis is a primary syntactic focal device. Further, the death-devil urgencies of the First Sermon demand choices (suggested by "chief things"), exemplified in the "all things lawful, not all things helpful" *sententia*. In the Second Sermon Luther explains the important and sometimes frustrating qualification (*force is wrong even for "musts"*) by using a pair of Latin *termini technici*—"right to speak" [*jus verbi*] but not the "power to do" [*executionem*].

In the Third Sermon, Luther returns to the bolder approach because he talks about "images," a topic he clearly places among the "free"; therefore, coercive legislation is even more wrongheaded. Further, Luther exploits many resources in arguing (largely through dramatic dialogue) a policy of tolerance toward images— apart from any coercive action he or his fellow reformers might take toward their removal. On this issue he emphasizes the complexity of scriptural authority in an effort not so much to embarrass those who dogmatically ground their position in the Old Testament, but to show how force hamstrings itself: Those who use it ignore or misunderstand the "must"/"free" distinction. The unwelcome result is recalcitrance, not faith. Luther then returns to his *preach, don't force* principle, applying scriptural precedents in a way that seems clear and sensible in contrast to the bewildering cacophony of voices heard in the Old Testament exegesis of Luther's opponents in dialogue.

Throughout this sermon, Luther is aggressive and confident, dispatching several problem topics related to the clergy (celibacy, cloisters, vows) by relegating them to the "free" category, showing his previous principles sufficient for dealing with them. That is to say, because these are "free" matters, human ordinances controlling them are contrary to God. One must, instead, be faithful to one's own conscience, which must be able to endure trials. Endurance will have to depend on nothing less than Scripture.[2] Nonetheless, Luther discusses "vows" [*gelübte*] without referring to Scripture, which implies that vows have no authorization from the Bible. Indeed, Luther argues in the first section that one should follow one's conscience [*gewyssen*], summarized nicely in the twofold "without harm and for love of his neighbor."

In the second half of the sermon—the "images" portion—Luther, without using the word "conscience," shows (1) that one can quickly and easily twist the faithful heeding of conscience into imposing one's conscientious scruples on others and (2) that even the attempt to ground conscientious beliefs in Scripture is problematic. Here we see the preacher using a strategy apparently quite different from his previous use of "clear, strong" texts. Here he demonstrates the error of dogmatically interpreting Scripture.[3] Then, showing the objectors' scriptural support to be unclear and, therefore, shaky, Luther exhibits virtual control of the agenda. In this Third Sermon, he makes no concessions and offers no compliments!

In summary, the broad structure of the sermon is as follows:

• Introductory review (538.16–22): A summation of the "musts" described in the first two sermons.

• Section I (538.22–541.20): Functions as development of the "free" category, particularly as it extends to clerical problems of vows.

• Section II (541.22–542.32): Takes up images[4] in a dialogic argument that engages and subsequently dispatches the objectors' Old Testament position.

• Section III (542.32–543.19): Moves toward a conclusion, returning to the positive preaching supported by apostolic-precedent themes of the previous day, reasserting a New Testament position on images, and closing with yet another antithetical *sententia*.

## INTRODUCTION (538.16–22)

The introduction's function is to provide a stable base by providing clarification of previous points between speaker and audience through a retrospective look at the first two sermons. Luther reiterates that private masses belong to the category "musts." The central enthymeme (538.17–20) suppresses a premise from the previous day: that private masses are a human work of merit. Luther clearly wants no misunderstanding about which Mass he means and, less clearly here, why the Mass is wrong. "But" [*Aber*] (538.20) even such "musts" do not justify force, and Luther establishes this principle in strong terms in a second enthymeme. In particular, he (1) uses two negatives [*keynen*] in 538.20f.; (2) provides vivid descriptions that circumscribe a range of forceful actions ("dragged to them or away from them by the hair . . . drive no man to heaven or beat him into it with a club" (51:79) [*mit den haren dauon oder darzu(o) thu(o)n / . . . gen hymel treyben / oder mit knu(o)tlen darzu(o) schlagen*] (538.20f.); and (3) employs a final, succinct pair of clauses that plainly put this matter to rest, transferring the responsibility from speaker to audience: "I said this plainly enough; I believe you have understood what I said" (51:79) [*diß ist grob genug gesagt. Jch meyne, jr habt es verstanden*] (538.22). So beginning with "we have heard," Luther quickly establishes a foothold, having rendered the audience carefully attentive.

## SECTION I (538.22–541.20)

The speaker now turns to the "frees" and discusses matters of clergy vows. The arguments and exhortations in this section are not elaborate or complex; they are repetitive as Luther moves rapidly from assertion to exhortation and back to assertion. The strategy is not to offer new insight into these clerical issues, but to let the issues illustrate the principle ("must"/"free"), presenting the issues of vows in such a way that they become examples of the principle.[5] By exhaustively approaching these issues from the "must"/"free" principle, Luther shows that vows are forceful encroachments upon free things, and he condemns any strictures of force placed upon vows. Thus, through the only Scripture citation he uses in this section, Luther avoids a detailed exegetical proof on these matters. His use of Paul (1 Tim 4:1–3) is a shrewd *exemplum*, emitting suspicion at every attempt to legislate such issues through ordinances. By making his principles more present, now illustrated concretely in the clerical problems, Luther not only resolves these issues, but he prepares the way for the same principle to be applied to "images" in the next section.

In 538.22–539.7 Luther's objective is to displace fear of disobeying God's ordinance with appreciation for the role of one's conscience in times of trial. Three times Luther mentions God—the first two in connection with freedom, the third with judgment. Thus, the argument flows from general assertions about God's ordaining the "frees" (positive), through a reminder about violating that ordinance (negative), to the final mention about judgment. The clear implication is that these "free" matters are not a threat; rather, they are God's means of assisting and preparing the believer. The next transition introduces the trial-testing theme. That Luther has elevated one's own conscience to primary concern can be seen in the movement of this part of the section, particularly in how (1) at 538.24ff. he defines the "frees"—as illustrated in "marry or not?" "leave cloister or not?" issues—and how (2) at 539.1–3 he takes the above definition and makes application of it, one that shows marriage as optional (though actually discussing only one option—to keep the celibacy vow). The option taken, however, cannot include making a "must" of the matter for others. Then the other option—to forsake the vow of celibacy—is presented (539.4f.) So the argument moves from defining through two applications that concretely display the two possible actions that let everyone (except a dogmatist) off the hook. Note the following expressions that particularly stress individual concern for the person (51:79): "without a burdensomeness to you" [*on dein beschwerunge*] (539.2); "each should be free" [*sol ein yeder frey sein*] (539.3); "that your conscience be relieved" [*das deynem gewyssen geradten werde*] (539.5).

Since Luther has already introduced a trial-testing theme (which continues to 539.14), this theme reveals not only that coming to grips with the marriage issue is but a small part of one's Christian maturity (which is the real issue), it further recalls the battle-death urgency of the opening of the First Sermon as Luther returns the conscience to a responsible, not reckless or careless, position. The enemy, or threat, in this theme is not God (indeed, "stand before God" suggests affirmation) nor death, it is the devil. It is the devil's threatening presence (note the *repetitio* at 539.7, 11, 14) that provokes the remark at 539.8 ("It is not enough to say . . ." [*Es ist nicht genu(o)g*]), which is strongly antithetical to Luther's earlier statement at 538.22 ("I said this plainly enough" [*diß ist grob genug gesagt*]). Clearly Luther was finished with the "musts." But here, with the "frees," Luther wants to develop the urgency much more because the threat is greater. Accordingly, he begins a pointed confrontation, one in which the second singular pronoun occurs seven times in as many lines! He uses the same terms (though in a different order) about the need to ground one's conscience in Scripture that he had used in the First Sermon: *starcken, klaren spruch*. This is what is held alongside the other kind of defense, one that Luther makes present by having a character speak, first in a stammering whine of desperation and blame, then by a specific (and implicitly cowardly) excuse wherein he heaps blame on individual leaders for influencing the multitudes. By invoking these names (Karlstadt, Zwilling), Luther clearly heaps scorn upon these men and their influence in Wittenberg, Karlstadt especially because his title also is given.[6] But of greater interest to us than "who" is *how* the names function within this argument. First, the names are on the lips of a character making lame excuses. That the excuses are insufficient to the devil's testing can be seen in a progressive tracing of blame—from crowds, to a doctor and a monk, to an archangel.[7] This crescendo of excuses (51:80), despite the final reference as "preaching," is answered by "Not so" [*Neyn*] (539.10). Clearly Luther will not allow the preaching of others to be an excuse for blame; one's own conscience must be convinced, which comes from Scripture. In addition to introducing a well-selected text for the occasion ("heeding devils, in opposition to what God created"—the broader application fits too[8]), two devices augment Luther's paraphrase: (1) A parenthetic *correctio* at 540.2. sets up the paraphrase, portraying the Scripture passage as like a tip of the iceberg. (2) In a second parenthesis, more a *litotes*, Luther uses an expression that, spoken as a thought uttered aloud, becomes understatement (51:80): "I think St. Paul is outspoken enough here!" [*jch meyne sant Pauls habs grob gnu(o)g außgestochen*] (540.4f.). All these devices reinforce the presence of the authority of Paul and the Scriptures.

In 540.8–13 Luther begins his exhortation, which is actually a continuation of the preceding conclusion, in third person. But now, after picturing the possibility of one standing victoriously upon Scripture, Luther can repeat his instruction about following one's conscience, and it can be more positively considered. Indeed, by choosing third singular injunctives ("let him" or "one should"), the speaker can broaden his focus to greater possibilities. The singulars (540.8–11) give way to repetitive, emphatic plurals as the audience can listen to Luther's desires:

> Would to God all monks and nuns could hear this sermon and properly understand this matter and would all forsake the cloisters, and thus all the cloisters in the world would cease to exist; this is what I would wish. (51:80) [*vnd wolte got alle Münch vnd Nonnen ho(e)rten diese predig vn(d) hetten den verstandt vnd lieffen alle auß den klo(s)tern vn(d) ho(e)rten alle klo(e)ster auff die in der gantzen welt seind / das wolte ich.*] (540.11–13)

A closer look at these thoughts shows more, however, because the transposition from assertive to optative alters the speaker's stance.[9] Here, I think, the shift does far more than express Luther's private value opinion. Indeed, his *exclamatio* [*wolte got*] and final optative [*das wolte ich*] become ways of talking indirectly to the audience. They suggest preferences; they imply that the audience should agree. Especially can we see this in "could hear this sermon and properly understand this matter" because that is exactly the purpose of the sermon. Indeed, that is preaching's purpose and goal: hearing leads to faith and understanding.

Then at 540.22–541.5 Luther concludes his focus on clerical issues with a powerful segment because the emptying of the Augustinian cloister and subsequent confusion over clerical vows required a strong position. Augustinian monk Martin Luther appeared tonsured and wearing his cowl, arguing vehemently for tolerance toward decisions other than his. This portion features resources he has not yet used: (1) The endearing direct address appears twice here—*Also lieben freünde* (540.22) and *lieber bru(o)der* (541.2). (2) A series of four "this . . . therefore, all" erroneous accusations are put into the mouth of the audience and answered each time with "Not at all" [*noch nit*]. These have the effect of an antiphony, as might be led by an actor goading an audience. They cover specific issues: marriage (540.25), cloisters (540.26), images—an issue Luther will turn to next and that is answered the most emphatically (541.2)—and marriage again. At this point (541.3), Luther takes a position opposite his previous one at 539.11ff. Collectively, these four accusations magnify the presence of what Luther had ironically uttered earlier (51:81): "I have said it clearly enough" [*es ist klar genu(o)g gesagt*] (540.22f.). Following that antiphonal chorus, he calmly portrays in the marriage issue (51:81) the positive principle concisely put at 540.23: "[N]ot make liberty a law" [*keyn gebott auß der freyheit machen*]. He uses two balanced clauses that support the notion that both, when performed conscientiously, are right (51:81): "For they who cannot retain their chastity should take wives, and for others who can be chaste . . ." [*dan(n) die keüscheyt nit halte(n) künden / nemen weyber / welche aber keüscheyt halten . . .*] (541.3f.). The statement ends, affirming those who keep their vows. Luther uses a scriptural allusion that obviously contrasts with the 1 Timothy 4 passage used earlier (540.2): "It is good that they restrain themselves, as those who live in the Spirit and not in the flesh" (51:81) [*den ist es gu(o)t das sie sich mu(o)gen enthalte(n) / da in die leben jm geyste / vnd nicht jm fleysche*] (541.4f.). Luther's affirmation about living in the Spirit provokes the transition to the remainder of this section, which takes up "vows" (541.5–20). First, he uses an enthymeme, showing that a vow involving what God has declared "free" is not only nothing to be concerned about, but instead justifies ridicule.

Luther has nearly completed his argument on vows and clerical matters, returning to the "you" exhortation. He then completes the discussion of vows, showing how a vow to keep an obvious wrong would be ridiculous (541.12–16). He uses "example" [*gleychnyß*],[10] following a premise that could be disbelieved ("your vow . . . contrary to God"). Following the easily acceptable analogy—a vow to assault or steal means breaking commandments—the speaker directly confronts through his rhetorical question (51:81), "Do you believe God would be pleased with such a vow?" [*Meynstu das got würde ein wolgefallen darjnnen habe(n)*] (541.13f.). Then Luther quickly makes the analogy explicitly fit the vow issue, supplying the *interpretatio* himself, "For God has in both cases . . ." (541.16). So *gleychnyß* is surely an "illustrative example" rather than an "argumentative example."[11] Yet that is not to say that the "example" is merely explanatory. Rather, it plays a significant role in a chain of argumentation: "Your vow is contrary to God" refers to the vows of chastity, obedience, poverty. That is what Luther is seeking to establish. The example offers a case of a vow agreeably "contrary to God." Even without knowing the commandments, one could follow the rhetorical question; the protasis that follows clinches it for us. The apodosis shows the preacher moving back into the arguable, seeking a connection; the example has become the starting point for his enthymeme (541.15ff.), which functions as *contrarium*. All the "I"s represent any person, and Luther's final "I" mentions a vow new to the discussion—"eating flesh." The last statement, in third person, refers to monastic orders that were afraid to eat meat. This judgment indicates Luther is done with this point because he has turned away from the audience and from his example, implying that he and they are now in agreement.[12]

## SECTION II: "IMAGES" (541.22–542.32)

The overall purpose in this section is to start from the assertion that images belong to the "free" category (541.23f.), arguing that legislation is, therefore, inappropriate (542.2). This argument, thus, responds to Karlstadt's arguments in *Von Abtuhung*, though we have no real evidence that Luther had read that work.[13] The balance of the section amplifies and supports that purpose by (1) citing some history of the Byzantine iconoclastic controversy as evidence that people have violated the "free" category (541.25ff.) and by (2) amplifying into a cacophonous dialogue (542.1ff.) on how God really is working through images, and subsequent human actions in response to them. This illustrates how futile it is to presume "to do things differently from the way the supreme majesty has decreed" (51:82) and how wise it is to leave such things alone. How does Luther accomplish this purpose?

First, we note at 541.22 the earlier strategy in twice mentioning "images." The first instance[14] was casual when, at 536.28ff., Luther explicitly applies the story of Paul at Athens to problems of the Mass. But it is Paul's actions and not Athenian beliefs that are the focus. However, the mention of altars in the temple—altars that Paul declared (51:77) as "nothing but idolatrous things" [*eytel abgo(e)ttereisch ding*] (536.32)—might have caught the audience's attention; they expected Luther to address the topic of images. So the Wittenbergers have, by this Third Sermon, already heard Luther favorably mention Paul's tolerance of idolatrous structures. The second foreshadowing[15] of images came in this sermon (541.1), an explicit, exclamatory denunciation of the violent destruction and burning [*gebrochen vnd verbrant*] of images.

Yet these foreshadowings merely hint at the wrong actions regarding images and do not necessarily imply that images themselves are "free." And that is exactly what Luther asserts at 541.23, surely a highly controversial assertion ("they are unnecessary . . . and we are free to . . ."). He delays his supporting arguments, instead granting concessions that put him in a more strongly communal position with the audience. The concessions are twofold. The first is a concession about images and everyone. The second is a personal confession (51:81): "[A]lthough it would be much better if we did not have them at all. I am not partial to them" [*wie wol es besser were wir hetten sie gar nicht. Jch bin jn auch nit holt*] (541.24). After clarifying his own feelings (perhaps responding to previous accusations that reached Wartburg), Luther's next statement further diverts any negative attention from himself and onto the topic he introduces. The historical evidence Luther cites, told in indirect discourse (narrative), seems an issue analogous to the present dilemma at Wittenberg, but more important, it illustrates the "must"/"free" division. It provides evidence that dovetails with the assertion just made (51:81)—that is, the "free to have or not have" [*wir mügen sie haben oder nicht haben*] rings true when one hears about the "great controversy" [*grosser streyt*] between emperor and pope. Luther rules them both wrong, even before finishing his story; in other words, they were wrong in principle, apart from the consequences of their actions. He finishes the story—a story of bloodshed, winner, and loser—then uses a rhetorical question, and we see that Luther tells just enough. He blends story with his own *interpretatio*, limiting the implications to no more than he himself will reveal. In this way the rhetor Luther molds audience expectations.

Luther explains the story's lesson, quickly moving from third to second person, from "they" to "God" to "you" (plural). The persuasive force of the lesson application derives from a *contrarium* in which pope and emperor (the two greatest world powers) erred. To paraphrase: How then can you [lesser persons] act the same [as they] without avoiding [greater] error? The error of emperor and pope is magnified (51: 82) by "This God cannot tolerate" [*Das kan got nit leyden*] (542.1), but even more so for the audience's potential error because "supreme majesty has decreed" and "cannot tolerate" indicate continuing jurisdiction. This historical narrative resembles the patristic (Jerome-Augustine) evidence from the previous day because it suggests the idea that the lessons of history reveal that force has a dismal record.

At 542.2 Luther begins a long argument from the Old Testament that shows not only the Law's ambiguity (and the futility of presuming to know God's motives), but also displays the recalcitrance of both dogmatic sides. Luther concludes at 542.29 that this "force" won't work. The first argument is based on Exod 20:4. It begins in a most intriguing manner as the preacher entices his audience to follow him through this and subsequent Scripture passages. Luther strings the audience along with a neutral lead-in, inserts the Scripture quotation, bringing the hearers along step-by-step, using present tense, giving no indication of where this is headed. In fact, Luther has lured the audience to relax. He then uses dialogue, visualizing the uncertainty caused by taking sides, that is, emphasizing one text or idea over another, showing how futile it is to act on such tenuous doctrine. To begin, this is implicit ("they say . . . they say . . ."); later it becomes emphatic with rhetorical questions. We further notice how Luther maintains his stance in all this. First, he aligns with his audience, but after the first response to the adversaries [*widersa(e)cher*], the speaker seems nowhere to be found. What remains are two competing sides, resulting in uncertainty. It is as though Luther stepped out of the fray, playing off "they say" against "you say," wherein both sides are citing the text (consecutive commandments of the Decalogue, in fact).[16] The force of this dialogue is not in its logic, but in the presence of its confusion; it exemplifies wavering uncertainty, which is the antithesis of one taking his "stand" [*grundt*] on a biblical text. The dialogue is summarized at 542.9f., indicating a stalemate (51:82): "You shall not make any images [*Du solt keyn bilder machen*] . . . You shall not worship" [*Du solt nit anbetten*]. The strategy in all this is now apparent: Luther is sympathetic with those in the audience who think that images are nothing but trouble! Yet he has shown the difficulty of making an authoritatively solid exegetical argument. Certainly no decisive persuasion of the heart will come of this!

Although the preceding dialogue developed somewhat of a crescendo, we see at 542.12 that there are even more rungs in the ladder, more layers to the argument. The opposition begins to grow bolder, using more Old Testament texts, summoning examples (Noah, Abraham, Jacob) from the patriarchs, mingling textual paraphrase with interpretive confrontation. Luther sticks closely with the audience this time because there is no dialogue—only the opponents' assault and the preacher's turning to the audience to express mutual frustration and helplessness, his and theirs. The opponents' argument gets so strong that it bears all the marks of the devil's earlier accusations (First Sermon, 533.16ff.). The speaker's response on his audience's behalf begins in helpless silence, then grants concessions, and culminates in a broad interpretive concession that begins with the opponents' text and ends with Luther himself adding a scriptural example. The result is that both sides can be shown to be equally valid (to 542.22). Today it is not easy for us to tell from the printed sermon text where the opponents' statements end and the narrator's begin. But we do not need to know because the speaker created opponents. If Luther has characterized them plausibly from the start, an audience will not demand (nor be capable of) rigid separation of speaker from character, though that might be necessary with an audience hostile to its speaker.[17]

The third layer of the argument (542.22–32) concludes this section. Thus far, Luther has shown his audience that only uncertainty results from efforts to base a dogmatic position regarding images on (1) explicit, clear prohibition of images in the Decalogue or (2) all practices of the patriarchs or Moses or the kings. Now Luther will show that even worship of images, something everyone agrees is a violation, cannot be corroborated empirically in experience, that is, "prove they're doing it." He signals each layer of his argument with *Nun*—previously "Let us now see" (542.5) and "Let us now go farther" (542.12)—(51:82), "Now who will be so bold and say, when challenged to answer: 'They have worshipped the images' " (542.22–24). We notice the editors rightly did not use a question mark because Luther has his audience following him. Also the rhetorical question unravels so gradually that immediate response to this matter is unlikely. Luther has subjected his hearers to a substantial pattern by now; they will listen because we recall and still observe that Luther is their spokesman, not their accuser. He immediately follows his "question" with an accusing interrogative spoken by the adversaries. He then reveals the nature of their challenge at 542.25–29, where the pronouns show the close communion Luther maintains with his audience. Four times "they" emphasized the distance between adversaries and audience. When he uses *Ich*, the speaker is thus drawn toward the audience. The more a speaker denounces an enemy, the greater an audience develops affinity for the speaker.

The problem Luther shows in all this is that accusations do not bring about change of a person's heart, only recalcitrance. He again lets the adversary speak, thus displaying that attitude of defensiveness. Each response by the adversaries to accusations has revealed a preoccupation with the persons rather than the positions. These forceful challenges, then, inevitably become insoluble, bitter *ad hominem* battles. Further, we see that Luther used the second response, along with his explanatory setup, to function as a *contrarium*, an argument advancing its conclusion from less to more certain. This *contrarium* has a dual function: (1) Explicitly, it argues that if the adversaries balk when charged with faith without works (and they did), so even more will they reject a charge of worshiping images. (2) Implicitly, it argues that if Luther's condemnation failed (less likely), then theirs certainly will (more likely). At 542.29 Luther calls this matter to a halt, and we note that this entire image business has been a matter of "force," the action so strongly condemned earlier.

## SECTION III (542.32–543.19)

In this section Luther begins with the failure of force already discredited, reasserting the necessity of preaching. He offers as support (1) his own record (brief); (2) Paul's action at Athens (same story from Acts 17 as he used the previous day), against which he confronts the Wittenbergers with their record; and (3) another Pauline action, not previously discussed. Support for preaching begins at 51:83 where Luther not only claims he has already shown what to do, but that it is what Paul also did: "*That* is what *I* did" [*als ich gethan habe*],[18] (542.34), "*that* is what *Paul* did in Athens" [*also tha(e)te Paul zu(o) Athen*] (543.1). When speaking of Paul, we notice that Luther narrates freely, slipping in the words "their *churches*," obviously contemporizing the Athenian context, as is his penchant in translation.[19] So the preacher has imported Paul to 16th-century Wittenberg and, implicitly, himself back to first-century Athens! Using a graphic expression,[20] Luther describes Paul's actions in Athens: what the apostle did not do ("strike on his mouth") and what he did (preached).[21] The final piece of evidence is an *exemplum* whereby the recognized authority is, again, Paul. The story told here of Paul's tolerance of images on the ship transporting him to Rome is new. We notice how Luther unveils the story, breaking the flow of the first premise (Paul traveled in a ship having images). Luther later mentions the author (Luke) by name, alerting us to the appeal he is making to the Lukan credibility, thereby increasing the power of the example (two witnesses—Paul and Luke—instead of one). Because he argues that Luke understood Paul's tolerance for images and wanted to convey the reasons for that in his text, Luther directs his audience to the corroboration of Scripture. All these reasons won't go unnoticed by those such as Karlstadt who value the Gospels and Acts more highly than the Pauline Epistles.[22]

To summarize, Luther has, to this point, begun with his conclusion that private masses must be abolished, but they must be abolished through preaching rather than force (the First and Second Sermons). He has argued for tolerance on clerical issues such as marriage, vows, cloisters, and even foods. The justification for tolerance is that these are "free" matters. Luther has likewise argued tolerance for images, showing (1) that the Old Testament prohibitions are difficult to interpret scrupulously and impossible to enforce equitably, and (2) New Testament evidence that the apostles tolerated images.

The "must"/"free" dichotomy is Luther's greatest argumentative resource. He carefully establishes it, first, by showing love and patience to be essential in practice and inseparable from faith (First Sermon); next, by repetitively developing and using the "must"/"free" dichotomy. He varies the terms, occasionally using "necessary"/"unnecessary," and Luther employs antitheses to develop presence. He employs dichotomies, often through antitheses such as "right to speak, not power to do" and "all things lawful, not all things helpful." Throughout the first three sermons, Luther has argued the important antithesis of action: *preach, don't force*. He has supported this heavily through scriptural examples, mostly of Paul, and through his own prior practices. We have seen, then, Luther skillfully develop his argument through repetition and recapitulation. The recapitulation is unmistakable, especially considering that he used all of the Second Sermon to reinforce arguments from the First Sermon. Repetitions of themes (such as Paul's refusal to use force) were used often in the scriptural stories. By preaching every day, Luther has a unique opportunity to sustain and develop an argument by accretion.

## THE FOURTH SERMON (LW 51:84–88; LSTA 2:543–47)

In the first two-thirds of this sermon, Luther completes the analysis and exhortation on images that he began in the previous sermon. In the final third, he presents a discussion on eating meats. Concerning images, Luther had already (1) argued the premise that they are a "free" item, amplifying the ambiguous exegesis of Old Testament texts that some say forbid them; and (2) stressed that the New Testament advocates preaching against images but supports a tolerant, rather than forceful, action toward them. That foundation was primarily an exploration of the issue behind the historical problem images had been for the church; secondarily, Luther was asserting the proper solution—preaching.

Luther proceeds in this sermon (at 543.26) to clarify what he contends is a sound scriptural basis for abolishing images, specifying in more contemporary, concrete situations what a proper course should be. Providing tools for sorting out

various situations, he suggests—but does not explicitly follow up in this sermon—
the Christian's motivation for doing the right thing. Thus the overall strategy for
Luther's treatment of images, begun in the Third Sermon, has been to start with
the strongest objections and undermine them. Luther then (at 544.11) introduces
the benefit-of-neighbor theme as further argument *against* image destruction and
*for* preaching against images.

In the section on eating meats (546.5–547.25),[23] Luther employs a clear,
didactic style of teaching. He argues, through an enumeration of three proposed
situations, that eating is a matter of Christian liberty to be decided within the context of one's own and other people's consciences. The exception to this is the case
of extreme personal need, wherein a possible offense to others should be ignored.
He quickly dispatches this possibility first and does not elaborate it with subsequent discussion, perhaps because it represents a situation of rare occurrence.
Luther's primary focus is the elaboration by example of possibilities two (standing
firm in one's liberty, that is, noncompliance when forced) and three (foregoing
one's liberty in hopes of not offending—thus, overcoming—the ignorance of others). In this sermon, then, Luther has returned to the neighbor-brother theme,
arguing that other people's needs must be considered when deciding how to act
within "free" categories.

## INTRODUCTION (543.22–26)

The first five lines of the sermon orient the hearers to what has gone before
and what yet awaits. While Luther makes no attempt to set off these remarks from
what follows, doing so will make our analysis easier. The preacher recalls again the
"must" and "free" categories, mentioning a specific "must"—the Mass. Recalling
the "free" category by antithesis, Luther then specifies by examples already treated in this sermon series—marriage, monastic life, and images. At 543.25, he recapitulates these four subjects as alike (51:84), with "love is the captain" [*die liebe
hierjnn der haüptman ist*].[24] And *die liebe* complements the opening [*LJeben freünde*],
creating a climate of tender concern between speaker and audience. Beyond this,
there are no additional endearments in this sermon. What we do see is Luther reasoning with his audience, appealing to their own observations, attempting to show
there are no real grounds for abolishing images.

## SECTION I: IMAGES, CONTINUED (543.26–546.3)

This section occupies roughly two-thirds of the sermon and moves in the following manner: In 530.17–531.5 Luther clarifies when/why images should be
abolished—"only when worshipped." In 543.31–544.10 he contrasts that situation
with a plausible instance in which images ought not be abolished—namely, when
they are "useful" to a person. In 544.11–19 he offers his recommendation for
both of these situations: Rather than abolish all or even some images, whether for
the best reason ("downright idolatry" [*rechte abgo(e)tterey*]) or the worst reason (the
mere presence of images), Luther advocates preaching that images are nothing to

God. By so doing, they (images) will fall of themselves (51:85). At 544.20–545.10 Luther exhorts his audience to reject the temptation to condemn images merely because they are abused, expanding the argument against rejection with three analogies. He shows the inconsistency of an abuse-requires-rejection rule, using an enthymeme that reveals the greatest enemy to be self, not objects. At 545.11–23 he dramatizes, filling the possible void left by the confusion that his rejection analogies had produced. Here Luther makes an offensive against the devil, pinning him back with dialogue and questions to demonstrate greater gains (benefiting one's neighbor) over lesser evils to be avoided (believing that images are something useful to God). In 545.23–546.3, Luther concludes the images section, continuing to use himself (begun by "I" at 545.12) to climax his argument because he has uncovered the mistaken emphasis and enthusiasm by the Wittenbergers. Now let us follow the persuasive action more carefully.

At 543.26 we see that Luther will stay with images as a concrete example of "free" things. He has begun with the "must"/"free" principle, enumerated the subjects in which they are manifested, and inserted "love" as a preferred motivation. Throughout the Invocavit Sermons, and in each of the eight sermons in particular, Luther tries to balance principle and problem. In this images section, we see evidence of that because the introductory and the concluding parts emphasize principle (must/free/love) while the core of the section stresses the particular problem (images). The term "images" [*byldern*] is more prevalent in the center than at the periphery of this section. Moreover, as indicated earlier, with Luther's turn toward a sharper focus on images at 543.26, he provides a signal in a manner consistent with what we have already seen: "On the subject of images, in particular" (51:84) [*Sonderlich von den byldern*].

Clarifying is the early task of this first section, and Luther clarifies the legitimate basis for abolishing images, beginning with antithesis (51:84): "abolished when they are worshiped; otherwise not" [*das die abgestelt sollen sein. Wie sie angebetten sollen werden / sonst nicht.*] (543.26f.). To show the seriousness of worshiping images, he not only claims they cause abuses, he also heightens this with personal testimony: His own preference is to be rid of images ("I wish they were" [*wie woll ich wolt*]). He manages his credibility deftly, however, hastening to show that his preference is grounded on something the Wittenbergers have overlooked. What he argues in this section, then (51:84), is essentially a new *definitio* of idolatry, which concludes at 543.30 with "which is downright idolatry" [*welchs dann rechte abgo(e)tterey*]. Luther's claim is that a person does not of necessity commit idolatry when he finds an image useful; instead, idolatry is the delusion that one thinks he is doing God a service in placing an image. In other words, the crucial issue regarding images has been overlooked by the Wittenbergers. The audience needs to rethink their position (previously shattered in the Third Sermon) in light of this replaced priority.

Luther's *definitio* is worth noting for a couple reasons. First, it is boldly presumptive—"For whoever places an image in the church imagines . . ." (51:84).

The speaker will need to (and does) support that contention with arguments designed to appeal to audience experience, as well as to justify his own claims to know what others are thinking (including the devil). Second, what one "imagines" [*meynet*] is subtle enough to appear harmless—that one has performed a good service to God and a good work (543.30).[25] Finally, Luther's final clause ("[you have] fastened on the least important reason of all") destroys any illusion. Turning from the idolatrous practice to less malevolent uses of images begins at 543.31 with an antithesis—the "greatest"/"least." A rather innocent attitude toward images is illustrated with reference to *d(as) crucifix*. Luther points (note the demonstrative *das da steet*) to an image still remaining in the church, an example on which the audience should be united. This serves as a helpful tension-reliever and a clearly acceptable example that does two things: (1) It amplifies the nature of God, thereby explaining the offense of idolatry. (2) It shows the contrast between a crucifix as "only a sign" [*sonder nur ein zeychen*] and Luther's previous definition of idolatry. Luther is helping divert audience attention from others' alleged idolatry to their own admitted harmless piety. The gentleness with which he offers the example shows his strategy (51:84): "For I suppose there is nobody, or certainly very few, who do not understand . . ." [*Dan(n) ich vermeyn es sey kein mensch oder jr gar wenig / der nit den verstandt hab . . .* ] (543.32f.). Although the central argument is less about showing idolatrous use of images and more about making present the "useful" [*braüchen*] purposes of images, Luther continues to juxtapose one against the other in an effort to argue for discriminating tolerance. He wants his audience to be Christian brethren, not judges.

But at 544.3 Luther returns to his earlier premise and uses examples of people trying to do service to God. He mentions actual persons of importance, this time through rhetorical question, delegating to the audience the same privilege of "supposing" that he had himself done in his presumptive assertion at 543.29ff. Luther names well-known benefactors and collectors of relics (especially Elector Frederick[26]), a suggestion that these examples affirm the point. Yet just as when he has the audience discovering error even among their leaders, Luther again inserts his primary point in this part of the section: Even the worst particular abuse cannot mandate a general rejection of images! He makes this point, recalling the argument by *repetitio* (through a reminder that the greatest "reason" [*sach*] is still not sufficient "grounds" [*vrsach*] for abolishing). The "not enough"[27] elicits the tripled compound verbs that instantiate the rejection as harm of abolishing, destroying, and burning all images [*alle bilder abzuthu(o)n, zu(o)reyssen vnd verbrennen*] (544.8). However, the assertion is highly contestable at this stage, and Luther—realizing this—expresses the interrogative *Warumb?* that would be on his hearers' lips. The notion that images are useful, suggested earlier by the illustrative crucifix, is perhaps more acceptable now. And Luther's language thus far shows a willingness to share in the feelings of his audience, whether in surprise or exasperation or even condescension, yet having even grudgingly to admit the need for "patience" (though he does not use the word): "We must admit that there are

still some people . . . (51:84)" [*dan(n) wir müssens zu(o)lassen. Es seind noch menschen
. . .* ] (544.9). The *correctio* and the conclusion both show Luther standing beside
his audience with an appeal for toleration of images for the sake of even their
slightest use to a person.

To this point Luther has worked with the distinction between idolatrous
actions that images tend to produce and the innocent usefulness that their mere
presence provokes. How much wrongdoing is to be ignored or how seldom people might benefit from images are secondary considerations not discussed. At
544.12 Luther argues a second distinction (antithesis)—the superiority of preaching over condemning. He does so on the premises already established in the first
antithesis, as well as by recovering the outcomes-prediction theme used in earlier
sermons.

The exhortation in first plural ("we") that began at 544.8 shifts at 544.12 to
second plural. Beginning with two balanced negative clauses, this exhortation
builds an accumulation that makes present the futility of images. This accumulation is all negative and begins to present the positive side of the antithesis at
544.15 with two more antitheses, the first highlighted by alliteration (even in
translation) and having a sententious flavor (51:85): "better to give a poor man a
goldpiece than God a golden image" [*wan(n) sie einem armen mensche(n) einen
gulden geben / dan(n) gotte ein gulden bilde*] (544.15f.).[28] The entire set of nega-
tive/positive antitheses is an enthymeme, with the supporting premise (51:85)
being "for God has forbidden the latter, but not the former" [*dan(n) diß hette got
verbotten / jhens nit*] (544.16). By arguing so closely, with the strong contrast
between the discredited action and the supported action, Luther relieves some of
his audience's tension; he shows them a solution. He then supplies his prediction
of preaching's success, an opportunity to remind his hearers how he previously
condemned their disturbances, something he has by now more fully explained.
The argument concludes at 544.18f. with Luther's claim that images are already
starting to wane, an implicit promise/threat that I paraphrase as: *Resume preaching
because it is working on its own; stop preaching, and you will halt what has started*, that
is, the demise of images.

At 544.20 Luther embarks on a course designed to heighten the presence of
the former antithesis that he has been arguing—namely, to ignore even idolatrous
worship by some people: "[D]o not risk destroying God's creation [those people
for whom images are useful] because of it." Luther employs analogies from experience to show how even scriptural commands must be obeyed in a manner that
prevents chaos. He then seeks to prepare the audience to better understand and
appreciate the wisdom and power of his preaching recommendation by continuing to undermine confidence in their solution (namely, to abolish images).
Through the Word of God proclaimed, Luther is wearing down his audience's
self-reliance (544.20–545.10) so he can fill the void with his own pastoral leadership and biblical solutions (545.10–23). We discover the uncertainty and mistrust

Luther pursues in his audience by looking to the last line of this part: ". . . what [mischief] would we *not* do?" (51:85 [*my emphasis*]).

Luther's transition to the next part appears awkward. The editors of the Weimar Edition[29] start a new paragraph at 544.20 because despite "therefore" [*Derhalbe(n)*], the injunction that one should be on guard against the devil has little connection to the previous context. The device used is *praeteritio*, foreshadowing the devil's reemergence at the end of this section and implying that the three analogies that follow are representative of "all his [the devil's] craft and cunning" [*allerlistigiste / vnd spitzegiste*] (544.21) and "his apostles" (51:85). The vividness of those rhyming synonyms, combined with the ironic use of the term *aposteln*,[30] mark this statement as a strongly important transition. The principle Luther wants to attack is carefully qualified at 544.21 ("Now, although it is true" [*nu(o)n wie wol es war ist*]) and leads to a premise that is strengthened by synonymy through parenthesis. But despite the evil use of images, Luther continues to argue that because images are abused does not necessarily demand that they be rejected. And he mocks the abuse-requires-rejection principle: "This would result in utter confusion" (51:85). The three analogies Luther uses to demonstrate the inconsistency of that principle involve beginning with scriptural commands.

The first analogy ("God has commanded us in Deut. 4" [*Gott hat gebotte(n) Deu. 4*]) is an Old Testament *exemplum*. Luther expands it through paraphrase into an enthymeme so the full reasoning behind God's command is exposed (544.24f.). Then Luther appears to give ground, granting the existence of abuse, in language similar to the previous concession. The preacher dangles that response to the granted abuse before his audience with a rhetorical question and answer.[31] His question (51:85) uses hyperbole ("pull the sun and stars from heaven"), eliciting his corresponding *litotes*: "we had better let it be" [*wir werde(n)s lassen*] (545.2). While the first analogy sprang from scriptural *exemplum*, the second alludes to a sententious adage.[32] The first analogy dealt with worship of sun and stars (the spiritual realm); the second deals with misuse of wine and women (the social realm). The rhyme and meter of these analogies and their ridiculous responses is interesting. Surely the audience was amused.

The third analogy makes no attempt to sound scriptural or even wise: "Again, gold and silver cause much evil, so we condemn them?" [*Weytter. Golt vn(d) silber stifft vil bo(e)ses / darumb wollen wirs tadlen*] (545.4f.). The hyperbole is missing in this analogy, however, and as we think back over the three analogies, we realize Luther has moved from (1) the ridiculous ("pull down sun and stars") to (2) the not-unheard-of (in principle—"kill women, dump wine") to (3) the somewhat common ("condemn gold and silver"). The impact of these analogies comes primarily through their verbs, and the verb of the third analogy is the *repetitio* of the point Luther is making: Not to condemn images because of "abuse" [*tadeln*] (544.23) [*tadlen*] (545.5). Rather, the logic of that would mean we'd have to kill ourselves to rid the world of evil.

Luther uses an *exemplum* of scriptural evidence, supplying quite explicitly a statement from Jeremiah [*Als der prophet Jere. am xvij. sagt.*] (545.8). The quotation begins at the point of the enthymeme ("for we have no greater enemy than our own heart")—"The heart of man is crooked" [*das mensche(n) hertz ist krum(m)'*]—and Luther uses his *correctio* ("or, as I take the meaning" [*oder wie ichs meyne(n) soll*]) to regain leadership for this argument, supplying his interpretation of the key term "crooked" to apply it to the context. His interpretation of Jer 17:9 conjures up an image of misdirected activity, a deviation from the true course. The adverbial phrase "And so on" characterizes the series of analogies by tarring them all with the same brush. Luther has thus led his audience down an amusing road to despair—or at least to perplexity. And he has done it all in first plural to avoid any loss of communion with his audience. Luther has them waiting, as we saw in the rhetorical question (51:85): "[W]hat would we not do? [*was würden wir außrichten*] (545.10). That "question" has no obvious answer because it freezes an audience's objections, fostering further silent speculations: *Indeed, there would be no end to our misdeeds!*

The next part (545.10–23) functions as a vivid, dramatic presentation of the truth and effectiveness of Luther's criticism of images, one that would ask the *right* questions and condemn the *important* wrongs. While not using the terms "preach" and "teach," Luther employs the device of dialogue, using the devil as interlocutor to help him portray an action more effective than condemning images (which is ineffective and hurts the wrong people). The devil is present throughout the remainder of the images section. In this part, he is present primarily through his appearance at 545.11 and as the continuing antecedent (or referent) of Luther's third-person singular pronouns—15 of them in 10 lines (545.11–20)! In the remaining part of the section, the preacher mentions *teuffel* four times. At 545.11 he picks up the devil motif (foreshadowed at 544.20) by an enthymeme that is highly figurative. Luther then shows his audience the proper way to deal with a slippery character (devil) through another staged dialogue, something of a favorite strategy of Luther by this point. The use of "I" does not stress Luther's authority as much as it representatively models proper Christian conduct, showing that verbal activity is more effective than force. So the verbs of the preface to the first question to the devil are as significant as the content of the question itself (51:85): "But I can catch [*fahen*] him by asking [*spreche*]" (545.13). The question forces the devil to admit what Luther wants and has been arguing as the more important and neglected point: the idea that one is doing God a service by placing images. That a concession is obtained from the devil is significant because in the First Sermon the devil was clever and claimed that he (Luther) had a weapon against him (533.20f.). The subsequent discussion in the First Sermon showed that only the Word could be effective against the devil. So in one sense, Luther is again demonstrating how the Word can be effective. In another sense, Luther is showing how he the preacher is effective because surely even the most obviously representative "I" produces speaker credibility. All Luther needs to show is that he succeeds against the devil while, by implication, the audience does not because the devil is slippery. The "neighbor" theme will be much more extensively used in later sermons. For now, Luther uses it to continue demonstrating the slipperiness of the devil. The resolution to the audience suspense is provided by the speaker's response, first in an enthymeme that ends with a rhetorical question, implying an obvious answer (the minor premise), and second in Luther's use of alliterative *sententia* from 544.15f.

The final part of the images section draws a conclusion to the matter. Luther intensifies the distinction between Wittenberger foolishness and his own authority and judgment. He continues to draw upon the devil's presence as a problem to be dealt with, for example, through Luther's own leadership. Maintaining his credibility and the Word's authority, Luther declares at 545.33 what harm the devil causes ("scattered us"). He lays upon the audience the responsibility for the harm caused by the devil. And despite the use of *vns* at 545.33 to hint at communion, Luther ends the section with a scolding exhortation whose central amplifying clause reverberates with rhyme (51:86): "If you want to fight the devil you must know the Scriptures well and, besides, use them at the right time" [*derhalben mu(o)ß man die schriefft wol wissen / darneben zu(o)r rechten zeytten gebrauchen / so man mit dem teüffel fechten will*] (546.1–3). In this way the preacher continues to appeal to his audience's feelings, alternating anxiety and relief, then enlivening their nerves again. The matter of images is thus disposed of. Luther, however, has more work to do.

## SECTION II: MEATS (546.5–547.21)

The section on "meats" is interesting for its role as a bridge between the difficult issues involving controversies over doctrine (that is, What is the scriptural truth concerning the Mass and images?) and the most controversial issue of all—the blessed Sacrament. Luther will devote sermons 5, 6, and 7 to that topic. Then he will be able to deal with confession last because he will have already dispatched confession as a supposed prerequisite to participation in the Sacrament. The eating of meats is an opportunity, then, to build from agreement, preparing the audience for the difficult topic of "Sacrament."

Luther treats "meats" (51:86) in a straightforward fashion: 546.5–10 functions as an introductory *distributio*. The presumed truth that the eating of meats is a "free" matter is seen in the three repetitions at 546.6–8: "It is true . . . . This no one can deny. . . . this is true" [*Es ist ja war . . . das kan ja nyemandts laügnen . . . das ist war*]. He begins at the security and assurance of Christian freedom (note the *repetitio* of "free"/"freedom" at 546.6, 7, 8), and he maintains close communion with the audience (*wir* at 546.5, 6; *vns* at 546.7, 9). This is disturbed by the antithesis aligning responsibility with freedom. This mandate ("must use our liberty") for action will be decided on the basis of the situation, that is, the attitude of others. The succeeding discussion (51:86) is in this way signaled and made emphatic (second singular): "Observe, then, how you ought to use this liberty" [*Nu(o) merck du wie du dieser freyheit brauchen solt*] (546.10).

The discussion set up by the *distributio* proceeds thus: First, the desire to eat could be a personal necessity; therefore, one can disregard any consequences to others (546.11–16). Second, should one be forced to eat, then one is obligated by freedom to resist the force through disobedience (546.16–28). Third, the weakness of some people may require one's tolerance of them, calling for deference of one's liberty for the benefit of the weak (546.28–547.21). Each situation and its discussion is progressively longer. The movement among these three distinct situations by way of *expeditio* shows the *third* situation—patient deference to the weakness of others—to be the most significant.

Part one [*Zum ersten . . .*] presents a hypothetical situation of personal need. Luther presents it in second singular, having established it in the previous paragraph. If one is sick or unable to abstain, one then has legitimate grounds for eating anything. This freedom, already made explicit in the *distributio* with asyndeton in a list of examples ("any kind of food, meats, fish, eggs, or butter" [*alle speyß / fleysch / fisch / eyr oder butter*] [546.6f.]), is here expressed by paraphrasis: "whatever you like" [*was dich gelust*] (546.12). Following those grounds and permissible actions, the consequences are presented through successive conditional clauses. First, the easy cases are presented (51:86): When physically in need of nourishment—because of illness or hunger—eat whatever you like, and "if anyone takes offense, let him be offended" [*Erger sich darab wer do wo(e)lle.*] (546.12). The individual hearer can be confident in this right to liberty, yet he or she will be reminded that God is the giver.

The second part [*Zum andern*] continues in the second singular and begins like the first—a hypothetical, singular situation. Yet the first situation remained abstract because it had no concrete examples to instantiate the hypothetical principles. This second situation is in second singular, but as we soon see, it does not represent an extreme (rare) situation. Both the first and second problems are common but not the most urgent topic. So as Luther becomes more concrete, he shows the greater likelihood of each possibility, especially because this second situation represents the viewpoint of a neighbor or brother who is a victim of force and/or ordinances, charges of which the audience has already been accused. Hence, Luther must make the second more present. But (and here the American Edition obscures the German syntax)[33] he aligns himself with his audience by immediately adding parenthetical examples (with epithets):

> as the Pope has done with his fool's laws, that you should not on Friday eat meat, but rather fish, or to eat fish during Lent and not eggs or butter. (*my literal translation*) [*wie dan(n) der Bapst getha(n) hat mit seinen nerrische(n) todte(n) gesetze(n) / du solt nit vff den freytag fleysch essen / sond(ern) fische / fisch in der faste(n) vn(d) nit eyr oder bu(o)tter.*] (546.16–19)

These particular foods are familiar to an evangelical audience—especially because they had begun observing Lent that very week—and Luther uses them to characterize this kind of situation. He then tells what legitimate practice, which makes clear the action and the reason, is allowed (51:87): "Because you forbid . . . I will eat . . . ." The preacher advocates disobedience to papal law only if one focuses on the grounds (and consequences?). The action is then generalized to a higher level of abstraction, making it an exemplary action: "And thus you must do in all other things which are matters of liberty" [*Also saltu jm in alle(n) andern dinge(n) tho(n) die da frey sein*] (546.23f.). Then Luther develops his principle of action with another example, both broadening the principle (beyond foods) and authenticating his personal practice, showing that it is consistent with what he preaches. The example [*Nym(m) ein exe(m)pel:*] concerns the wearing of the cowl [*kappe*], which Luther has previously discussed (Third Sermon) when addressing monastic vows. In the example, he hypothetically presumes that the cowl is required, then he argues that force alone, regardless of its human source, permits one to disobey *in defiance* ("out of spite") [*zu(o) tru(o)tz*]. Yet Luther is careful to qualify the exact nature of such force, that it must be restrictive enough to imply that the culprit is making something out of nothing. Luther does this with a demonstrative: "*that* [cowl] and none other" [*das vn(d) kein anders*] (546.25f.).[34]

At 546.28, the third [*Zum dritten*] and most important situation begins. This one has an even greater likelihood, so Luther abandons the singular for a plural, broader, "you." He refers to those of concern to him as "some [*seindt etliche*] who are weak in faith." These are the *schwachen* and are to be distinguished, according to 546.9f., from the "stubborn" [*halß starcken*]. Luther has consistently urged consideration for these people, regardless of how few they might be. Here he uses accumulation to develop the presence of their need and to tie it, and them, to the preaching-teaching solution; hence, Luther varies and accumulates appropriate verbs and continues to describe "them" with reference to "us." This last phrase opens the possibility that preaching can succeed, achieving faith and unity, because he establishes the basis for a first plural exhortation that draws strength from juxtaposed descriptors (51:87): "such good-hearted men"; "the stubborn" (546.32). Following that "we must" [*müssen wir*] is another injunction ("we should" [*so(e)lle(n) wir*]), one that articulates, through accumulation, the kind of action called for: "bear patiently . . . and not use our liberty" [*gedult tragen vns vnser freyheit enthalten*] (547.1), which is a positive/negative antithesis. Then, having already established (1) the need-motivation (expectation) at 546.28–31 and (2) the action (fulfillment) at 546.31ff., Luther suggests the results (visualization) at 547.2ff. This procedure will generate further presence, and Luther does this first by arousing reassurance; then, by igniting excitement; and finally, by awakening fear. Notice the expansive style of the initial phases (51:87), employing doubled expressions ("peril or harm," "body or soul," "brothers and sisters"):

[S]ince it brings no peril or harm to body or soul; in fact, it is rather salutary, and we are doing our brothers and sisters a great service besides. [*Die weill es vns keynen schaden oder gefa(e)r weder an leyb noch seel bringt / Ja mer fürderlich darnebe(n) wir vnßern brüdern vnd schwestern ein grossen frum(m)en thon.*] (547.1–4)

This "doubling" seems a favorite device of Luther because he often uses two words when one would seem to suffice.[35] These doublings aid in showing the harm to the weak. Yet hurting the weak is not all because Luther hastens to argue that these folk, in time, would have been won. Hence, he intimates there is both actual harm and potential loss. The negative results are added through accumulation, with offense [*zum ergernyß*] to one's neighbor at the center of a movement that begins with use of freedom and ends with loss. Thus Luther builds a crescendo of emotion. The entire accumulation, which takes up approximately two-and-one-half lines of text, uses *vnser* three times and *wir* twice. The preacher's handling of the third situation is strongly communal.

At 547.5, Luther turns to *exempla* that can reinforce the presence of the attitude toward the weak and the action he advocates. This will allow his audience some diversion from their anxiety over the undesirable results Luther has just sketched. Besides that, the *patient deference* solution (my term) he proposes for the third situation needs support to keep the hypothesized results from arousing disbelief. The scriptural evidence Luther imports—Acts 16—is all derived from the activity of Paul, the apostle so frequently used in the earlier sermons, especially the Third Sermon, in which Pauline action comprises the sermon's final supporting argument. In the Second Sermon, Luther had said virtually the same thing as Paul: *What's the harm?* Here he relates three separate incidents but mentions no texts.

The first incident illustrates the preceding *patient deference* principle. Its telling is brief, yet Luther makes the story's action present by allowing the audience to hear *Paul's* thoughts, thus visualizing *Luther's* proposed, preferred action. Syntactically, we note, however, that Luther gradually unveiled the details of Paul's circumcision of Timothy, beginning with an abstract, blanket remark, then revealing the attitudes (first, of the Jews, then, of Paul), delaying mention of circumcision until last.[36] The diction also shows Paul maintaining control, allowing others to function (that is, do the circumcising). Hence, the grammar portrays the deference or relinquishing of one's own rights. Luther's gradual telling of this scriptural story (And which time in Scripture does he mean? The Jews were often offended in the New Testament!) keeps the audience listening, and it models the patience the speaker advocates. That is to say, it gives people some benefit of doubt. That attitude is verbalized in Paul's thoughts as he attributes the problem to ignorance [*vnuerstandts*]—therefore, the problem is solvable—rather than stubbornness (which the reflexives might suggest).

The second Pauline *exemplum* illustrates the stubborn-resist (second) situation. Luther continues in a narrative fashion, making the disjunction and beginning slowly. The new attitude is explicated by a doublet ("ought and must" [circumcise Titus]) that acts as a *correctio* (547.11).[37] Luther then portrays the firmness with which this attitude must be taken. No contemplation is called for, he says, only resolute, purposeful action. The third *exemplum* further illustrates the second situation. It opens plainly enough as an additional illustration. It bears the same repetitive *Da* (at 547.12, 14) as the first two *exempla* (547.7, 10), but we soon see this story is rather more involved. "He did the same when St. Peter" cues a narrative of successive temporal events in much the same way it did in Luther's previous narrative *exempla*. Therefore, the *Da* serves much the same function as the *waw*-consecutive in the Hebrew Old Testament or the initial *kai* in the Greek New Testament and the Septuagint.[38] The American Edition of Luther's Works inserts "It happened in this way:" [*durch die weyse*] as a clue to the fact that Luther begins an illustrative narrative at this point.[39] The story weaves several elements of this section's three attitudinal situations. Luther shows St. Peter using his freedom, and it ultimately resulted in a bad effect for the Gentiles—they acquired an "evil understanding" [*ein bo(e)sen verstandt*] (547.12), a strikingly vivid expression.

For an audience not thoroughly familiar with each of these biblical episodes (and they come, after all, from different books of the Bible), the initial clause arouses curiosity because Luther keeps Paul's action—"stood his ground"—in the foreground. He develops presence (51:87) for the harmlessness of eating meat through his contemporary, humorous "pork and sausages" [*schweyne(n) fleysch vn(d) würste*] and through the *prosopopeia* that effectively expresses the wrong view, both cognitively and affectively.[40] The expression "to the injury of evangelical freedom" [*zum nachtheyl der Euangelischen freyheit*] (547.18f.) completes the necessary details of the episode, and Luther again uses dialogue to make vivid the momentousness of the occasion, what he epithetically calls "an apostolic lecture" [*ein alte lection*] (547.20).[41] This time, I think, the preacher is not being as ironic as he is emphatic! The dialogue carefully quotes from Gal 2:14. The quote completes the sequence of the three *exempla* and the section on meats as well. So the power of Paul's rhetorical question derives from its manner of involving the audience in the answer. Coming as it does from the lips of Paul, Luther's question suffices as a warning, implying that using liberty ought not be taken lightly; even apostles make mistakes! The choice of the *exempla* (circumcision and food laws) is significant because not only might these issues seem (at least, to us) more theologically crucial than were Catholic food laws, but they represent the Law itself, thereby symbolizing for the audience the possibilities both of overcoming the Law (as in Peter's freedom) and the danger of reverting to it (as in Peter's equivocation). Luther also cannot help being identified with Paul, and the Wittenbergers may see their own leaders as resembling Peter—leaders they followed in good faith only to witness them caught in inconsistency. "Leaders" themselves may see Peter in the mirror![42]

To summarize, Luther has now fulfilled audience expectations about images. He has discredited misguided efforts to force their removal because images may prove useful to the weak. He then employs that same "deference" theme in his discussion of foods. By distinguishing different situations, especially as reinforced through biblical examples, the preacher demonstrates how important weak brethren are. Their welfare constitutes a genuine concern, one calling for patience and preaching rather than force and haste. Force, in particular, Luther implicates as an ineffective tactic, one that provokes rebellion rather than compliance; it does not foster faith.

## CONCLUDING EXHORTATION (547.21–25)

Following the quotation of Gal 2:14, Luther exhorts his audience, in first-person plural. His exhortation is succinct, carefully coalescing with the introduction to the foods section. He has used the synonymous "[right and][43] proper time" [*rechter vnd bequemer zeyt*] to summarize the three situations above, though he omits the "stubborn" here. Further, Luther expands "weak" with the doublet "brothers and sisters" for effect, broadening the "principle" from *Euangelischen freyheit* (547.19) to *Christenlichen freyheit* (547.23). Freedom from the Jewish law becomes the model for contemporary Christian freedom, as we recall from the opening sermon, the *haüptstuck* of a Christian.

# CHAPTER 5

# THE FIFTH AND SIXTH
# INVOCAVIT SERMONS

## THE FIFTH SERMON (LW 51:88–91; LStA 2:547–51)

The Fifth Sermon concerns the "blessed Sacrament," the Eucharist, the next-to-last issue of controversy addressed in these sermons. As a topic of discussion, the Sacrament occupies all of the Fifth and Sixth Sermons. The Seventh Sermon is on the "fruit of the sacrament, which is love" (555.28f.). The Eighth Sermon, the last one, takes up confession—a topic closely related to the Sacrament because confession (and fasting) had been papal prerequisites for sacramental observance. Recent reform activities in Wittenberg during late 1521 and into early 1522, especially Karlstadt's Christmas Day (1521) "evangelical" Mass, exacerbated the controversy of the Eucharist. Confusion over how to behave and who could partake of the blessed Sacrament (and to what extent) prompted Luther to respond in these sermons.[1] As we have seen, he has already in the Fourth Sermon discussed meats without reference to the Sacrament because he will discuss the Sacrament in the Sixth Sermon.

Luther devotes more time to the topic of the Sacrament than any other. In this Fifth Sermon, he returns to some approaches he used in the opening sermon: (1) The endearing *lieben freünde* occurs five times (six times in the First Sermon); thus, 11 of the 16 occurrences of this term in the Invocavit Sermons are in these two sermons. (2) Luther uses strong first-person singular in emotional testimony. (3) Luther employs *ad hominem* confrontations with ample use of "you." Further, he renews a dramatized exegetical debate with the devil, a tactic used in the Second and Fourth Sermons. This Fifth Sermon, then, provides some of the most vivid and striking examples of speaker stance toward the audience thus far observed. Luther is able to build upon the communion already established in earlier sermons. Similarly, as he progresses he continually recapitulates themes discussed earlier. In this way he claims rhetorical jurisdiction over each new territory.

The structure of this sermon is, moreover, easier to follow than the others have been. The movements in the message are crisp and well signaled. These clear movements indicate not only shift in subject (as with the topic heading at 550.9 [*Von beyderley gestalt des Sacraments*]), but more often adjustment in emphasis (that is, presence or emotion). The sermon falls into two distinct sections, nicely set up by a brief review of what has gone before and signaled by a distinctive thematic sentence (548.2) that serves as *distributio* for the two sections of the sermon. Specifically, if we paraphrase the thematic expression ("observing the sacrament"), the two sections focus on the action and its object, respectively: Section I—"Observing," that is, "handling" (548.3–550.8); and Section II—"the Sacrament," that is, "both kinds" (550.9–551.16). However, both sections are primarily concerned with "observing," more with the action of the communicant than with the essence of the Sacrament.[2] Both sections, then, develop virtually the same point—*force has no place in the blessed Sacrament.* Luther first emphasizes the force in "taking with hands"; then he deals with force as insisting on "both kinds," that is, bread *and* wine.

Section I (548.3–550.8) admonishes the Wittenbergers to cease their requirement that everyone handle the Sacrament. The strategy of this argument begins with the pope's "foolish laws" (and their inconsistencies) (548.3–14), laws that, when violated—Luther argues—constitute no threat of sin (548.15–19). However, Luther accuses the Wittenbergers of making their own foolish laws with their mandatory Sacrament reform (548.19–549.7). Then he offers a *prolepsis* that shows, through dialogue with the devil, that literally "taking" (with hands) cannot be supported in Scripture as a clear command (549.7–27), whereupon Luther concludes and exhorts his audience to abandon this reform ordinance (549.27–550.8). One might liken the first part of the strategy in this section to that of Nathan the prophet (2 Sam 12:1–25). Prior to confronting King David for his sins against Bathsheba and Uriah, Nathan told the king a story. In doing so, that is, by leading David into granting acceptable premises ("*That man* deserves to die," David raged), Nathan aroused the king's emotions against the story's villain. At that point Nathan made his confrontation explicit—"*Thou* art the man."[3]

Section II (550.9–551.16) moves toward a conclusion—that taking both kinds was instituted by the Lord and is "necessary" but that this fact should be preached rather than forced. This section contains three discernible parts: first, what should be done and why (550.10–20); next, vehement accusations and personal criticism (550.21–551.7); last, final warnings (551.8–16). It is apparent that the burden of persuasive effort to change belief is in Section I and that Section II seeks commitment, mostly by exhorting and threatening the audience, admonishing them to stop the use of force. Hence, Luther has developed a two-stage argument. First, he shatters audience confidence in the validity of their position, then he affectively challenges the audience to modify their behavior.

The opening paragraph acts as a reminder of the context and a reinforcer of the categories ("necessary"/"unnecessary" and "must"/"free"), as well as the action principle *preach, don't force* that has operated thus far in the sermon series. Then a thematic sentence provides transition to Sections I and II. Luther is not merely orienting particular audience attention, but he is generating a repetitive form through these sermon openings, attenuating the idiosyncrasy of each issue while strengthening the unity and coherence of the overall scheme. He begins and ends the review—the opening paragraph—in first plural, thereby continuing the communion from the end of the Fourth Sermon. The review (547.28–548.2) is one sentence—six-and-one-half lines in German—and it itemizes the categories "necessary"/"unnecessary" [no(e)ttigk/vnno(e)ttig], as well as their examples. "Meats" has been omitted because that had been treated the day before. The latter half of the review sentence uses antithesis and amplification to recall the action principle—*preach, don't force.*

The diction and flow of the review sentence (51:88) inheres in a logical form similar to the "know"/"be armed" movement of the First Sermon's opening: "We have *heard* about the things . . . how one should *treat* them" (547.28f. [*my emphasis*]). That is to say, one's knowledge must be manifested in behavior. Luther's *preach, don't force* antithesis is applied to both categories of things. Hence, the action principle is made more emphatic than is the category of which one speaks. The same logic is used in the thematic sentence: The topic is unveiled, then the kind of consideration to be taken, which focuses the topic (away from essence of Sacrament and toward behavior in observing it). Thus "keeping" has recency for the hearers: "Let us now consider how we must observe the blessed sacrament" [*Nu(o)n wo(e)llen wir sehen / von dem hochwirdige(n) Sacrament wie man sich in dem halten soll*] (548.2f.). Let us examine the strategy in greater detail.

## SECTION I, FIRST PART: "FOOLISH LAWS" (548.3–550.8)

Luther begins with papal regulations on handling the Sacrament and labels them "foolish," reminding the audience that they know this from his preaching and should be thankful for this enlightened position. Then the preacher attacks, accusing the audience of making their own reform a foolish law! The attack is confrontational and personal. The argument showing the foolishness of papal regulations hinges on generating maximal presence through detail, so inconsistencies cannot escape notice. For example, a "pure" nun [*ein reyne Nonne*] cannot wash the altar linen unless a "pure" priest [*eynem reynen priester*] has already washed it. By *repetitio*, using the same adjective [*reyne*] and verb [*wa(e)schen*], the focus is on the inconsistency of the papal rule. "Pure" becomes ironic, especially because in the Third Sermon Luther treated priests and nuns the same with respect to their vows.[4]

A second example of foolish papal law regarding the Sacrament comes at 548.8f. It becomes clearer now that Luther is playing off verbs, distinguishing the harmless and gentle from the violent and rough: Someone "touches" [*angerürt*] the body of Christ and priests "come running" [*fürn*] "to scrape" [*zu(o) vn(d) beschnytten*] his finger. And these inconsistencies are not only vivid, but numerous (51:88): "and much more of the same sort" [*vn(d) der gleichen vil meer*]. Luther's own sympathies cannot be disguised as he utters these in tones conveying how extreme things are. Further discussing papal foolishness, at 548.9f. the speaker shifts [*Aber wen(n)*] his emphasis from papal pettiness to papal neglect. Luther holds these up against the former extremes: (1) vivid details—through adjective and rhyme [*einem nackenden pfaffen geschlaffen*]—characterize the offense, then (2) the papal response is shown vividly to be lenient, even for more serious cases (548.11f.). This latter expression of papal laxity is sharply contrasted with another papal extreme, thus producing the contrast. Then Luther returns to another papal laxity. So through various details, vivid contrast is generated, showing papal law to be inconsistent, that is, overly scrupulous with trivial matters yet careless with serious ones.

At 548.14 Luther uses the same descriptive expression ("foolish law") to rally his audience, summing up their agreement regarding "such foolish law" [solliche nerrische gesetz], which they were rightfully "against" [wider], by preaching and exposing (548.14). He began the section with "I" and now uses "we" to disclose [offenbart] his position (and that of the audience) against such inconsistent papal strictures. This content comes like a proclamation in its own right, as Luther (unlike Nathan) reminds his audience what they strongly hold as evangelical truth. This is a celebration of their "great knowledge" [grosse erkentnyß] (548.18). He will spend much of this section and the next on "touch with hands," but now Luther emphasizes the lofty import of the proclamation. However (lest we forget Nathan), there is not as much compliment as implicit warning—the audience's "great knowledge" is pitted against a great lack because others are not so enlightened (51:89): "You should give thanks to God that you have come to such clear knowledge, which many great men have lacked" [in dem solt jr ja gotte dancken / das jr in solche grosse enkentnyß kom(m)en seyt / das vilen grossen leüten gemangelt hat] (548.17–19).

Luther initiates a confrontation, exploiting his already-established communion, by shifting to direct accusations at 548.19. Thus, the Nathanian strategy: (1) 16 lines of leading the audience to celebrate now shifts to (2) 17 lines of confrontation and exhortation. The accusation begins with comparison ("become as foolish as the pope" [gleich so nerrisch als der Bapsts], then is delineated, showing that Wittenberger Sacrament reforms violated the "must"/"free" categories (51:89): "you think that a person must touch the sacrament with his hands" [jr meynet es mu(o)ß seyn / das man das sacrament mit den hende(n) angreiffe] (548.20f.). We recall, of course, that Luther did not begin this discussion of the Sacrament by categorizing it as a "must" or a "free," but he started with particular regulations, which every listener would readily agree were "foolish." The accusation now hinges on how convinced the audience is that their stampede to the Sacrament was as wrong as their being denied access to it. That proof will follow later (543.7f.). Here Luther wants to attack the motives of the audience, generating proper fear and repentance before God. The accusation at 549.7ff. plays on the terms "hands" and "handled," between literal object and figurative action. It culminates in a fearful hyperbole whose verb ("struck") spins off the earlier verb ("handled"), initiating the dread that something has been started that is now out of control. This must have startled the audience, and Luther holds audience attention with that affect by directing the focus toward their error (not the pope's). He does this with antithesis: "the other, maybe, but this [Aber das], No."

Now (548.24) the "blessed sacrament" (earlier at 548.3) begins to become more present as Luther supports his speculation about the severity of the Wittenbergers' offense by referring to God, an *exemplum* that is highly demonstrative. The reference to God's displeasure actually forms an enthymeme, ending with "you have made a compulsion out of it" [*jr ein gezwang darauß habt gemacht*] (548.25f.). This confrontation ("you" occurs 11 times in 12-and-one-half lines [548.17–549.1]) started with the audience's correct knowledge, shifted to their false understanding and false motives or desires, then discussed risking consequences from God. Now at 548.26 Luther makes a personal threat, one he has not used since the First Sermon. He threatens with the possibility of leaving Wittenberg, and he heightens the presence of the threat through comparisons, implying that the audience and he are on opposite sides of a "battle."

At 549.2–6 Luther begins to desist from confrontation while still striking a blow. He compares Wittenberger "handling" of the Sacrament to the actions of Herod and Pilate. This is Luther at his brutal best before an audience. Sarcasm and vivid crescendo bring this first part of the section to its conclusion (51:89): "[If] you want to show you are *good Christians* . . . and have fame around the world? Then are Herod and Pilate the *very best* Christians: I mean, [because] *they* have the body of Christ *truly handled* (549.2–5 [*my literal translation and emphasis*]). The sarcasm starts with rhetorical question and climaxes with *antastet*, a pivotal, ironic verb that means "touch" or "violate." What follows is sober and marks the most blatant "laxity" of all: "when they had him nailed to the cross and put to death" [*wen(n) sie haben yn lassen anß creütz schlagen vnd to(e)dten*] (549.5f.). Luther's previous use of *schlagen* (548.24) now becomes more meaningful because he knew he would later (here, at 549.5) use the crucifixion imagery. The crescendo of feeling that is sustained through a dozen lines, then, is followed by a compression of thought, beginning with the endearing signal *Neyn, lieben freünde*.

The concluding thought is precise, but it broadens the previous discussion to a major, acceptable premise. Note the significant scriptural allusions in the terms "kingdom of God," "external things," and "faith" that surround their antithesis ("touch or feel") and that are not merely synonymous but accumulative (51:89): "The kingdom of God does not consist in outward things, which can be touched or perceived, but in faith [Luke 17:20; Rom. 14:17; I Cor. 4:20]" [*Das reych gottes stehet nit in eüsserlichen dingen das mann greyffen oder empfinden kan / sond(ern) jm glaübe(n)*] (549.6–7). So Luther rescues his audience at their point of despair by directing their attention to faith, the element of hope for relief.

## SECTION I, SECOND PART: TESTING THE ASSERTION

Luther's previous strategy becomes more apparent here because he openly takes up the issue that traditionally had been a hotly contested theological issue— Jesus' "institution" of the Lord's Supper. An *evangelische* position, though by no means a matter of consensus among them,[5] tended to regard the words of Jesus in Matt 26:26 ("Take, eat, this is my body") as authoritative for all believers, not only for priests. While much debate raged over Jesus' declaration [*Hoc est corpus meum* (Vulgate)]—its meaning and implications—Luther focuses on Jesus' first command ("Take") because that action is what he uses to praise and blame, mostly to blame![6] All the physical "touching" verbs Luther used in discussing papal foolishness have prepared the audience for blaming these mistakes on excessive literalism. We will now observe how Luther accomplishes this.

Luther grants his audience a chance to collect their thoughts, allowing objections to be expressed. He uses dialogue to give the *prolepsis* presence, and he employs second singular for concreteness, as if taking on a single interlocutor who is acting as spokesperson. The doubled objection is concise (51:89): "we live and we ought to live *according to the Scriptures*" (*my emphasis*). It sounds sententious. The participle *der geschrifft* allows a gradual unfolding of the argument's force, more than would a solitary Scripture citation; "according to the Scriptures" is a battle cry, a claim of broad consensus. That Luther has inaugurated a proleptic debate is clear from 549.10: "The answer is this." His response, in first singular, is careful and conditional because he liberally acknowledges historical agreement and permissable application, but he is loathe to compel others—what might seem a frustrating, even contradictory, position. Staying with the "I," Luther maintains two certainties (confidence and resolve) while conceding little. As has been his habit, the preacher then reveals his motivation: *vrsach: wen(n) der teüffel . . .* (549.13). The devil's appearing, then, accounts for the predicament. Further, we quickly see that "I" is not uniquely Luther but has broader application, parenthetically, "when he really pushes us to the wall" [*als er vns genach su(o)chtt*]. Luther allows the devil to speak, intensifying the dilemma in which the whole audience, represented by *Ich*, is caught. The dilemma is verbalized in question form precisely, "Where have you in the Scriptures read . . . ?" So Luther has satisfied some frustration by hinting that he is not advocating that one back down from truth; rather, we begin to realize the ambiguity of the audience's understanding of the "truth," thus, the invalidity of the action based upon it.

At this point it sounds as if Luther is nit-picking, but he quickly shows there is further challenge coming. His diction shows him standing with his audience (51:89): "How will I support and defend it, yea, how will I respond to him [the devil] . . . ?" The doubled verbs connote ineptitude [*beweren vnd erhalten*] against those verbs of the devil's fierce assault (549.15). The devil's case is shown to be a problem for the philological point Luther has, as an instance of living "according to the Scriptures," generated on behalf of the Wittenbergers. The devil claims, through concrete examples, that "take" can have other meanings: "that 'take' does not mean to receive with the hands only, but also to convey to ourselves in other ways" (meaning the traditional placing on the communicant's tongue by the priest) [*Das nemen nicht alleyne mit den hende(n) empfahen heyst / sonder durch ander weyse*] (549.17f.). Then the devil speaks again (51:89), this time with a subtle, but condescending, epithet ("Listen to this, my good fellow" [*ho(e)restu gesell*]) that begins a question that raises counterexamples of the word "take," followed by a confrontation that demands an admission. Luther then expresses the admission in his own words; for the consideration of the audience he does this. We have seen this sort of approach before—acting out a dialogue that portrays the progression of the argumentation, which gives the audience freedom to "listen in," to observe, rather than to feel put on the spot.[7] The devil keeps it up, quoting a Scripture passage in Latin (Luke 7:16), then in German translation. So far no texts are cited, yet Luther admits the devil has him because the quotations from Scripture (not the devil's authority) stop him. Synonymous verbs and the parenthetic *correctio* (at 549.25f.) lend finality to the admission, ending with Luther's restated conclusion that the word "take" has wider uses in Scripture.

At 549.27 Luther uses the preceding *prolepsis* to exhort the audience to apply their new belief about the Sacrament to what he has been trying to teach regarding liberty and the weak. Summoning closer attention and beginning with another endearment [*Darumb lieben freünde*], the initial conclusion draws its strength from the presence of the devil's threat. Note (51:90) the theme of vigilance to the devil's challenge, vigilance that comes only from knowledge of Scripture—its clarity (the First Sermon) and also its complexities (the Third Sermon): "we must be on firm ground, if we are to withstand the devil's attack" [*müssen wir auff eyne(n) gewissen grundt stan das wir vor des teüffels anlaüff besteen mügen*] (549.28f.).[8] Luther then pleads with his audience through rhetorical question, clarifying how the Sacrament fits into the "liberty" and "weak" themes. His stance is direct, coming in second singular, repeatedly driving itself upon the hearer as the rhythm builds, then tapers. The speaker has managed to redirect his hearers' thoughts to the sententious conclusion about being good Christians (548.21) through his use of "weak in faith" [*schwachglaübigen*] (549.33). Section II will pursue the broader plea for Christian witness to others.

The final part of Section I (550.2–8), in which Luther exhorts his audience to abandon their reforms, consists of two pairs of injunctives in the pattern: imperative, exhortative; imperative, exhortative. The diction is sober and elevated, but the tone is urgent. The first imperative looks back, drawing a broad conclusion of high standards, a conclusion that applies to all the topics of these sermons. The first imperative employs a new term, "new practices" [*neüwckeyt*], making (1) preaching the basis for reforms and (2) understanding the measuring stick for preaching's success (51:90): "unless the gospel has first been thoroughly preached and understood, as it has been among you" [*das Eua(n)gelium sey dan(n) durch vnd durch geprediget vnd erkant. Wie eüch geschehen ist*] (550.3f.). The polysyndeton indicates how exact Luther's terms are, and the dependent clause invites agreement. The exhortation, then, points forward ("On this account, dear friends, let us . . ." [*der wegen. Lieben freunde last vns seüberlich vnnd weyßlich*]), specifying through accumulation the broad terms of Christian conduct.[9] Luther has made the crucial stipulation that the Wittenbergers, especially those who can identify themselves as enlightened (as he has been trying to compliment them into believing), must consider themselves the strong. It is others who do not yet *thoroughly* understand (not because they are stubborn but because they have not been preached to by the Wittenbergers) who are weak. The weak are not to be forsaken or run over; they are to be helped.

## Section II (550.10–551.16)

This section follows an emotional curve similar to Section I: Begin with teaching and points of agreement, then move into disagreement and indictment. Throughout the section, especially throughout the latter parts, Luther is careful to blend sarcasm and solidarity. After bringing his audience through an indictment of "handling" the Sacrament, he now clarifies his position on "both kinds," conceding an historical point but disallowing use of force. Through accumulation he builds a case for the role and results of the alternative—preaching. Following that, Luther recounts some Wittenberger activities with which he is unhappy as a means of generating greater presence for both the value and urgent need of preaching, as well as the consequences from its lack. This section concludes with additional instructions. The entire section refers strongly to the public consequences of Sacrament observance, much more than did Section I.

In the first part (550.10–20), the speaker-to-audience stance is somewhat remote, with nearly everything in third-person assertive. Luther is teaching a distinction. The premise that one should observe the Sacrament in both kinds is the concession granted in the dependent clause of "Although I hold that it is necessary that the sacrament should be received in both kinds" (remembering that Luther has already "loosened" the semantic meaning of *nemen* ["take"]). We observed at the outset of this sermon that Luther was careful to avoid bracketing the sacramental observance within either the "must" and "necessary" or "free" and "unnecessary" categories. Now we see that this is because he continually has framed the matter in concessional terms. He does this again, granting provisional "necessary" [*von no(e)tten*] status to the "Lord's institution" [*auffsetzu(n)ge des herrn*], drawing his antithetical line at "force" (direct and indirect). The alternative Luther urges is "preaching the Word," which is expressed through amplification: "promote and practice and preach" [*treyben / vbe(n) vnd predige(n)*] (550.13f.). Then Luther amplifies the presence of preaching's results, visualizing for the audience not only the power of the Word, but also the responsibility that freedom brings to the hearers. This responsibility suggests a tension between preaching and the "understanding" stipulation: "be . . . preached . . . and *understood*" (550.4 [*my emphasis*]), a tension that Luther later needs to resolve. Notice the doublet of consequences (51:90)—"result and execution"—and the "everyone" theme (reminiscent of the opening of the First Sermon): "then afterwards leave the result and execution of it entirely to the Word, giving everyone his freedom in this matter" [*dannocht darnach / die folge vn(d) treybu(n)ge dem worte heym gebe(n) oder stellen / vn(d) jederman hierjnnen frey lassen*] (550.14f.). Another antithesis follows, and Luther defines[10] this sacramental observance—when it is forced upon people—with epithetical terms: "an outward work and a hypocrisy" [*ein eüsserlich werck darauß vn(d) gleißnerey*] (550.16). We recall, now, that those terms are not of the "kingdom of God" [*reych gottes*] (549.6), and Luther widens the disparity more by interpreting the devil's wishes. To this point, then, Luther has presented and expanded the distinction between his way and the way of the Wittenbergers.

The final lines of this part are built around another antithesis. Luther has alternated between points of the *preach, don't force* antithesis several times: *Preach . . . don't force . . . preach*. The case here for the Word (51:90) is a mini-*narratio*. First, it contains a brief *correctio* ("free course and is not bound" [*frey lest vnd bünde es an ein werck*]), then a carefully, approvingly spoken *gradatio*: "takes hold of one today and sinks into his heart, tomorrow it touches another, and so on" [*so ru(o)rt es heüte den(n) vn(d) felt jm jns hertze / morge(n) dem andern vn(d) so fürhien*] (550.18f.). The case for preaching the Word concludes, drifting aloft in a mood of admiration and awe. The synonymous, sibilant doublet "quietly and soberly" [*still zu(o) vnd seüberlich*] (550.19) describes the work of preaching, corresponding to the earlier, accumulative "soberly and wisely" [*seüberlich vnnd weyßlich*] (550.5) that described the general activities and posture [*handeln*] called for. Here, then, Luther uses doubled adverbs to increase presence. Even the consonance of the first German clause's last four words complements the smoothness, assurance, and mystique of the statement (51:90): "Thus *quietly and soberly* it does its work, and no one will know how it all came about" [*so geet es feyn still zu(o) vnd seüberlich. Vnd es wirdt nyemandts gewar / wie es dan(n) angefangen wa(e)re / vnd ho(e)rtte es gantz gerne*] (550.19–21). Obviously, that prolonged pause (a full stop not properly indicated in the translation), coupled with a slowed pace and softening voice, would depict God's mysterious power at work behind the scenes.

In the second part (550.20–551.7) Luther picks up that quiet note ("no one will know") with his revelation that he was originally glad when hearing that the Sacrament in both kinds was being taken by some. Then he begins several confrontational assertions that, in second plural, contrast Wittenberger hasty action with what might have been. Notice how Luther pins "you" at the vortex of these positions (51:91): "[T]o receive the sacrament in both kinds. You should have allowed it to remain thus and not forced it into a law" [*das Sacrament in beyderley gestalt zunemen in dem braüch ha(e)ttet jrs so(e)llen lassen bleyben / jn keyn ordnunge gezwunge(n) habe(n)*] (550.22f.). Luther will keep the pressure on, intensifying the presence of the frenzy of which he accuses the Wittenbergers. Luther is drawing a wide disparity between what they did (hasty force) and what they should have done (patient preaching).

The curtain is suddenly dropped on this scene as Luther tersely jolts his audience to attention: "Thus will you fail, dear friends!" [*Do werd jr felen liebe(n) freünde*] (550.25).[11] Then he hurls a stinging rebuke, a real scolding. In all, our preacher makes three rebukes in this section. Two are conditional threats ("if . . . then"), and the third is an insult from others. The first rebuke pits Wittenberger motivation against Luther's own assessment. Instead of becoming "good Christians above [*vor*][12] all others" (550.26), they become "to me bad Christians" [*schlecht Christen*] (550.27f.). Luther then intensifies that personal assessment with further insult (51:91): "even a sow could be a Christian, for she has a big enough snout to receive the sacrament outwardly." The general effect has to be shock. Insult of this kind the Wittenbergers heard in the First Sermon ("even an ass can intone the lessons").[13] But these are not divisive, mean-spirited attacks because we see Luther follow the "sow" comparison with his measured instruction: "We must deal soberly with such high things" [*derhalbe(n) thut wol vn(d) seüberlich in den hochen sache(n)*] (550.30). Significantly, another *Lieben freunde* precedes the instruction (the previous endearment was only six lines earlier), and Luther warns his audience that their relationship with him is in jeopardy. Holding them to a choice, Luther thinks about consequences—his regret at having preached "one sermon here"—that show the conflict between "you" and "I." In particular, the 13 lines of 550.20–551.1 contain nine "I" pronouns and 10 "you" pronouns, not to mention the two endearments! He repeats the charge made earlier that this is the most serious offense of all Wittenberger problems, and his frequent references to this have been both from God's vantage and his own. The twice-used "mockery" [*schympff, schimpffen*] (550.6, 31) clearly reveals Luther's strong feelings about this matter because he condemns "mockery" more strongly than he had "downright idolatry" (at 543.30).[14]

Luther's final attempt to shame the audience is to show them they are even objects of public ridicule (51:91): "Those other things could have been overlooked. But this cannot be, for *you* have made it too bad . . ." (*my translation and emphasis*). Luther makes this present through "speaking in character," as town gossip, something surely embarrassing if not horrifying to the Germans of Wittenberg. He has previously mentioned other cities: In the Fourth Sermon, he mentions Halle, the site of Albrecht's relics; in the Third Sermon, Luther mentions Nuremburg, where the Imperial Council of Regency had convened. Luther compared Wittenberg to biblical Capernaum (the First Sermon). So the preacher often assaults his audience's pride. The gossip is related in a sarcastic tone, and it fulfills Luther's earlier warning of "mockery." One can easily imagine the mocking voice as Luther assumes the role of a wagging tongue: *ja zu(o)Wittenberg . . . .* The gossip finished, the speaker returns, restoring communion as he brings near the objects of concern—the weak. Note Luther's accumulating synonyms of sympathy ("weak and well-meaning people" [*die schwache gu(o)thertzigen menschen*])[15] while he reminds his audience of the responsibility of their position. Even here, we observe Luther returning to first plural in a thoughtful, poignant moment. Not that he has calmed down all that much, but actual harm to the weak is far worse than what some are saying. The former is unnerving; the latter is cause for grief.

In the third part (551.8–16), a final warning comes with a last-straw proviso. Luther both warns and stipulates, granting "permission" to handle the Sacrament. He distinguishes between private permission and public refraining (551.9).[16] How sarcastic Luther is depends in part on what variant reading we accept. The Amer-

ican Edition reads "so smart" and for *greyff es / das es genu(o)g hette*: "let him handle it to his heart's content."[17] The sarcasm might well be moderate since it turns
into more sincere, yet strong, confrontation—offense to "our brothers . . ."—but
offered in first person! Everyone shares this loss. The pervasiveness of the loss can
further be seen in the four first plural pronouns in the two lines of 551.11–13.
Certainly the asyndeton amplifies the presence of those objects of concern
("brothers, sisters, and neighbors" [*brüdern schwestern vn(d) nachpaüern*]), and
hyperbole magnifies their feelings (51:91): "so angry with us they are ready to kill
us!" (551.13). If Luther *is* overstating the seriousness of the matter, he is careful to
side *with* the Wittenbergers.

Looking back, we realize this sermon is unique because it is the first in the
series to develop only one issue—the Sacrament. All previous sermons have developed general principles and/or applied them to specific issues, usually more than
one issue. Because in the earlier sermons instruction, clarification, and exhortation
had to be distributed for each issue, the affect was more widely distributed. After
carefully setting in place both issues and principles, Luther "lets it all out" in this
sermon. He blasts supposed scriptural support (via the devil); he charges his audience with their greatest offense; he claims the most serious harm done. And all
along the problems could have been avoided, he avers, had the Wittenbergers
used the alternative—preaching. Luther's humiliating insults are stronger in this
sermon—"even a sow"—than in the First Sermon ("an ass can almost intone").
His claims of being hurt—his thought of leaving and his feelings of regret—are
more focused. Luther emotionally exhausts himself and his audience in this sermon.

Yet he alternates anxiety and relief, and he blends communion with teaching.
Moreover, the structural moves do not indicate that Luther is losing control. One
suspects the strategy would have failed had it not been properly set up in the previous sermons. The prophet Nathan condemned the king's sin and proclaimed his
sentence. John the Baptist warned and rebuked a segment of his audience (specifically, the scribes and Pharisees), distinguishing between genuine and counterfeit
repentance for the entire audience. This is more a conflict than a contest; here is
a leader warning the troops that they are not only on maneuvers. Luther provides
a powerful example of biblical preaching.

# THE SIXTH SERMON (LW 51:92–95; LSTA 2:551–54)

The Sixth Sermon brings respite from the intense personal confrontation
Luther generated in the Fifth Sermon, confrontation that is resumed in the short
Seventh Sermon. Whereas a day earlier he had focused on how believers were
behaving at the Sacrament—especially how Wittenbergers had participated in
and administered innovations in sacramental observance—the Sixth Sermon
addresses *individual* thinking and decisions. As speaker, then, the prosecutor has
yielded to the teacher-advisor. Today's message resembles that of the Second Ser-

mon, especially in its more didactic, controlled stance, as exemplified by a complete absence of endearments (the Second Sermon had only one) and much less
use of first- and second-person constructions. The third singular assertive pre-
vails, and when Luther does use the second person, he is not scolding; rather, he
maintains a close communion with his audience, vigorously praising their faith.
When using the first person, Luther is usually standing with his audience (first
plural) or offering a concrete instance for them (first singular). The message contains no chastisements at all. Instead,  the sermon is much closer to a *lutherische*
theology (Gospel and faith) than any of the other sermons in this series. This one
time, then, we do not witness Luther in an adversarial relationship with his audience.

Yet the preacher is still dealing with an issue of controversy—namely, the
Sacrament, which is, for Luther, the most important issue. He has previously disposed of the pragmatics of the problem; he must here do the teaching necessary
for the confrontation yet to come, one concerning "love." Just as castigating the
failures of others' children is far easier than providing guidance for one's own, so
preaching "faith" and "love" takes creative strategy and energy. Hence, Luther
employs a patient, encouraging role. This sermon is intense in its content, replete
with expectation and fulfillment of audience understanding. The next day Luther
will again confront!

Although its nine concise paragraphs in the modern editions suggest a clearly discernible design, the actual structure of the sermon proves more subtle than
the typography suggests. Perhaps this is in part because it is a more unified sermon than the previous several sermons, which have had topical divisions often
cutting the message into two separable parts. Noteworthy is Luther's refusal to
rigidly separate his discussion of Sacrament observance into two distinct sections.
Although he clearly signals his intention of discussing "how [*wie*] to receive" and
"who [*welche*] should receive," there is no easily discernible break between these
parts. As it happens, Luther sees the two parts as indivisible, and he frequently
implicates the "who" when discussing the "how." Indeed, there is also a turning
back on itself in the sermon, the speaker not completely disposing of a topic but
always returning to it. This is fairly common in other sermons as Luther reintro-
duces themes from the preceding ones. A rough outline that attempts to discern
functional, as well as temporal, structure would be: Introduction— (551.19–22);
Section I—"How to receive" (551.22–553.5); Section II—"Who should receive"
(553.5–554.19).

In greater detail, Section I first dispatches "outward" reception as inferior
(551.22–32). Then, Luther shows "inner" reception occurring in faith
(551.32–552.18). There are three moves to this argument: (A) Faith authenticates
reception as a sign of God's acceptance (551.32–552.6). (B) Faith trusts Christ
(552.6–12). (C) Faith empowers believers (552.12–18). As we shall see, these three
moves are by no means laid out so neatly by the speaker. After this argument
Luther makes "outward" reception present through a *prolepsis*, arguing that papal

forcing of sacramental observance is an example of outward reception (552.18–32). Luther then celebrates the victory found in inner reception (552.32–553.5). In Section II Luther argues that the one who is "prepared" through suffering is the one who should receive the Sacrament. When "unprepared," one should abstain. This argument also develops in three stages. Then, in drawing the sermon toward a close, Luther gives this claim presence through an example from Scripture (554.7–15).

## INTRODUCTION (551.19–22)

These two sentences constitute an orientation and a partition for the sermon. The orientation starts in the now familiar formula, "You have now heard."[18] We can see three stages of focus in the orientation. First, a reminder of the "chief things" [*von dem haüptstück*]; then, the extent of progress therein ("up to the . . . of sacrament, where we now are"); last, the orientation subtly sets up an important perspective on the Sacrament—the "receiving" of it [*empfahen*]. This orientation becomes clearer as Luther signals the direction he will go along this line ("yet further" [*noch weytter*]) with his partition at 551.20. He points his audience in two directions: (1) "How [*wie*] we should conduct [*halten*] ourselves" and (2) "Who [*welche*] are permitted [*geschickt sein*] to the reception [*empfahung*]." A third possible direction—"Who belongs there" [*darzu(o) geho(e)ren*]—is, on first hearing, ambiguous because we cannot be sure whether "belongs" is synonymous with "permitted," or an amplification of it, or to be distinguished from it. Later it becomes more clear that we want to take as signals of direction only the first two key terms: "how" and "who." Luther's major purpose in this sermon is to encourage faithful preparations for all believers in receiving the Sacrament. The audience's persistent concern with prerequisites for receiving the Sacrament, which Luther does address, especially with papal laws, becomes engulfed and transformed by a shift from "outward" standards—that is, as judged by observers—but also "outward" in the general, physical sense (for example, "hands"). Thus the grammar of Luther's thematic sentence, which I am calling a partition, shows an unwrapping, a going further and deeper along the same—not a different—direction: "yet further, how . . . even who is permitted and belongs."[19]

One more thing may be important in the introduction. Luther has begun his discussion of Sacrament with the words "receiving" [*empfahen*] and "reception" [*empfahunge*]. This is a subtle, but significant, shift from the previous day's preoccupation with "taking" [*nemen*]. In the Fifth Sermon, he began with "taking" and its resultant disturbances; he attacked the scriptural support for an overly literal and single-minded translation that "take" has to mean "with the hands." Luther used the verb "receive" [*empfahen*] in the Fifth Sermon (at 549.17). In this Sixth Sermon he seeks to fulfill the expectation that the *sententia* suggested (51:89): "The kingdom of God [resides] . . . not in externals one can grasp [*greyffen*] or perceive [*empfinden*] but in faith." Although the audience would, at this point, have little reason for attaching great significance to "receive," the emergence in the opening line is important in establishing expectation. The predominant way Luther proceeds is by repetitive form, generated early in this sermon; eight times "receive" is used in the first 15 lines!

This first section, which develops the "*how* one should receive," cannot be separated from the "*who* should receive." The broad distinction between "outward" and "inner" reception makes clear that the "how" issue is not a matter of ritual, procedure, or protocol. Indeed, the "how" is a matter of faith and is thus intrinsically wedded to the "who" issue. In fact, Luther nowhere says he will *first* develop the "how," and we could make a case that "how to partake" is a central focus of the second section and not the first. Or we could see Section I as a *definitio* of inner, faithful "reception" and Section II as an operationalizing of that for the believer—that is, Section I: Theory of Reception; Section II: Practice of Reception. However we segment this sermon, Luther does seek to respond to the two aspects of the same issue.

## SECTION I (551.22–553.5)

The dominant strategy of the sermon, especially in this section ("how"), is to distinguish "outward" from "inner" reception. This distinction carries over in Section II ("who") as one of "unprepared"/"prepared." In 551.22–32 Luther announces this distinction as important [*ein grosse vnterscheyd*]. Previous inklings of "outward" [*eüsserliche*] occurred in the Second Sermon where Luther claimed that force produces hypocrisy and sham.[20] Here he distinguishes "outward" from "inner" in several ways, showing the former to be inferior. Were we not to hear more about "outward" later (regarding papal laws), we might consider this strategy a variant of an *expeditio*. However, for Luther, distinctions—especially important ones—cannot be abandoned or dispatched; rather, they need to be ever close at hand. So he amplifies both terms, respectively, first (51:92) with an amplifier and a doublet each (". . . inner and spiritual reception. Bodily and outward reception . . ."). Then—and I am disrupting his syntax—Luther makes "outward" reception present by the verbal action portrayed in "that in which a man receives with his mouth the body of Christ and his blood" [*wen(n) ein mensch den leichnam Christi vnd sein plu(o)t mit seim munde empfacht*] (551.25f.). The nouns are all anatomical; hence, they develop a case for "outward" to be characterized by "body." Even "body and blood of Christ" assists in this eventually pejorative characterization, starting its negative descent with "by mouth." Luther's case picks up logical force in the next clause by showing what outward reception lacks. Indeed, "without faith and love" [*on glaübe(n) vnd liebe*] forces back on the earlier "with his mouth" [*mit seim munde*] a gluttonous or animalistic connotation. Luther also shows the ubiquity of such reception; hence, there is an ever-present danger and need for vigilance: "any man can receive the sacrament in this way."

Luther next freezes this commonness (or carelessness) with his terse, pivotal assertion (51:92), "But this does not make a man a Christian" [*die macht aber keyn Christen mensch nit*] (551.28). This assertion should catch its hearers because it challenges the *haüptstück* to be those of a Christian and not only common things.[21] Further, it corresponds to the previous remark that "even a sow could be a Christian . . . outwardly." The negative characterization of "outward" reception gets more reinforcing presence when Luther uses the mouse [*die mauß*] to jolt his audience into thinking about the locus of importance in receiving the Sacrament. His use of the vivid, also somewhat phonemically consonant [*munde, machten, menschen, mauß*], "mouse" is mostly affective; it evokes shame, yet it is humorous, less insulting than "ass" or "sow." Notice how (51:92) Luther uses adverbs to slow the action, alerting the audience to see the similarities between human and animal motion ("for it [mouse] can the bread also eat, can also truly, from the cup drink" [*my translation*]). The slowing role is clear in the next terse sentence—"It is such a simple thing to do" [*Ey das ist ein schlecht ding*] (551.30)—a locution bringing no new content but prompting backward reflection.

This characterization of the reception of the Sacrament—as purely physical *motion*—has been gentle and thought-provoking.[22] Luther's purpose was not to condemn, but to shift the focus from external "touching" to a new focus. That purpose becomes clear now where a turn [*Aber die*] from the "outward" shows that there is more, in a statement of expectation that leads into the next argument. Note the asyndeton that drives, with hammer blows, the distinctiveness of what is to come. This is a sentence of major importance for the rest of this sermon and the next sermon (51:92): "But the true, inner, spiritual reception is a very different thing, for it consists in the right use of the sacrament and its fruits" [*Aber die jnnerliche geystliche rechtliche empfahunge / ist vil ein ander ding / wan(n) sie steet in der vbunge / gebraüch vnd früchten*] (551.30–32). *Ein ander ding* is, of course, a counterpoint because the speaker rhythmically juxtaposes two parallel expressions—"a simple thing" [*ein schlecht ding*] and "a very different thing" [*ein ander ding*]—in rhythm, each coming at the end of its clause. Luther thus closes one door and opens another.

After establishing "outward" reception as a foil against which he has introduced "inner" reception, Luther now builds a case for this "inner" reception throughout the rest of the section. He does this in several phases, for which the controlling *distributio* is 551.32f.: "I would say in the first place that this reception occurs in faith and is inward and will have Christ" [*Zum ersten wol wir sagen die geschicht in dem glaüben / vn(d) ist jnnerlich / vnd wirt Christum haben*]. This argument portrays "faith," a controlling term that appears no less than nine times in the next 19 lines, (1) as having already entered as an "inner" thing, which is further contrasted to "outward" (551.32–552.6); (2) as looking to Christ (552.6–12); (3) as empowering the believer (552.12–18). The argument in general amplifies the opposition "outward"/"inner." More subtly, the argument portrays "faith" by rotating audience attention inward, upward, and back again to self. The first shift—inward—moves one "into" the faith relationship. The second and third shifts alternate perspectives from within. The first shift is an amplified antithesis in which Luther concedes a certain signifying function to the Sacrament. It distinguishes—that is, shows—that Christians are different from others. The second shift is an *accumulatio* on "faith" as trust in Christ. Here Luther articulates what God has done, thus pointing attention to Christ, but from the self's vantage. Notice how Luther generates celebratory audience communion in a strong use of first plurals. In five lines there are seven pronouns; the first three are *wir* ("what we do"), and the last four are *vns* or *vnser* ("what *we* receive"). At 552.11f. the paraphrasis ("He who has this faith") not only encapsulates the previous content of faith, but it foreshadows the emphasis in Section II ("who"). Hence, Luther has fashioned a *definitio* of faith, which he then begins to explore. So besides didactically proposing faithful (inner) reception, Luther is promoting and encouraging it.

A further ramification of the benefits of faith, begun with the "we"/"our" above, is God's protection. This shows God's empowering of the believer in the face of the feared trio: *teüffel / hell / noch sünde* (552.12) These entities of evil are Luther's way of talking big, of bragging or scaring. These terms form a circumscribing, though more by expanding than by delimiting.[23] He uses these terms—which are ever-present realities to him and which he speaks of frequently—to temper the audience's enthusiasm, which is generated by all those first plurals. These terms strengthen the value and applicability of faith by showing to the believer its vulnerability and strength. I say "believer" because Luther shifts to first singular in 552.12ff., and we see at 552.15 ("us in Christ") that he means *any* believer. The strong claim—that none of the dreaded trio can harm one—gives Luther the opportunity to set up his support through the interrogative *Warumb*. What follows, then, is the premise of the enthymeme. Notice the first-person pronouns (51:92f.):

> Because God is his protector and defender. And when *I* have this faith, then *I* am certain God is fighting for *me*. *I* can defy the devil, death, hell, and sin, and all the harm with which they threaten *me*. (*my emphasis*) [*dann gott ist sein schütz vnd rückhalter / vnd wenn ich sollichen glaüben habe / dafür ichs gewyß halte / gott streyttet für mich / tru(o)tz dem teüffel / todt / helle / vnd sünde / das sie mir schaden.*] (552.12–15)

As the argument continues, faith is again made more present by Luther's boasting assertions that describe both negatively (note the rhyme and the use of "grasp")—"no man can describe or grasp in words" [*keyn mensch mit worten ergreyffen noch erreyche(n) kan*] (552.16)—and positively—"This is the great, inestimable treasure" [*das ist der hoche vberschwencklich schatz*] (552.15). The amount of morphemic rhyme in this exciting description is striking—similar thoughts in similar sounds. Luther then narrows the focus with antithesis—a look ahead ("who"), as well as back ("outward"). He has frozen attention at *glaüb*, then suspensefully holds attention there for the next argument. Notice the inverted syntax (subject in final position) and the excluding modifiers ("only" and "alone") in the first clause (51:93): "Only faith can take hold of the heart, and not every one has such faith [2 Thess.

3:2]" [*auch kans hertze ergreyffen alleyn der glaüb / vn(d) den glaübe(n) habe(n) ja nit alle leüte*] (552.17).

At 552.18 Luther initiates ("therefore" [*daru(m)b*]) a *ratiocinatio*, arguing that a law requiring Sacrament observance is doomed to fail because it violates the very standard of Sacrament for which he has been arguing: the inner reception of faith. The *ratiocinatio* thus functions as a *prolepsis*, testing the validity of the previous claim that "only faith can take hold of the heart, and not everyone has this faith" (552.17). Yet Luther is not questioning his own claim; rather, he stands with his audience in seeking agreement against the pope's laws. His assertion at 552.19 ("the most holy father, the pope") is sarcastic, appearing to attribute *allerheiligst* to the pope. Since he has not so reverently spoken of *bapst* anywhere else in these sermons, we suspect sarcasm. Moreover, Luther uses "holy" three times in this argument, concluding with the last use (551.4) where he points out that the law failed to produce holiness! Thus "the most holy father" makes a proclamation for "holy Eastertide" that ends up causing great sin among "[those who] want to be most holy" [*am aller heiligsten sein wollen*]. Luther further articulates his and the audience's feelings for the papal laws with his epithets: "fool's commandment" [*nerrische(n) gesetze(n)*] (552.19), "foolish law" [*nerrisch gebot*] (552.22), and "unChristian command" [*vnchristliche(n) gebots*] (552.27). He uses the rhetorical question to orchestrate expectation, then he responds to it with a concise enthymeme that ends in a *sententia* (51:93):

> Is not this a foolish law which the pope has set up? Why? Because we are not all alike; we do not all have equal faith; the faith of one is stronger than that of another. [*ist d(as) nit ein nerrisch gebot / durch den bapst vffgericht waru(m)b? wen(n) wir sind nit alle gleich / habe(n) auch nit alle gleich eine(n) glaübe(n) / dan(n) einer hat eine(n) starcke(n) glaube(n) den(n) d(er) ander.*] (552.22–24)

Luther now capitalizes further on his audience's disposition, and the emotional peak of this proleptic argument comes soon after those now familiar verbs "drive and force" [*zwinge(n) vn(d) tringe(n)*] (552.28). He turns to *gradatio*, developing a crescendo of condemnation: "And if [all] robbery, usury, unchastity, and all sins were cast upon one big heap" [*wen(n) auch alle rauberey / wu(o)cherey / vnkeüscheit vn(d) alle sünd vff ein haüffen gereche(n)t würde*] (552.28). The argument ends with Luther's restatement of the claim he began with ("Only faith can . . . and not every one has such faith,"). This time, however, he puts it more concretely and more boldly: "The pope can see into no one's heart to see whether he has faith or not." That may rally enthusiasm, but it also involves compromising some personal responsibility, and Luther wants his audience to feel this tension. At 552.32–553.5 he picks up that tension and seeks to resolve it by renewing the confidence created earlier where he used the first singular in a display of certitude. Using second singular, Luther exhorts the believer with more of that militaristic imagery, using *sermocinatio* (dialogue) to heighten the presence of God's offered protection.

Many of Luther's previous uses of dialogue have already been designed to heighten the devil's presence. Here Luther names all the enemies twice more. The first time (553.1) the asyndetic list comes from the lips of God, who speaks to the believer. The second list (553.4) comes from Luther's own lips. So, in all, he has named the enemies four times in this sermon: "devil, hell nor sin" (552.12); "devil, death, hell and sin" (552.14); "devil, death, sin and hell and all creation" (553.1f.); "devil, hell, sin nor death" (553.4). A repetitive form is generated, and these occurrences resound not so much because they imply a need to be vigilant, but because they appear boldly confident! In fact, looking at Luther's second singular and first singular pronouns (six and five, respectively, in 552.32–553.5), we see that these pronouns all refer to the believer and to God. Hence, Luther has brought the two parties together through his dialogue. His diction portrays those victorious ones marching behind their committed leader. For instance, notice how Luther vividly prefaces God's remarks (51:93): "God steps in for you and stakes all he has and his blood for you" [*got tret für dich vn(d) setze all sein gu(o)t vn(d) blu(o)t für dich*] (552.32f.). Luther uses "for you" [*für dich*] three times, accompanied by "behind me" [*hinder mich*]. The images "rearguard" [*schützhalter*] and "vanguard" [*vorgeer*] visualize the beneficiaries [*für*] and their surroundings, circumscribing a perimeter of protection. Luther even credits dialogue to God himself, what Frederic Baue calls *quasi dicat*, putting words into God's mouth.[24] And we should not be surprised because many preachers have done that.

Luther then brings this section to a degree of closure, adding his own third-person assent to the dialogue. Just as he had earlier ("he who has this faith"), he puts the matter paraphrastically, "He who believes" [*wer d(as) glaubt*] (553.3). This answers what, in the initial partition [*welche*], Luther had earlier promised to investigate. The present rhetorical question completes the paraphrasis and alludes to Rom 8:31, though no editor includes this passage. Indeed, Luther has built this *sermocinatio* around the notion of "for you": "if God fights for him, what can you do to him?" [*dan(n) got streyt für jn / wie wilt jm nu(o) thon.*] (553.4f.). Therefore, the argument has already moved from discredited "outward" reception to valued "inner" reception. Luther has directed audience expectations beyond "how to" receive and toward his celebration here, which extends directly into developing the "who" more fully.

## SECTION II (553.5–554.19)

This portion of the sermon grows out of themes established in the first portion and is not, strictly speaking, independent of the first section. The paraphrastic "whoever has [such] faith," used twice already, appears again (553.5) in a modified form ("He who has such faith has his rightful place" [*der in ein solche(n) glaube(n) stat*]), which allows us to see how this portion continues the exposition of that expression. Whereas in Section I Luther described the faith largely in terms of those things residing *outside* the believer—namely, external enemies and forces (pope, devil, death, hell, sin, and law)—here he describes the faith from the perspective *within* the believer. He speaks of attitudes.

Beginning from where he left off—the person "standing" in such faith—Luther responds to the ambiguous third question in his introductory partition ("who belongs here"), even using the verb "take."[25] Luther uses polysyndeton to generate synonyms of accumulation, articulating the goal to which believers strive: "the sacrament as an assurance, or seal, or sign to assure him of God's promise and grace" [*das sacrame(n)t als zu(o) einer sicheru(n)g od(er) sigel oder verzeihu(n)g / d(azs) er der go(e)tliche versprechu(n)g vn(d) zu(o)sagu(n)g gewiß sey*] (553.6–8). Thus, through a rhyming look back, the Sacrament as assurance provides a departure for the next argument. In 553.7–21 Luther returns to the premise that he has created—that faith is an inward thing, therefore, manifested differently among persons. He will now make a case for both the scarcity and the abundance of faith. First, "such faith" (note *repetitio* at 553.5, 8) is scarce. Luther emphasizes this point by *praeteritio* (51:93): "But, of course, we do not all have such faith; would God one-tenth of the Christians had it!" [*ja solche(n) glauben habe(n) wir nit all / wolt got es het jn der .x.theil*] (553.8). This claim suggests a paradox in which God's abundant grace cannot be everyone's possession, surely a puzzling claim for the audience to accept or even follow. However, Luther maintains a strong communion with his audience (note "we" not "they" or "you"), directing their attention toward his inclusive claim with an imperative ("See, such rich, immeasurable treasures" [*secht solche reyche vberschwencklich schetze*]) and strengthening its presence with a *translatio* ("which God . . . showers upon us" [*mit welche(n) wir vo(n) got vberschüt*] [553.9f.]). The paradox, moreover, continues as a veiled antithesis at 553.10 ("cannot be the possession of everyone, but only of those who . . ." [*künde(n) nit jederman gemeyn sein / den(n) allein dene(n)*]), one rich in rhyme and turning into a *distributio* (51:93):

> those who suffer tribulation, physical or spiritual, physically through the persecution of men, spiritually through despair of conscience, outwardly or inwardly . . . . [*die widerstandt habe(n) / es sey leiplich od(er) geistlich / leiplich durch v(er)folgung der mensche(n) / geistlich durch verzagung der gewissen / eüsserlich od(er) jnnerlich . . . .*] (553.11–13)

After taking his audience from joy to despair—or at least to puzzlement—Luther now, using second person, mentions the devil to generate the presence of this feeling of need for faith's strength. Notice how Luther begins with asyndeton, pressing home several short, balanced clauses with second-person pronouns (51:94): "when the devil causes your heart to be weak, timid, and discouraged, so that you do not know how you stand with God, and when he casts your sins into your face" [*wen(n) er dir dein hertz schwach blo(e)d vn(d) verzagt macht / das du nit weyst wie du mit got dran seyst / vn(d) helt dir dein sünd für*] (553.13–15). Even the way Luther locates his dative and genitive pronouns deepens the despair of this statement because coming in succession, the "you" experiences the pressure: The devil casts *"your* sins into *your* face."

At 553.15f. Luther uses an *exemplum* from Scripture, something—in this sermon—quite rare! Moreover, this is his most explicit citation of Scripture in the past few sermons. The terms "terrified and trembling hearts" [*erschrocke(n) zitterden hertze(n)*] are participles (rarely used by Luther in these sermons, but which are useful for providing vividness because of their continuing action) and further deepen the despair of the paradox, which Luther proceeds to clarify. He uses what looks like an enthymeme, yet it is delivered as a rhetorical question. It provides much needed explanation to the paradox. Specifically, note the role of asyndeton as the preacher juxtaposes God's resources with the believer's recognition of need. This is especially present through a strong rhyme (51:94):

> For who desires a protector, defender, and shield to stand before him if he feels no conflict within himself, so that he is distressed because of his sins and daily tormented by them? [*dan(n) wer begert einen schirmschutz oder rückhalter / d(er) vor jm steet / wen(n) er bey sich kein widerstandt empfindt / d(aß) jm sein sünd leyd sind / vn(d) beist sich teglich mit jn*] (553.16–19)

Those images of militarism, which treat the conflict of the *distributio* on "suffering" as an inner one with terms such as "grief" [*leid*] and "sting" [*beist*], are terms ambiguous enough to cover both spiritual and physical suffering. The pains are a necessary part of belonging at the Sacrament, which Luther has been stating in the negative (that is, "without these, one cannot . . ."). He concludes the argument at 553.19, shifting the imagery of the Sacrament to a new one—"food" [*speyß*].[26] Luther uses *repetitio* and participles (rare for these sermons)[27] to strengthen the presence, constructing another enthymeme (51:94):

> That man is not yet ready for *this food. This food* demands a hungering and longing man, for it delights to enter a hungry soul, which is constantly battling with its sins and eager to be rid of them. (*my emphasis*) [*d(er) ist noch nit d(er) zu(o) dieser speyß geho(e)rt / diese speiß wil ein hu(n)gerige(n) vn(d) verla(n)gende(n) mensche(n) haben / dan(n) in ein hu(n)gerige seel get sy gern / die stets mit den sünde(n) streit vn(d) wer jr gern loß.*] (553.19–21)

Thus, Luther has continued to explore and exploit audience expectations, showing the need for dependence on God. He has satisfied one need only to create another. One who would properly receive, then, must both "suffer" and "hunger." We would be remiss if we failed to mention the demonstrative "this" (food) [*dieser speyß*], which is twice repeated previously and appears again at 553.22 [*vo(n) diesem sacrame(n)t . . . diese speiß*] and 554.15 ("this bread") [*diß brot*]. One can visualize the *Prediger* gesturing with his hand and emphasizing with his voice. Clearly he has been developing a case for a new scriptural perspective on the Sacrament, and he has done it through antithesis (*this, not that*). Many interrogative pronouns (*wer*, [who] especially) and substantives (for example, *der*, "*that one* is not yet fit for this food") acted as prior foils for *diese*.[28] In other words, Luther uses his grammatical style to carry his point. First, he probes, confuses, challenges; then, he clarifies, ratifies, emphasizes.

The argument in 553.21–554.2 moves from the previous paradox to the advice for dealing with it. Here we have the "how" and "who" issues as closely intertwined as anywhere in the sermon. Luther explains how one should approach the Sacrament. First, he advises one to abstain if not "prepared" [*nit befindt*], employing the *repetitio* ("this"). He completes this with a conditional sentence, warning against coming unprepared. There is strong presence generated from monosyllables with vocalized pauses (51:94): "this sacrament, for this food will not enter a sated and full heart, and if it comes to such a heart, it is harmful" [*dan(n) diese speiß wil nit in ein sat vn(d) vol hertze. kom(m)t sy aber dahin / so ist sie mit schaden da*] (553.23f.). The pacing of that warning directs attention to a slowing of action—a danger ahead! Surely to hear of possible spiritual danger at the Sacrament is sobering and startling for audience members who had been indoctrinated and commanded by canon law to attend annually at Easter. Luther's use of *hertze . . . sie* as synecdoche shows the third person, the distant, formulaic quality of his warning—a prediction more than a confrontation. He intended this news to be sobering.[29] He then responds to the audience need to hear of an escape—with the first plural; he uses seven inclusive pronouns in five lines (553.24–28). Employing accumulation, Luther encourages his audience to see the possibilities, to feel communion in his desire to encourage and unite with them. The summary comes at 553.26ff., providing another perspective on "fitness" [*schickligkeit*] for the Sacrament. Luther says an individual believer's daily life is an uneven matter; one is sometimes "fit" and sometimes not. Understandably, he shows this in first singular (51:94):

> So we do not always find that we are fit; today I have the grace and am fit for it, but not tomorrow. Indeed, it may be that for six months I may have no desire or fitness for it. [*so finde(n) wir vns all zeit nit geschickt / jch hab heüt die gnad vn(d) bin geschickt darzu(o) morge(n) aber nit / es kan kome(n) d(aß) ich in eim halbe(n) jar nit ein v(er)lange(n) vn(d) ein schickligkeit darzu(o) hab.*] (553.28–554.2)

This kind of clarification is a reassurance to Luther's audience, both of the possibilities for them and of the support they sense from him. The feel of his remark is more like that of an encouragement ("Let us do this") than a scolding.

Luther's conclusion to the argument of "who" belongs at the Sacrament comes at 554.3–7. He clearly marks it [*daru(m)b*]; it is a single-sentence assertive. The terms are bold and strong: three negative universals—"cannot harm" (note *repetitio*) and "nothing can uproot"—surrounded, again, by those enemies ("death and devil" [554.3]; "death, devil, sin" [554.6f.]). These enemies highlight the paradox, which clarifies the startling conclusion on the Sacrament: "best prepared [are those] who are constantly assailed." So Luther has done a lot of teaching, clarifying a particular "spiritual" perspective on the Sacrament. He has kept the audience highly involved not through direct confrontation, but by his peaks and valleys of emotion, by celebrating their mutual (his and the audience's) opportunities, and by arousing fears of dreaded dangers.[30]

The final part of Section II is 554.7–15, an example from Scripture that Luther presents as *narratio* of Christ's method in instituting the Sacrament. In several ways this part is a strong climax to the section and the whole sermon: (1) To this point, this is the second time in these sermons the preacher has dared to use Christ's action as paradigmatic. Luther has previously used mostly Paul and himself. (2) Although the audience may not have been conscious of this at first hearing, using the example of instituting [*auff setze(n)*] the Sacrament is strategic. It responds to the chief objection Luther had offered earlier to the sacramental reform that required Wittenbergers to "take" with their hands—that Jesus' words of institution essentially constituted a command that Christians must take the Sacrament in their hands. (3) The style of this part of the sermon manipulates emotion in a climactic manner. The *narratio* is indexed by the temporal connectors *do* or *da* (four times), but Luther often interrupts it with his interpretations. He uses *sermocinatio* once, allowing Jesus to speak. Luther follows that with a rhetorical question, an "order question," with an obviously affirmative answer (51:94): "Do you think that that did not . . ." [*meynet jr nit . . .*] (554.11). This draws his audience into participating in the interpretation.[31] Notice the emotions made present in the expressions: "he frightened his disciples sitting there and wanted to shake them in their hearts . . . ." [*erschreckte er seine jünger fast seer vn(d) erschottert in jre hertzen gar wol zuuor*] (554.8f.). The effect of these expressions is obvious, especially given the alliterative verbs, the emphatic initial verb in first position, and the *abusio* of the second verb. Luther then shares Christ's words—first, as indirect discourse colored with vivid diction ("painful [*peinlich*] to them"). Then he follows with direct discourse. He allows the syntax of his quote to prolong the uncertainty (agony) of the revelation (51:94): "One of you will betray me" [*Einer vnd(er) eüch wirt mich verratte(n)*] (554.10f.).

Luther's interpretive question uses another emotional appeal—*abusio*: "cut them to the heart" [*d(aß) jene(n) das sey zu(o) hertze(n) gangen*] (554.11). Then he continues the suspensive narrative, telling "what happened." He adds terms that make the result quite specific because Luther uses *transgressio* ("traitors to God"), the same word Christ had used. The narrative ends with accumulating expressions of hope, which are designed to respond to the emotions of despair generated earlier. Luther again uses *transgressio* to begin his description of the Sacrament (51:95): Jesus "institute[d] the blessed sacrament as a comfort and comforted them again" (*my translation*) [*Da setzt er aller erst d(as) hochwirdige sacrame(n)t vff / zu(o) einem trost / vnd tro(e)ste sie wider*] (554.14f.). Then follows a striking series, using asyndeton in metaphorical phrases that contain more of those infrequent participles. Here Luther uses participles to represent all the persons for whom he wants the Wittenbergers to be concerned. And in the present context, the Wittenbergers themselves are included. He begins with the final use of the demonstrative "this bread," picking up at the three repetitions of *trost*. Notice a pattern to the meter of the clauses—6, 6, 7, 8, 12 (51:95): "a comfort for the sorrowing" [*ein trost der betrübten*]; "a healing for the sick" [*ein artzney der krancken*]; a life for the dying [*ein leben der sterbende(n)*]; "a food for all the hungry" [*ein speyß aller hungerigen*]; "and a rich treasure for all the poor and needy" [*vnd ein reycher schatz aller armen vn(d) dürfftigen*] (554.15–17). The anaphora and asyndeton also aid the balance and progression of that climax. With that, Luther stops, giving a concise restatement of the topic of the day.

Those metaphors are recapitulatory because they compress into tight expressions what Luther has been arguing. All the previous emotions of the sermon—the threat and distress—he responds to with these metaphors. His narrative on Jesus' institution of the Sacrament crystallized in slow motion the feelings for the audience; thus, his listeners are prepared for the responding summary. Moreover, the final line fulfills the promise implied early in the sermon—that true, inner, spiritual reception consists in the "right use of the sacrament and its fruits" (551.32). "Fruits" particularly pertains to the Seventh Sermon, where Luther will begin with this metaphor (at 554.28) immediately after his introductory recap. The metaphors here are each ambiguous enough to cover physical and spiritual adversity, though "food" and "treasure" are more obviously metaphorical. Indeed, Luther expanded the perspective on Sacrament, reconstructing a *definitio*—from the "body" of the Lord, to the "bread" of the Sacrament, to "food" for the soul.

So Luther has, in these last two sermons, moved audience attention significantly. From its fixation with "handling," which elicited vigorous scriptural argumentation that produced audience confusion and uncertainty (the Fifth Sermon), Luther moved on to a deeper significance and attitude in Sacrament observance (in the Sixth Sermon), employing a few scriptural allusions. In this way he appeals to audience values not so much as evidence, but as reference—for praise and blame. The sermon ends in an elevated style, as though the blessed Sacrament has risen to a new level. And Luther has set the stage for his next sermon because where standards are high, expectations are also high. Hence, he can move into serious accusations.

# CHAPTER 6

# THE SEVENTH AND EIGHTH INVOCAVIT SERMONS

## THE SEVENTH SERMON (LW 51:95–96; LStA 2:554–55)

This Seventh Sermon is short but not sweet; indeed, its very brevity plays a role in its function. At least at the beginning, Luther continues the theme of Sacrament observance, commencing with a review of key claims from the previous day (554.22–28). But this recapitulation is no mere restatement. Rather, the preacher not only nicely recaps the *who should come/how to come* themes of the previous day, but he also contextualizes the Sacrament observance. Specifically, Luther shows how fear of death and the devil can be constructively used to personal benefit—by preparing one to partake of the Sacrament. The emphasis on this "preparation" implicitly works to soften the audience for what is to come. As Luther moves toward a new assertion—that "love" [*die liebe*] is the "fruit" of the blessed Sacrament (554.28–555.3)—he resumes a strongly communal stance with his audience.[1] This section, like much of the Sixth Sermon, is another celebration of what God has provided for his believers.

But at 555.3, what began as communal has, in fact, set up a confrontation. Luther suddenly turns upon his audience, initiating a vigorous confrontational accusation—that he finds no evidence of love in Wittenberg (555.3–26)! This section resumes the accusation from the First Sermon (531.3–5), which we recall (51:71):

> And here, dear friends, have you not grievously failed? I see no signs of love among you, and I observe very well that you have not been grateful to God for his rich gifts and treasures. [*Alhie lieben freündt ist es nitt fast gefelt / vn(d) spür in keynem die liebe / vnd merck fast woll / das jr gott nit seyt danckpar gewesen vmb solchen reichen schatz vnd gabe.*] (531.3–5)

Moreover, in this sermon Luther develops indictments from 1 Corinthians 13, paraphrasing at some length. In this way he calls on some of the scriptural authority of Paul. The abrupt and forceful shift in speaker stance—from one rejoicing (in Section I) to one prosecuting (in Section II)—is clearly evidenced in the obvious transition from first plural to second plural pronouns. Section III (555.27–34) continues in second plural, arguing that the Wittenbergers' lack of "love" will be their downfall. What Luther implicitly argues in the course of this sermon is that love, by his definition, is a reciprocal relationship between believer and God, who

starts the chain reaction. Hence, the claim in this sermon is a playing out of implications resulting when the reciprocal relationship is aborted; the speaker would
redirect the congregation's attention from Sacrament to love. In brief, Luther's
argument moves along the lines of a temporal progression: Section I—Love *has
always been* the fruit of the Sacrament (554.28–555.3); Section II—Love *is* stillborn
in you (555.3–26); Section III—Love *will be* your nemesis (555.27–34).

The connection between this sermon and the early part of the First Sermon
is so strong that it is almost as though the intervening controversial issues (Mass,
images, foods, Sacrament observance) were diversions, that "faith" and "love"—
received through and practiced through preaching—were the dominant theme.
Rhetorically, this sermon is, by design, a brief, uncomfortable meeting of speaker
and audience. This is a "visitation," something never pleasant, something to be
endured and finished as soon as possible.[2] This sermon sets the stage for the final
message; ultimately, the *success* of the entire series depends on how effective
Luther's bitter medicine in this Seventh Sermon goes down.

## Introduction (554.22–28)

As he did in the Second and Sixth Sermons, Luther begins with "you" plural
[*IR*],[3] and in this review he reiterates the two planks of his previous sermon—
"who" is worthy and "how" to partake. We note in the opening sentence how consonant synomymy is used to heighten the affect of these early remarks: "holy,
blessed sacrament" [*heylige(n) hochwirdige(n) sacraments*] (554.22f.), "timid and
despairing consciences" [*verzagte gewissen / vnd fo(e)rchten*] (554.24), "for the
strengthening of their weak faith and the comforting of their conscience" [*zu(o)
stercken jren schwachen glaüben vmb tro(e)stung jrs gewissens*] (554.25f.). One function
of the review is to reinforce or even extend what has been said the day before, and
Luther does this the same way as he did in his introduction to the Sixth Sermon—
through a *distributio* and its amplification. Hence, following the "who" [*in welchen*]
comes the "how" (554.24–26).

Next, Luther compresses the two planks in a concluding statement that combines "who" and "how" with the concise expression "true use and practice" (51:95)
[*diß ist der rechte braüch vn(d) vbunge diß Sacraments*] (554.26). We cannot miss the
*repetitio* [*diß*] and the synonymy, which are used to draw close the preferred point
of focus. Such a declaration has an unmistakable sound of finality, yet it is followed
by the application: ". . . let him [the unprepared one] refrain from coming until
God also takes hold of him and draws him through his Word" (51:95). Indeed,
Luther moves ahead, and the nouns "use" and "practice" drop out entirely because
those terms are part of what is but a phase in the flow of the argument. He will not
continue a discussion on how to administer the Sacrament. Luther now expands
the "true use and practice" in Section I, thus setting the stage for the subsequent
indictment strategy: First, locate the target; then, "zoom in" on the target; finally, reveal the miss. Unfortunately, the Wittenbergers had been shooting at the
wrong target!

## SECTION I (554.28–555.3)

Luther moves away from the third-person assertive and initiates a strongly communal, celebratory *definitio* of love. The first plural pronoun dominates these lines—six of them in the first five lines. But the preacher is doing more than celebrating. Luther's transitional thematic statement clearly signals a shift in the discussion, and it asserts a strong claim, one that he repeats at the first line of the next section. Thus the shift of focus from Sacrament to "love" is the point of this section. Notice Luther's syntax (51:95):

> We shall now speak of the fruit of this sacrament, which is love; that is, that we should treat our neighbor as God has treated us. . . . Love, I say, is a fruit of this sacrament." [*Nu(o) wo(e)llen wir von der frucht dieses sacraments / welche die liebe ist reden das wir vns also lassen finden gege(n) vnserm na(e)chsten / wie es von got geschehen ist . . . Die liebe sag ich / ist ein frucht dieses sacrame(n)ts.*] (554.28–555.3)

Within those lines, Luther repeats *liebe* three times, stressing the bond between *liebe* and *frucht*. He explains "love" first through a golden-rule principle—"that we should also treat our neighbor as God has treated us." So the focus has moved—from Sacrament, to love, to a picture of love as relating to others.

Luther then amplifies and supports part of that picture—God's action toward "us." But he does not concretely support it with lower levels of abstraction. Rather, he asserts with sweeping claims, seeking to gain adherence through a strongly directed style that is still communal. Notice how this section's three sentences begin: *Nu(o) wo(e)llen wir . . .* (554.28); *nu(o)n haben wir . . .* (554.30); *Die liebe sag ich / ist . . .* (555.3). Luther also uses various vivid expressions to show God's action: (1) synonymous nouns with a strong adjective—"nothing but love and favor" [*eyttel liebe vnd wolthat*] (554.30), "full of love" [*foller liebe*] (555.2); (2) *repetitio* of adjectives [*alle*] in different expressions; and (3) a pregnant verb, "poured out," [*außgeschüttet*] (554.32). So the impact of these devices, which are linked through first plural pronouns, is to powerfully describe God's action, then to testify about it through negative "tests." Note the accumulative verbs and consonance ["k"] (51:95) in "which no man can measure and no angel can understand or fathom" [*welche nyemants ermessen kan / keyn engel kan sie begreyffen noch ergründe(n)*] (555.1). Then Luther caps his description with a strong locution whose vivid participial ("glowing furnace" [*glüender backofen*]) ends with unexpected directions ("from earth to heaven"). I say "unexpected" because Luther has been developing the flow of blessings downward—God to "man"—and "glowing furnace . . . earth to heaven" reverses the direction. Indeed, we see the reversal, the change of focus—to human outpouring: *der da reichet vo(n) der erden biß an den hym(m)el* [555.2f.] ("which then reaches from the earth even up to heaven"). Now, the theme of "giving as you have received" has been taught before (the First Sermon), so Luther here holds that principle before his audience. That is, "we" should be reproducing the "kindnesses" [*güter*] (555.14, 18) from God in actions toward others.[4]

## Section II (555.3–26)

This section, essentially the heart of the sermon and by far its longest section, confronts the Wittenbergers with their lack of love. It is here that Luther resumes the supremacy-of-love motif from the First Sermon. It is here that he deftly corrals many of the controversial issues previously treated into a discriminating, antithetical indictment, as if to say: "You do *those*, but you don't do *these*." And he picks up the Pauline material of 1 Corinthians 13, waving the authoritative standard before his audience. Reducing the argument, then, we can paraphrase Luther as charging: "You don't love, and you ought to, as Paul says . . . you could have done . . . [Luther supplies examples], and you didn't."

Along with the continued abundance of "you" throughout the rest of this sermon, Luther varies his confrontation with negatives—namely, the third singular pronoun "nobody" [*niemant*] and the adjective "no" [*keynen*]. In 555.17–24 this is particularly striking. There are two "you" pronouns and seven negatives. So both positively and negatively, as if looking *at* them and speaking *of* them, Luther confronts his audience. The effect on the audience surely is cumulative and devastating; there is no respite because the variation allows Luther to insert the Wittenbergers into the scriptural mandate, then to find them lacking. The "you" makes a charge; the "nobody" asserts evidence of the charge, evidence that even the audience can examine. In particular, the opening of the confrontation is striking for its burst of pronouns (four "you" pronouns) and the way it introduces details of culpability. These are especially seen through Luther's conjunctions "although" [*wiewol*] and "nevertheless" [*doch*] and the temporal adverb "not yet" [*noch nit*]. Notice how the initial "you" is quite specific ("among you here in Wittenberg" [*eüch alhie zu(o)Wittenberg*] (555.4), how Luther antithetically—*this [God's love] is [important], but this [your love] is not [present]*—syntactically juxtaposes the assertion repeated from the first section to its antithesis in the second section (51:96):

> Love, I say, is a fruit of this sacrament. But this I do not yet perceive among you here in Wittenberg, even though you have had much preaching and, after all, you ought to have carried this out in practice. [*Die liebe sag ich / ist ein fruch dieses sacrame(n)ts / die spür ich noch nit vnder eüch alhie zu(o) Wittenberg / wiewol eüch vil gepredigt ist / in welcher jr eüch doch fürderlich vben solt.*] (555.3–5)

I "notice" or "perceive" [*spür*] is, of course, a term seldom used in this sermon series, but one that is picked up from the First Sermon (at 531.3, followed at 531.6 by "see" [*sihe*]). Back on Sunday that remark was a harmless aside, not to be taken as a serious challenge; here, though, it has more menacing implications. It represents a fatal flaw, a deficiency discovered by an acknowledged authority.

Another key term from that First Sermon [*haüptstück*] comes next, applied singularly and supremely to "love" (51:96): "This is the chief thing, which is the only business of a Christian man" [*das sind die haüptstück die alleyn eim Christen menschen zu(o)steen*] (555.5f.). This recalls and recaps the encompassing theme that drives the series—the "chief things" of a Christian. So to pinpoint it here in so dramatic a way ("the chief . . . the only thing") is to hold it aloft above all else. Hence, the demonstrative *das* operates as an oral signal for the audience.

Luther then prepares for the argument of the scriptural *exemplum*—Paul in 1 Corinthians 13, where Paul's argument of verses 1–3 is one of *expeditio*: "love" overshadowing every other desirable action. But Luther first recalls the "necessary"/"unnecessary" categories of earlier sermons because the early part of 1 Corinthians 13 itself bears an antithetical structure.[5] He first asserts, then raises questions, each mode having the effect of condemning the audience (first, positively; then, negatively) for faulty priorities (51:96):

> But nobody wants to be in this, though you want to practice all sorts of unnecessary things, which are of no account. If you do not want to show yourselves Christians by your love, then leave the other things undone, too . . . . [*hierjn(n) wil niemandt / vnnd wo(e)lt eüch sunst vben in vnno(e)ttigen sachen / daran nit gelegen ist / wo(e)lt jr eüch nit in der liebe erzeyge(n) / so last die andern auch anstan . . . .*] (555.6–8)

The use of 1 Corinthians 13 functions mostly to generate presence for the futility of "unnecessary" things, worthy though they may be, more than it does to speak directly about love. I say that because Luther only quotes from the first three verses of 1 Corinthians 13, verses that offer, in turn, potent competitive challenges to love only to be eventually humiliated by Paul's vivid denials. In the First Sermon Luther avoided many of those vivid Pauline expressions, using only Paul's "I am nothing." Here, however, Luther uses more of them. Notice first how carefully he documents his source: *dan(n) S(ankt) Pau(lus) .1. Corin. 11. spricht* (555.8f.). He quotes the dual expression "tongues of men and of angels" [*engelischen vn(d) menschen zungen*] more completely than he did in the First Sermon, here reversing the order of terms from the Pauline text. He interrupts after verse 1 to give an interpretation, then resumes his quotation, paraphrasing quite thoroughly verses 2–3. This is the longest quotation of Scripture in the eight Invocavit Sermons.

In brief, Luther uses the vivid, concrete expressions, combined with the modifiers "all" (thrice) and "even" ([*auch*], twice), to build an astounding antithesis that is ineluctable by virtue of the "without love" and "have no love." Surely the implications of such strong language have deeply impressed him since he realizes that these "are such terrifying words of Paul" [*das sind so erschrockenlichen wort Pau(li)*] and still he utters the saying.[6] Luther is obviously lavish here, possibly because he has so thoroughly prepared for this indictment in the preceding sermons. Any confusion his audience might have experienced regarding where all this was heading is now dispelled.

At 555.15 Luther begins mercilessly applying the scriptural standards to his audience. To do that, he slips out of the Pauline first-person singular, but he does not do so abruptly. Rather, Luther bridges the gulf between the exemplary "I" (of 1 Corinthians 13) and the problematic "you" (for the Wittenbergers) with his connector "so far as this . . ." [*so weyt seyt*]. Hence, he resumes the second person, then concisely presents his sweeping conclusion in a rhyming monosyllabic, "Not yet have you come so far as this" [*so weyt seyt jr noch nicht kom(m)en*], which obviously needs amplifying. First, Luther concedes the abilities of the Wittenbergers, though his concession is a lure to admitting culpability. Note the "g" consonance (51:96): "though you have received great and rich gifts from God, the highest of which is a knowledge of the Scriptures" [*wiewol jr grosse gabe gottes habt / vnd der vil habt / das erkenen der schrifft ho(e)chlich*] (555.16f.). This implies, and Luther later develops the idea, that among the Wittenbergers the reproductive chain of love has become sterile. Yet as we notice more concessions at 555.17 ("It is true, you have [the true Gospel]" [*das ist ja war / jr habt . . .*]), we also see that the speaker is being careful not to overplay his hand, to alienate his audience by appearing unfair (or unorthodox), that he not be caught contradicting his earlier praise of his audience (in the First Sermon) and their Gospel knowledge. Moreover, as indicated previously, conceding their gifts from and knowledge of God [*war Euangeliu(m) / vnd das laüter wort gots*] (555.17f.) does not excuse the audience. In fact, those advantages make the Wittenbergers' failures more ignominious. Harvesting empty ears of corn is worse than taking no ears at all!

The shift to the third person begins at 555.18 as Luther itemizes the failings of the Wittenbergers. His grammar again employs those cold, remote, impersonal pronouns: "nobody," "everyone," "anybody." Not only does 1 Corinthians 13 show that even great "deeds" pale before love, but the Wittenbergers cannot claim even the deeds! Notice how the "treasures" [*gu(o)ter*] of God (554.32) are now the "goods" [*güter*] of Paul (555.14) and Luther (555.18). Further, distinguishing between "things" and "love" [*die ding on die liebe*] (555.19), the preacher contextualizes the matter of love within the practice of Sacrament. Luther starts in second plural and shifts to third singular, almost as if to turn his back to the Wittenbergers, as he confronts them with a convicting antithesis (51:96):

> You are willing to take all of God's goods in the sacrament, but you are not willing to pour them out again in love. [*jr wo(e)lt vo(n) got all sein gu(o)t jm sacrament nemen / vnd wo(e)llent sie nit in die liebe wider außgiessen / keyner wil dem andern die hende reychen / keyner nympt sich des andern erstlich an.*] (555.20–22)

So Luther has alternated between confrontations with second person and accusations using third person.

Luther then turns back to a hypothetical *narratio*—a typical scenario—where the boundary between indirect and direct discourse is obscured by his irony. Surely the audience catches the significance of "take" and "hand," recalling their crucial importance in the Fifth Sermon on the Sacrament ("take with hands"). This is another masterful piece of recapitulation of an earlier theme; the cumulative effect is not only to remind, but to hold the audience accountable—for *every* theme. Notice the assonance of Luther's sarcastic mimicry—"lets everything else go hang" [*laßt gan was da gat*]—his balanced clauses with *repetitio* ("if someone is helped, let them be helped," [*wem da geholffen ist dem sey geholffen*] [555.23f.]), and a pun on repetition of the word "poor" [*armen/erbarmen*] (". . . no one seeks the poor, how you might help them; this is a pity" [*niemant sicht vff die armen / wie jn von eüch geholffen werde / das ist zu(o) erbarme(n)*] [555.24f.]).

Thus, irony persists throughout this indictment, an irony provoked especially by the three repetitions of *geholffen*. As might be expected, the speaker's stance becomes more confrontational as the sarcastic discourse collides with *das ist . . . das ist . . .* (555.25). It is intentional, not incidental, "help" that Luther wants his listeners to initiate, and he ends (1) by claiming that they knew this—from its centrality in his books and preaching (555.25f.)[7] and (2) by sustaining one last time his claim that "love" (and faith) is the sum total of what his preaching strives for and what the Wittenbergers' lives should produce.

## Section III (555.27–34)

The goal and purpose of "urging to faith and love" [*den glaüben vnd leibe zutreybe(n)*] (555.26) remains at the forefront of the concluding part of the sermon. Luther keeps his focus on love, allowing only a brief pause. Beginning there,[8] he shifts toward the future (51:96): "And if you will not love one another, God will send a great plague upon you" [*vnd werdent jr nit einander lieb habe(n) / so wirt got ein grosse plage vber eüch lassen gan*] (555.27f.). The second plural continues, and we see the warning element in orienting the thought toward the future with the past and present in view; all three tense forms are manifest. Moreover, the entire sermon is structurally designed along a temporal progression. Luther has maintained that love *has always been* a God-initiated reciprocity, which is brought to mind (and, it is hoped, to subsequent action) in the Sacrament (Section I). Then the indictment (Section II) argues that love *is not* occurring, resulting in Luther's warning (Section III) that God *may send* a "great plague."[9] This warning mingles the temporal considerations, fluctuating from future threat to present indictment to (for) past responsibility (51:96):

[F]or God will not have his Word revealed and preached in vain. You are tempting God too far, my friends; for if in times past someone had preached the Word to our forefathers, they would perhaps have acted differently. [*dan(n) got wil nicht vergebens sein wort offenbart haben vnd gepredigt / jr versücht got all zu hart / mein freünde / dan(n) wer das wort vnsern vorfarn vor ettlichen*]

*zeytten gepredigt hette / sie hette(n) sich villeicht wol anders hierjnne gehalten.*]
(555.28–31)

*Repetitio* is a forceful element in this section, generating presence of the authority of God (*got*, four times; *wort*, twice; *gepredigt*, thrice). Even the diction aids the warning. The conditional adverb "perhaps" [*vielleicht*] in the comparison to "fore-fathers" shifts to a more certain possibility with "poor children in the cloisters": ". . . if it were preached . . . they would receive . . . more joyfully [*vil fro(e)licher*] than you, for you are not heeding it at all . . ." (555.30–32).

The comparison to children is a stinging one because it brings not only the accusation of the Wittenbergers' *omissions*, but also of *commission*—their preoccupation with "tomfoolery" (51:96). Luther's diction, moreover, is ironic also, for *gaückelwerck* indicates a game (juggling) and certainly is a *contrarium* to the more sober terms (*got, wort, gepredigt*). And it is described as vacuous: "which does not amount to anything" [*welchs nicht von no(e)ten ist*] (555.34). At every level of description, then, the point is driven home.

## CLOSING (555.34)

The extremely terse closing, coming on the heels of *von no(e)ten*, establishes an ominous ending—omitting "that is enough; tomorrow we will . . . ." and through its rhyme ("I commend you to God" [*Seyt got beuolhen*]). Although this is a common way for Luther to close—indeed, virtually formulaic[10]—here it is more than "good-bye" or "God be with you." Given the devastating confrontation that preceeds it, this close becomes more literally, "[You are busy with trivia]; God help you."

# THE EIGHTH SERMON (LW 51:97–100; LSTA 2:556–58)

This final sermon is a teaching on confession and closes with an exhortation deriving from and supporting the entire sermon series. As such, what we have here does not provide a big finish, nor should it because the preacher has loose ends to pull together. Moreover, Luther also faces a defeated audience that needs encouragement and instruction. He did not come to crush a rebellion but to redirect one. Lest we concede too hastily that Luther concluded with a whimper instead of a bang, consider the following. First, the concise way in which he moves immediately into the topic of confession suggests that any expectation we have of a strong climax will be unfulfilled. Whether the audience would have such expectations is hard to say because we cannot tell if they even knew with any certainty this would be the last sermon of the series.[11]

After the previous sermon on "love," one might puzzle over the logic and wisdom of returning to a didactic message that specifically deals with an issue such as private confession. It would seem that treating "love"—and its close companion "faith"—would be a more climactic way to end. However, Luther saw the blessed Sacrament as the issue most seriously being violated through the Wittenberg

Ordinance, and he approached his treatment of sacramental observance through his previously established focus of "must" and "necessary"/"free" and "unnecessary." Because his development of the arguments on the blessed Sacrament required him to move from particular to general—physical "taking" to "inner" reception to "fruit" of love—Luther could not interrupt that sequence to take up confession.[12] Although Catholic Christians generally confessed during Lent so they could receive the Eucharist during Holy Week, Luther takes up this topic last.[13]

Luther's approach to confession is to subsume the topic within the broader conception of God's "comfort," a reality he has already established in the Sixth and Seventh Sermons as an "outpouring" available to Christians and that should be reciprocated with neighbors. In fact, in this sermon Luther claims there are *three* confessions, not only one. Moreover, rather than ending the series on the negative, ominous note of the Seventh Sermon, Luther redirects audience attention from their lack of love shown to others to the love available from God and through others. In this way Luther describes a Christian economy where God, neighbor-brother, and Christian can flourish amid threats from outside. Karlstadt had denigrated confession in his *Christag Predig*, claiming that dependence on it showed that one was denying the forgiving power of the Sacrament. Moreover, people had stopped going to confession. But "Luther thought that to go to a minister of the word, unburden your conscience, and hear him pronounce absolution was a comfort essential to poor sinful Christians. He would never abolish that opportunity, he said, and he proved his sincerity by confessing to Bugenhagen frequently throughout his life."[14]

But we may misconstrue Luther's intentions if we fail to consider another matter—the question of textual integrity. As it happens, we simply cannot know if we have all of Luther's remarks on Reminiscere (March 16). Because it was Sunday, we have to wonder what became of the normal procedure of reading and expounding the Gospel for the day. Augustus Steimle argues that Luther may have preached on the Gospel lection before taking up what we now have as this Eighth Sermon.[15] Considering the title given to the sermon in our text, "A Brief Summary of the Sermon of D [r.] M [artin] L [uther] Preached on Reminiscere Sunday on Private Confession," one might guess that more was said preceding this but that the purposes of publishing the sermon series prevailed in the textual tradition. That is to say, witnesses hearing the sermons may have intended to focus on his attention to the Wittenberg controversy—its agenda and outcomes—rather than on preserving all of Luther's remarks. Thus we might have (1) only the last part of what Luther said; (2) only an outline, a reworking, of what Luther said; or (3) both. Steimle and the Weimar Edition editors rely heavily on Johann Kesler's account of how, in the opening sermon (Sunday, March 9, Invocavit Sunday), Luther had first dealt with the Gospel text, then moved to the issues of controversy.[16] Had Luther followed the same procedure the next Sunday (Reminiscere), several matters would seem accounted for: (1) the absence, in the First Sermon, of a more formal introduction to the overall series; (2) the lack of such an introduction in the last sermon; and (3) the editors' use of the term "brief summary" as a title to describe the Eighth Sermon, which is actually longer than the previous sermon. At any rate, the American Edition makes no reference to this textual problem.

Regarding the theory that the text is a mere reconstruction, it ought to be observed that the functional and structural sophistication and coherence show this sermon to work too suitably to be a mere secondary rewrite. If it is, the redactors are indistinguishable from the speaker. The structure of the Eighth Sermon is easily discernible: three forms of confession, each developed, in turn, in a similar three-fold manner; a section that develops all three forms and that enlarges the scope of confession; and a conclusion to this and to all eight sermons. Although there is no explicit initial *distributio*, each form of confession discussed is clearly signaled: *Zum ersten* (556.4–30); *Zum andern* (556.30–557.13); *Zum dritten* (557.13–558.9). The remainder of the sermon (558.9–34) moves toward a conclusion. Specifically, it is more helpful to see this section as developing the features common to all forms of confession, showing the logic of a reconception of "absolutions" as having an interpersonal sense of "comfort" and "strengthening" rather than the prevailing legal sense of "pardon." The later stage of the conclusion claims more than the prior stage because Luther's argument advances from the availability of these "comforts" to their necessity. Also easily seen is the fact that throughout the sermon Luther uses a rich and precise vocabulary, aided by *repetitio* of several kinds, to magnify the portrait he paints of the Christian struggle. A reader is struck by the sheer variety of terms used for "sin" and "righteousness." The speaker's stance is overwhelmingly communal rather than confrontational. Thus both repetitive and progressive form develop.

## SECTION I (556.4–30)

This section [*Zum ersten* . . .] argues the case for confession as "brotherly admonition" [*brüderliche ermanu(n)ge*], what I shall refer to as confession$_1$, which I shall argue involves a horizontal dynamic. Luther claims that it is scripturally commanded yet lost—thus it needs recovery. Indeed, he may have introduced this notion of confession first because he felt it to be the most neglected. He strongly implies, as seen in his first and final statements, that the audience falls far short: "There *is* a confession grounded in Scripture (556.4 [*my emphasis*]) . . . That [reinstating this form of confession] would be Christian, but I cannot do it alone" (556.30). Briefly, this kind of confession is explained (556.4–8), justified (556.8–10), and contextualized, that is, it has "been neglected" (556.10–14) and so should be practiced as follows . . . (556.14–30). This progressive format—from *is* to *why* to *ought*—is followed in principle, if not to the letter, in each of the first three sections [*Zum ersten* . . . *Zum andern* . . . *Zum dritten* . . .]. Priority given to scriptural authorization is evident in the way Luther unveils this first form of confession because his listeners are confused about the nature, purpose, and practice of confession.[17] So the syntax in 556.4f. shows Luther's claim to be an assertion for getting his audience's attention by taking a firm, controversial position—"There *is* a confession grounded in Scripture" [*es ist ein beichte gegründt in der schriefft . . .*]—while delaying his revelation of what that confession is. Of course, the presumption of the audience was, *There isn't any confession grounded in Scripture.* The demonstrative syntax of the rest of 556.4f. [*vn(d) ist die*] freezes their attention, then, so the preacher can gradually explain to them this first form of confession—the one grounded in Scripture—in the most favorable light. Luther uses a kind of *narratio*, describing a hypothetical situation clearly found in Scripture (51:97): "When . . . then . . . and if . . . then . . . but if not . . . then . . ." [*wen(n) nyemandts . . . so wardt . . . stünd er das abe / so . . .wolt er aber . . . so wa(e)r . . .* ] (556.5–8).[18] He then supports his case for "this confession," continuing with demonstratives for sharp focus. He cannot allow this argument to drift—from the domain he prescribes—toward other contours of "confession." Luther is, therefore, recasting his audience's conception of confession. The support is, as we would expect, a clear citation and quote from Scripture. Earlier, *gegründt* marked the support; here, Luther uses "commanded by God" and quotes Matt 18:15 ("If your brother sins, . . . go and tell him his fault . . ." [RSV]). His syntax parallels the "if, then" format used earlier.[19]

The logic of the first three sections of the sermon is quite straightforward—explain, justify, contextualize. Luther moves in a rapid, concise manner. He is hastening through a string of strong assertions to get to his extended *narratio* of how this confession should be conducted (556.15–30). There he will connect the threads he has dangled as the progressive form Luther creates moves from (1) focus—he explains; to (2) presence—he justifies; to (3) affect—he dramatizes. The contextualizing (affect) portion of this section develops as follows: First, Luther strongly asserts that this form of confession has been neglected. Especially prominent is his *repetitio* of the demonstrative "this confession" [*diese beycht . . . dieser peichte(n) . . . diese beicht . . . diese stück*] (556.9-15). He is obviously discussing the entire "brotherly admonition" event synecdochically, by its last and first phases. Through antithesis Luther makes the assertion that Wittenberger priorities are misplaced (51:97): "Here you should have . . . and let the other alone" [*Alhie solt jr eüch . . . vn(d) die ander lassen ansteen*] (556.14–15). So the desired reform—the one they missed—Luther places twice before his audience through *repetitio*: ". . . whoever would have re-established . . . you should have re-established" (556.13–14). Next, he uses the directional lever of his demonstratives, aided by the previous antithesis, to describe the proper procedure for this first form of confession. Luther uses the assertive/injunctive modal variations ("if he does . . . you should . . .") used previously to teach—that is, to prescribe an instructional standard. Luther begins the procedure in second plural, presumably because he holds all his listeners accountable for this responsibility (51:97): "When you see . . . , you should go to him in secret . . ." [*wan(n) jr sehent . . . so solt jr . . .* ] (556.17). The sibilant, rhyming asyndeton that catalogs a quick list of sinners one might encounter ("a usurer, adulterer, thief, or drunkard" [*einen wu(o)cherer / eebrecher / raüber / saüffer*]) also hints at the individual encounters one might imagine. The single pronoun *einen* governs all four nouns, showing that the list is a compression of discrete possibilities. Hence, Luther's style conveys his sense of a conditional imperative: "When you see . . . go . . . ." He has addressed the audience through the collective "you," and he has covered all the bases.

However, Luther soon changes to second singular as his prescription proceeds to the matter of the sinner's refusal to listen—a possibility introduced earlier. Whereas the preponderance of this sermon is about restoring sinners through a confession of sin, this particular passage is an opportunity to discuss punitive measures.[20] The second singular, then, is needed to focus upon a concrete case, especially because this activating of confession must be initiated by an individual. Through *repetitio*—"admonish" [*vermane(n)*] (556.18); [*ermane(n)*] (556.20); [*ermanu(n)ge*] (556.24)—Luther shows how the initiating believer should maintain consistent behavior toward the recalcitrant brother, though the entire episode may include a progression of witnesses (Matt 18:15ff.). By contrast, the brother's attitude is retrogressive—stubborn and rebellious: "pays no heed" [*keret er sich nit*] (556.19), "scorns" [*verachten*] (556.21). The preacher makes present the public accusation [*ansagen*] that opened this discussion through *sermocinatio*. He repeats the "pastor" [*pfarrer*] four times at 556.21–27—in the context of confession as "brotherly admonition" and as the only mention of that term in the sermon. The pastor's role seems to be that of an interlocutor—hearing the testimony from the witnesses as they address him, "Dear pastor" [*lieber herr pffarrer*]—and of a judge, who then renders his decision.

Yet Luther continues to stress the responsibility of the congregation's members. Their physical presence, pictured at the scene of accusation and banishment,[21] is justified because they need to be present at the second and third stages. The inclusive pronouns show the commitment a believer must have to engage a sinner ("our brotherly admonition"; "with my witnesses who heard this"). Significantly, the decisive point in the deliberative process comes when the stakes are revealed. The benefit of the congregation is first [*von wegen des haüffens*] (556.28), but the reclaiming of the brother is also in view (51:98): "until he comes to himself and is received back again" [*biß das er sich erkent vn(d) wider angenom(m)en würde*] (556.29).[22] Luther's picture is not merely a formula to follow, but it argues for a pastoral, psychological sensitivity for brotherly closeness, for better or worse. He sees this as a badly needed remedy to irresponsible radicalism in Wittenberg, and he closes the section, leaving the responsibility upon his hearers.

Interestingly, Luther only once in this section mentions God—at 556.10, where he first introduced his topic ("this confession is commanded by God"). The implication, obviously, is that the command is clear and sufficient for justification. The demonstrative ("this") aids the implication that neglect has occurred because it diverts attention from the remote (the wrong) to the near (the right). The absence of "God" conveys a sense of responsibility to the audience because both confession₁ (brotherly admonition) and confession₃ (private confessing) are largely horizontal—they are authorized by God but executed primarily within human relationships. Confession₂ (prayer of confession) is, by contrast, more vertical. The point I am making is that even Luther's various ways of developing the three forms of confession assist in supporting his claim that many "absolutions" or "comforts" are available and that to summarily dismiss all confession is hasty and shortsighted. So he closes with (51:98): "This would be Christian. But I cannot undertake to carry it out single-handed" [*diß wer Christlich / d(as) getrew ich aber alleyne nit außzurichten.*] (556.30). And the conclusion we draw is that Luther wanted to divert his hearers from what they *thought* was Christian to what *is* Christian. The irony of that distinction is unmistakable.

## SECTION II (556.30–557.13)

This section is a short argument, an explanation, and a justification of the second form of confession—confession to God [*eyne beicht vns vo(n) no(e)ten*] (557.1). The argument is another attempt, similar to that in the previous section, though much looser, to redefine a previously held conception of confession. Here Luther shifts to a definition of confession as a vertical (person to God), intimate activity: "prayer." Yet he does not spend much time on this form of confession because it is a version with little obvious social dimension, so he makes no contextualizing comment. But confession₂ functions as a counterpoint to Section I, which argues for the accountability of one person to another and to the congregation. This section, instead, describes accountability to God. Whereas the former section starts with the awareness [*erkündigunge*] of a brother's public [*offentlich*] sin, this section permits one to deal with private sins—sin prior to its notice by others and confessed in "a corner" [*einen winckel*]. Again Luther presents a scenario of sin, this one culminating in a more restorative result.

The most important difference between the two sections is Luther's exclusive focus in this section on the individual person's responsibility for himself.[23] The style changes accordingly. Possessive and reflexive pronouns are dominant, and the more powerful and final Scripture *exemplum* (Ps 32:5f.)—a section replete with scriptural language—is in first and second singular: *Ich* and *du*. Because Luther begins with inclusive ("we"/"our") pronouns, we take his later use of singulars as representative rather than personal; the speaker is a teacher-reporter who describes and quotes. Even Luther's brief explanation of prayer as "confessing to God himself" [*got selber beichte(n)*] (557.1f.) shows the private, reflective, vertical perspective—as seen in the pronouns and adjectives. He presents a universal need for intimacy, note (1) "by ourselves" [*alleine*]; (2) "when we" [*wan(n) wir*]; (3) "all our faults" [*allen vnsern gebreche(n)*]; (4) "into a corner" [*in einen winckel*]; (5) "to God himself" [*got selber*]. And we must not miss how Luther puts this need, as overlooked by the American Edition: "a confession needed *by us*" [*vns von no(e)ten*] (*my emphasis*). In addition to clarifying the roles of participants, Luther describes the action of the second kind of confession. He shifts from the noun "confession" [*beicht*] to the verb "confess" [*beichte(n)*], returning to the imagery of the Seventh Sermon with the conjoined verb "pour out" [*schütte(n) da auß*]. It is this action of the one confessing to God that Luther explores. He restores *got* to the discussion,[24] and the familiar verb "pray" [*bitten*] is not used until late in the paragraph (at 557.10, 13). So the speaker has enlivened this picture of confession by reinforcing the presence of the listener (God) and the expressing of the sinner. Luther brings in three scriptural *exempla*, all of which he offers as evidence for his claim that "this [confession] is also commanded" [*die ist auch gebotte(n)*] (557.2f.). But he uses Scripture in a way much different from the previous section's particular, procedural instructions (Matt 18:15ff.). The emergence of Latin phrases suggests that this form of confession was an issue of controversy, or at least of tradition.

The first *exemplum* is a quotation in Latin from Gen 18:19, which Luther simply calls "the familiar word in Scripture" [*das gemeyne wort in der schriefft*] (557.3). The first part of the quote, *Facite judiciu(m) et iusticiam*, was undoubtedly a maxim.[25] The second part, which is Luther's *interpretatio* of the first part, he also gives in Latin.[26] He then adds the second *exemplum* from the German translation of Ps 106:3. Luther intended his citation here—"As it is written" [*Als geschriebe(n) steet.*] (557.5)—to be stronger than the former citation—"from this comes" [*doher kompt auch*]. The reason, as we shall soon see, is that Luther's interpretation of the second *exemplum* rewrites an understanding of the first one, making manifest in the second what is only latent in the first. The goal, at first broadly delegated to believers, becomes concretely possible with action. Luther translates the action of "knowing" oneself into something positive, not ugly (for example, as in "conscience stricken"). He uses terms that have always been positive for him: "humility" [*demütickeit*] and "self abasement" [*selbs ernyderu(n)g*] (cf. the Sixth Sermon). Further, he transforms the action of "knowing self" in "righteousness" [*gerechtickeit*] through his parallel construction of another clause (51:98): "praying to God for the mercy and help" [*gnade vnd hülff vo(n) got bittet*] (557.10), culminating in the raising up by God [*von got erhabe(n) wirt*]. Hence, Luther has syntactically fused "justice" [*gerichte*] and "righteousness" [*gerechtickeit*] through the action of confession as prayer, by which a restorative, three-step progression occurs: (1) knowing self, (2) praying to God, and (3) being raised up by God. This restorative progression stands in contrast to the retrogressive scenario of the recalcitrant sinner in Section I.

Luther visualizes the restorative process—that is, actualizing it through a concrete example—in a third, climactic *exemplum*, one from the same author as the second: David. This quote is vivid (in first singular); is vocal (using *serminocinatio*—"when he says" [*do er sprach*]); and is transparent. It avoids problematic subtleties, blending key terms from the entire section. Further, it bridges back to the first section with the use of *gesündiget* ("sinned") and *sünde* ("sin"—here unconditional admission of sin, so absent in Section I). It also bridges ahead to Section III with its voluntary approach to God, so urged in remaining sections. Here is Luther's quote from David's Ps 32:5–6 (51:98):

I have sinned; I will confess my transgressions to the Lord and thou didst forgive the guilt of my sin; for this all thy saints shall pray to thee. [*Jch habe gesündiget / ich wil bekenne(n) gott wider mich meine vngerechtickeit / vnd du hast erlassen mir meine vntugent meiner sünde / für dieselbige(n) werde(n) bitten alle deine heylige(n).*] (557.11–13)

This quotation unites the person with God as an exemplary action, one available only through highly reflective determination (note Luther's seven first-person singular pronouns in three lines!). So we see that Luther has diverted whatever preoccupation with the sins of others his audience may have had, directing them to be concerned for their own sins. We have already seen in Section I how, by furnishing a concretely supported scriptural dictum, he challenges any hasty tossing out of confession. So instead of throwing confession away, Luther gives it a new prominence.

## SECTION III (557.13–558.10)

Clearly, Luther's overall strategy in this sermon enlarges the scope of confession, converting a narrow conception of *der beichte* as ritual or act into three perspectives on confession as process. Each is *ein beichte*, almost as if to promote confession by characterizing it according to potential results—"absolution." By returning to the devil-struggle motif, Luther subsumes his discussions of confession within the personal and urgent realm of Christian living. He has delayed until last the most controversial form of confession. The previous two sections each upheld a confession at once (1) necessary, (2) commanded in Scripture, and (3) beneficial.[27] Luther's positions on this third form of confession parallel the conditioned responses (*stubborn, then resist; desire, then partake*) used in connection with the theme of "meats" in the Fourth Sermon.

The threefold strategy of Sections I and II is also used here. First, Luther introduces the species of confession—a third kind—by explaining it (557.13f.); second, he discusses its apparent justification, that is, its authority—here, the pope (557.16–20); third, disregarding the authority of the pope, Luther ultimately argues for its need because it is so valuable and has scriptural basis (557.20–558.10). Because this kind of confession requires the most maturity to master, Luther needs to be quite careful how he treats it. He distinguishes, then, between the value of confession itself and the pollution brought to it by the pope's force. As he introduces this confession, its identity as the one particularly at issue is temporarily delayed by Luther's use of hypothetical-typical language (51:98)—"one takes another aside and tells what troubles one . . . ." Even when he explains the purpose and results ("so that one may hear from him a word of comfort" [*Auff d(aß) er vo(n) jm ho(e)re ein tro(e)stlich wort*] (557.15), the notion of "the confessional" is not all that obvious. As Luther then supplies this confession's justification, he breaks the repetitive cycle: Scripture is not the authority, the pope is! He allows to go unstated a comparison between God's command of the two previous kinds of confession (556.9; 557.1) and the pope's (558.16). Then Luther begins to probe, to consider the strengths and weaknesses of papal "justification"—namely, force. In other words, Luther begins to praise and to blame: "this urging and forcing . . ." [diß no(e)tten vnd zwingen . . .] (557.16f.). Hence, the demonstrative and synonymy focus sharply on the pope's negative action (not his person). Luther also clarifies those actions of "condemning" [verworffen] and not going to confession as exclusively [Allein daru(m)b] (557.17) provoked by illegitimate force. Moreover, he clearly states that his "wish" stems from the illegitimacy of the pope's actions (51:98): "which he has not the power to do" [welches er nit macht hat / darauß mache(n)] (557.19f.). So far, then, in objecting to the pope's authority, Luther has gone along with what his audience already thinks.

But in mid-sentence (557.20), Luther shifts [aber dannocht] his discussion to its third stage—the *need* for private confession. Here he begins to adjust for his audience's presumptions. The fact that Luther shifts with sustained vehemence is important becaues he cannot give his audience the impression that he is half-hearted about this need.[28] Hence, he uses strong expressions in 557.21—"allow no man to take" [niemants lassen neme(n)]—and hyperbole—"for all the treasures in the world" [vmb der gantze(n) welt schatz]—through an enthymeme. The minor premise ("since I know what comfort and strength it has given me" [dan(n) ich weyß was trost vn(d) stercke sie mir gegebe(n) hat] (557.22) contains the doublet "comfort and strength," which is the goal-purpose-result of Christian living. These two terms [trost vn(d) stercke] are important repetitions in the rest of the sermon. The major premise of the enthymeme (*whatever brings God's comfort and strength we should retain*) is, in various forms, an implicit premise of the entire sermon series, but it is more obvious here. Luther has often bolstered the plausibility of that premise by using himself both explicitly, as example, and implicitly, through his ubiquitous first singular, as he does here.[29] He clarifies and justifies the use of the personal argument ("from me"; "I will"; "I know") at 557.22f. by reintroducing the theme of a Christian's struggle with the devil. This example (51:98) of the Christian who has struggled ("No one knows what it can do for him except one who has struggled often and long with the devil" [Es weiß niemants was sie vermag / den(n) wer mit de(m) teüffel gefochte(n) hat] [557.22f.]) has been used before in this series of sermons.

To this point, then, Luther gradually develops a case for the need of private confession. He does so in a nonconfrontational manner by a weaving together third-person assertives and first-person elaboration. The emergence of the devil, in first-person testimony at 557.23, signals the stronger development of a more positive case. Luther juxtaposes the danger Satan poses to a Christian to the nurture available in private confession through the choice of both his nouns and his verbs: teüffel/beichte, erwürgt/erhalten. The latter antithesis, the emphasis on the verbs having the same prefix but opposing outcomes, is new. The devil as catalyst for the argument is no longer useful, so the preacher ends it and continues to develop the "need"—its urgency and its familiarity—as separate dead ends (51:98): "can neither reach nor ascertain by himself" (*my translation*).[30] Thus,

Luther has met the audience expectation by (1) ratifying conscientious resistance of the pope's force and by (2) surprising the audience in supporting the worth of private confession, both personally and representatively.

Luther then narrates a positive outcome of this confession—that one receives "comfort" from another, as though from God himself. However, Luther employs the rhetorical question to present the same principle found in the Fourth Sermon—of relinquishing liberty—in similar provocative terms (51:99): "What harm . . . ?" [*was schadet jm*] (557.27). Strategically, he suggests to his audience that they give this "confession" the benefit of doubt because his rhetorical question challenges them to prove him wrong. Notice how Luther uses his verbs. Specifically, he injects the term "harm" with content intended to evoke an obvious, though not immediate, thought (*Why, no harm, I suppose*) through the use of two verbs, the first of which he had previously used as an important idea—in noun form—at 557.8 ("true justice," [*ware demütickeit*]). Here he uses it as a verb [*demütiget*] (557.28). The second verb makes a rhyming play on the noun "harm" [*schadet . . . zu(o) schande(n)*] (557.27–28). The third verb of the question, "awaits" [*warte*], forms the pivot, so the question is already developing a progressive form (in 557.28f.) of (1) "humbles [himself a little]"; (2) "puts [self to shame]"; (3) "awaits [a word of comfort]." This progression culminates in (4) "takes [it]" and (5) "believes in it" (51:99). Luther uses a weighty, modifying clause ("as if he were hearing it from God himself" [*als wan(n) er sie vo(n) gott ho(e)rte*] (557.29) to project divine authorization and participation, which has been so distressingly absent thus far in this section, onto the whole process of confessing. Moreover, Luther does not wait to support that *as if* suggestion; he supplies his *exemplum* (51:99): "as we read in Matt. 18" [*wie wir dan(n) habe(n) .Mat. 18.*] (557.30). The quotation is a loose paraphrase of Matt 18:19, suggesting that God, too, is involved in this confessing process, though thus far in Section III *got* has appeared only once. Luther eventually uses *got* three more times in this section by inserting positive concern about God as he continues to develop this *as if God* plausibility. This is a way Luther displaces the audience's negative fixation on papal force.

At 557.31 Luther introduces "absolution" as a term in this argument for the need of confession as "private confession" (557.20; 558.8, 18f.). He uses the term "absolution" almost as a substitute for "confession," as we hear him signaling the advancement of the argument: *Wir müssen auch vil absolution habe(n)*. The word "absolution" may evoke its legal, technical use, but here, through its repetitive uses (six times in 557.31–558.27),[31] Luther gives it new meaning. He has prepared the audience for the term with his previous arguments.[32] The significance of his introduction of "absolutions" is not further explained until he picks it up again at 558.10. We see (51:99) from the strong modals—"must" [*müssen*], "should" [*sol*]— and especially from the strong, universal negative conclusion ("Therefore, no man shall forbid the confession nor keep or draw any one away from it" [*darumb . . . niemant . . . auch niemants . . .*] ) that Luther is serious about the need for this confession. In addition to the strong prohibition, he goes beyond the explicit "forbid" [*verbiete(n)*]; his more subtle doublet "keep or draw away" [*halten oder zye-hen*] (558.2) condemns both those who would restrain and those who would entice others from confession. The picture drawn is of a voluntary, urgent need for brotherly acceptance and God's healing. It counters any prior, mistaken concep-tion of confession, such as a dreaded cowering before one's human superior, that is, the confessor. Luther wants to make it clear that it is God, not the confessor, who confers absolution.

Luther represents the case for God being at work within the confessing process by repetition and progression of *speaking* expressions (51:99): A "sure word" [*gewissen spruch*] (558.3), "what he says to him" [*was er jm darüber sprechen wirdt*] (558.4), "let him take it as if God himself had spoken it through the mouth" [*das neme er an als wen(n) es gott selber gesprochen hett / durch den mu(n)dt*] (558.4f.). Thus, using the reflexive [*selber*], Luther explicitly suggests what he has more sub-tly hinted at earlier—"as though God himself."

At 558.5 Luther begins an apparent *prolepsis*, an imagined exception to the preceding case. The conjunction *aber* alerts listeners to a discrepancy (and inter-ruption) in the need for private confession, and the remainder of the statement gives the conditions and permission to bypass or forego the confession to others. The "strong, firm faith" [*starcken festen glaübe(n)*] is completed by the sybillant triplet *sein sünd sein* ("his sins are [forgiven him]"), and the exception allowed by this *prolepsis* seems legitimately provided by Section II, as if one need go to no one but God alone. However, Luther quickly shows this possibility as unlikely (51:99): "But how many have such a strong faith?" [*ja wie vil habe(n) soliche(n) starcken glaübe(n)?*] (558.7). Therefore, it is but a pause in (and a reinforcing of) his case.[33] The question momentarily freezes the flow, allowing the audience to ponder, with the answer obvious only being realized upon reflection. Luther has, particularly through his use of *glaübe(n)*, lured his audience into briefly entertaining the notion that, for some people, confession might not be needed. Then he reminds them of his constant theme of the series—those "weak in faith." The conclusion to the sec-tion begins at 558.8 ("Therefore, as I have said," [*derhalben wird ich . . .*]) and forms a dual prohibition: *Don't take it [confession] from me; don't force [it on anyone]*. Final-ly, through three first-person pronouns, Luther makes present the value of the confession. He supports the prohibition against force with a clause that assigns responsibility to the audience member (51:99): "But I will not have anybody forced to it" [*sonder eim jeden frey heym gestelt habe(n)*] (558.9–10).

## SECTION IV (558.10–25)

In the remainder of the sermon, Luther continues to develop his notion of confession as "absolution," arguing that God has provided many absolutions (from Section III) and exhorting his audience to use them for the battle (in Sec-tion IV). By doing this, Luther explains that confessions are God-given helps to be embraced, not pope-ordained obstructions to be resisted. Luther's argument describing absolutions asserts first that they are abundant (558.10–13), then he gives five examples as support (558.13–25). The claim that "absolutions" are abundant provides a new perspective, first revealing absolutions as manifestations of God's generosity, not as papal repressions. To aid his idea, Luther adopts a communal posture, using first plural pronouns and celebrating intimacy rather than distance. He then challenges the presumption that God is "niggardly" [*karg*]. Finally, Luther's key terms of Section III ("comfort and strength" [*trost od(er) stercke*]) oppose the prevailing audience view: that God's forgiveness is available only through the pope's confessional absolution. In its entirety, the claim recasts "absolution" as available in many ways, aligning the instrument of absolution as the Gospel [*euangelio*]. Such a claim can appeal to *evangelische* values by removing the papal taint from absolution, transferring it from "his" (pope and clerics) to "ours." Luther's important strategic claim throughout these sermons is: *Take your eyes off the pope, and look to Scripture, self, and neighbor.* And he immediately furnishes examples to support his claim.

The first two are *exempla* from the Sermon on the Mount. The first example describes the conditional basis for forgiveness, quoting Matt 6:14; hence, it illustrates the "private confession" of Section III and provides a much stronger justification and scriptural authority than did the Matthew 18 *exemplum* of that section. Luther's example here even more accurately illustrates confession as "brotherly admonition" (Section I) because both clauses of Matt 6:14 use "you" plural and the term for "sins" is *schüldigern* ("debts"), which closely corresponds to *beschüldigu(n)g*, the term used in Section I (556.27).[34] The second example, the Lord's Prayer [*vatter vnser*] (558.15), illustrates confession as the "private prayer" of Section II and holds out the possibility of audience identification—all can participate in it. Even today, what the English-speaking world calls the Lord's Prayer (Matt 6:9–13), Germans refer to as the *Unser Vater* because of its opening line: "*unser Vater in Himmel.*" In Luther's third example, he does not cite Scripture; rather, he continues to express himself in first plural, thus sustaining the inclusive focus on the many absolutions. "The third is baptism" [*Die tritt ist die tauff*] (558.16) again illustrates how Luther uses numerals elliptically, in repetition of the same idea—of *trost* (558.11), of *and(er) tro(e)stung* (558.15). To generate presence for clarifying how Baptism can be a "comfort," Luther uses dialogue between himself and God. "I" and the possessive pronouns represent any person (51:99): "when I reason thus:" [*wan ich also gede(n)ck*] (558.16). His discourse portrays a believer in response to God. Luther employs the significant verb *gewyß sey* ("be assured") and a prominent noun (*barmhertzigkeit* ["mercy"] at 558.17.[35] Again, then, Luther has taken a familiar Christian concept and talked it out with God, thus recasting Baptism in a new light, as absolution.

Luther presents the fourth example, "private confession" (*die heymlich beichte*), in first person. Again he uses himself as the representative example. Through *repetitio* and *accumulatio*, he strongly enacts the results of this confession. Notice how the oral rhythm of the phrases—with five, five, and eight beats—accelerates toward a crescendo: "as if God himself spoke it, so that I may be assured that my sins are forgiven" [*als sprech got selber d(aß) ich gewyß sey mein sünd seyen mir vergeben*] (558.19f.). But that fitting crescendo notwithstanding, Luther is not yet finished. His final example [*zu(o) lezts*] is the blessed Sacrament. He uses first singular to portray the action of partaking. This time his diction employs the vivid terms *co(e)rper* and *blu(o)t* ("body" and "blood"), neither of which he has used previously.[36] These terms are used in balanced expressions (51:99)—"when I eat his body and drink his blood" [*esse sein co(e)rper vnd trincke sein blu(o)t*] (558.21f.)—locutions that rhythmically direct, through formulaic familiarity, attention to the new material that is the objective of those actions: "as a sign that" [*zu(o) eyne(m) zeychen*] (558.22). The inward "sign" is a celebration that is assurance "that I am rid of my sins" [*das ich meiner sünde loß sey*] (558.22). We have now seen Luther brilliantly recapitulate earlier themes, recontextualizing—literally and decisively, in the final example—several of the sacraments as threads in God's fabric of "comforts." Furthermore, Luther has subtly slipped in, as but the final absolution—the fourth in a list—auricular confession. He did so smoothly, incorporating the same assurance ("as if God himself") earlier attested to, in a strongly persuasive manner, and remaining silent regarding any controversy over confessing to a papally sanctioned priest.

To reinforce the presence of this particular Gospel comfort (the blessed Sacrament), Luther mentions the recipient's feelings of assurance first (using "I") and the gift second. He further begins to explain this assurance at 558.17–18, where he claims that the purpose of God's giving the Sacrament was to provide assurance (51:99): "in order to make me sure of this, he gives me . . ." [*damit er mich gewyß ma(e)chte / gibt er mir . . .*] (558.23). Then Luther's final clause employs a modal doublet to emphasize assurance: "I shall not and cannot doubt . . ." [*das ich jo nit verzweyfflen mag noch kan*] (558.24f.). Even the repetition through consonance ("g" sound) in these latter two examples aids the embodiment of this "assurance"; Luther establishes its reality through repeated sounds: *gee . . . gewyß* (558.19); *got . . . gewyß . . . vergeben* (558.20); *hochwirdige* (558.21); *gott . . . gebrechen gefreyet . . . gewyß . . . gibt* (558.22-23); *gnedige(n) got* (558.25). In other words, Luther brings together syntax, feeling, and form in a particularly impressive piece of composition.

So throughout this sermon, Luther has distinguished among several forms of confession, arguing their legitimacy and utility. Further, he has broadened "confession" by removing it from the narrow confines of the confessional and of papal restrictions and by placing it within the scope of God's multifaceted "comforts" or "absolutions." Imagine a dramatic pause at the end of the passage described above. Now Luther is ready to conclude. Now he is ready to close the entire series by returning to the broadest appeal of all—Christians' needs and the devil's threats.

## SECTION V: CONCLUSION (558.25–34)

The conclusion, like all the previous sections in this sermon, moves in three steps. First, Luther rounds off his case for the genus "confession" in all its types.

Next, he leads straight into an exhortation to the audience to be prepared for battle, using the "absolutions" and other gifts from God. Third, he ends with renewed warnings about possible dangers, especially in view of the audience's lack of experience and commitment. Further, as we observe Luther's communion with the audience, we see that his reminder to retain confession and his warnings about the devil are cast in second-person plural. The warnings concerning the Wittenbergers' ignorance are emphasized in first singular. The exhortation to be prepared is in first plural. Moreover, Luther uses militaristic imagery (51:100), the "paraphernalia" I mentioned previously—"weapons" [*waffen*], "armour" [*harnasch*] "equipment" [*rüstunge*]—the last one echoed by its rhyming predicate [*vnuerrückt bleybe(n)*] ("keep intact").[37] The entire exhortation contains six first plural pronouns in four lines (558.26–29)! Thus Luther has placed his final, personal cap on the developing argument for God's "comforts" and "assurances."

The section closes with Luther summing up the reasons for the exhortation (indeed, for the entire sermon series), casting it in second plural. As before, he does not arbitrarily move from exhortation to warning (or vice versa); most often there is some lack in the audience or a threat from outside that accounts for his moves. The epithet at 558.29 ("our enemies" [*vnser feinde*]) triggers Luther's final warning. He wants to leave his audience with a healthy, fearful respect for their task, and he does so by returning to the "you . . . not yet" expression, repeating the verb "struggle" [*streytte(n)*], and by using a new term—"labor" [*mühe*]. This assertion, then, is supported by antithesis of comparison, something done in the First Sermon. Luther contrasts the audience's deficiency with his own experience ("you do not yet know . . . but I know . . ."). Therefore, Luther opens and closes the sermon series with a strongly authoritative stance. The prominent term in the closing warning is the adverb *wol* ("[I know him, that is, the devil] *well*"), found four times in 558.31–33. This repetition provides a strong foil to contrast with *noch nit* ("not at all"), the lack of the audience. And Luther returns to second-person plural to document his major evidence for this lack of preparedness: the rejection of confession. This is the only explicit accusation he makes in this sermon. His previous charge—"Here is where you should have exerted yourselves and re-established this kind of confession" (51:97)—was much more vague, but this one is precise, leaving him and the audience at odds. By doing this, Luther wants and requires that the Wittenbergers do something, that they make some changes. Merely hearing him out cannot be the end of the matter. To the audience now falls the burden of showing how effective is this preaching.

# CHAPTER 7

# CONTRIBUTIONS OF LUTHER'S INVOCAVIT SERMONS

## "RECEIVING BOTH KINDS IN THE SACRAMENT" (APRIL 1522)[1]

On March 30—exactly two weeks after completing the preaching of the Invocavit Sermons—Luther wrote a letter to Georg Spalatin, chaplain and private secretary to the Elector Frederick, at the Lochau residence. At the close of the brief correspondence, Luther told Spalatin that he had "in hand a little tract on the evangelical communion. The matter is giving me a great deal of trouble, but I am not afraid of it; Christ lives, and for His sake we must be not only 'a savor of death' to some and 'a savor of life' to others, but we must even be put to death."[2] A week later (April 5) Luther wrote to Count Lewis of Stolberg, a former student at Wittenberg, at the request of Melanchthon. In the opening paragraph of the letter, Luther refers to "my book," which Preserved Smith and Charles Jacobs believe is "Receiving Both Kinds in the Sacrament." Obviously, then, the "Both Kinds" document handles more than the issue of the Sacrament because Luther referred to the book as sufficient for the count's questions on images: "Philip has asked me to write you about the matter of the images, of which your Grace wrote to him, and although your Grace can gather my opinion well enough from my book, I have wished to grant his request and do your Grace a service, and so write to you myself."[3] Twelve days later (April 17), Luther wrote his Augustinian brother Gabriel Zwilling, who had left Wittenberg and was living in retirement in Düben, that he should accept the call to preach, if and when the city council of Altenburg asked him. (Luther had recommended Zwilling when the council asked "for a preacher of the Gospel.") In the letter, Luther advises Gabriel on what type of attitude and message to bring to the situation. As we recall that Zwilling had earlier been the firebrand preacher most responsible for many of the monastic and Mass reforms in Wittenberg, this is what Luther now advised him:

> May the Lord make you to increase unto thousands of thousands. See to it, above all things, that you are moderate, and wear the dress of a priest, putting off that broad-brimmed hat of yours for the sake of the weak, remembering that you are sent to those who must be fed with milk and released from the snares of the Pope. To do this you must work only with the Word, as you have heard from me, and as you will read in my new book.[4]

Thus, within a month after the Invocavit Sermons, Luther published his views for a wider audience outside Wittenberg, where he had not only stabilized the situation with a kind of apostolic authority, but also suggested that elsewhere the same guidance from a strong, authoritative preaching priesthood was needed.[5] We should expect to find those views on the Sacrament, images, and other issues organized in such a way as to assist the weak.

Primarily addressing the matter of the Sacrament, Luther's essay takes a forward look at most of the church reforms being faced by Wittenberg and surrounding towns and cities in the spring of 1522.[6] I say "forward" because of its contrast to the published Invocavit Sermons, which take a more backward look, examining each issue of controversy with respect to what—in Luther's absence— had happened, what was done wrong, what he would have done differently, and what ought now to be done. The sermons are supposed to be a record of Luther's remarks to Wittenbergers upon his sudden and unannounced (to most of them) return from Wartburg. In this essay, however, Luther presumes that his readers (outside Wittenberg) mostly agree on the rightness of both kinds (a subject he had addressed in the Fifth Invocavit Sermon [LW 51:90f.]), and with almost no air of animosity toward his evangelical opponents in Wittenberg—save for the delicate matter of trying to keep the one remaining recalcitrant, Karlstadt, out of print[7]— Luther lays out a recommended future course of action that is based on the policy already in place in Wittenberg.

The course of action includes 10 steps, five of which deal with the Sacrament and its context within the Mass, identifying proposals not spelled out in the Invocavit Sermons. The latter five steps cover other issues of church reform, and these do not radically advance the positions taken in the Invocavit Sermons (step 9— roughly 3 percent of the tract—handles images explicitly). Thus, Luther need not spend as much effort in this document rallying support for his own authority and leadership; rather, he can concentrate on outlining the policy's rightness, rationale, and effectiveness. Consequently—and perhaps consistent with the adaptation of oral, face-to-face address into written form—there is far less personal indignation by the speaker, not as much direct confrontation with the audience, and relatively less exhortation and admonition than in the Invocavit Sermons. There are still present, however, many indicators in the essay that Luther sees his role, and that of his readers, as resembling those of Paul the Apostle addressing New Testament churches.

The first two-thirds of the essay deals mostly with the Sacrament, while other issues (private masses, confession, images, vows, and foods) are taken up in the final one-third. For the entire essay's scope and plan, Luther can be much clearer in his organizational design than in the Invocavit Sermons. He provides distinct reading signals at key transition points; in identifying positions, arguments, and evidence; and in indicating shifts in topic. For example, the essay is divided into "Part I" and "Part II," with the implementation plan of the latter consisting of 10 steps, each an enumerated item. Luther needs such distinctive markers because the length of the piece precludes the use of the introduction and conclusion, which each respective sermon in the Invocavit series contains, wherein the introductions usually recapitulate the progress to that point, making the gist of the previous arguments all the more concise and clear. In this essay the internal summaries have to be strategically inserted rather than simply being demanded by each of the Invocavit Sermons' introductions.

In Part I Luther uses a biblical argument for the right of Christians to partake of both kinds that is not found in the Invocavit Sermons: Jesus' claim of authority over the Sabbath as evidence for believers' lordship over the Sacrament and as illustration of how humans often obstruct God's design when they rank Sabbath over man and sacramental elements over Christians. In Part II Luther employs two arguments from circumstances that are not found in the Invocavit Sermons, using biblical motifs. These arguments work as explanatory metaphors, rendering problematic circumstances more clear: (1) the wineskins image (from Matthew 9), wherein Luther argues that many German Christians are like old wineskins—their consciences simply cannot handle the new freedoms (such as partaking in both kinds) and that they will have to become new wineskins, which can only happen through preaching to them; and (2) the Babylonian captivity image (with which many should have been familiar), wherein Luther maintains that conditions are controlled by papists, whereby weak Christians' consciences are held in captivity—limited in their ability to handle the new reforms. Consequently, these conditions constrain the pace at which reforms can be effected.

In addition (and effectively, I believe, unless his assessment of the matter is flawed), Luther justifies his call for a moderating pace—a kind of temporary holding action. This justification helps sort out Christian priorities by making important and difficult distinctions:

1. The companion qualities of faith and love—as they apply to the reformers in the German church in 1522—are characterized in ways that show them helpfully distinct. Namely, faith addresses (clings to, fights for) truth and opposes the enemy (Satan and papists) while love properly pertains to (embraces, tolerates, helps) people—specifically, the weak (their consciences and actions).

2. Luther clearly holds, in several places and ways in the essay, that the present situation with respect to Sacrament and other church reforms is a matter for love's prevailing because those people most in jeopardy are friends, not enemies. In this essay, far more than in the Invocavit Sermons, Luther makes a convincing case for understanding more precisely what love and faith are and where and how they can both be applied. Moreover, what aids his case is a clear and reasonable description of weak persons, rather than a flimsy presumption of their importance that lacks sympathetic evidence on which to base such a presumption. In this essay, Luther has returned to arguments he made in "A Sincere Admonition."[8]

## SUMMARY OF THE INVOCAVIT SERMONS

We have analyzed Luther's response to a fluid, evolving situation, a response that entails specific issues: (1) his own printed book ("Both Kinds") and (2) a version of his preached sermons published by others (Invocavit Sermons). So what have we learned about the preacher Luther from our examination of his style, especially when we compare it to the style of Karlstadt? Why did Luther return to Wittenberg? What were the problems he simply had to deal with in person? How effective were the Invocavit Sermons for dealing with the problems?

In the Invocavit Sermons, Luther questioned, challenged, and condemned every forceful administrative reform initiated in Wittenberg during his absence. This seems the central concern of historians and theologians who have written about these sermons. However, Luther agreed with many of the reforms as goals even as he challenged the forceful means of bringing them about because he urged preaching as a superior means of reform. That Luther had strong personal and professional relationships, that is, similarities, with some in his audience and that he needed to speak to other serious differences are important factors to keep in mind. In particular, he had deep roots with this audience, so the several references to them as "dear friends" are much more than politeness. On the other hand, Luther's direct confrontations with the audience are not attacks upon an enemy; they are attempts to draw attention to serious distinctions for the benefit of friends. Luther the preacher sought to speak God's truth in love (Eph 4:15). Although he does not say so, we should note that Luther challenged his hearers to regard their Christian responsibilities and roles as those of planters and cultivators rather than harvesters. He said they must preach to other people and support them, not legislate for them and demand from them. Despite such emphases (which seem more immediate and less preoccupied with results), Luther also urged looking to the future because one of his frequent arguments in support of preaching and against force was that preaching would be more effective in bringing change. So Luther urged his hearers to forego short-term results for more enduring, long-term benefits.

We must examine now more carefully the manner in which these tasks emerge in the actual discursive encounter. I argue that Luther prepares his audience for the tasks they face, and he also equips them for handling those tasks. We begin to discover Luther's assessment of the situation at Wittenberg when we observe his manner of preparation and equipping, and it is a surprising phenomenon, one not at all obvious: Luther's assessment of the controversial issues differs from everyone else's!

First, as he prepares his audience for their tasks, Luther sets a precedent that, especially in the First Sermon, helps determine what the audience understands its role to be, though we must acknowledge also that the constraints of occasion, place, and events leading up to the sermons will figure into the mix as well. To regroup the Wittenberg movement and regain leadership, Luther must succeed in presenting a viewpoint that is plausible to his audience. He attempts this by redirecting the audience's attention and recasting their mission: They must look to a leader who is authentic and dedicated—to God and to them. They must look to their own blessings from God rather than to their grievances against Rome. Accordingly, they must consider the needs of others following in their footsteps rather than fixating on instant change. In brief, the Wittenbergers must proceed more cooperatively and cautiously. Luther turns the focus from inexorable reforms toward personal growth as he suggests to them in the middle of the First Sermon:

> Therefore we must not look upon our own, but upon our brother's powers, so that he who is weak in faith, and attempts to follow the strong, may not be destroyed of the devil. Therefore, dear brethren, follow me; I have never been a destroyer. And I was also the very first whom God called to this work. I cannot run away, but will remain as long as God allows. I was also the one to whom God first revealed that his Word should be preached to you. I am also sure that you have the pure Word of God. Let us, therefore, act with fear and humility, cast ourselves at one another's feet, join hands with each other, and help one another. I will do my part, which is no more than my duty, for I love you even as I love my own soul.[9]

Consider also how Luther equips the audience for their tasks. How can he succeed in this turn toward conservativism and a slowed reforming pace? How shall he face his most ardent supporters who have stood with him until now? Does he want to proceed as if in a debate or trial? Or does he wish to find a better—less adversarial, more subtle—way to address the issues within the broader context of a sermon series? In the First Sermon, Luther frames the message by beginning with a reminder that his concern in these sermons is with "chief things" that every Christian must know and be ready to use. He ends this reminder with a warning that misery awaits his audience if they persist in their actions, actions that are responsible for the fact that he had to risk his life to return to them to speak publicly regarding these things. Thus, these "chief things"—not the consensual issues of controversy—are addressed first. These chief things are used as prolegomena for the controversial issues.

The first policy issue is, of course, the Mass, but what Luther develops first is an antithetical heuristic for presenting each issue: whether something is a "must" or a "free." He uses this heuristic to condemn many of the actions Wittenbergers have taken, claiming that their lack of patience, lack of love, and forceful legislation have essentially violated the "free" nature of one's obligations stemming from these issues. In the first two sermons, Luther continues this overall heuristic in an adroit fashion. He proceeds to each new issue of discussion in the same manner: He begins by naming and explaining the issue, then he presents the scriptural authority for it. Only after these have been discussed does Luther turn to any "charges" or "compliments" with regard to how the Wittenbergers measure up. Thus, before making either accusations or praise, Luther starts with the agreeably accepted standard of "ought," against which he measures his audience and himself—the "is"—and from which he applies his evaluations and exhortations. Consequently, Luther furnishes both a practical argumentative context for the issues of controversy and a workable relational context in which he can provide teaching and correction. For the four "chief things," Luther finds that his audience is doing fine on the first two—knowledge of sin and faith in Christ. Both of these are beliefs based on scriptural knowledge, which Luther takes some credit for providing, but for which he also acknowledges his audience's own achievements, thereby anticipating and implicitly rebutting any possible audience pleas of ignorance. But the third and fourth things—love and patience—are actions growing out of the first two beliefs. Luther grounds all four things as scripturally sanctioned, and it is in love and patience that he finds the audience lacking.

To summarize Luther's astounding strategy for addressing the controversial issues: None of the "issues" of controversy is itself a "chief thing"; knowledge of sin, faith in Christ, love of neighbor, and patience with the weak are each of greater import than any of the issues. Yet the latter two things—love and patience—are the keys to handling every issue. Every action that Luther henceforth condemns in the eight sermons is tied to these two behavioral principles—love and patience—which he shows as crucial to the kingdom. Love is necessary to show that faith is genuine, and love is not only words, but action (deeds). Further, the object of love is one's neighbor, and loving one's neighbor requires patience. These latter two things are not options, but they are integrally involved in the prior two things. Hence, all four chief things subsume all controversial issues, providing a way to handle them, a way that seemed to escape everyone before Luther returned. Therefore, Luther has radically extended his evangelical view of the Christian life to include loving deeds that are an outgrowth of faith. With these four "chief things" anchoring every thought and deed of a believer (and every subsequent argument he makes), Luther proceeds to deal with the policies concerning the Mass, vows, images, foods, the Sacrament, and confession. For the most part, Luther has found as "free"—optional with respect to literal scriptural obligation—what Karlstadt, Zwilling, and even Melanchthon thought were obligatory "musts." The Wittenberg Movement had just applied the brakes (both tactical and theological) . . . hard! Grounding the Invocavit Sermons with this theological underpinning, Luther champions the cause of humanitarian service done in the name of Christ.[10] And his rationale for refusing to remove images maintains this theological position—namely, that thinking one can do a work for God and thereby reap salvific benefits for himself is foolish and more unbiblical than violating any Old Testament proscriptions against making images. Without discussing the doctrines of justification and sanctification, Luther has nonetheless in his sermon distinguished the two: Justification is Christ's work of accomplishing salvation for us; sanctification is the believer's loving response to grace and new life.

# LUTHER'S REASONS FOR RETURNING TO WITTENBERG

Why did Luther return to Wittenberg? To answer the historical and theological questions, we need to compare Luther's sermonic discourse with his (and some observers') correspondence. Therefore, we will look at Luther's own stated reasons for returning as recorded in his March 7–8 letter to Elector Frederick and compare the reasons given there with evidence from the Invocavit Sermons—particularly with respect to Luther's claim of being summoned by the congregation. Second, for drawing conclusions about style, we will compare Luther's *ethos* in the sermons, using the external reports of witnesses. For both of these issues—Luther's authority in returning, and his credibility in preaching—we will discuss them in connection with the shifting rhetorical situation in Wittenberg and surrounding towns.

Luther's letter of March 5 to Elector Frederick stated, in mostly vague and extreme language, his determination to return. When he arrived, Luther was instructed to put into writing—with the editorial assistance of the lawyer Jerome Schurff—more detailed and specific reasons behind his choice to end his confinement at the Wartburg. While willing to disregard the Elector's wishes and instructions to stay put, to pursue more urgent concerns, Luther did acknowledge the edited version of his letter's contents as reflecting an acceptable summary of his intentions. In the letter (written March 7 or 8) Luther outlines three major reasons for returning, each of which he defends with a brief argument.

The first reason is an argument from authority:

> I am called by the whole congregation at Wittenberg in a letter filled with urgent begging and pleading. Since no one can deny that the [present] commotion has its origin in me, and since I must confess that I am a humble servant of the congregation . . . I had no way of refusing [this call] without rejecting Christian love, trust, and obedience.[11]

Luther invokes what he regards as a legitimate, written summons "filled with urgent begging and pleading" from the Wittenberg congregation, to whom he feels a sense of obligation not only to answer their plea for help, but also because of his part in originally provoking some of what had happened. In the First Sermon (51:73) Luther twice invokes the original call to preach in Wittenberg ("whom God first called" [532.26]; called "by the council to preach" [*von dem radt zu(o) predige(n)*] [533.22]) while still chastizing the congregation for not consulting him. Presumably, he means that he was not consulted prior to some of the reforms undertaken during his absence. As to the written summons to return, Luther does not refer to it explicitly, but he does so only vaguely at the close of the First Sermon, invoking not the formal request but the urgent likely outcome if he did not come: "Therefore, I could no longer remain away, but was compelled to come and say these things to you" (51:75). In the Wolfenbüttel Manuscript, no mention whatsoever of the summons to return can be found. In "Both Kinds"

Luther plainly tells others, after the fact, that the policy he recommends is now in place in Wittenberg. In all probability, then, Luther did receive a request from the congregation, though we simply do not have a copy of it.[12] If the congregation was generally aware of such a summons, there would be no need to mention it aloud to them; hence, the silence in the Wolfenbüttel Manuscript could reflect a general knowledge and acceptance by most Wittenbergers of Luther's summons to return. For a subsequent reworking of the Invocavit Sermons for later publication, however, it might be helpful to include arguments about the legitimacy of Luther's return, couched both in authority and urgency, legality and duty.

Luther's second reason to return is an argument for the need of a face-to-face opportunity to fend off Satan's presence, which has broken out in the church: "Satan has intruded into my fold at Wittenberg. The whole world shouts it abroad . . . that Satan has injured some [sheep] which I cannot heal with my writing. I have to deal with them personally via mouth and ear."[13] Luther's argument not only stresses his desire for a more effective communication setting, but it keeps invoking his perceived pastoral duty to (and relationship with) the congregation, which he describes as "my flock,"[14] "my fold," "my children in Christ": "Had I been able to help things by writing letters, as I did until now, so that it would not be necessary to be called back, why should I not willingly consent to stay away from Wittenberg even for good, since it is also my duty to die for my neighbor's sake?"[15] Such a desire to be able to face his parishioners is understandable and was wise, and I shall attempt to summarize in the second section of this chapter a few of the ways in which Luther was so effective at situated oral discourse.

Luther's third stated reason for his return is that he feared actual widespread rebellion in the land. He believed that responsibility for this danger lay with the "fleshly sense" in which the common people tended to receive the Gospel. However, he also blamed the leaders for not heading this off. The people know the Gospel is true, but they "do not want to use it correctly. Those who should calm such rebellion only aid it. They attempt to put out the light by force, not realizing that they are only embittering the hearts of men by this and stimulating them to revolt."[16] Regardless of whether "by force" refers to leaders in Wittenberg—for their aggressive reform legislation—or to the Imperial Council of Regency in Nuremberg (for its attempt at judicial halting of reforms), Luther indicates that his notion of how the Gospel should operate requires his physical presence in the city. He saw the whole problem in Wittenberg in cosmic proportions—Satan and his minions against Christ and His Gospel. When persons obstructed the Gospel, they were playing into the hands of the opposition. However, Luther's pastoral heart saw the common people, the weak, the neighbor as precious souls caught between these forces. That accounts for so many warnings in the Invocavit Sermons to watch out for the devil and to be concerned for one's neighbor. As early as 1520, Luther had found evidence in Psalm 15 (Psalm 14 in the Vulgate) for his arguments about dealing differently with the weak than with the strong:

(1) LORD, who shall abide in thy tabernacle? who shall dwell in thy holy hill? (2) He that walketh uprightly, and worketh righteousness, and speaketh the truth in his heart. (3) He that backbiteth not with his tongue, nor doeth evil to his neighbour, nor taketh up a reproach against his neighbour. (4) In whose eyes a vile person is contemned; but he honoureth them that fear the LORD. He that sweareth to his own hurt, and changeth not. (5) He that putteth not out his money to usury, nor taketh reward against the innocent. He that doeth these things shall never be moved. (Ps 15:1–5)

These lines prompted Luther to ponder the relationship between worship rituals [*Zeremonien*]—seemingly suggested by verses 1, 5b—and the ethical-righteous behavior of faith and love elaborated in verses 2–5a. Luther came to believe that no person or institution could get along without ceremony but that eventually one might not need them. Meanwhile, ceremonies nourish people's faith, and those who are farther along in their development must bear with, not force, others who are coming along more slowly.[17]

A situated, oral-visual encounter gave Luther the chance to present a variety of appeals in a way that parishioners could experience again the pastoral concern they knew before—through the tracts and the preaching—from one who had faced the devil himself at Leipzig and Worms and now had returned from Patmos. Tangible effects from people's response to the oral and written Word preached—from Luther, Karlstadt, and Zwilling—had, in some cases, outrun their faith and love, resulting in confusion and offense. Now Luther believed it would take a powerful dose of the preached Word—in person. The Invocavit Sermons take their listeners first to principles of faith and love and concern for the weak, then they provide examples—usually those of biblical characters and of Luther himself—of how to implement those principles. As Adam Weyer puts it, "The confrontation with the principles of faith stands before the demanded practice of these principles."[18] Most effective of all, perhaps, is that Luther's sermons embodied those principles and examples: "The Wittenbergers hear the resolute preacher Luther, who wants to meet them with love and patience."[19]

## LUTHER'S *ETHOS*

In the Invocavit Sermons, Luther managed to embody both pastoral love and apostolic authority. It was this unique blend of love and truth that people saw as emanating from the Spirit of God, not simply from the Augustinian monk just back from the Wartburg, with his fresh tonsure and new cowl. The effects produced by this discourse are variously described. Karlstadt especially saw the results as tragic, as a betrayal of those "strong" evangelicals who, despite Luther's enriching of the notion of love, were now not receiving love. But for those who found the discourse convincing, one term may be most fitting—the scriptural notion of repentance.

Participants reporting a change of heart as a direct result of Luther's preaching include Hieronymus (Jerome) Schurff, whose March 15 letter (late in the week of the Invocavit Sermons) to Elector Frederic is worth quoting in part:

> I humbly wish your Grace to know that there is great gladness and rejoicing here, both among the learned and the unlearned, over Doctor Martin's return and over the sermons with which, by God's help, he is daily pointing us poor deluded men back again to the way of truth, showing us incontrovertibly the pitiful errors into which we have been led by the preachers who forced their way among us. It is plain as day that the Spirit of God is in him and works through him, and I have no doubt that it is by the special providence of the Almighty that he has come to Wittenberg just at this time. Even Gabriel [Zwilling] has confessed that he has erred and gone too far. Dr. Capito was here for two nights and heard two of Doctor Martin's sermons, in which he showed what gross errors had been committed against the Holy Sacrament of the Altar and its use. He was delighted with them, as he himself says. Since, then, the work that has been begun here comes, beyond all doubt, from God, He will protect it and will provide that it shall not be overthrown either by the devil or by his followers, if we only commend it to Him in true confidence and with real humility and fear.[20]

That attitude of repentant submission—to the conviction of the Holy Spirit at work in Luther—of which Schurff speaks is what Luther had been hoping for, even that Karlstadt would submit, though Luther knew "It will be hard for Carlstadt to give up his views, but Christ will force him to do so if he does not yield of his own accord."[21] Confirmation that Luther reached Capito is corroborated in a letter of Albert Burer to Beatus Rhenanus (27 March 1522), which is included in Nikolaus Müller's collection and a portion of which is available in Smith and Jacobs. The letter summarizes the impact of the Invocavit Sermons and their immediate context from the perspective of one who has tried to analyze, yet is convinced by, Luther's prowess and authority.

> On March 6 Martin Luther returned to Wittenberg in equestrian habit, accompanied by several horsemen. He came to settle the trouble stirred up by the extremely violent sermons of Carlstadt and Zwilling. For they had no regard for weak consciences, whom Luther, no less than Paul, would feed on milk until they grew strong. He preaches daily on the Ten Commandments. *As far as one can tell from his face the man is kind, gentle and cheerful. His voice is sweet and sonorous, so that I wonder at the sweet speaking of the man. Whatever he does, teaches and says is most pious, even though his impious enemies say the opposite. Everyone, even though not Saxon, who hears him once, desires to hear him again and again, such tenacious hooks does he fix in the minds of his auditors.* In short there is nothing lacking in that man which makes for the most perfect Christian piety, even though all mortals and the gates of hell may say the contrary. On March 12, Fabritius Capito came to Wittenberg to be reconciled to Luther, whom he somewhat offended by his letters, so that, it is said, he was called a poisonous beast by Luther. Now, I hear, they are entirely at one. What dis-

pleased Capito has begun to please him. He heard Luther preaching in the Wittenberg parish church, in which he saw him by chance. . . .[22]

In our analysis we must be cautious not to be so driven by these external reports that they dictate every detail we observe in Luther's discourse. However, Burer's observations are not mere flattery, nor are they simply impressionistic, adjectival evaluations. While strongly suggestive of the observer's frame of mind, they also attempt to describe the preacher's nonverbal demeanor and behavior, his oral qualities, and his argumentation. Much as one would amass and assess sign evidence—gathering observations, then holding them up to standards—Burer suggests that what he saw and heard fit those qualities described especially by the Apostle Paul, particularly Luther's teaching about Spirit-filled believers and his strategy (albeit forced upon him) of teaching the basics to those of weak conscience [ratione infirmorum]: milk [lacte], not meat.[23] We recall that Burer's earlier letter to Rhenanus (19 October 1521)[24] had also reported exciting news about reform activity in Wittenberg—a favorable report about Zwilling's preaching and Karlstadt's erudition. So Burer could be totally malleable and unreliable as a witness-analyst; if so, we might have to similarly charge not only Burer but Zwilling, Amsdorf, Melanchthon, Jonas, and many others. It is equally plausible, I think, that Burer (and the others) were even more persuaded by Luther's preaching than they had earlier been convinced of their former conclusions and positions. Moreover, we know that Luther saw the situation in Wittenberg in apostolic (Pauline) terms. For example, consider his letter of March 5 to the Elector: "Your Electoral Grace knows (or if you do not, I now inform you of the fact) that *I have received the gospel not from men but from heaven only*, through our Lord Jesus Christ, so that I might well be able to boast and write as a minister and evangelist [*Knecht und Evangelisten*], as I shall do in the future."[25]

## LUTHER'S STYLE

What can be learned about the preacher Luther from our examination of his style? In looking at Luther's preaching for the chief characteristics of his eloquence (not limited to whatever Burer meant by *suauiloquentiam*), I want to review four features that made Luther's discourse compelling, features that derive from his familiarity with Scripture: (1) his use of biblical passages, (2) his use of dialogue, (3) his pronoun manipulation, and (4) his use of doublets.

Luther's method of using Scripture differed considerably in these sermons from many of his other published sermons. He did not start from a prescribed pericope, as he does, for example, in the Wartburg Postils. Rather, in the midst of arguments intended to resolve problems, he made excursions to biblical passages,[26] and this tactic is itself important. As a practice, Luther's repetitive custom of recalling (alluding to, quoting, and paraphrasing)[27] Scripture—of condensing narratives and compressing centuries of time—set an example for the audience of what he, in fact, was preaching to them. In one sense Luther was demonstrating the finished product in himself: a Christian believer conversant in and comfortable with Scripture, one empowered by the Word of God to live victoriously amid threats from the devil, one sensitive to the needs of brethren, with teaching rather than force being the greatest need. We see Luther incorporating brief and varied themes from Scripture in a way that suggests not only a powerful command— memorization—of many texts, but also an understanding of Scripture's canonical and theological coherence. Moreover, unlike Karlstadt's tendency in *Von Abtuhung*, Luther seldom piles on ubiquitous Scripture citations as proof texts.[28] When he wanted to make rapid progress, consolidating agreement already available, Luther incorporated Scripture in a bold, concise manner, appealing to the clarity of a text.[29] However, when he needed to secure agreement with a controversial claim, one challenging the audience's position, Luther appealed to Christian charity, particularly when asserting caution, patience, and deference. When facing a "free" issue, Luther depicted ill-advised interpretations of Scripture as a poor shield behind which to hide. "[P]recisely because of his willingness to reformulate his argument according to the context, Luther was often successful in persuading his various audiences to agree with his position."[30]

In the Third Sermon, when discussing images (541.22–543.19), Luther directly introduced *controversia* into the argument, producing the kind of presence he desired—in this case, an eroding confidence in a mistaken position. And in an effort to break down a false sense of security, he did not merely string together scattered texts from separate contexts. He did that, to be sure; but prior to that (at 541.25–43.2), he set up his exegesis with a story about historic controversy between emperor and pope over images. In other words, Luther suggested the idea of controversy before displaying it from Scripture. In fact, as the argument unfolds, the "free" and "unnecessary" category easily lends itself to controversy because what some people think are "musts," others regard as "free."[31] Beginning at 541.22, Luther argued: "But now we must come to the images, and concerning them also it is true that they are unnecessary . . . ." Then he shared the story of emperor and pope, concluding at 541.29, "What was it all about? They wished to make a 'must' out of that which is free. This God cannot tolerate. Do you presume to do things differently . . . ?" (51:81f.). Then, Luther turns to Scripture passages that might be used to support a stand against images, producing in the next two dozen lines a "shaking of foundations" and "uncertainty." Moreover, he did this kind of thing later with the blessed Sacrament (the Fifth Sermon); using *controversia*—specifically in the matter of Christian freedom—he created presence. As we have seen, then, when Luther wanted to create presence for "musts," he turned to the clarity and firmness of Scripture. When developing presence in the "free" areas, he exploited the controversies of Scripture and its interpreters. Whichever use of Scripture is made, we should note, the one who directs attention to Scripture (Luther, the speaker) is potentially in the position to gain credibility.

When we look carefully at the places of scriptural *controversia* mentioned above—on images (the Third Sermon) and on the blessed Sacrament (the Fifth Sermon)—we observe yet another factor contributing to the ability of *controversia* to create presence. Luther does not merely act as a lecturer who identifies the ambiguities; he enacts them, that is, he embodies these clashes in dialogue. Thus, he enlarges the setting in which the controversy develops. In the case of images (the Third Sermon [51:81f.]), Luther produces several voices along the lines of: (1) "You" (the audience) assert a textual claim (542.2); (2) "our adversaries" reply (542.5–7); (3) Luther's own (narrator's) voice interjects comments (542.7–9); (4) the Scripture speaks, as uttered from the mouth of either side (542.12–15), and so on. Surely Luther would use vocal techniques to vivify these voices[32] because to miss that opportunity would minimize the effect these different voices could have—their various moods, tones, and pace. In the Fifth Sermon (51:88–90), Luther again produces dialogue between "you" (audience) and himself. By personally participating in the debate, Luther switches his auditor from the audience to the devil. But beyond enlarging the scope of the controversy, we might ask what is the value in producing these various voices?

In the matter of the blessed Sacrament (the Fifth Sermon), the dialogue is used not only to create presence through additional voices, and it does not merely enact scriptural *controversia*; rather, the *controversia* in dialogue executes a *prolepsis*. Luther uses the participation of the audience, engaging them through their invocation of their purported textual support, to directly challenge his own claim. He has, so to speak, summoned several expedients in his task of directly assaulting his opponents' proud accomplishment—taking the Sacrament in their own hands. That this is no straw-man objection is clear because Luther puts the objection squarely on the lips of the audience ("But you say . . ."). It is a brute fact to be reckoned with, an apparently clear command of Scripture—indeed, a "must"—standing firmly in the path of Luther's alleged "free." To summon the kind of presence needed for adherence to a thesis not at all easily accepted, Luther uses the direct approach, an all-out proleptic dialogue, one that allows him to control the outcome. Of course, *prolepsis* is always under the speaker's control; both sides in the dialogue ultimately issue from the same speaker. But dialogue enacts a means of cloaking this bias; if well done, it performs a big share of the persuasive work.

Certainly a characteristic (and distinctly functional) feature of these sermons is their intensity and intimacy. Luther used first- and second-person pronouns frequently yet skillfully, without succumbing to the pitfalls of mere flattery, insult, melancholia, or braggadocio. We notice that he sometimes used the first-person singular to put distance between himself and his audience. Here he uses the hammer of the Word to convict. "I" refers to Luther himself, and in the First Sermon (51:71) the shift from an inclusive (*we-us*) to exclusive (*I/you*) stance is rapid, in part because of the transition from the writer Paul to the speaker Luther, both of whom use the first person:

> [W]e must also have love and through love we must do to one another as God has done to us through faith. For without love faith is nothing, as St. Paul says (I Cor. 2 [13:1]): If I had the tongues of angels and could speak of the highest things in faith, and have not love, I am nothing. And here, dear friends, have you not grievously failed? I see no signs of love among you, and I observe very well that you have not been grateful to God for his rich gifts and treasures.[33]

Later in the same sermon, Luther uses the "I" repeatedly, in the same syntactic position, to drive home the distance between himself—as worthy of emulation—and his audience, to emphasize that the audience is falling short (51:72f.): "Therefore, dear brethren, follow *me*; *I* have never been a destroyer. And *I* was also the very first whom God called to this work. *I* cannot run away, but will remain as long as God allows. *I* was also the one to whom God first revealed that his Word should be preached to you. *I* am also sure that you have the pure Word of God" (*my emphasis*).

However, Luther at other times creates and celebrates intimacy and agreement. Here is where he woos, wins, and even challenges wounded hearts that have been bruised by the chastizing rod of preaching. He particularly uses this tactic to advantage when exhorting his audience to act affirmatively on his recommendations (to preach and nurture others). He uses the inclusive first plural at the close of the first sermon (51:74f.):

> Let *us*, therefore, feed others also with the milk which *we* received, until they, too, become strong in faith. For there are many who are otherwise in accord with *us* and who would also gladly accept this thing, but they do not yet fully understand it—these *we* drive away. Therefore, let *us* show love to *our* neighbors; if *we* do not do this, *our* work will not endure. *We* must have patience with them for a time, and not cast out him who is weak in faith; and do not omit to do many other things, so long as love requires it and it does no harm to *our* faith. If *we* do not earnestly pray to God and act rightly in this matter, it looks to me as if all the misery which *we* have begun to heap upon the papists will fall upon *us*. (*my emphasis*)

Luther uses the first plural to celebrate acknowledged premises, to generate momentum that will carry on to exhortations. Notice in the Seventh Sermon (51:95) how no second-person pronouns invade. The focus is on celebrating:

> *We* shall now speak of the fruit of this sacrament, which is love; that is, that *we* should treat *our* neighbor as God has treated *us*. Now *we* have received from God nothing but love and favor, for Christ has pledged and given *us* his righteousness and everything he has; he has poured out upon *us* all his treasures, which no man can measure and no angel can understand or fathom, for God is a glowing furnace of love, reaching even from the earth to the heavens. (*my emphasis*)

When a proliferation of second-person pronouns is found, it can help generate confrontation. Luther gives the "you" a sorry character that is very unpleasant (51:95f):

> But this I do not yet perceive among *you* here in Wittenberg, even though *you* have had much preaching and, after all, *you* ought to have carried this out in practice. This is the chief thing, which is the only business of a Christian man. But nobody wants to be in this, though *you* want to practice all sorts of unnecessary things, which are of no account. If *you* do not want to show *yourselves* Christians by *your* love, then leave the other things undone, too . . . . (*my emphasis*)

Hence, Luther pushes away the second person to such an extent that it fades into the third person. He follows this negative "you" with a quote of Paul in 1 Corinthians 13 (containing several "I"s), then more "you"s and "nobody"s. In all, at 555.15–29, he utters six "you"s, six "nobody"s, and the adverbs "not yet" and "as yet." So we see how Luther uses pronouns—first- and second-person pronouns especially—to help convey the closeness and comfort, or the distance and discomfort, that the ideas he works with can elicit: positive and negative emotions, praise and blame, celebration and exhortation.

Luther's style, especially in the way he handles pronouns, is not unlike Pauline argumentation. For example, consider Paul's argument in 1 Cor 15:3–19. Before becoming more aware of the stylistic features of pronoun usage, I might have taken the argument to be reducible to a tightly constructed logical progression—namely, the following conundrum: (1) Christ has been raised (vv. 3–11); (2) But some say there is no resurrection of the dead (v. 12); (3) Then Christ is not raised (v. 13). Then in verses 14–19, Paul explores the implications of that negative conclusion. Yet this reconstruction and its conception as a "logical argument" obscures—even distorts—a great deal of what is going on in the rhetorical action.[34] This "argument" does not occur in a vacuum; indeed, its beginning (v. 3) shows that the whole matter of resurrection operates as an enthymematic datum—the supporting reason in a rhetorical syllogism[35]—intended to demonstrate Paul's earlier claim (v. 2) that the Gospel's saving power (resurrection of the dead) consists in the factual veracity of Christ's resurrection. In other words, the context of (purpose for, human connection to) the "argument" endows the argument with meaning and significance. And Paul's pronoun usage helps us see that (beginning with "For I delivered *unto you* . . ." [*my emphasis*]). Merely a glance at Paul's strategic use of pronouns reveals several interesting stylistic features, beginning with how he initially presses hard to show the audience's personal stake ("unto you") in the apostolic authority of the message ("I declare/preached/ delivered"): "Moreover, brethren, I declare unto you the gospel which I preached unto you, which also ye have received, and wherein ye stand; By which also ye are saved, if ye keep in memory what I preached unto you, unless ye have have believed in vain" (1 Cor 15:1–2). Then he uses (1) a cluster of "I"s in verses 3–11, wherein Paul the speaker surrounds himself with a panoply of authoritative witnesses. (2) At verse 11, the expectation—that the audience attests to everything previously stated—is shifted from Paul to the Corinthians (listeners). That is, he now "throws the ball" to them: "Therefore whether it were I or they [witnesses], so we preach, and so ye believed." (3) At verse 12f. Paul uses several "you"s to vocalize the counterargument that "there is no resurrection." (4) At verse 14f. Paul uses first-person plural pronouns to summarize the devastating outcome—for everyone, himself included, no exceptions: "Then is our preaching vain, and your faith is also vain. Yea, and we are found false witnesses." So the audience is trapped and reels between contraries; they face their own self-inflicted dismantling after going from confidence in a resurrected Lord, to devastation at realizing He is an unrisen Christ, to shame/destruction in bearing the guilty sentence of a false witness (which, for Jews, would be stoning to death). My point is that Paul does far more in the passage than simply outline the necessary consequences of Corinthian premises; neither does he merely present the Corinthians with a contradiction in their premises. He isolates his audience from the fellowship of significant others—from himself, from their own beliefs, from their own tradition. He enacts a movement from acknowledged, confident celebration to alarming despair. The argument does not only speculate (or even assert) about death, the discourse effects a drama. Without looking closely at the style, we miss that.

However, Luther's use of personal pronouns need not have been influenced solely by Paul because the manner in which form gets into a discourse is never easy to determine. For that matter, it is probably a natural feature of human language that emotion—especially as it tries to express the way ideas affect human relationships—simply finds its way into our discourse. Auditors may not be initially drawn to notice the pronouns, but they are there nonetheless; critics pick them up, and so may sensitive listeners or readers. Sometimes personal pronouns are not simply repetitive or shifting from one person to another to mark changing relationships; at other times they are strategically positioned in the rhetor's syntax. They cannot only be frequent, but prominent in emphasis.

Psalm 22 is an example, one that Luther would not have missed. Any reader remotely familiar with this psalm knows that its solitary, haunting perspective on isolation from God and persecution by others was powerful enough that Jesus used the opening verse to express his own anguish on the cross: "My God, my God, why hast thou forsaken me?" (Ps 22:1; Matt 27:46; Mark 15:34). One of the striking stylistic features of Psalm 22 (Psalm 21 in the Vulgate) is that many of the personal pronouns are positioned for emphasis—either at the front or the rear of statements. This phenomonon is even more clear in the Vulgate where word order plays a greater role in Latin (for showing emphasis) than in English. The psalmist tends to pile up pronouns in clusters to convey a sense of isolation. Sometimes the first singular (I/me/my) appears repeatedly, then the second-person singular (thee/thou/thine) piles up. The frequency, position, and sudden shift all drive the protagonist's (and the rhetor's) point: I am in despair, and it feels even worse when I closely consider whom I was counting on (God); neither does it help when I consider those others persecuting or laughing at me (third-person pronouns emerge). Here is a small sample, where the strategically placed pronouns occur mostly at front positions—where the emphasis is greatest—with some at the rear. The idea is that I (subject) see only trouble, often at my (object) expense:

(1) My God, my God, why hast thou forsaken me? why art thou so far from helping me, and from the words of my roaring? [*Deus Deus meus quare dereliquisti me longe a salute mea verba rugitus mei*] (2) O my God, I cry in the daytime, but thou hearest not; and in the night season, and am not silent. [*Deus meus clamabo per diem et non exaudies et nocte nec est silentium mihi*] (3) But thou art holy, O thou that inhabitest the praises of Israel. [*et tu sancte habitator Laus Israhel*] (4) Our fathers trusted in thee: they trusted, and thou didst deliver them. [*in te confisi sunt patres nostri confisi sunt et salvasti eos*] (5) They cried unto thee, and were delivered: they trusted in thee, and were not confounded. [*ad te clamaverunt et salvati sunt in te confisi sunt et non sunt confusi*] (6) But I am a worm, and no man; a reproach of men, and despised of the people. [*ego autem sum vermis et non homo opprobrium hominum et dispectio plebis*] (7) All they that see me laugh me to scorn: they shoot out the lip, they shake the head, saying, [*omnes videntes me subsannant me dimittunt labium movent caput*] (8) "He trusted on the LORD that he would deliver him: let him deliver him, seeing he delighted in him." [*confugit ad Dominum salvet eum liberet eum quoniam vult eum*] (9) But thou art he that took me out of the womb: thou didst make me hope when I was upon my mother's breasts. [*tu autem propugnator meus ex utero fiducia mea ab uberibus matris meae*] (10) I was cast upon thee from the womb: thou art my God from my mother's belly. [*in te proiectus sum ex vulva de ventre matris meae Deus meus es tu*] (Ps 22:1–10)

Just a bit later—though the English syntactic requirements obscure it—we find the first singular pronoun occurring at the rear—the second most emphatic position. The idea is that "me" is the object of negative action.

(12) Many bulls have compassed me; strong bulls of Bashan have beset me round. [*circumdederunt me vituli multi tauri pingues vallaverunt me*] (13) They gaped upon me with their mouths, as a ravening and a roaring lion. [*aperuerunt super me os suum quasi leo capiens et rugiens*] (14) I am poured out like water, and all my bones are out of joint: my heart is like wax; it is melted in the midst of my bowels. [*sicut aqua effusus sum et separata sunt omnia ossa mea factum est cor meum sicut cera liquefacta in medio ventris mei*] (15) My strength is dried up like a potsherd; and my tongue cleaveth to my jaws; and thou has brought me into the dust of death. [*aruit velut testa fortitudo mea et lingua mea adhesit palato meo et in pulverem mortis detraxisti me*] (16) For dogs have compassed me: the assembly of the wicked have inclosed me: they pierced my hands and my feet. [*circumdederunt me venatores concilium pessimorum vallavit me vinxerunt manus meas et pedes meos*] (17) I may tell all my bones: they look and stare upon me [*numeravi omnia ossa mea quae ipsi respicientes viderunt in me*] (Ps 22:12–17)

Luther knew the Psalms as a book where the reader is able to "*hear* the saints speak," unlike other religious books that present the saints "with their *tongues tied*."[36] He often saw the Psalms as the "christological hymnbook of the Bible,"[37] depicting, promising, and proclaiming Christ, but Luther always (after his second lecture course in 1519–21) approached the Psalter as a laboratory in which to practice that proper relationship to God while praying the text, calling it "a training room for the feelings."[38] He could not but be affected by the syntax of the Vulgate, its patterns and rhythms working their way into his memory, ready to be deployed when his own preaching required similar rhetorical tasks.[39] David, filled with the inspiring joy of God, revels endlessly in " 'new figures of speech' and in the beautiful clothing of figurative poetic language."[40] Anyone who doubts Luther's understanding of structure and stylistic devices needs to read Helmar Junghans's indispensable study of Luther's rhetorical remarks in the *Dictata super Psalterium*[41] or any of several studies of Luther's discourse by Birgit Stolt.[42] Of course, the poetic structure one finds embedded in verse should not all be orally enacted, lest the reading become overtly mechanical, thereby allowing form's total subjugation of the information. But when I find such overwhelmingly obvious patterns—be they pronouns or any other repetitive device—I try to evoke those images in my oral presentation of the piece. Such faithful rendering of what is an integral part of the coherence of a message normally does not produce mistaken judgments about the speaker ("what a good reader he is! etc."); rather, it elicits rapt attention to the discourse. Luther naturally received praise—from Burer and others. But such praise will be short-lived and will prove ill-conceived, unless audiences are moved to conviction by the message—not dazzled by the messenger.

Luther's sermons also display the frequent use of a stylistic feature I have called doublets. While there are several variations possible, doublets usually connect two words of the same grammatical form—finite verbs, adjectives or adverbs, and substantives—with a coordinate conjunction. Luther usually uses the conjunction *and* (*und*) or *or/nor* (*oder, noch*), though he often asyndetically omits these, using mere pauses (commas). Most often the two or three terms are highly alike in meaning—though occasionally they are contrasting—and sometimes they rhyme. It appears that when he uses doublets Luther has an important point to make, and these doublets are one of the tools he uses to make the point. A similar structure is the *triplet*, though in Luther's case doublets outnumber them seven to one. The following is an example from the First Sermon:

> Let me illustrate. The sun has two properties, *light and heat.* No king has power enough to *bend or guide* the light of the sun; it remains fixed in its place. But the heat may be *turned and guided*, and yet is ever about the sun. Thus faith must always remain [pure and immovable] in our hearts,[43] never wavering; but love *bends and turns* so that our neighbor may *grasp and follow* it. There are some who can run, others must walk, still others can hardly creep [cf. I Cor. 8:7–13]. Therefore we must not look upon our own, but upon our

brother's powers, so that he who is weak in faith, and attempts to follow the strong, may not be destroyed of the devil.[44]

Luther's first doublet introduces what he maintains are two distinct (and for him, probably comprehensive) properties of the sun—light and heat—that may seem contiguous to us but which, in this rhetorical context, are opposites. Apparently, he refers to the property of light as static, radiating from a fixed point, while heat is dynamic and reaches down to the creation without losing its source in the sun. After establishing the actions of the sun's properties with the first verbal doublet, Luther chiastically uses the same doublet again—*bygen oder lencke(n)* . . . *lencken vnd byge(n)*—so what is impossible with, and not required of, light is expected of heat. Then Luther repeats each property's attribute, this time adding the recipient of the heat-bending love (neighbor) and the desired outcome of love in the neighbor—may "grasp and follow," which seems like a contiguous relation. Yet "grasp and follow" is not clearly contiguous, but it seems progressive; indeed, the progressive relation, whereby the second term is a product of the first, is characteristic of many of Luther's doublets of similarity. The "grasp and follow" doublet leads to tripled, ordered clauses of contiguous relation (*run/ walk/ creep*), each bearing the same repetitive term in German [*ettliche*] (*some . . . others . . . others*). Once he has established the process through explanation and teaching, Luther turns to exhortation ("Therefore, we must"), which seems especially timely because it comes on the heels of the previously demonstrated need ("hardly creep").

Luther is using the doublets to suggest a second term, like unto the first, wherein he makes another stab at his point. Once he has employed two terms, he can repeat them chiastically or even add a third term. While the discourse samples we have considered represent only some of the ways Luther uses doublets, we can generalize by saying he simply doesn't let go of a point until he is good and ready, until satisfied that he has milked its meaning and applications thoroughly, until he believes at least one of the terms has worked for listeners. "Luther knew the performative power of the words, and what he was seeking to drive (*was Christum treibt*) was not his own point of view but the same that Paul was seeking to promote, namely, Jesus Christ."[45]

Luther was accustomed to expounding on Scripture, and the more familiar he became with its broad theological coherence, the harder he worked to present—in celebration and application—its truths to others. The doublet or triplet became another tool for setting forth Scripture for audiences to "see," to comprehend. Despite his well-known depictions of Scripture as a "mouth-house," meant to be spoken and heard, Luther used doublets much in the way the *Ad Herennium* once refers to *enarratio*, in facilitating "*ocular* demonstration":

It is Ocular Demonstration when an event is so described in words that the business seems to be enacted and the subject to pass vividly before our eyes. This we can effect by including what has preceded, followed, and accompanied the event itself, or by keeping steadily to its consequences or the attendant circumstances . . . . Through this kind of narrative [*huiusmodi enarrationibus*] Ocular Demonstration is very useful in amplifying a matter and basing on it an appeal to pity, for it sets forth the whole incident and virtually brings it before the eyes.[46]

In the Invocavit Sermons, we do not simply discover the already obvious—that Luther was an effective preacher. Much more, we have seen specific ways in which he was effective because he was not simply in the right place at the right time with the right doctrine. Luther made the Scriptures work for his listeners because he knew the Word and he knew his listeners. "Luther represents here no image of rhetoric as [merely?] instrumental, but rather as one of emotion-binding. He looks for faith-binding agreement with his listeners."[47] Theology and care are most closely interrelated and mutually permeate each other.[48] Both the "I" of the preacher and the "you" of the community are significant. Luther is a pastoral preacher, his discourse profoundly affected by the needs of the community—the situation—as well as by his view of Scripture, God, and human nature. God is creator of both humankind and Scripture; he designed each for oral-aural, *affektgebundene*, interaction with the other.[49] In his discourse responding to the Wittenberg Movement, Luther's biblical and pastoral rhetoric coincides with characteristics of a Renaissance culture of oratory that relied heavily on persuasion rather than on coercion, on the inward assent of individuals to the Word of God preached.[50] In closely following the discursive action of Luther, it is hoped that we have also gained a greater sensitivity and appreciation for how preaching works. Perhaps we have even sharpened our ability to read all discourse.

# APPENDIX
# EIGHT SERMONS AT WITTENBERG
## 1522

[69]The title of the earliest printed version of these sermons reads: "Eight Sermons by Dr. M. Luther, preached by him at Wittenberg in Lent, dealing briefly with the masses, images, both kinds in the sacrament, eating [of meats], and private confession, etc."

In December, 1521, Luther returned secretly to Wittenberg from the Wartburg for a three-day conference on how to meet the turbulence and confusion caused by the radical reformers. Soon after his return to the Wartburg, Karlstadt put himself at the head of those who favored immediate abolition of Roman practices. At Christmas Karlstadt administered communion in two kinds for the first time in the parish church. (This had been done as early as September in the Augustinian monastery where Gabriel Zwilling conducted mass in the vernacular and abolished private masses.) Karlstadt also declared that confession before communion was unnecessary, that images were not allowable in the church, and that rules of fasting were not binding, and this led to outbreaks of actual destruction of images and altars. He also taught the doctrine of direct illumination by the Spirit, which made scholarship and learning unnecessary for the understanding of the Scriptures. The consequence was that the city schools were closed and the university threatened with collapse. Allied with Karlstadt's followers were the Zwickau prophets, Storch, Drechsel, and Stübner, adherents of Thomas Münzer.

Luther, who hitherto had relied upon Melanchthon's leadership to keep order, returned to Wittenberg on March 6. On March 8 he conferred with Melanchthon, Justus Jonas, Nicholas Amsdorf, and Hieronymus Schurf. On March 9, Invocavit Sunday, he mounted the pulpit in the parish church and preached each day from the ninth to the sixteenth. This remarkable series of sermons, which are powerful, inspired preaching of the gospel, had the effect of restoring [70] tranquility and order almost at once. His task was to lead his congregation away from fanatical enthusiasm back to the spirit of the gospel and to answer the questions that were agitating his people in the light of the gospel. (Further details may be found in an excellent introduction to the sermons in *PE* 2, 387–390 and in the biographies of Luther and the church histories.)

The sermons were transcribed by an unknown amanuensis and printed in many editions. Later versions by Stephan Roth, in the church postils, and Aurifaber, in the Eisleben edition, are simply free expansions of this oldest transcript.

The present translation is a revision of that by A. Steimle in *PE* 2, 390–425. The minor differences, apart from style, are due largely to the fact that Steimle more frequently resorted to the undependable Aurifaber text.

Text in German; *CL* 7, 363–387, compared with *WA* 10/3, 1–64 and *MA³*, 4, 33–58, 332–337.

# THE FIRST SERMON, MARCH 9, 1522, INVOCAVIT SUNDAY

The summons of death comes to us all, and no one can die for another. Every one must fight his own battle with death by himself, alone. We can shout into another's ears, but every one must himself be prepared for the time of death, for I will not be with you then, nor you with me. Therefore every one must himself know and be armed with the chief things which concern a Christian. And these are what you, my beloved, have heard from me many days ago.

In the first place, we must know that we are the children of wrath, and all our works, intentions, and thoughts are nothing at all. Here we need a clear, strong text to bear out this point. Such is the saying of St. Paul in Eph. 2 [:3]. Note this well; and though there are many such in the Bible, I do not wish to overwhelm you with many texts. "We are all the children of wrath." And please do not undertake to say: I have built an altar, given a foundation for masses, etc.

[71] Secondly, that God has sent us his only-begotten Son that we may believe in him and that whoever trusts in him shall be free from sin and a child of God, as John declares in his first chapter, "To all who believed in his name, he gave power to become children of God" [John 1:12]. Here we should all be well versed in the Bible and ready to confront the devil with many passages. With respect to these two points I do not feel that there has been anything wrong or lacking. They have been rightly preached to you, and I should be sorry if it were otherwise. Indeed, I am well aware and I dare say that you are more learned than I, and that there are not only one, two, three, or four, but perhaps ten or more, who have this knowledge and enlightenment.

Thirdly, we must also have love and through love we must do to one another as God has done to us through faith. For without love faith is nothing, as St. Paul says (I Cor. 2 [13:1]): If I had the tongues of angels and could speak of the highest things in faith, and have not love, I am nothing. And here, dear friends, have you not grievously failed? I see no signs of love among you, and I observe very well that you have not been grateful to God for his rich gifts and treasures.

Here let us beware lest Wittenberg become Capernaum [cf. Matt. 11:23]. I notice that you have a great deal to say of the doctrine of faith and love which is preached to you, and this is no wonder; an ass can almost intone the lessons, and why should you not be able to repeat the doctrines and formulas? Dear friends, the kingdom of God,—and we are that kingdom—does not consist in talk or words [I Cor. 4:20], but in activity, in deeds, in works and exercises. God does not want hearers and repeaters of words [Jas. 1:22], but followers and doers, and this occurs in faith through love. For a faith without love is not enough—rather it is not faith at all, but a counterfeit of faith, just as a face seen in a mirror is not a real face, but merely the reflection of a face [I Cor. 13:12].

Fourthly, we also need patience. For whoever has faith, trusts in God, and shows love to his neighbor, practicing it day by day, must needs suffer persecution. For the devil never sleeps, but constantly gives him plenty of trouble. But patience works and produces hope [Rom. 5:4], which freely yields itself to God and vanishes away in him. Thus faith, by much affliction and **[72]** persecution, ever increases, and is strengthened day by day. A heart thus blessed with virtues can never rest or restrain itself, but rather pours itself out again for the benefit and service of the brethren, just as God has done to it.

And here, dear friends, one must not insist upon his rights, but must see what may be useful and helpful to his brother, as Paul says, *Omnia mihi licent, sed non omnia expediunt,* " 'All things are lawful for me,' but not all things are helpful" [I Cor. 6:12]. For we are not all equally strong in faith, some of you have a stronger faith than I. Therefore we must not look upon ourselves, or our strength, or our prestige, but upon our neighbor, for God has said through Moses: I have borne and reared you, as a mother does her child [Deut. 1:31]. What does a mother do to her child? First she gives it milk, then gruel, then eggs and soft food, whereas if she turned about and gave it solid food, the child would never thrive [cf. I Cor. 3:2; Heb. 5:12–13]. So we should also deal with our brother, have patience with him for a time, have patience with his weakness and help him bear it; we should also give him milk-food, too [I Pet. 2:2; cf. Rom. 14:1–3], as was done with us, until he, too, grows strong, and thus we do not travel heavenward alone, but bring our brethren, who are not now our friends, with us. If all mothers were to abandon their children, where would we have been? Dear brother, if you have suckled long enough, do not at once cut off the breast, but let your brother be suckled as you were suckled. I would not have gone so far as you have done, if I had been here. The cause is good, but there has been too much haste. For there are still brothers and sisters on the other side who belong to us and must still be won.

Let me illustrate. The sun has two properties, light and heat. No king has power enough to bend or guide the light of the sun; it remains fixed in its place. But the heat may be turned and guided, and yet is ever about the sun. Thus faith must always remain pure and immovable in our hearts, never wavering; but love bends and turns so that our neighbor may grasp and follow it. There are some who can run, others must walk, still others can hardly creep [cf. I Cor. 8:7–13]. Therefore we must not look upon our own, but upon our brother's powers, so that he who is weak in faith, and attempts to follow the strong, may not be destroyed of the devil. Therefore, dear brethren, follow me; I have never been a destroyer. And I was **[73]** also the very first whom God called to this work. I cannot run away, but will remain as long as God allows. I was also the one to whom God first revealed that his Word should be preached to you. I am also sure that you have the pure Word of God.

Let us, therefore, let us act with fear and humility, cast ourselves at one another's feet, join hands with each other, and help one another. I will do my part, which is no more than my duty, for I love you even as I love my own soul. For here we battle not against pope or bishop, but against the devil [cf. Eph. 6:12], and do you imagine he is asleep? He sleeps not, but sees the true light rising, and to keep it from shining into his eyes he would like to make a flank attack—and he will succeed, if we are not on our guard. I know him well, and I hope, too, that with the help of God, I am his master. But if we yield him but an inch, we must soon look to it how we may be rid of him. Therefore all those have erred who have helped and consented to abolish the mass; not that it was not a good thing, but that it was not done in an orderly way. You say it was right according to the Scriptures. I agree, but what becomes of order? For it was done in wantonness, with no regard for proper order and with offense to your neighbor. If, beforehand, you had called upon God in earnest prayer, and had obtained the aid of the authorities, one could be certain that it had come from God. I, too, would have taken steps toward the same end if it had been a good thing to do; and if the mass were not so evil a thing, I would introduce it again. For I cannot defend your action, as I have just said. To the papists and blockheads I could defend it, for I could say: How do you know whether it was done with good or bad intention, since the work in itself was really a good work? But I would not know what to assert before the devil. For if on their deathbeds the devil reminds those who began this affair of texts like these, "Every plant which my Father has not planted will be rooted up" [Matt. 15:13], or "I have not sent them, yet they ran" [Jer. 23:21], how will they be able to withstand? He will cast them into hell. But I shall poke the one spear into his face, so that even the world will become too small for him, for I know that in spite of my reluctance I was called by the council to preach. Therefore I was willing to [74] accept you as you were willing to accept me, and, besides, you could have consulted me about the matter.

I was not so far away that you could not reach me with a letter, whereas not the slightest communication was sent to me. If you were going to begin something and make me responsible for it, that would have been too hard. I will not do it [i.e., assume the responsibility]. Here one can see that you do not have the Spirit, even though you do have a deep knowledge of the Scriptures. Take note of these two things, "must" and "free." The "must" is that which necessity requires, and which must ever be unyielding; as, for instance, the faith, which I shall never permit any one to take away from me, but must always keep in my heart and freely confess before every one. But "free" is that in which I have choice, and may use or not, yet in such a way that it profit my brother and not me. Now do not make a "must" out of what is "free," as you have done, so that you may not be called to account for those who were led astray by your loveless exercise of liberty. For if you entice any one to eat meat on Friday, and he is troubled about it on his deathbed, and thinks, Woe is me, for I have eaten meat and I am lost! God will call you to account for that soul. I, too, would like to begin many things, in which but few would follow me, but what is the use? For I know that, when it comes to the showdown, those who have begun this thing cannot maintain themselves, and will be the first to retreat. How would it be, if I brought the people to the point of attack, and though I had been the first to exhort others, I would then flee, and not face death with courage? How the poor people would be deceived!

Let us, therefore, feed others also with the milk which we received, until they, too, become strong in faith. For there are many who are otherwise in accord with us and who would also gladly accept this thing, but they do not yet fully understand it—these we drive away. Therefore, let us show love to our neighbors; if we do not do this, our work will not endure. We must have patience with them for a time, and not cast out him who is weak in faith; and do and omit to do many other things, so long as love requires it and it does no harm to our faith. If we do not earnestly pray to God and act rightly in this matter, it looks to me as if all the misery which [75] we have begun to heap upon the papists will fall upon us. Therefore I could no longer remain away, but was compelled to come and say these things to you.

This is enough about the mass; tomorrow we shall speak about images.

## THE SECOND SERMON, MARCH 10, 1522,
## MONDAY AFTER INVOCAVIT

Dear friends, you heard yesterday the chief characteristics of a Christian man, that his whole life and being is faith and love. Faith is directed toward God, love toward man and one's neighbor, and consists in such love and service for him as we have received from God without our work and merit. Thus, there are two things: the one, which is the most needful, and which must be done in one way and no other; the other, which is a matter of choice and not of necessity, which may be kept or not, without endangering faith or incurring hell. In both, love must deal with our neighbor in the same manner as God has dealt with us; it must walk the straight road, straying neither to the left nor to the right. In the things which are "musts" and are matters of necessity, such as believing in Christ, love nevertheless never uses force or undue constraint. Thus the mass is an evil thing, and God is displeased with it, because it is performed as if it were a sacrifice and work of merit. Therefore it must be abolished. Here there can be no question or doubt, any more than you should ask whether you should worship God. Here we are entirely agreed: the private masses must be abolished. As I have said in my writings,[1] I wish they would be abolished everywhere and only the ordinary evangelical mass be retained. Yet Christian love should not employ harshness here nor force the matter. However, it should be preached and taught with tongue and pen that [76] to hold mass in such a manner is sinful, and yet no one should be dragged away from it by the hair; for it should be left to God, and his Word should be allowed to work alone, without our work or interference. Why? Because it is not in my power or hand to fashion the hearts of men as the potter molds the clay and fashion them at my pleasure [Ecclus. 33:13]. I can get no farther than their ears; their hearts I cannot reach. And since I cannot pour faith into their hearts, I cannot, nor should I, force any one to have faith. That is God's work alone, who causes faith to live in the heart. Therefore we should give free course to the Word and not add our works to it. We have the *jus verbi* [right to speak] but not the *executio* [power to accomplish]. We should preach the Word, but the results must be left solely to God's good pleasure.

Now if I should rush in and abolish it by force, there are many who would be compelled to consent to it and yet not know where they stand, whether it is right or wrong, and they would say: I do not know if it is right or wrong, I do not know where I stand, I was compelled by force to submit to the majority. And this forcing and commanding results in a mere mockery, an external show, a fool's play, man-made ordinances, sham-saints, and hypocrites. For where the heart is not good, I care nothing at all for the work. We must first win the hearts of the people. But that is done when I teach only the Word of God, preach the gospel, and say: Dear lords or pastors, abandon the mass, it is not right, you are sinning when you do it; I cannot refrain from telling you this. But I would not make it an ordinance for them, nor urge a general law. He who would follow me could do so, and he who refused would remain outside. In the latter case the Word would sink into the heart and do its work. Thus he would become convinced and acknowledge his error, and fall away from the mass; tomorrow another would do the same, and thus God would accomplish more with his Word than if you and I were to merge all our power into one heap. So when you have won the heart, you have won the man—and thus the thing must finally fall of its own weight and come to an end. And if the hearts and minds of all are agreed and united, abolish it. But if all are not heart and soul for its abolishment—leave it in God's hands, I beseech you, otherwise the result will not be good. Not that I would again set up the mass; I let it in in God's name. Faith must not be chained **[77]** and imprisoned, nor bound by an ordinance to any work. This is the principle by which you must be governed. For I am sure you will not be able to carry out your plans. And if you should carry them out with such general laws, then I will recant everything that I have written and preached and I will not support you. This I am telling you now. What harm can it do you? You still have your faith in God, pure and strong so that this thing cannot hurt you.

Love, therefore, demands that you have compassion on the weak, as all the apostles had. Once, when Paul came to Athens (Acts 17 [:16–32]), a mighty city, he found in the temple many ancient altars, and he went from one to the other and looked at them all, but he did not kick down a single one of them with his foot. Rather he stood up in the middle of the market place and said they were nothing but idolatrous things and begged the people to forsake them; yet he did not destroy one of them by force. When the Word took hold of their hearts, they forsook them of their own accord, and in consequence the thing fell of itself. Likewise, if I had seen them holding mass, I would have preached to them and admonished them. Had they heeded my admonition, I would have won them; if not, I would nevertheless not have torn them from it by the hair or employed any force, but simply allowed the Word to act and prayed for them. For the Word created heaven and earth and all things [Ps. 33:6]; the Word must do this thing, and not we poor sinners.

In short, I will preach it, teach it, write it, but I will constrain no man by force, for faith must come freely without compulsion. Take myself as an example. I opposed indulgences and all the papists, but never with force. I simply taught, preached, and wrote God's Word; otherwise I did nothing. And while I slept [cf. Mark 4:26–29], or drank Wittenberg beer with my friends Philip² and Amsdorf,³ the Word so greatly weakened the papacy that no prince or emperor ever inflicted such losses upon it. I did nothing; the Word did everything. Had I desired to foment trouble, I could have brought great bloodshed upon Germany; indeed, I could have started such a game that even the emperor would not have been safe. But what would it have been? Mere fool's play. I did [78] nothing; I let the Word do its work. What do you suppose is Satan's thought when one tries to do the thing by kicking up a row? He sits back in hell and thinks: Oh, what a fine game the poor fools are up to now! But when we spread the Word alone and let it alone do the work, that distresses him. For it is almighty, and takes captive the hearts, and when the hearts are captured the work will fall of itself. Let me cite a simple instance. In former times there were sects, too, Jewish and Gentile Christians, differing on the law of Moses with respect to circumcision. The former wanted to keep it, the latter not. Then came Paul and preached that it might be kept or not, for it was of no consequence, and also that they should not make a "must" of it, but leave it to the choice of the individual; to keep it or not was immaterial [I Cor. 7:18–24; Gal. 5:1]. So it was up to the time of Jerome, who came and wanted to make a "must" out of it, desiring to make it an ordinance and a law that it be prohibited.⁴ Then came St. Augustine and he was of the same opinion as St. Paul: it might be kept or not, as one wished. St. Jerome was a hundred miles away from St. Paul's opinion. The two doctors bumped heads rather hard, but when St. Augustine died, St. Jerome was successful in having it prohibited. After that came the popes, who also wanted to add something and they, too, made laws. Thus out of the making of one law grew a thousand laws, until they have completely buried us under laws. And this is what will happen here, too; one law will soon make two, two will increase to three, and so forth.

Let this be enough at this time concerning the things that are necessary, and let us beware lest we lead astray those of weak conscience [I Cor. 8:12].

# [79] THE THIRD SERMON, MARCH 11, 1522, TUESDAY AFTER INVOCAVIT

We have heard the things which are "musts," which are necessary and must be done, things which must be so and not otherwise: the private masses⁵ must be abolished. For all works and things, which are either commanded or forbidden by God and thus have been instituted by the supreme Majesty, are "musts." Nevertheless, no one should be dragged to them or away from them by the hair, for I can drive no man to heaven or beat him into it with a club. I said this plainly enough; I believe you have understood what I said.

Now follow the things which are not necessary, but are left to our free choice by God and which we may keep or not, such as whether a person should marry or not, or whether monks and nuns should leave the cloisters. These things are matters of choice and must not be forbidden by any one, and if they are forbidden, the forbidding is wrong, since it is contrary to God's ordinance. In the things that are free, such as being married or remaining single, you should take this attitude: if you can keep to it without burdensomeness, then keep it; but it must not be made a general law; everyone must rather be free. So if there is a priest, monk, or nun, who cannot abstain, let him take a wife and be a husband, in order that your conscience may be relieved;[6] and see to it that you can stand before God and the world when you are assailed, especially when the devil attacks you in the hour of death. It is not enough to say: this man or that man did it, I followed the crowd, according to the preaching [80] of the dean,[7] Dr. Karlstadt,[8] or Gabriel,[9] or Michael.[10] Not so; every one must stand on his own feet and be prepared to give battle to the devil. You must rest upon a strong and clear text of Scripture if you would stand the test. If you cannot do that, you will never withstand—the devil will pluck you like a parched leaf. Therefore the priests who have taken wives and the nuns who have taken husbands in order to save their consciences must stand squarely upon a clear text of Scripture, such as this one by St. Paul, although there are many more: "In later times some will depart from the faith by giving heed to deceitful spirits and doctrines of the devil (I think St. Paul is outspoken enough here!) and will forbid marriage and the foods which God created" [I Tim. 4:1–3]. This text the devil will not overthrow nor devour, it will rather overthrow and devour him. Therefore any monk or nun who finds that he is too weak to maintain chastity should conscientiously examine himself; if his heart and conscience are thus strengthened, let him take a wife and be a husband. Would to God all monks and nuns could hear this sermon and properly understand this matter and would all forsake the cloisters, and thus all the cloisters in the world would cease to exist; this is what I would wish. But now they have no understanding of the matter (for no one preaches it to them); they hear about others who are leaving the cloisters in other places, who, however, are well prepared for such a step, and then they want to follow their example, but have not yet fortified their consciences and do not know that it is a matter of liberty. This is bad, and yet it is better that the evil should be outside than inside.[11] Therefore I say, what God has made free shall remain free. If anybody forbids it, as the pope, the Antichrist, has done, you should not obey. He who can do so without harm and for love of his neighbor may wear a cowl [81] or a tonsure, since it will not injure your faith. The cowl will not strangle you, if you are already wearing one.

Thus, dear friends, I have said it clearly enough, and I believe you ought to understand it and not make liberty a law, saying: This priest has taken a wife, therefore all priests must take wives. Not at all. Or this monk or that nun has left the cloister, therefore they must all come out. Not at all. Or this man has broken the images and burnt them, therefore all images must be burned—not at all, dear brother! And again, this priest has no wife, therefore no priest dare marry. Not at all! For they who cannot retain their chastity should take wives, and for others who can be chaste, it is good that they restrain themselves, as those who live in the Spirit and not in the flesh [Rom. 8:4; I Cor. 7:40]. Neither should they be troubled about the vows they have made, such as the monks' vows of obedience, chastity, and poverty (though they are rich enough withal). For we cannot vow anything that is contrary to God's commands. God has made it a matter of liberty to marry or not to marry, and you, you fool, undertake to turn this liberty into a vow contrary to the ordinance of God! Therefore you must let it remain a liberty and not make a compulsion out of it; for your vow is contrary to God's liberty. For example, if I vowed to strike my father on the mouth, or to steal someone's property, do you believe God would be pleased with such a vow? Therefore, little as I ought to keep a vow to strike my father on the mouth, so little ought I to abstain from marriage because I am bound by a vow of chastity, for in both cases God has ordered it otherwise. God has ordained that I should be free to eat fish or flesh, and there should be no commandment concerning them. Therefore all the Carthusians[12] and all monks and nuns are departing from God's ordinance and liberty when they believe that if they eat meat they are defiled.

## Concerning Images

But now we must come to the images, and concerning them also it is true that they are unnecessary, and we are free to have them or not, although it would be much better if we did not have them at all. I am not partial to them. A great controversy arose on the subject of images between the Roman emperor and the pope; the [82] emperor held that he had the authority to banish the images, but the pope insisted that they should remain, and both were wrong. Much blood was shed, but the pope emerged as victor and the emperor lost.[13] What was it all about? They wished to make a "must" out of that which is free. This God cannot tolerate. Do you presume to do things differently from the way the supreme Majesty has decreed? Surely not; let it alone. You read in the Law (Exod. 20 [:4]), "you shall not make yourself a graven image, or any likeness of anything that is in heaven above, or that is in the earth beneath, or that is in the water under the earth." There you take your stand; that is your ground. Now let us see! When our adversaries say: The meaning of the first commandment is that we should worship only one God and not any image, even as it is said immediately following, "You shall not bow down to them or serve them" [Exod. 20:5], and when they say that it is the worship of images which is forbidden and not the making of them, they are shaking our foundation and making it uncertain. And if you reply: The text says, "You shall not make any images," then they say: It also says, "You shall not worship them." In the face of such uncertainty who would be so bold as to destroy the images? Not I. But let us go further. They say: Did not Noah, Abraham, Jacob build altars? [Gen. 8:20; 12:7; 13:4; 13:18; 33:20]. And who will deny that? We must admit it. Again, did not Moses erect a bronze serpent, as we read in his fourth book (Num. 22 [21:9])? How then can you say that Moses forbade the making of images when he himself made one? It seems to me that such a serpent is an image, too. How shall we answer that? Again, do we not read also that two birds were erected on the mercy seat [Exod. 37:7], the very place where God willed that he should be worshipped? Here we must admit that we may have images and make images, but we must not worship them, and if they are worshipped, they should be put away and destroyed, just as King Hezekiah broke in pieces the bronze serpent erected by Moses [II Kings 18:4]. And who will be so bold as to say, when he is challenged to give an answer: They worship the images. They will say: **[83]** Are you the man who dares to accuse us of worshipping them? Do not believe that they will acknowledge it. To be sure, it is true, but we cannot make them admit it. Just look how they acted when I condemned works without faith. They said: Do you believe that we have no faith, or that our works are performed without faith? Then I cannot press them any further, but must put my flute back in my pocket; for if they gain a hair's breadth, they make a hundred miles out of it.

Therefore it should have been preached that images were nothing and that no service is done to God by erecting them; then they would have fallen of themselves. That is what I did; that is what Paul did in Athens, when he went into their churches and saw all their idols. He did not strike at any of them, but stood in the market place and said, "You men of Athens, you are all idolatrous" [Acts 17:16, 22]. He preached against their idols, but he overthrew none by force. And you rush, create an uproar, break down altars, and overthrow images! Do you really believe you can abolish the altars in this way? No, you will only set them up more firmly. Even if you overthrew the images in this place, do you think you have overthrown those in Nürnberg and the rest of the world? Not at all. St. Paul, as we read in the Book of Acts [28:11], sat in a ship on whose prow were painted or carved the Twin Brothers [i.e., Castor and Pollux]. He went on board and did not bother about them at all, neither did he break them off. Why must Luke describe the Twins at this point? Without doubt he wanted to show that outward things could do no harm to faith, if only the heart does not cleave to them or put its trust in them. This is what we must preach and teach, and let the Word alone do the work, as I said before. The Word must first capture the hearts of men and enlighten them; we will not be the ones who will do it. Therefore the apostles magnified their ministry, *ministerium* [Rom. 11:13], and not its effect, *executio*.

Let this be enough for today.

# [84] THE FOURTH SERMON, MARCH 12, 1522, WEDNESDAY AFTER INVOCAVIT

Dear friends, we have now heard about the things which are "musts," such as that the mass is not to be observed as a sacrifice. Then we considered the things which are not necessary but free, such as marriage, the monastic life, and the abolishing of images. We have treated these four subjects, and have said that in all these matters love is the captain. On the subject of images, in particular, we saw that they ought to be abolished when they are worshipped; otherwise not,— although because of the abuses they give rise to, I wish they were everywhere abolished. This cannot be denied. For whoever places an image in a church imagines he has performed a service to God and done a good work, which is downright idolatry. But this, the greatest, foremost, and highest reason for abolishing images, you have passed by, and fastened on the least important reason of all. For I suppose there is nobody, or certainly very few, who do not understand that yonder crucifix is not my God, for my God is in heaven, but that this is simply a sign. But the world is full of that other abuse; for who would place a silver or wooden image in a church unless he thought that by so doing he was rendering God a service? Do you think that Duke Frederick, the bishop of Halle,[14] and the others would have dragged so many silver images into the churches, if they thought it counted for nothing before God? No, they would not bother to do it. But this is not sufficient reason to abolish, destroy, and burn all images. Why? Because we must admit that there are still some people who hold no such wrong opinion of them, but to whom they may well be useful, although they are few. Nevertheless, we cannot and ought not to condemn a thing which may be any way useful to a person. You should rather have taught that images are nothing, that God cares nothing for [85] them, and that he is not served nor pleased when we make an image for him, but that we would do better to give a poor man a goldpiece than God a golden image; for God has forbidden the latter, but not the former. If they had heard this teaching that images count for nothing, they would have ceased of their own accord, and the images would have fallen without any uproar or tumult, as they are already beginning to do.

We must, therefore, be on our guard, for the devil, through his apostles, is after us with all his craft and cunning. Now, although it is true and no one can deny that the images are evil because they are abused, nevertheless we must not on that account reject them, nor condemn anything because it is abused. This would result in utter confusion. God has commanded us in Deut. 4 [:19] not to lift up our eyes to the sun [and the moon and the stars], etc., that we may not worship them, for they are created to serve all nations. But there are many people who worship the sun and the stars. Therefore we propose to rush in and pull the sun and stars from the skies. No, we had better let it be. Again, wine and women bring many a man to misery and make a fool of him [Ecclus. 19:2; 31:30]; so we kill all the women and pour out all the wine. Again, gold and silver cause much evil, so we condemn them. Indeed, if we want to drive away our worst enemy, the one who does us the most harm, we shall have to kill ourselves, for we have no greater enemy than our own heart, as the prophet, Jer. 17 [:9], says, "The heart of man is crooked," or, as I take the meaning, "always twisting to one side." And so on—what would we not do?

He who would blacken the devil must have good charcoal, for he, too, wears fine clothes and is invited to the kermis.[15] But I can catch him by asking him: Do you not place the images in the churches because you think it a special service to God? And when he says Yes, as he must, you may conclude that what was meant as a service of God he has turned into idolatry by abusing the images and practicing what God has not commanded. But he has neglected God's command, which is that he should be helpful to his neighbor. But I have not yet caught him, though actually he is caught and will not admit it; he escapes me by saying: Yes, I help the poor, [86] too; cannot I give to my neighbor and at the same time donate images? This is not so, however, for who would not rather give his neighbor a gold-piece than God a golden image? No, he would not trouble himself about placing images in churches if he did not believe, as he actually does, that he was doing God a service. Therefore I must admit that images are neither here nor there, neither evil nor good, we may have them or not, as we please. This trouble has been caused by you; the devil would not have accomplished it with me, for I cannot deny that it is possible to find someone to whom images are useful. And if I were asked about it, I would confess that none of these things give offense to one, and if just one man were found on earth who used the images aright, the devil would soon draw the conclusion against me: Why, then, do you condemn what may be used properly? Then he has gained the offensive and I would have to admit it. He would not have got nearly so far if I had been here. Proudly he scattered us, though it has done no harm to the Word of God. You wanted to blacken the devil, but you forgot the charcoal and used chalk. If you want to fight the devil you must know the Scriptures well and, besides, use them at the right time.

### Concerning Meats

Let us proceed and speak of the eating of meats and what our attitude should be in this matter. It is true that we are free to eat any kind of food, meats, fish, eggs, or butter. This no one can deny. God has given us this liberty; this is true. Nevertheless, we must know how to use our liberty, and in this matter treat the weak brother quite differently from the stubborn. Observe, then, how you ought to use this liberty.

First, if you cannot abstain from meat without harm to yourself, or if you are sick, you may eat whatever you like,[16] and if anyone takes offense, let him be offended. Even if the whole world took offense, you are not committing a sin, for God can approve it in view of the liberty he has so graciously bestowed upon you and of the necessities of your health, which would be endangered by your abstinence.

[87] Secondly, if you should be pressed to eat fish instead of meat on Friday, and to eat fish and abstain from eggs and butter during Lent, etc., as the pope has done with his fool's laws, then you must in no wise allow yourself to be drawn away from the liberty in which God has placed you, but do just the contrary to spite him, and say: Because you forbid me to eat meat and presume to turn my liberty into law, I will eat meat in spite of you. And thus you must do in all other things which are matters of liberty. To give you an example: if the pope, or anyone else were to force me to wear a cowl, just as he prescribes it, I would take off the cowl just to spite him. But since it is left to my own free choice, I wear it or take it off, according to my pleasure.

Thirdly, there are some who are still weak in faith, who ought to be instructed, and who would gladly believe as we do. But their ignorance prevents them, and if this were preached to them, as it was to us, they would be one with us. Toward such well-meaning people we must assume an entirely different attitude from that which we assume toward the stubborn. We must bear patiently with these people and not use our liberty; since it brings no peril or harm to body or soul; in fact, it is rather salutary, and we are doing our brothers and sisters a great service besides. But if we use our liberty unnecessarily, and deliberately cause offense to our neighbor, we drive away the very one who in time would come to our faith. Thus St. Paul circumcised Timothy [Acts 16:3] because simpleminded Jews had taken offense; he thought: What harm can it do, since they are offended because of their ignorance? But when, in Antioch, they insisted that he ought and must circumcise Titus [Gal. 2:3], Paul withstood them all and to spite them refused to have Titus circumcised [Gal. 2:11]. And he stood his ground. He did the same when St. Peter by the exercise of his liberty caused a wrong conception in the minds of the unlearned. It happened in this way: when Peter was with the Gentiles, he ate pork and sausages with them, but when the Jews came in, he abstained from this food and did not eat as he did before. Then the Gentiles who had become Christians thought: Alas! we, too, must be like the Jews, eat no pork, and live according to the law of Moses. But when Paul learned that they were acting to the injury of evangelical freedom, he reproved Peter publicly and read him an apostolic lecture, saying: "If you, [88] though a Jew, live like a Gentile, how can you compel the Gentiles to live like Jews?" [Gal. 2:14]. Thus we, too, should order our lives and use our liberty at the proper time, so that Christian liberty may suffer no injury, and no offense be given to our weak brothers and sisters who are still without the knowledge of this liberty.

# THE FIFTH SERMON, MARCH 13, 1522, THURSDAY AFTER INVOCAVIT

We have heard of the things that are necessary, such as that the mass is not to be performed as a sacrifice, and of the unnecessary things, such as monks' leaving the monasteries, the marriage of priests, and images. We have seen how we must treat these matters, that no compulsion or ordinance must be made of them, and that no one shall be dragged from them or to them by the hair, but that we must let the Word of God alone do the work. Let us now consider how we must observe the blessed sacrament.

You have heard how I preached against the foolish law of the pope and opposed his precept,[17] that no woman shall wash the altar linen on which the body of Christ has lain, even if it be a pure nun, except it first be washed by a pure priest.[18] Likewise, when any one has touched the body of Christ, the priests come running and scrape his fingers, and much more of the same sort. But when a maid has slept with a naked priest, the pope winks at it and lets it go. If she becomes pregnant and bears a child, he lets that pass, too. But to touch the altar linen and the sacrament [i.e., the host], this he will not allow. But when a priest grabs it, both top and bottom, this is all right.

Against such fool laws we have preached and exposed them, in order that it might be made known that no sin is involved in these **[89]** foolish laws and commandments of the pope, and that a layman does not commit sin if he touches the cup or the body of Christ with his hands. You should give thanks to God that you have come to such clear knowledge, which many great men have lacked. But now you go ahead and become as foolish as the pope, in that you think that a person must touch the sacrament with his hands. You want to prove that you are good Christians by touching the sacrament with your hands, and thus you have dealt with the sacrament, which is our highest treasure, in such a way that it is a wonder you were not struck to the ground by thunder and lightning. All the other things God might have suffered, but this he cannot allow, because you have made a compulsion of it. And if you do not stop this, neither the emperor nor anyone else need drive me from you, I will go without urging; and I dare say that none of my enemies, though they have caused me much sorrow, have wounded me as you have.

If you want to show that you are good Christians by handling the sacrament and boast of it before the world, then Herod and Pilate are the chief and best Christians, since it seems to me that they really handled the body of Christ when they had him nailed to the cross and put to death. No, my dear friends, the kingdom of God does not consist in outward things, which can be touched or perceived, but in faith [Luke 17:20; Rom. 14:17; I Cor. 4:20].

But you may say: We live and we ought to live according to the Scriptures, and God has so instituted the sacrament that we must take it with our hands, for he said, "Take, eat, this is my body" [Matt. 26:26]. The answer is this: though I am convinced beyond a doubt that the disciples of the Lord took it with their hands, and though I admit that you may do the same without committing sin, nevertheless I can neither make it compulsory nor defend it. And my reason is that the devil, when he really pushes us to the wall, will argue: Where have you read in the Scriptures that "take" means "grasping with the hands"? How, then, am I going to prove or defend it? Indeed, how will I answer him when he cites from the Scriptures the very opposite, and proves that "take" does not mean to receive with the hands only, but also to convey to ourselves in other ways? "Listen to this, my good fellow," he will say, "is not the word 'take' used by three evangelists when they described the Lord's taking of gall and vinegar? [Matt. 27:34; Mark 15:23; Luke 23:36]. [90] You must admit that the Lord did not touch or handle it with his hands, for his hands were nailed to the cross." This verse is a strong argument against me. Again, he cites the passage: *Et accepit omnes timor*, "Fear seized them all" [Luke 7:16], where again we must admit that fear has no hands. Thus I am driven into a corner and must concede, even against my will, that "take" means not only to receive with the hands, but to convey to myself in any other way in which it can be done. Therefore, dear friends, we must be on firm ground, if we are to withstand the devil's attack [Eph. 6:11]. Although I must acknowledge that you committed no sin when you touched the sacrament with your hands, nevertheless I must tell you that it was not a good work, because it caused offense everywhere. For the universal custom is to receive the blessed sacrament from the hands of the priest. Why will you not in this respect also serve those who are weak in faith and abstain from your liberty, particularly since it does not help you if you do it, nor harm you if you do not do it.

Therefore no new practices should be introduced, unless the gospel has first been thoroughly preached and understood, as it has been among you. On this account, dear friends, let us deal soberly and wisely in the things that pertain to God, for God will not be mocked [Gal. 6:7]. The saints may endure mockery, but with God it is vastly different. Therefore, I beseech you, give up this practice.

## Concerning Both Kinds in the Sacrament

Now let us speak of the two kinds. Although I hold that it is necessary that the sacrament should be received in both kinds, according to the institution of the Lord, nevertheless it must not be made compulsory nor a general law. We must rather promote and practice and preach the Word, and then afterwards leave the result and execution of it entirely to the Word, giving everyone his freedom in this matter. Where this is not done, the sacrament becomes for me an outward work and a hypocrisy, which is just what the devil wants. But when the Word is given free course and is not bound to any external observance, it takes hold of one today and sinks into his heart, tomorrow it touches another, and so on. Thus quietly and soberly it does its work, and no one will know how it all came about.

[91] I was glad to know when some one wrote me, that some people here had begun to receive the sacrament in both kinds. You should have allowed it to remain thus and not forced it into a law. But now you go at it pell mell, and headlong force every one to it. Dear friends, you will not succeed in that way. For if you desire to be regarded as better Christians than others just because you take the sacrament into your hands and also receive it in both kinds, you are bad Christians as far as I am concerned. In this way even a sow could be a Christian, for she has a big enough snout to receive the sacrament outwardly. We must deal soberly with

such high things. Dear friends, this dare be no mockery, and if you are going to follow me, stop it. If you are not going to follow me, however, then no one need drive me away from you—I will leave you unasked, and I shall regret that I ever preached so much as one sermon in this place. The other things could be passed by, but this cannot be overlooked; for you have gone so far that people are saying: At Wittenberg there are very good Christians, for they take the sacrament in their hands and grasp the cup, and then they go to their brandy and swill themselves full. So the weak and well-meaning people, who would come to us if they had received as much instruction as we have, are driven away.

But if there is any one who is so smart that he must touch the sacrament with his hands, let him have it brought home to his house and there let him handle it to his heart's content. But in public let him abstain, since that will bring him no harm and the offense will be avoided which is caused to our brothers, sisters, and neighbors, who are now so angry with us that they are ready to kill us. I may say that of all my enemies who have opposed me up to this time none have brought me so much grief as you.

This is enough for today; tomorrow we shall say more.

## [92] THE SIXTH SERMON, MARCH 14, 1522, FRIDAY AFTER INVOCAVIT

In our discussion of the chief things we have come to the reception of the sacrament, which we have not yet finished. Today we shall see how we must conduct ourselves here, and also who is worthy to receive the sacrament and who belongs there.

It is very necessary here that your hearts and consciences be well instructed and that you make a big distinction between outward reception and inner and spiritual reception. Bodily and outward reception is that in which a man receives with his mouth the body of Christ and his blood, and doubtless any man can receive the sacrament in this way, without faith and love. But this does not make a man a Christian, for if it did, even a mouse would be a Christian, for it, too, can eat the bread and perchance even drink out of the cup. It is such a simple thing to do. But the true, inner, spiritual reception is a very different thing, for it consists in the right use of the sacrament and its fruits.

I would say in the first place that this reception occurs in faith and is inward and will have Christ. There is no external sign by which we Christians may be distinguished from others except this sacrament and baptism, but without faith outward reception is nothing. There must be faith to make the reception worthy and acceptable before God, otherwise it is nothing but sham and a mere external show, which is not Christianity at all. Christianity consists solely in faith, and no outward work must be attached to it.

But faith (which we all must have, if we wish to go to the sacrament worthily) is a firm trust that Christ, the Son of God, stands in our place and has taken all our sins upon his shoulders and that he is the eternal satisfaction for our sin and reconciles us with God the Father. He who has this faith is the very one who takes his rightful place at this sacrament, and neither devil nor hell nor sin can harm him. Why? Because God is his protector and [93] defender. And when I have this faith, then I am certain God is fighting for me; I can defy the devil, death, hell, and sin, and all the harm with which they threaten me. This is the great, inestimable treasure given us in Christ, which no man can describe or grasp in words. Only faith can take hold of the heart, and not every one has such faith [II Thess. 3:2]. Therefore this sacrament must not be made a law, as the most holy father, the pope, has done with his fool's commandment: All Christians must go to the sacrament at the holy Eastertide, and he who does not go shall not be buried in consecrated ground.[19] Is not this a foolish law which the pope has set up? Why? Because we are not all alike; we do not all have equal faith; the faith of one is stronger than that of another. It is therefore impossible that the sacrament can be made a law, and the greatest sins are committed at Easter solely on account of this un-Christian command, whose purpose is to drive and force the people to the sacrament. And if robbery, usury, unchastity, and all sins were cast upon one big heap, this sin would overtop all others, at the very time when they [who come to the sacrament] want to be most holy. Why? Because the pope can look into no one's heart to see whether he has faith or not.

But if you believe that God steps in for you and stakes all he has and his blood for you, as if he were saying: Fall in behind me without fear or delay, and then let us see what can harm you; come devil, death, sin, and hell, and all creation, I shall go before you, for I will be your rear guard and your vanguard [Isa. 52:12]; trust me and boldly rely upon me. He who believes that cannot be harmed by devil, hell, sin, or death; if God fights for him, what can you do to him?

He who has such faith has his rightful place here and receives the sacrament as an assurance, or seal, or sign to assure him of God's promise and grace. But, of course, we do not all have such faith; would God one-tenth of the Christians had it! See, such rich, immeasurable treasures [Eph. 2:7], which God in his grace showers upon us, cannot be the possession of everyone, but only of those who suffer tribulation, physical or spiritual, physically through the persecution of men, spiritually through despair of conscience, outwardly [94] or inwardly, when the devil causes your heart to be weak, timid, and discouraged, so that you do not know how you stand with God, and when he casts your sins into your face. And in such terrified and trembling hearts alone God desires to dwell, as the prophet Isaiah says in the sixth chapter [Isa. 66:2]. For who desires a protector, defender, and shield to stand before him if he feels no conflict within himself, so that he is distressed because of his sins and daily tormented by them? That man is not yet ready for this food. This food demands a hungering and longing man,[20] for it delights to enter a hungry soul, which is constantly battling with its sins and eager to be rid of them.

He who is not thus prepared should abstain for a while from this sacrament, for this food will not enter a sated and full heart, and if it comes to such a heart, it is harmful.[21] Therefore, if we think upon and feel within us such distress of conscience and the fear of a timid heart, we shall come with all humbleness and reverence and not run to it brashly and hastily, without all fear and humility. So we do not always find that we are fit; today I have the grace and am fit for it, but not tomorrow. Indeed, it may be that for six months I may have no desire or fitness for it.

Therefore those who are most worthy, who are constantly being assailed by death and the devil, and they are the ones to whom it is most opportunely given, in order that they may remember and firmly believe that nothing can harm them, since they now have with them him from whom none can pluck them away; let come death, devil, or sin, they cannot harm them.

This is what Christ did when he was about to institute the blessed sacrament. First he terrified his disciples and shook their hearts by saying that he was going to leave them [Matt. 26:2], which was exceedingly painful to them; and then he went on to say, "One of you will betray me" [Matt. 26:21]. Do you think that that did not cut them to the heart? Of course they accepted that saying with all **[95]** fear and they sat there as though they had all been traitors to God. And after he had made them all tremble with fear and sorrow, only then did he institute the blessed sacrament as a comfort and consoled them again. For this bread is a comfort for the sorrowing, a healing for the sick, a life for the dying, a food for all the hungry, and a rich treasure for all the poor and needy.

Let this be enough for this time concerning the use of this sacrament. I commend you to God.

## THE SEVENTH SERMON, MARCH 15, 1522, SATURDAY BEFORE REMINISCERE

Yesterday we heard about the use of this holy and blessed sacrament and saw who are worthy to receive it, namely, those in whom there is the fear of death, who have timid and despairing consciences and live in fear of hell. All such come prepared to partake of this food for the strengthening of their weak faith and the comforting of their conscience. This is the true use and practice of this sacrament, and whoever does not find himself in this state, let him refrain from coming until God also takes hold of him and draws him through his Word.

We shall now speak of the fruit of this sacrament, which is love; that is, that we should treat our neighbor as God has treated us. Now we have received from God nothing but love and favor, for Christ has pledged and given us his righteousness and everything he has; he has poured out upon us all his treasures, which no man can measure and no angel can understand or fathom, for God is a glowing furnace of love, reaching even from the earth to the heavens.

Love, I say, is a fruit of this sacrament. But this I do not yet **[96]** perceive among you here in Wittenberg, even though you have had much preaching and, after all, you ought to have carried this out in practice. This is the chief thing, which is the only business of a Christian man. But nobody wants to be in this, though you want to practice all sorts of unnecessary things, which are of no account. If you do not want to show yourselves Christians by your love, then leave the other things undone, too, for St. Paul says in I Cor. 11 [I Cor. 13:1], "If I speak in the tongues of men and of angels, but have not love, I am a noisy gong or a clanging cymbal." This is a terrible saying of Paul. "And if I have prophetic powers, and understand all mysteries and all knowledge, and if I have all faith, so as to remove mountains, but have not love, I am nothing. If I give away all I have, and if I deliver my body to be burned, but have not love, I gain nothing" [I Cor. 13:2–3]. Not yet have you come so far as this, though you have received great and rich gifts from God, the highest of which is a knowledge of the Scriptures. It is true, you have the true gospel and the pure Word of God, but no one as yet has given his goods to the poor, no one has yet been burned, and even these things would be nothing without love. You are willing to take all of God's goods in the sacrament, but you are not willing to pour them out again in love. Nobody extends a helping hand to another, nobody seriously considers the other person, but everyone looks out for himself and his own gain, insists on his own way, and lets everything else go hang. If anybody is helped, well and good; but nobody looks after the poor to see how you might be able to help them. This is a pity. You have heard many sermons about it and all my books are full of it and have this one purpose, to urge you to faith and love.

And if you will not love one another, God will send a great plague upon you; let this be a warning to you, for God will not have his Word revealed and preached in vain. You are tempting God too far, my friends; for if in times past someone had preached the Word to our forefathers, they would perhaps have acted differently. Or if it were preached even now to many poor children in the cloisters, they would receive it more joyfully than you. You are not heeding it at all and you are playing around with all kinds of tomfoolery which does not amount to anything.

I commend you to God.

# [97] THE EIGHTH SERMON, MARCH 16, 1522, REMINISCERE SUNDAY

A Short Summary of the Sermon of D[r.] M[artin] L[uther] Preached on Reminiscere Sunday on Private Confession

Now we have heard all the things which ought to be considered here, except confession. Of this we shall speak now.

In the first place, there is a confession which is founded on the Scriptures, and it is this: when anybody committed a sin publicly or with other men's knowledge, he was accused before the congregation. If he abandoned his sin, they interceded for him with God. But if he would not listen to the congregation [*häuffen*], he was cast out and excluded from the assembly, so that no one would have anything to do with him. And this confession is commanded by God in Matt. 18 [:15], "If your brother sins against you (so that you and others are offended), go and tell him his fault, between you and him alone." We no longer have any trace of this kind of confession any more; at this point the gospel is in abeyance. Anybody who was able to re-establish it would be doing a good work. Here is where you should have exerted yourselves and re-established this kind of confession, and let the other things go; for no one would have been offended by this and everything would have gone smoothly and quietly. It should be done in this way: When you see a usurer, adulterer, thief, or drunkard, you should go to him in secret, and admonish him to give up his sin. If he will not listen, you should take two others with you and admonish him once more, in a brotherly way, to give up his sin. But if he scorns that, you should tell the pastor before the whole congregation, have your witnesses with you, and accuse him before the pastor in the presence of the people, saying: Dear pastor, this man has done this and that and would not take our brotherly admonition to give up his sin. Therefore I accuse him, together with my witnesses, who have heard this. Then, if he will not give up and willingly acknowledge his guilt, the pastor should exclude him and put him under the ban before the whole **[98]** assembly, for the sake of the congregation, until he comes to himself and is received back again. This would be Christian. But I cannot undertake to carry it out single-handed.

Secondly, we need a kind of confession when we go into a corner by ourselves and confess to God himself and pour out before him all our faults. This kind of confession is also commanded. From this comes the familiar word of Scripture: *Facite judicium et justitiara.*[22] *Judicium facere est nos ipsos accusare et detonate; justitiam autem facere est fidere misericordiae Dei.*[23] As it is written, "Blessed are they who observe justice, who do righteousness at all times" [Ps. 106:3]. Judgment is nothing else than a man's knowing and judging and condemning himself, and this is true humility and self-abasement. Righteousness is nothing else than a man's knowing himself and praying to God for the mercy and help through which God raises him up again. This is what David means when he says, "I have sinned; I will confess my transgressions to the Lord and thou didst forgive the guilt of my sin; for this all thy saints shall pray to thee" [Ps. 32:5–6].

Thirdly, there is also the kind of confession in which one takes another aside and tells him what troubles one, so that one may hear from him a word of comfort; and this confession is commanded by the pope. It is this urging and forcing which I condemned when I wrote concerning confession,[24] and I refuse to go to confession simply because the pope has commanded it and insists upon it. For I wish him to keep his hands off the confession and not make of it a compulsion or command, which he has not the power to do. Nevertheless I will allow no man to take private confession away from me, and I would not give it up for all the treasures in the world, since I know what comfort and strength it has given me. No one knows what it can do for him except one who has struggled often and long with the devil. Yea, the devil would have slain me long ago, if the confession had not sustained me. For there are many doubtful matters which a man cannot resolve or find the answer to by himself, and so he takes his brother aside and tells him his trouble. **[99]** What harm is there if he humbles himself a little before his neighbor, puts himself to shame, looks for a word of comfort from him, accepts it, and believes it, as if he were hearing it from God himself, as we read in Matt. 18 [:19], "If two of you agree about anything they ask, it will be done for them."

Moreover, we must have many absolutions, so that we may strengthen our timid consciences and despairing hearts against the devil and against God. Therefore, no man shall forbid the confession nor keep or draw any one away from it. And if any one is wrestling with his sins and wants to be rid of them and desires a sure word on the matter, let him go and confess to another in secret, and accept what he says to him as if God himself had spoken it through the mouth of this person. However, one who has a strong, firm faith that his sins are forgiven may let this confession go and confess to God alone. But how many have such a strong faith? Therefore, as I have said, I will not let this private confession be taken from me. But I will not have anybody forced to it, but left to each one's free will.

For our God, the God we have, is not so niggardly that he has left us with only one comfort or strengthening for our conscience, or only one absolution, but we have many absolutions in the gospel and we are richly showered with many absolutions. For instance, we have this in the gospel: "If you forgive men their trespasses, your heavenly Father will also forgive you" [Matt. 6:14]. Another comfort we have in the Lord's Prayer: "Forgive us our trespasses," etc. [Matt. 6:12]. A third is our baptism, when I reason thus: See, my Lord, I have been baptized in thy name so that I may be assured of thy grace and mercy. Then we have private confession, when I go and receive a sure absolution as if God himself spoke it, so that I may be assured that my sins are forgiven. Finally, I take to myself the blessed sacrament, when I eat his body and drink his blood as a sign that I am rid of my sins and God has freed me from all my frailties; and in order to make me sure of this, he gives me his body to eat and his blood to drink, so that I shall not and cannot doubt that I have a gracious God.

Thus you see that confession must not be despised, but that it is a comforting thing. And since we need many absolutions and assurances, because we must fight against the devil, death, hell, and **[100]** sin, we must not allow any of our weapons to be taken away, but keep intact the whole armor and equipment which God has given us to use against our enemies. For you do not yet know what labor it costs to fight with the devil and overcome him. But I know it well, for I have eaten a bit of salt or two with him. I know him well, and he knows me well, too. If you had known him, you would not have rejected confession in this way.

I commend you to God. Amen.

# ABBREVIATIONS

| | |
|---|---|
| *ARG* | *Archiv für Reformationsgeschichte* |
| Benzing | Benzing, Josef. *Lutherbibliographie: Verzeichnis der gedruckten Schriften Martin Luthers bis zu dessen Tod.* Baden-Baden: Librarie Heitz, 1966. |
| *CL* | Luther, Martin. *Luthers Werke in Auswahl.* Edited by Otto Clemen et al. Bonn, 1912–33; Berlin, 1955–56. |
| *CS* | Burke, Kenneth. *Counter-Statement.* 2d ed. Berkeley: University of California Press, 1968. |
| Freys-Barge | Freys, E., and H. Barge, "Verzeichnis der gedruckten Schriften des Andreas Bodenstein von Karlstadt." *Zentralblatt für Bibliothekswesen* 21 (1904): 153–79, 209–43; 305–31. |
| *Inst.* | *Institutio oratoria* |
| *LQ* | *Lutheran Quarterly* |
| LStA | Delius, Hans-Ulrich, ed. *Martin Luther: Studienausgabe.* Vol. 2. Berlin: Evangelische Verlagsanstalt, 1982. |
| LW | Luther, Martin. *Luther's Works.* American Edition. General editors Jaroslav Pelikan and Helmut T. Lehmann. 56 vols. St. Louis: Concordia, and Philadelphia: Muhlenberg and Fortress, 1955–86. |
| *MA³* | Luther, Martin. *Martin Luther.* Ausgewählte Werke. München, 1948–. |
| *Neot* | *Neotestamentica* |
| *NR* | Perelman, Chaim, and Lucy Olbrechts-Tyteca. *The New Rhetoric: A Treatise on Argumentation.* Translated by John Wilkinson and Purcell Weaver. Notre Dame; University of Notre Dame Press, 1969. |
| *PE* | Luther, Martin. *Works of Martin Luther.* Philadelphia, 1915–43. |
| *Rhet. Her.* | *Rhetorica ad Herennium* |
| WA | Luther, Martin. *D. Martin Luthers Werke. Kritische Gesamtausgabe. Schriften.* 68 vols. Weimar: Hermann Böhlaus Nachfolger, 1883–1999. |
| *WB* | Müller, Nikolaus, ed. *Die Wittenberger Bewegung 1521 und 1522: Die Vorgange in und um Wittenberg wahrend Luthers Wartburgaufenthalt.* 2d ed. Leipzig: M. Heinsius, 1911. |
| WABr | Luther, Martin. *D. Martin Luthers Werke. Kritische Gesamtausgabe. Briefwechsel.* 18 vols. Weimar: Hermann Böhlaus Nachfolger, 1930–85. |

WATr         Luther, Martin. *D. Martin Luthers Werke. Kritische Gesamtausgabe. Tischreden.* 6 vols. Weimar: Hermann Böhlaus Nachfolger, 1912–21. Reprinted in 2000.

# NOTES

## INTRODUCTION

1. According to Bernd Moeller, 682 publications (singly and as collections) of Luther's works appeared in a total of 3,897 editions during his lifetime; cf. Bernd Moeller, "Luther in Europe: His Works in Translation 1517–46," in *Politics and Society in Reformation Europe: Essays for Sir Geoffrey Elton on His Sixty-Fifth Birthday* (ed. E. I. Kouri and Tom Scott; New York: St. Martin's, 1987), 236.

2. Mackinnon's lament was that there was "no exhaustive treatise" and that a systematic study of Luther's sermons remained "a desideratum" (James Mackinnon, *Luther and the Reformation*, 4 vols. [London: Longmans, Green & Co., 1930], 4:318).

3. Five years after Mackinnon's remark, Kiessling took up the challenge; see Elmer Carl Kiessling, *The Early Sermons of Luther and Their Relation to the Pre-Reformation Sermon* (1935; New York: AMS, 1971).

4. Birgit Stolt, *Studien zu Luthers Freiheitstraktat mit besonderer Rücksicht auf das Verhältnis der lateinischen und der deutschen Fassung zu einander und die Stilmittel der Rhetorik* (Acta Universitatis Stockholmiensis: Stockholmer Germanistische Forschungen 6; Stockholm: Almqvist & Wiksell, 1969); "*Docere, delectare*, und *movere* bei Luther: Analysiert anhand der 'Predigt, daß man Kinder zur Schulen halten solle,' " *Deutsche Vierteljahrsschrift für Literaturwissenschaft und Geistesgeschichte* 44 (1970): 433–74, now included in Birgit Stolt, *Wortkampf: Frühneuhochdeutsche Beispiele zur rhetorischen Praxis* (Acta Universitatis Stockholmiensis: Stockholmer Germanistische Forschungen 13; Frankurt on the Main: Athenaeum, 1974), 31–77. Professor Stolt uses the theories and prescriptions of the classical rhetorical handbooks to analyze Luther's sermons.

5. Klaus Dockhorn, "Luthers Glaubensbegriff und die Rhetorik," *Linguistica Biblica* 21/22 (1973): 19–39.

6. Ulrich Nembach, *Predigt des Evangeliums: Luther als Prediger, Pädagoge und Rhetor* (Vluyn: Neukirchener, 1972).

7. John W. O'Malley, "Luther the Preacher," *Michigan Germanic Studies* 10 (1984): 3–16, repr. in Gerhard Dünnhaupt, ed., *The Martin Luther Quincentennial* (Detroit: Wayne State University Press, 1985), 3–16. Both O'Malley and Nembach find Luther to be heavily influenced by Quintilian.

8. Knut Alfsvag, "Language and Reality: Luther's Relation to Classical Rhetoric in *Rationis Latomianae confutatio* (1521)," *Studia Theologica* 41 (1987): 85–126. For further specific, historical bibliography on Luther's connection with rhetoric, see Reinhard Breymayer, "Bibliographie zum Thema 'Luther und die Rhetorik,' " *Linguistica Biblica* 21/22 (1973): 39–44; for additional recent bibliography, especially from Scandinavian countries, see the endnotes of Alfsvag, "Language and Reality," 115–26.

9. Birgit Stolt, "Lieblichkeit und Zier, Ungestüm und Donner: Martin Luther im Spiegel seiner Sprach," *Zeitschrift für Theologie und Kirche* 86 (1989): 297f.; Stolt, "*Docere, delectare*, und *movere* bei Luther," in *Wortkampf*, 61ff., convincingly demonstrates some of Luther's "skill with audiences" [*Publikumszugewandtheit*]. See also C. Joachim Classen, "Cicero orator inter Germanos redivivus," *Humanistica Lovanien-*

*sia* 37 (1988): 79–114; and C. Joachim Classen, "Redivivus II," *Humanistica Lovaniensia* 39 (1990): 157–76.

10. While favoring different methods of the selection of sermon texts (Calvin chose linear exposition of biblical books while Luther followed the lection), both Luther and Calvin share a commitment to the centrality of preaching in the life of the church. Luther is noted for his insistence on a strong role for the sermon in the worship service. See Helmut Schanze, "Problems and Trends in the History of German Rhetoric to 1500," in *Renaissance Eloquence: Studies in the Theory and Practice of Renaissance Rhetoric* (ed. James J. Murphy; Berkeley: University of California, 1983), 105–25. See Jaroslav Pelikan, *Divine Rhetoric: The Sermon on the Mount as Message and as Model in Augustine, Chrysostom, and Luther* (Crestwood, N.Y.: St. Vladimir's Seminary Press, 2001), 81, 89; Helmar Junghans, "Die Werte Christi geben das Leben," in *Wissenschaftliches Kolloquium "Der Mensch Luther und sein Umfeld"* (Warburg-Jahrbuch; Sonderband 1996; Eisenach: Wartburg-Stiftung, 1996), 154–75.

11. Robert Scribner, "Oral Culture and the Diffusion of Reformation Ideas," *History of European Ideas* 5 (1984): 238 (*Scribner's emphasis*). See also Peter Blickle, *From the Communal Reformation to the Revolution of the Common Man* (trans. Beat Kümin; Leiden: E. J. Brill, 1998), 187 [SMRT 65].

12. Lewis W. Spitz, "The Course of German Humanism," in *Itinerarium Italicum: The Profile of the Italian Renaissance in the Mirror of Its European Transformations: Dedicated to Paul Oskar Kristeller on the Occasion of His 70th Birthday* (Studies in Medieval and Reformation Thought 14; ed. Heiko A. Oberman and Thomas A. Brady Jr.; Leiden: E. J. Brill, 1975), 385–87.

13. LW 51:xii. Luther's own statement about how much he preached is found in WATr 5, no. 6434.

14. O'Malley, "Luther the Preacher," 8; cf. John W. Doberstein, Introduction, LW 51:xiii.

15. "*Wort-besessen*" (Ulrich Bubenheimer, "Luther als Prediger," public lecture at Ehrenkinker Evangelische Kirchengemeinde [30 October 1988]).

16. I thank Ulrich Bubenheimer for an insightful tour of the *Lutherhalle* (old *Augustinerkloister*), *Stadtkirche*, and Wartburg castle. I thank Erika Schulz (former librarian at the Evangelisches Predigerseminar Bibliothek) for a tour of the *Schloßkirche*.

17. See Heiko A. Oberman, "Preaching and the Word in the Reformation," *Theology Today* 18 (1961): 16–29; David W. Lotz, "The Proclamation of the Word in Luther's Thought," *Word and World* 3 (1983): 344–54.

18. Alfsvag, "Language and Reality," 90f., though he slightly overstates the matter, is generally on target when he says that "the question of origin is never important in understanding Luther (or whoever it may be). It is . . . how Luther works with the concepts as means to solve his problems that really matters . . . ."

19. Donald C. Bryant, "Of Style: Buffon and Rhetorical Criticism," in *Essays on Rhetorical Criticism* (ed. Thomas Nilsen; New York: Random House, 1968), 50–63.

20. Fred W. Meuser, *Luther the Preacher* (Minneapolis: Augsburg, 1983), 35f., without attribution, says: "He usually took into the pulpit with him what he called his *Konzept*: a brief outline or plan—written in German—of how he would proceed."

21. See a discussion of textual verification techniques in literary studies, classical philology, and biblical studies (and what these fields can offer speech criticism) in Neil R. Leroux, "Text Criticism: Prerequisite to Rhetorical Analysis," (paper presented at the annual convention of the Speech Communication Association, Chicago, Ill., November 1992).

22. LW 45:57; *Eine trew Vermahnung zu allen Christen, sich zu hütten vor Aufruhr und Empörung* (Wittemberg: Melchior Lotter, 1522), Aii; cataloged in Benzing, no. 1047.

23. Bubenheimer, "Luther als Prediger," finds that the Invocavit Sermons exemplify the major issues in Luther's preaching: (1) the role of preacher, (2) the content of the sermon, and (3) the community that is the audience of preaching.

24. A. Skevington Wood, "Luther as a Preacher," *Evangelical Quarterly* 21 (1949): 112f., quoting a lengthy section of the Seventh Sermon, one of only two substantive quotes in the article.

25. For example, Theodore G. Tappert, ed., *Selected Writings of Martin Luther, 1520–1523* (Philadelphia: Fortress, 1967).

26. For example, the most recent conference on Karlstadt to be held in Germany, the Wissenschaftliches Kolloquium in Karlstadt am Main vom 24. bis 26. September 1998. The papers from that conference are found in Ulrich Bubenheimer and Stefan Oehmig, eds., *Querdenker der Reformation: Andreas Bodenstein von Karlstadt und seine frühe Wirkung* (Würzburg: Religion and Kultur, 2001).

27. Sergiusz Michalski, *The Reformation and the Visual Arts: The Protestant Image Question in Western and Eastern Europe* (London: Routledge, 1993), 1–50; cf. Sergiusz Michalski, "Aspekte der protestantischen Bilderfrage," *Idee: Jahrbuch der Hamburger Kunsthalle* 3 (1984): 66.

28. James Samuel Preus, *Carlstadt's "Ordinaciones" and Luther's "Liberty": A Study of the Wittenberg Movement 1521–1522* (Harvard Theological Studies 26; Cambridge: Harvard University Press, 1974), 2.

29. Against the view that Luther simply reacted to events in Wittenberg that alarmed him, Helmar Junghans, "Luther on Reform of Worship," *LQ* 13 (1999): 315–33, argues that Luther held a carefully conceived view of worship and that he implemented reforms in a gradual manner in Wittenberg.

30. WA 10/3:lvii–lxiii.

31. Ulrich Bubenheimer, "Unbekannte Luthertexte: Analecta aus der Erforschung der Handschrift im gedruckten Buch," *Lutherjahrbuch* 57 (1990): 220–41. Prof. Bubenheimer and I are now editing this text of Luther's.

# CHAPTER 1

1. Lloyd F. Bitzer, "Functional Communication: A Situational Perspective," in *Rhetoric in Transition: Studies in the Nature and Uses of Rhetoric* (ed. E. E. White; University Park: Pennsylvania State University Press, 1980), 21–38. Bitzer's original essay on rhetorical situation is "The Rhetorical Situation," *Philosophy and Rhetoric* 1 (1968): 1–14.

2. Herbert A. Wichelns, "The Literary Criticism of Oratory," in *Studies in Rhetoric and Public Speaking in Honor of James A. Winans* (ed. A. M. Drummond; New York: Century, 1925); repr. in Bernard L. Brock and Robert L. Scott, eds., *Methods of Rhetorical Criticism: A Twentieth-Century Perspective* (2d rev. ed.; Detroit: Wayne State University Press, 1980), 40–73. For a concise discussion of traditional criticism with selected samples, see Brock and Scott, *Methods of Rhetorical Criticism*, 7–132.

3. For a discussion of five dozen communication articles related to style, see Neil R. Leroux, *Style in Rhetorical Criticism: The Case of Martin Luther's Vernacular Sermons* (Ph.D. diss., University of Illinois, 1990), 2–20. Literary studies typically take style more seriously, but little of that has any bearing on rhetorical criticism as it has

come to be known. For example, Bennison Gray, "Style as the Speaker (The Rhetorician)," in *Style: The Problem and Its Solution* (The Hague: Mouton, 1969), 34–46, argues that applying the "categories and considerations of rhetoric" to literary works is highly problematic.

4. See C. Joachim Classen, "St. Paul's Epistles and Ancient Greek and Roman Rhetoric," *Rhetorica* 10 (1992): 319–44 (originally published as "Paulus und die antike Rhetorik," *Zeitschrift für die neutestamentliche Wissenschaft* 82 [1991]: 1–33), for a penetrating examination of the use of classical rhetorical handbook requirements in the criticism of Pauline Epistles; cf. Classen's recent remarks in "Review of R. Dean Anderson, Jr., *Ancient Rhetorical Theory and Paul* (Kampen: Kok Pharos Publishing House, 1996)," *Rhetorica* 16 (1998): 324–29.

5. Donald C. Bryant, "Of Style," *Western Speech* 21 (1957): 103–10.

6. Thomas M. Conley, "The Linnaean Blues: Thoughts on the Genre Approach," in *Form, Genre, and the Study of Political Discourse* (ed. Herbert W. Simons and Aram A. Aghazarian; Columbia: University of South Carolina Press, 1986), 73.

7. Donald C. Bryant, "Of Style: Buffon and Rhetorical Criticism," in *Essays on Rhetorical Criticism* (ed. Thomas Nilsen; New York: Random House, 1968), 62.

8. Bryant, "Of Style," 108, citing Russell H. Wagner, "The Meaning of *Dispositio*," in *Studies in Speech and Drama in Honor of Alexander M. Drummond* (ed. James Winans; Ithaca: Cornell University Press, 1944), 293, 289 (*Bryant's emphasis*).

9. Comte de DeBuffon, "Discourse on Style," in *The Art of the Writer* (ed. Lane Coope; Ithaca: Cornell University Press, 1952), 146–55. The "discourse" is titled "An Address Delivered Before the French Academy by M. DeBuffon Upon the Day of His Reception." Buffon (George-Louis Leclerc, 1707–88) is the source of the now-famous and often misquoted remark, "Style is the man himself."

10. Brian Vickers, *In Defence of Rhetoric* (Oxford: Clarendon, 1988), particularly, "The Expressive Function of Rhetorical Figures."

11. David Buttrick, *Homiletic: Moves and Structures* (Philadelphia: Fortress, 1987), 201 (*Buttrick's emphasis*).

12. Bryant, "Of Style," 110.

13. Classen, "St. Paul's Epistles," 322.

14. Classen, "St. Paul's Epistles," 328, 332. See John R. Schneider, *Oratio Sacra: Philip Melanchthon's Rhetorical Construal of Biblical Authority* (Lewiston, N.Y.: Edwin Mellen Press, 1990); and John R. Schneider, "Melanchthon's Rhetoric as a Context for Understanding His Theology," in *Melanchthon in Europe: His Work and Influence beyond Wittenberg* (ed. Karin Maag; Grand Rapids: Baker, 1999), 141–59. For a survey of modern scholarship, see R. Meynet, "Histoire de 'l'analyse rhétorique' en exégèse biblique," *Rhetorica* 8 (1990): 291–320.

15. Aristotle, *On Rhetoric: A Theory of Civic Discourse* (trans. and ed. George A. Kennedy; New York: Oxford University Press, 1991), Book III, chapter 3; Richard A. Lanham, *Analyzing Prose* (New York: Charles Scribner's Sons, 1983), chapter 1, "The Domain of Style." Lanham also eschews these prescriptions, what he calls the "C-B-S mentality" (clarity, brevity, sincerity).

16. Donald C. Bryant, "Rhetoric: Its Functions and Its Scope," in *Philosophy, Rhetoric, and Argumentation* (ed. M. Natanson and H. Johnstone; University Park: Pennsylvania State University Press, 1965), 47.

17. Stephen E. Lucas, "The Renaissance of American Public Address: Text and Context in Rhetorical Criticism," *Quarterly Journal of Speech* 74 (1988): 249 (*my emphasis*).

18. Interestingly, Burke is seldom mentioned in the communication periodical literature

I have surveyed. *The New Rhetoric* by Perelman and Olbrechts-Tyteca is completely ignored. However, both Burke and *The New Rhetoric* are extremely significant in much rhetorical criticism, though seemingly not when it comes to style.

19. Kenneth Burke, *Counter-Statement* (2d ed.; Berkeley: University of California Press, 1968).

20. Chaim Perelman and Lucy Olbrechts-Tyteca, *The New Rhetoric: A Treatise on Argumentation* (trans. John Wilkinson and Purcell Weaver; Notre Dame: University of Notre Dame Press, 1969).

21. I am indebted to Alister E. McGrath, "Evangelical Apologetics," *Bibliotheca Sacra* 155 (1998): 7, for the prism analogy.

22. *CS*, 124. This section derives from Neil R. Leroux, "Repetition, Progression, and Persuasion in Scripture," *Neot* 29 (1995): 21–25.

23. In a response to an article by Fredric Jameson, Burke said: "[T]he term 'persuasion' did not cover the ground that I felt should be part of a modern rhetoric. To this end I proposed the term 'identification,' not as a substitute for the traditional approach but as 'an accessory to the standard lore' (*A Rhetoric of Motives*, xiv)" (Burke, *A Rhetoric of Motives* [Berkeley: University of California Press, 1950; paperback, 1969]). See Kenneth Burke, "Methodological Repression and/or Strategies of Containment," *Critical Inquiry* 5 (1978): 403.

24. *CS*, 31.

25. Susan Sontag, "On Style," *Partisan Review* 32 (1965): 543–60.

26. Leland Ryken, *How to Read the Bible as Literature* (Grand Rapids: Zondervan, 1984), 28.

27. *CS*, 142.

28. *CS*, 141.

29. Here Burke seems to have in mind the definition of "aspect" in its grammatical domain: "the nature of the action of a verb as to its beginning, duration, completion, or repetition and without reference to its position in time" (*Merriam-Webster's Collegiate Dictionary* [10th ed.; Springfield, Mass.: Merriam-Webster, 1995]).

30. *CS*, 30.

31. Eugene Lowry, *The Homiletical Plot: The Sermon as Narrative Art Form* (Atlanta: John Knox, 1980), 15, 21.

32. Walter R. Fisher, "Narration as a Human Communication Paradigm: The Case of Public Moral Argument," *Communication Monographs* 51 (1984): 8; cf. Walter R. Fisher, *Human Communication as Narration* (Columbia: University of South Carolina Press, 1987).

33. Of course, influence of art upon "life" also occurs. Undoubtedly, most people's expectations for the apprehension of villains have been shaped far more by mediated art than by real-world experiences with murder.

34. This matter of expectation through progression still holds in inflected languages, where "grammatical meaning" is not completely dependent upon word order, as in English, contra R. Norrman, *Samuel Butler and the Meaning of Chiasmus* (London: Macmillan, 1986), 2; however, *emphasis* (certainly an important component of rhetorical force or impact) is an essential of meaning.

35. *CS*, 140.

36. *CS*, 140.

37. Sheron D. Pattison, "Rhetoric and Audience Effect: Kenneth Burke on Form and

Identification," in vol. 2 of *Studies in Interpretation* (ed. E. M. Doyle and V. M. Floyd; Amsterdam: Rodopi, 1977), 183–98.

38. Vernon K. Robbins, *Jesus the Teacher: A Socio-Rhetorical Interpretation of Mark* (Philadelphia: Fortress, 1984), 9; cf. Robert C. Tannehill, "The Disciples in Mark: The Function of a Narrative Role," *Journal of Religion* 57 (1977): 386–405; and Robert C. Tannehill, "The Gospel of Mark as Narrative Christology," *Semeia* 16 (1980): 57–95.

39. A study that finds both syllogistic and qualitative form in an autobiographical work is Charles J. G. Griffin, "The Rhetoric of Form in Conversion Narratives," *Quarterly Journal of Speech* 76 (1990): 152–63.

40. Robbins, *Jesus the Teacher*, 64; cf. Robert Alter, *The Art of Biblical Narrative* (New York: Basic Books, 1981), 88–113.

41. *Rhet. Her.* 4.42.54.

42. Bruce F. Kawin, *Telling It Again and Again: Repetition in Literature and Film* (Ithaca: Cornell University Press, 1972), 4.

43. Kawin, *Telling It Again and Again*, 5.

44. Robert Alter, "How Convention Helps Us Read," *Prooftexts* 3 (1983): 117; cf. Robert Alter, "Biblical Narrative," *Commentary* 61 (1976): 61–67.

45. LW 2:91, quoted by Peter Auksi, *Christian Plain Style: The Evolution of a Spiritual Ideal* (Montreal: McGill, 1995), 213, whose larger statement is worth noting: "What appears to be purposeless tautology or repetition in the language of Moses, for example, or in the mourning of David over Absalom proves upon Luther's analysis to be purposive. . . . and the repetition in Genesis artfully 'reflects the depth of Moses' feeling and the very great trouble of his soul.' "

46. Kawin, *Telling It Again and Again*, 7–8 (*my emphasis*).

47. David G. Buttrick, "Preaching on the Resurrection," *Religion in Life* 45 (1976): 279.

48. *CS*, 125.

49. Geoffrey N. Leech, *A Linguistic Guide to English Poetry* (London: Longmans, Green & Co., 1969), 92.

50. In Rom 8:38f., Paul is also working with doublet, bipolar pairs. "death/life"; "things present/things to come"; "height/depth." "Angels/principalities-powers" is a variant, disrupting the neatness of the list, probably because, for Paul, "principalities" and "powers" normally go together; cf. Eph 3:10; 6:12; Col 1:16; 2:15; and Titus 3:1.

51. W. E. Rickert, "Rhyme Terms," *Style* 12 (1978): 35.

52. Thomas M. Conley, "The Beauty of Lists. *Copia* and Argument," *Journal of the American Forensic Association* 22 (1985): 101 (*my emphasis*); cf. Thomas M. Conley, "Philo's Rhetoric: Argumentation and Style," *Aufstieg und Niedergang der Römischen Welt* 2.21.1 (1984): 343–71.

53. James Muilenburg, "A Study in Hebrew Rhetoric: Repetition and Style," *Vetus Testamentum Supplements* 1 (Congress Volume; Copenhagen, 1953; Leiden, 1953), 99; cf. James Muilenburg's seminal work, "Form Criticism and Beyond," *Journal of Biblical Literature* 88 (1969): 1–18.

54. See chapters 1 and 2 of Leroux, *Style in Rhetorical Criticism*.

55. Robert Alter, "Biblical Type-Scenes and the Uses of Convention," *Critical Inquiry* 5 (1978): 355–78.

56. *CS*, 204.

57. *CS*, 36.

58. *CS*, 40f.

59. Eugene A. Nida, *God's Word in Man's Language* (South Pasadena: William Carey Library, 1973).

60. Cf. John W. O'Malley, "Content and Rhetorical Forms," in *Renaissance Eloquence* (ed. J. J. Murphy; Berkeley: University of California Press, 1983), 239f.

61. *NR*, 142; cf. sections 36–38. My use of the term "style" and Burke's concept of "form" are, of course, to be contrasted to the more common denotations of these terms.

62. See Robert L. Heath, "Kenneth Burke on Form," *Quarterly Journal of Speech* 65 (1979): 401, commenting on Burke in *A Rhetoric of Motives*.

63. *NR*, 142.

64. While certainly not a "philological work," Richard M. Weaver, "Some Rhetorical Aspects of Grammatical Categories," in *The Ethics of Rhetoric* (Chicago: Regnery, 1953), 115–42, offers a significant exception to the dearth of such material. For another example of grammatical insights from a rhetorical perspective, see Conley's discussion of Philo's use of the optative in "Philo's Rhetoric," 346–48.

65. *NR*, section 39, 156–60.

66. *NR*, 160. Much of the work done on tense is by structuralists, for example, Emile Benveniste, "The Correlations of Tense in the French Verb," in *Problems in General Linguistics* (trans. M. E. Meek; Coral Gables: University of Miami Press, 1971), 205–15; cf. Gerard Genette, "Frequency," in *Narrative Discourse: An Essay in Method* (Ithaca: Cornell University Press, 1980), 113–60.

67. *NR*, 161.

68. *NR*, 162.

69. *NR*, 163.

70. *NR*, 163 (*my emphasis*).

71. Anne M. O'Donnell, "Rhetoric and Style in Erasmus' *Enchiridion militis Christiani*," *Studies in Philology* 77 (1980): 30. O'Donnell calls this the "assertive 'I.' "

72. O'Donnell, "Rhetoric and Style," 30.

73. Leech, *Linguistic Guide to English Poetry*, 74.

74. Conley, "Philo's Rhetoric," 351f. Perelman and Olbrechts-Tyteca use the term "choice," but I consider that term somewhat ambiguous because it might divert attention toward prior inventional decisions rather than focusing upon what the speaker does in the present discourse.

75. *Presence* is "the displaying of certain elements on which the speaker wishes to center attention in order that they may occupy the foreground of the hearers' consciousness" (*NR*, 142).

76. Louise A. Karon, "Presence in *The New Rhetoric*," *Philosophy and Rhetoric* 9 (Spring 1976): 97, argues that presence has at least five effects or characteristics: (1) It is a felt quality in the auditor's consciousness. (2) It fixes audience attention while altering audience perceptions and perspectives. (3) Its strongest agent is the imagination. (4) Its purpose is to initiate action or disposition of the audience toward action or judgment. (5) It is created chiefly through techniques of style, delivery, and disposition. See also John M. Murphy, "Presence, Analogy, and *Earth in the Balance*," *Argumentation and Advocacy* (1994): 1–16.

77. William J. Brandt, *The Rhetoric of Argumentation* (Indianapolis: Bobbs-Merrill,

1970), 153, considers "stance" the writer's attitude toward the subject and as involving some sort of definition of the writer.

78. The *sine qua non* of modern handbooks on figures of speech in the Bible is E. W. Bullinger, *Figures of Speech Used in the Bible, Explained and Illustrated* (London: Eyre & Spottiswoode, 1898; repr., Grand Rapids: Baker, 1968). Scholars now have access to one of the earliest vernacular treatises of rhetorical figures, Richard Rex, ed., *A Reformation Rhetoric: Thomas Swynnerton's* The Tropes and Figures of Scripture (Cambridge: Renaissance Texts from Manuscript, 1999).

79. See *NR*, 504f., on "division"; cf. *Rhet. Her.* 3.30.47; cf. Quintilian on "partition," in *Inst.* 4.5; 7.1.11.

80. *Rhet. Her.* 4.29.40, on "elimination"; *Inst.* 9.3.99 and 5.10.66ff., on "successive removals."

81. *NR*, 169f., 501; *Inst.* 9.2.16f.; 6.3.100.

82. Indeed, Arthur Quinn defines *asyndeton* as "the omission of an expected conjunction" (Arthur Quinn, *Figures of Speech: Sixty Ways to Turn a Phrase* [Salt Lake City: G. M. Smith, 1982], 7).

83. Elizabeth Blettner, "One Made Many and Many Made One: The Role of Asyndeton in Aristotle's Rhetoric," *Philosophy and Rhetoric* 16 (1983): 52.

84. Quinn, *Figures of Speech*, 11.

85. Richard A. Lanham, *A Handlist of Rhetorical Terms* (2d ed.; Berkeley: University of California Press, 1991), 10. A transparent example of *anadiplosis* in Scripture can be found in Joel 1:4: "What the *cutting* locust left, the *swarming* locust has eaten. What the *swarming* locust left, the *hopping* locust has eaten, and what the *hopping* locust left, the *destroying* locust has eaten" (RSV; *my emphasis*).

86. Alter, *Art of Biblical Narrative*, 95–96. Alter disguishes among motif, *Leitwort*, theme, and sequence of actions.

87. LW 51:77.

88. LStA 2:537.3.

89. The first position is the strongest position of emphasis in Koine Greek. There are actually two participles in the sentence: "teaching" [διδάσκων] occurs six words closer to the final adverb, thus the adverb modifies both actions. For more discussion on Acts 28:31, see Gerhard Delling, "Das Letzte Wort der Apostelgeschichte," *Novum Testamentum* 15 (1973): 193–203.

90. *Paraphrasis* also affects communion because the scrutiny to which one holds up an object, as my examples show, can be a view of suspicion and skepticism (distance), as well as affirmation and closeness; cf. 1 Cor 10:12, "Wherefore let him that thinketh he standeth take heed lest he fall."

91. Jeanne Fahnestock, "Series Reasoning in Scientific Argument: *Incrementum* and *Gradatio* and the Case of Darwin," *Rhetoric Society Quarterly* 26.4 (Fall 1996): 13–40, shows how these two figures are conceptual in nature and how they advance an argument.

92. Leech, *Linguistic Guide to English Poetry*, 79.

93. Leech, *Linguistic Guide to English Poetry*, 84.

94. William Shakespeare, *The Merchant of Venice*, 4.1.182.

95. Leech, *Linguistic Guide to English Poetry*, 85.

96. Martin U. Brecht, *Doctor Luther's Bulla and Reformation: A Look at Luther the Writer* (Gross Memorial Lecture 1990; Valparaiso, Ind.: Valparaiso University Press, 1991), 1. The full treatment of this topic is Martin U. Brecht, *Luther als Schriftsteller: Zeug-*

*nisse seines dichterischen Gestaltens* (Stuttgart: Calwer, 1990).

97. Helmar Junghans, *Martin Luther in Two Centuries* (trans. Katharina Gustavs and Gerald S. Krispin; St. Paul, Minn.: Lutheran Brotherhood Foundation Reformation Research Library/Luther Northwestern Theological Seminary, 1992), 12; cf. Timothy Kircher, *Luther's Conception of Language: Forms of Religious Expression in Late Medieval and Renaissance Europe* (Ph.D. diss., Yale University, 1989), 22.

98. LStA 2:530.11.

99. Roger Brown, *Words and Things* (Glencoe, Ill.: Free Press, 1958), 56.

100. I. A. Richards, *The Philosophy of Rhetoric* (New York: Oxford University Press, 1936; repr., 1981), 59. Richards is following Leonard Bloomfield, *Language* (New York: Henry Holt, 1933), in his guarded discussion of the resemblance of sound and sense.

101. By *synonymy*, I simply call attention to a plethora of ways to amplify an idea through the addition of terms. For more theoretical interest in the concept of synonymity, see E. D. Hirsch Jr., "Stylistics and Synonymity," *Critical Inquiry* 1 (1975): 559–79.

102. Leech, *Linguistic Guide to English Poetry*, 97; Leech is following Karl J. Shapiro and Robert L. Beum, *A Prosody Handbook* (New York: Harper & Row, 1965), 14f.

103. Leech, *Linguistic Guide to English Poetry*, 100.

104. Buttrick, *Homiletic*, 191.

105. *NR*, 331, on "personification"; *NR*, 176, on "imaginary direct speech"; *Rhet. Her.* 4.53.65, on *prosopopeia*; *Rhet. Her.* 4.52.65, on *sermocinatio*; *prosopopeia* and *sermocinatio* are inseparable in *Inst.* 9.2.29.

106. Luther's rhetoric, particularly in comparison to that of Erasmus, has a reputation as assertive and monologic, as Thomas Conley, *Rhetoric in the European Tradition* (New York: Longman, 1990), 120–24, points out. However, in the Invocavit Sermons there are several times when we see another side of Luther, a side strategically presenting *controversia*, which, as defined by Conley, is the management of uncertainty. Conley's *Rhetoric*, it should be noted, is the only major contemporary work in English on the history of rhetoric to pay Luther any note whatsoever!

107. The Vulgate begins each question identically (*numquid omnes*), while Luther's 1522 *Newe Testament Deu(o)tzsch* varies the diction (the first four begin with *sind sie alle*, the next two with *haben sie alle*, then *reden sie alle*, and last *kunden sie alle*).

108. *Inst.* 9.2.37f.; and *Rhet. Her.* 4.15.22, on *apostrophe*.

109. There are, of course, shades of sincerity and irony to be weighed, but the communion term still applies.

110. This grammatical case form in Greek unmistakably indicates direct address. In New Testament Greek, the nominative case, often with the article, is normally used. That direct address is being employed is easily discernible from the punctuation and context.

111. See H. G. Haile, "Luther and Literacy," *Publication of the Modern Language Association* 71 (1976): 820: "Proverbs . . . are convincing not only because they seem to distill the wisdom of the ages which is beyond dispute but also because their use certifies the native son, a fellow countryman who can make a special claim on credence."

112. See Rom 10:15, where Paul is more faithful to the context of Isa 52:7 than I am with his context.

113. For a discussion of these types of problems, see Thomas M. Conley, "The Linnaean Blues: Thought on the Genre Approach," in *Form, Genre, and the Study of Political*

*Discourse* (ed. Herbert W. Simons and Aram A. Aghazarian; Columbia: University of South Carolina Press, 1986), 59–78.

114. Gérard Genette, *Figures of Literary Discourse* (trans. Alan Sheridan; New York: Columbia University Press, 1982), 56.

115. Moisés Silva, *Biblical Words and Their Meaning: An Introduction to Lexical Semantics* (rev. & expanded ed.; Grand Rapids: Zondervan, 1994), 117.

# CHAPTER 2

1. Lloyd F. Bitzer, "The Rhetorical Situation," *Philosophy and Rhetoric* 1 (1968): 1–14.

2. Neil R. Leroux, "The Rhetor's Perceived Situation: Luther's Invocavit Sermons," *Rhetoric Society Quarterly* 28.1 (1998): 49–80; cf. E. M. Cornelius, "The Relevance of Ancient Rhetoric to Rhetorical Criticism," *Neot* 28 (1994): 457–67.

3. LW 31:17–33.

4. LW 31:77–252.

5. Heiko A. Oberman, *Luther: Man between God and the Devil* (trans. Eileen Walliser-Schwarzbart; New York: Doubleday [Image Books], 1989), 144: "His Augustinian brethren were the ones who had not contented themselves with seeking their own perfection in Observantism, but had decided instead to fashion their monasteries into staging areas from which to reach out for the betterment of the church and world."

6. Carter Lindberg, *The European Reformations* (Oxford: Blackwell, 1996), 56–70. Helmar Junghans, "Wittenberg," in *The Oxford Encyclopedia of the Reformation* (ed. Hans J. Hillerbrand; New York: Oxford University Press, 1996), 4:283, says Luther held the lectorship in moral philosophy in 1508–09, and in 1512 he was made professor of biblical studies. "Soon after" that, Luther accepted the office of municipal preacher [*Prädikamt*]. On Luther's doctorate, see Pfarrer Steinlein in Ansbach, "Luthers Doktorat," *Neue Kirchliche Zeitschrift* 23 (1912): 757–843.

7. LW 54:206 (WATr 3:341.8–11, no. 3472); cf. Ulrich Bubenheimer, "Luther als Prediger," public lecture at Ehrenkinker Evangelische Kirchengemeinde (30 October 1988). Martin Brecht, "Luther's Reformation," in *Handbook of European History 1400–1600: Late Middle Ages, Renaissance, and Reformation* (ed. Thomas A. Brady Jr., Heiko A. Oberman, and James D. Tracy; Grand Rapids: Eerdmans, 1996), 2:130, says Luther assumed the pulpit duties of the city church in 1514.

8. Lindberg, *The European Reformations*, 60. On Staupitz's influence on Luther, see Lothar Graf zu Dohna, "Staupitz and Luther: Continuity and Breakthrough at the Beginning of the Reformation," in *Via Augustini: Augustine in the Later Middle Ages, Renaissance, and Reformation: Essays in Honor of Damasus Trapp* (Studies in Medieval and Reformation Thought 48; ed. Heiko A. Oberman and Frank A. James III; Leiden: E. J. Brill, 1991), 116–29.

9. Heiko A. Oberman, *Luther: Man between God and the Devil* (trans. Eileen Walliser-Schwarzbart; New Haven: Yale University Press, 1989), 128–44.

10. Oberman, *Luther: Man between God and the Devil*, 172.

11. LW 44:115–217; WA 6:404–69.

12. The remarks about the "three walls" are in LW 44:126; Oberman, *Man between God and the Devil*, 46; and Harry Loewen, *Luther and the Radicals* (Waterloo, Ontario: W. Laurier University, 1974), 17.

13. LW 36:35–126; WA 6:497–573.

14. LW 31:329–77; WA 7:42ff.

15. Timothy J. Wengert, "Martin Luther's Movement toward an Apostolic Self-Aware-ness as Reflected in His Early Letters," *Lutherjahrbuch* 61 (1994): 87. My own perusal of WABr 2 shows that Luther commonly signed off as "Augustinian" (to all non-Augustinians; he could refer to a brother of his order in the *salutatio*) until March 1521, then such a signature becomes infrequent for the next couple months and virtually stops by October 1521.

16. Bengt Hoffman, ed., *The Theologia Germanica of Martin Luther* (New York: Paulist, 1980), 53–54; cf. LW 31:75 (WA 1:378–89).

17. Luther had no really personal relationship with Frederick, claiming in 1524 that he had only seen the Elector once in person (see "Against the Heavenly Prophets" [LW 40:102]). Nearly all Luther's correspondence to the Elector was directed through Georg Spalatin, Frederick's chaplain.

18. Heinrich Böhmer, *Luther in Light of Recent Research* (trans. Carl F. Huth Jr.; New York: The Christian Herald, 1916), 147.

19. James Samuel Preus, *Carlstadt's "Ordinaciones" and Luther's "Liberty": A Study of the Wittenberg Movement 1521–1522* (Harvard Theological Studies 26; Cambridge: Harvard University Press, 1974). This is one of the few studies in English that pays close attention to the content of the Invocavit Sermons.

20. Besides his doctorate in theology, Karlstadt held doctorates in civil law and canon law, which he earned in Rome while on sabbatical from Wittenberg. On Karlstadt's legalistic side, see Ulrich Bubenheimer, *Consonantia Theologiae et Iurisprudentiae: Andreas Bodenstein von Karlstadt als Theologe und Jurist zwischen Scholastik und Refor-mation* (Tübingen: J. C. B. Mohr [Paul Siebeck], 1977).

21. Amsdorf, Jonas, and Hieronymus Schurff (Luther's attorney) were the three Luther chose to accompany him on the dangerous journey—under the emperor's safe-keep-ing king-of-arms Karspar Sturm—to Worms; cf. De Lamar Jensen, *Confrontation at Worms: Martin Luther and the Diet of Worms* (Provo: Brigham Young University Press, 1973), 95. Amsdorf was probably Luther's closest friend next to Melanchthon; cf. Robert Kolb, *Nikolaus von Amsdorf 1483–1565: Popular Polemics in the Preservation of Luther's Legacy* (Bibliotheca Humanistica and Reformatorica 24; Nieuwkoop: B. de Graaf, 1978).

22. Martin Brecht, *Martin Luther: Shaping and Defining the Reformation, 1521–1532* (trans. James L. Schaaf; Minneapolis: Fortress, 1990), 25.

23. E. G. Schwiebert, *Luther and His Times: The Reformation from a New Perpective* (St. Louis: Concordia, 1950), 524.

24. As we might expect of a person in hiding, almost no letters addressed *to* Luther dur-ing this period have survived. However, we have many letters Luther wrote during this time, and perusal of them indicates that he was kept well informed of events in Wittenberg.

25. For a concise summary of what I have liberally borrowed from in my sketch of these groups, see Preus, *Carlstadt's "Ordinaciones,"* 5–8; cf. Steven E. Ozment, *The Refor-mation in the Cities: The Appeal of Protestantism to Sixteenth-Century Germany and Switzerland* (New Haven: Yale University Press, 1975), 138–45; and the documents collected in Nikolaus Müller, ed., *Die Wittenberger Bewegung 1521 und 1522: Die Vorgange in und um Wittenberg wahrend Luthers Wartburgaufenthalt* (2d ed.; Leipzig: M. Heinsius, 1911).

26. Preus, *Carlstadt's "Ordinaciones."* 6; Harold J. Grimm, "The Relations of Luther and Melanchthon with the Townsmen," in *Luther and Melanchthon* (ed. Vilmos Vajta; Philadelphia: Muhlenberg, 1961), 37f.

27. Böhmer, *Luther in Light of Recent Research*, 146–75.

28. Some disturbances also occurred at the Franciscan cloister.

29. The standard catalogue of Karlstadt's works is E. Freys and H. Barge, "Verzeichnis der gedruckten Schriften des Andreas Bodenstein von Karlstadt," *Zentralblatt für Bibliothekswesen* 21 (1904): 153–79; 209–43; 305–31.

30. The All Saints' Chapter was, according to Helmar Junghans, the "only institution of the medieval church in Wittenberg that closed its mind to the Reformation"; cf. Helmar Junghans, "Wittenberg and Luther: Luther and Wittenberg," in *Martin Luther in Two Centuries* (trans. Katharina Gustavs and Gerald S. Krispin; St. Paul, Minn.: Lutheran Brotherhood Foundation Reformation Research Library/Luther Northwestern Theological Seminary, 1992), 22.

31. Leopold von Ranke, *History of the Reformation in Germany* (ed. Robert A. Johnson; trans. Sarah Austin; London: George Routledge & Sons, 1905), 248–63.

32. "The Misuse of the Mass" [1521] (LW 36:127–230; WA 8:482–563).

33. "The Blessed Sacrament of the Holy and True Body of Christ, and the Brotherhoods" [1519] (LW 35:49–73; WA 2:742–58).

34. Hermann Barge, *Andreas Bodenstein von Karlstadt*, 2 vols. (Leipzig, 1905), 1:265ff., cited in Schwiebert, *Luther*, 524.

35. "The Blessed Sacrament " (LW 35:49–73; WA 2:742–58).

36. Brecht, *Shaping and Defining the Reformation*, 26; Ronald J. Sider, *Andreas Bodenstein von Karlstadt: The Develoment of His Thought 1517–1525* (Studies in Medieval and Reformation Thought 11; Leiden: E. J. Brill, 1974), 144.

37. Sider, *Andreas Bodenstein von Karlstadt*, 145.

38. Among these other problems, in particular, were the use of Latin (versus vernacular) in the Mass and perhaps the most significant issue to be addressed by Luther, though not explicitly debated in writing: Who, if anyone, is responsible (and to what extent and at what pace) for making changes in church practice?

39. *Von der Beicht. ob der Papst Macht habe sie zu gebieten* (WA 8:140ff.). The dedication of the tract is a letter to Franz von Sickingen in which Luther says, "In order to demonstrate that I am not idle in this wilderness and in my Patmos, I, too, have written a Revelation for myself and will share it with all who desire it. . . . It is a sermon *On Confession* . . ." (LW 48:246 [Letter 82]).

40. LW 48:277–82 (Letter 91 [WABr 2:370–72, no. 424]).

41. Preserved Smith and Charles M. Jacobs, eds., *Luther's Correspondence and Other Contemporary Letters* (Philadelphia: The Lutheran Publication Society, 1918): 2:58 (Letter 506).

42. Brecht, *Shaping and Defining the Reformation*, 26.

43. Böhmer, *Luther in Light of Recent Research*, 155.

44. Brecht, *Shaping and Defining the Reformation*, 26.

45. Sebastian Helmann to Johann Hess at Bresslau (8 October 1521): "Behold, God has raised up unto us another prophet [Zwilling] of the same order [Augustinians], who preaches the Gospel so sincerely and candidly that he is dubbed the Second Luther by all. Melanchthon neglects no sermon . . . . Accordingly, we Wittenbergers do not hear masses. We hear the Word of God diligently; also we do not communicate in one kind, but in both, and we do it often. Philip Melanchthon with all his pupils communicated in both kinds in the parish church on Michaelmas, and now this is done in all the churches" (Smith and Jacobs, *Luther's Correspondence*, 2:59f. [Letter 507]).

46. Smith and Jacobs, *Luther's Correspondence*, 2:60f. (Letter 508).

47. Albert Burer, in a letter to Beatus Rhenanus (19 October 1521), attests to the October 13 preaching of Zwilling, adding that Karlstadt also conducted a debate on the abolition of masses following the sermon (Smith and Jacobs, *Luther's Correspondence*, 2:62f. [Letter 511]); cf. Siegfried Hoyer, "Zwilling, Gabriel," in *The Oxford Encyclopedia of the Reformation*, 4:319f.

48. LW 44:251–400; WA 8:577–669.

49. LW 36:127–230; WA 8:482–563.

50. Smith and Jacobs, *Luther's Correspondence*, 2:78f. (Letter 517).

51. LW 48:325–28 (Letter 103 [WABr 2:402f., no. 438]).

52. LW 48:329–36 (Letter 104 [WA 8:573–76]). For an analysis of this letter, see Scott H. Hendrix, "Luther's Loyalties and the Augustinian Order," in *Augustine, the Harvest, and Theology (1300–1650): Essays Dedicated to Heiko Augustinus Oberman in Honor of His Sixtieth Birthday* (ed. Kenneth Hagen; Leiden: E. J. Brill, 1990), 236–58; repr. in Kenneth Hagen, *Tradition and Authority in the Reformation* (Collected Studies 535; Aldershot: Variorum), 1996.

53. *WB*, no. 32, 73f.

54. *WB*, no. 33–34, 74–76.

55. LW 48:351f. (Letter 107 [WABr 2:409f., no. 443]): "Everything else that I hear and see pleases me very much. May the Lord strengthen the spirit of those who want to do right! Nevertheless I was disturbed on the way by various rumors concerning the improper conduct of some of our people, and I have decided to issue a public exhortation on that subject as soon as I have returned to my wilderness." What Luther was *not* pleased with was the delay in publishing some of his writings. Luther's "A Sincere Admonition" is found in LW 45:57–74 (WA 8:676–87).

56. *WB*, no. 36, 77f.; *WB*, no. 43, 84–90. The eight signatories were Hessus, Karlstadt, H. Schurff, Wild, A. Schurff, Melanchthon, Amsdorf, and Bockenheim.

57. Sigrid Looß, "Radical Views of the Early Andreas Karlstadt (1520–1525)," in *Radical Tendencies in the Reformation: Divergent Perspectives* (Sixteenth Century Essays and Studies 9; ed. Hans J. Hillerbrand; Kirksville: Sixteenth Century Journal Press, 1988), 47.

58. There had been disturbances in Erfurt also. It was, however, mostly reports and rumors of disturbances to which Luther had access.

59. LW 48:356f. (Letter 109 [WABr 2:413, no. 445]).

60. Smith and Jacobs, *Luther's Correspondence*, 2:80f. (Letter 519). Luther's earlier letter to Albert is Smith and Jacobs, *Luther's Correspondence*, 72–75 (Letter 515 [WABr 2:420f., no. 448]).

61. *WB*, no. 57, 123–26.

62. *Predig Andresen Boden. von Carolstatt tzu Wittenberg Von emphahung des heiligen Sacraments* (Freys-Barge, no. 76).

63. *WB*, no. 58, 128ff. (with extensive bibliography provided by Müller).

64. *WB*, no. 62, 135f.; *WB*, no. 65, 145f.

65. Jonas himself married shortly thereafter, on February 9, 1522; cf. Bob Scribner, "Anticlericalism and the Cities," in *Anticlericalism in Late Medieval and Early Modern Europe* (Studies in Medieval and Reformation Thought 51; ed. Peter A. Dykema and Heiko A. Oberman; Leiden: E. J. Brill, 1993), 153, n. 14. Luther, of course, remained unmarried until 1525.

66. *WB*, no. 64, 137–45. The role the "prophets" played and their contribution to troubles in Wittenberg, to Melanchthon's (and others') stability, and to Luther's return are highly controversial.

67. Susan C. Karant-Nunn, *Zwickau in Transition, 1500–1547: The Reformation as an Agent of Change* (Columbus: Ohio State University Press ), 6, 106–13.

68. Felix Ulscenius, in a letter to Wolfgang Capito at Mainz (1 January 1522), refers to Stübner's knowledge of Scripture and possession of "a great deal of the Spirit" (Smith and Jacobs, *Luther's Correspondence*, 2:82f [Letter 522]).

69. *WB*, no. 68, 151–64 (Wittenberg newspaper account).

70. *WB*, no. 67, 147–51.

71. *WB*, no. 72, 169; cf. Hoyer, "Zwilling, Gabriel," in *Oxford Encyclopedia of the Reformation*, 4:319f.

72. "To Amsdorf," LW 48:360–64 (Letter 111 [WABr 2:422f., no. 449]). "To Melanchthon," LW 48:364–72 (Letter 112 [WABr 2:424–27, no. 450]).

73. LW 48:364. For a discussion of the commonplace depiction of Melanchthon as weak-kneed during this period, see the review article by Heinz Scheible, "Luther and Melanchthon," *LQ* 4 (1990): 317–39.

74. LW 48:380f. (Letter 114 [WABr 2:443f., no. 452]).

75. The modern edition is Andreas Karlstadt, *Von Abtuhung der Bilder und das keyn Bedtler unther den Christen seyn sollen, 1522* (Kleine Texte 74; Bonn: A. Marcus & E. Weber, 1911).

76. From 1520 to 1570, the Leucorea was the most popular German university, reaching a peak enrollment (in 1570) of 3,351 students. From 1520 to 1525, enrollment declined from 1,714 to 1,069 students; cf. Helmar Junghans, *Wittenberg als Lutherstadt* (Berlin: Union, 1979), 180.

77. *WB*, no. 81, 177f.

78. *WB*, no. 83, 180f.

79. *WB*, no. 95, 201–05.

80. *WB*, no. 99, 206–11.

81. Mark Edwards, *Luther and the False Brethren* (Stanford: Stanford University Press, 1975), 16: "The Elector's refusal to accept the compromise presented the Wittenbergers with a dilemma: They must either undo the reforms or defy the Elector."

82. LW 48:388–93 (Letter 117 [WABr 2:454-457, no. 455]).

83. Carter Lindberg, *Beyond Charity: Reformation Initiatives for the Poor* (Minneapolis: Fortress, 1993), 201f. The other articles pertained to poor relief and begging.

# CHAPTER 3

1. For my analysis of the collected eight Invocavit Sermons, I examined—and will normally quote—the text of LW 51:70–100, edited and revised by John W. Doberstein, which is a revision of the text of Augustus Steimle, ed., *Luther's Works* (Philadelphia: A. J. Holman, 1918), 2:390–425. The text is based on the critical edition printed on the upper portion of pages 1–64 of volume 10/3 of WA, which remains the standard critical edition for all Luther's works. In view of the recent challenge offered by Kenneth Hagen, *Luther's Approach to Scripture as Seen in His "Commentaries" on Galatians 1519–1538* (Tübingen: J. C. B. Mohr [Paul Siebeck], 1993)—that the

Weimar Edition ought not always be trusted and that for some Luther writings (particularly those based on his exegetical lectures) there may be marginal authorial notes and punctuation that ought to be considered—I have also checked 16th-century prints in microfilm, namely, Josef Benzing, *Lutherbibliographie: Verzeichnis der gedruckten Schriften Martin Luthers bis zu dessen Tod* (Baden-Baden: Librairie Heitz, 1966), no. 50, which is classified as "B" in the WA introduction and apparatus (Augsburg: Heinrich Steiner, 1523). This represents one of the two earliest recensions of the text of the collected eight sermons. In addition, I have checked a microfilm version of the "Sermon on Images" (Benzing, no. 1320), which is identified in the apparatus as "a" (Augsburg: Melchior Ramminger, 1522), and is the earliest printed form of any of the sermons. The WA has a full (and cumbersome) *apparatus criticus* that cites variant readings and their witnesses, while two other recent critical editions—*Luthers Werke in Auswahl* (3d ed.; ed. Otto Clemen; Berlin: W. de Gruyter, 1962), 362–87 (*CL* 7:363–87; and Helmar Junghans' edition in LStA 2:530–58 (1982)—employ more abbreviated *apparati critici* that cite variants more sparingly and use what are essentially footnote systems, mostly for biblical references. Both *Luthers Werke in Auswahl* and LStA carefully crossindex their texts to the WA. LStA is now clearly the most useful study text edition [*Studienausgabe*] for rhetorical scholars (particularly those whose native language is not German) because this edition not only provides a concise and helpful introduction, but also employs a modern font. Editors insert full-sized vowel diacritical marks (only the u-umlaut [ü] is retained) and omitted consonants (the result of abbreviations) in parentheses, making the text in some ways more authentic, even more readable, and citing numerous interpretive cross-references to the WA in the footnotes. The text also retains the original punctuation for partial stops and pauses, the slash [ / ], while using the modern period [ . ] for the full stop. The editors have eliminated most paragraph indentations that the 16th-century printers used, enabling the reader to exercise personal judgment about such things based on the author's (not the printer's) text/context. That means, of course, that rhetorical signals of dispositional units are neither clarified nor obscured by paragraph indentations. The text-critical apparatus is radically reduced (compared to the WA), omitting all variants except the major recensions. At the same time, however, the critical apparatus (in footnotes) is greatly expanded for the general scholar, incorporating historical and theological references. Thus, the text of the Invocavit Sermons that has had scholarly consensus for the past century can be found in numerous contemporary publications (*Luthers Werke in Auswahl*, WA, LStA), and LStA is the most up-to-date.

2. Luther probably began by reading and expounding the Gospel reading for the day, Matt 4:1–11. There is external evidence that he did this, and such practice would be consistent with Luther's habit on Sundays. The themes in the Gospel reading—the temptation of Jesus—would provide a backdrop for Luther's focus on the issues of controversy because in that scriptural pericope, Jesus faces testing at the hands of the devil, and Scripture ("It is written . . .") is what stabilizes the one tempted. For the "eyewitness" testimony that Luther first took up the Gospel, see WA 10/3:lii (from which I quote in my discussion of the Eighth Sermon).

3. Because there are no line numbers in LW, I will cite LStA by page and line number.

4. Luther mentioned death in two letters to Frederick: March 5 (Preserved Smith and Charles M. Jacobs, eds., *Luther's Correspondence and Other Contemporary Letters* [Philadelphia: Lutheran Publication Society, 1918], 2:93–96 [Letter 529]; LW 48:388ff.; WABr 2:453–59, no. 455) and March 12 (Smith and Jacobs, eds., *Luther's Correspondence*, 2:99 [Letter 532]).

5. The first word of the Latin introit [*invocavit*] suggests a theme of being summoned. This became part of the Lenten tradition. How "he shall call" [*invocabit*] became

"he has called" [*invocavit*] is a mystery, but it is the name that stuck for the Sunday and the sermons. Luther had nothing to do with assigning the term *invocavit* to the sermons, and I doubt any of his followers did either. It was common at that time to date one's letters as so many days since/before *Inuocauit*. See Paul Zeller Strodach, "Invocavit, the first Sunday of Lent," in *The Church Year: Studies in the Introits, Collects, Epistles and Gospels* (Philadelphia: United Lutheran Publishing House, 1924), 107–11.

6.  Luther was quite adept and bold in his creative use of personal pronouns. According to Robin Leaver, in his creedal hymn *Wir glauben*, Luther transformed the first-person singular language of the Latin *credo* ("I believe in God, Father Almighty" [*Credo in deum patrem omnipotentem*]) to the first-person plural ("We all believe in one God" [*Wir gelauben all an einen Gott*]). See Robin A. Leaver, "Luther's Catechism Hymns 3: Creed," *LQ* 12 (1998): 79–88; cf. Timothy J. Wengert, "Wittenberg's Earliest Catechism," *LQ* 7 (1993): 247–60. In his "Table Talk" (1531), Luther even discussed the importance of personal pronouns: "So this one word 'your' or 'our' is the most difficult of all in the whole Scripture. It's like the word 'your' in the first commandment, "I am the Lord your God [Exod. 20:2]" (LW 54:9, no. 81).

7.  Luther's use of the second singular pronoun *du* is a common and often significant feature in these sermons. Although there is some uncertainty among scholars as to whether the modern distinction between the "intimate" and "formal" can be ascertained in the pronouns of the Renaissance, we can distinguish singular [*du*] from plural [*ihr*]. I am presuming that, in general, singular is more "intimate" than the plural, but I will treat each situation carefully. See Roger Brown and Albert Gilman, "Pronouns of Solidarity and Power," in *Style in Language* (ed. T. A. Sebeok; Cambridge: MIT Press, 1960), 253–76. For discussion of some significant uses of first- and second-person pronouns, see Hartwig Thyen, *Der Stil der Jüdisch-Hellenistischen Homilie* (Forschungen zur Religion und Literatur des Alten und Neuen Testaments; Göttingen: Vandenhoeck & Ruprecht, 1955), 90–100.

8.  *NR*, 158–60.

9.  *NR*, 158–60.

10. *NR*, 176.

11. Later we will see, in retrospect, how Luther himself does this very thing in the Invocavit Sermons, that is, "confront the devil with many passages." In a letter to Spalatin dated March 13, Luther says: "Do pray for me, and help me to tread underfoot that Satan who, in the name of the Gospel, has set himself up here in Wittenberg against the Gospel. We are fighting against an angel of darkness who has transformed himself into an angel of light. It will be hard for Carlstadt to give up his views, but Christ will force him to do so if he does not yield of his own accord" (Smith and Jacobs, *Luther's Correspondence*, 2:101f [Letter 533]).

12. In Matt 11:23, which is enclosed in brackets in LW 51:71, Jesus had scolded the villagers of Capernaum for failing to recognize his wondrous deeds. Hereafter, I will cite LW references to the Invocavit Sermons as 51:xx.

13. In the brief synopsis that the "eyewitness" Johannes Kesler gives, concern for one's "neighbor" [*nechsten*] is mentioned. See WA 10/3:lii.

14. Luther quotes the Vulgate directly.

15. Kesler's summary mentions three passages Luther presumably used in the sermons, of which this is the first. Kesler carefully preserves Luther's German translation.

16. According to C. A. Pater, *Karlstadt as the Father of the Baptist Movements: The Emergence of Lay Protestantism* (Toronto: Toronto University Press, 1984), 15, this text had been a favorite of Karlstadt. Here Luther uses one of Karlstadt's "primary" texts

against him. Pater, *Karlstadt*, 22, argues that Karlstadt's scriptural preferences were based on a two-level structure: "primary" texts (Genesis through Deuteronomy; Matthew through Acts) and "secondary" texts (the Prophets and the Pauline Epistles). Luther honors no such distinctions between texts.

17. Richard Lanham, *Analyzing Prose* (New York: Charles Scribner's Sons, 1983), 33–52, on *parataxis*. Here the *et* drives a deep wedge between "they" (the disturbers in Wittenberg) and "I" (God, Luther). The "right-branching" direction clearly implies who is the apex of authority, that, for the Wittenberg ordinance, authoritative sanction is found wanting.

18. This rebuke is especially sharp because the observation is in present tense, because the Spirit's leading was a boast of some radicals (especially the Zwickau Prophets), and because Luther's own teaching at Wittenberg had been that the Spirit is available through Scripture.

19. These are essentially the themes summarized by Kesler.

20. As we shall more directly see in this sermon, Luther is not merely quibbling over the pace of the reforms. Rather, he approaches their implementation (practice) by framing the practices in a theoretical context. For Luther, "force" is not merely an imprudent strategy, but it is based on a false theology (theory); it tries to do God's work. Cf. Steven Ozment, "Pacing the Reforms," in *The Reformation in the Cities: The Appeal of Protestantism to Sixteenth-Century Germany and Switzerland* (New Haven: Yale University Press, 1975), 138–45.

21. One way chiasmus, or reverse parallelism, can function is by effecting a turn at the point where the reverse parallelism begins (the "pivot"). Thus, it can be a more precise way to guide listeners along the path of an antithesis; see Neil R. Leroux, "Repetition, Progression, and Persuasion in Scripture," *Neot* 29 (1995): 1–25.

22. Luther enlivens this story by paraphrasing Acts 17:16–32, modernizing it for his audience, making the story seem like a situation analogous to Wittenberg's, and telling it with humor: "kicked with his foot."

23. Cf. a similar remark Luther had made in "A Sincere Admonition": "Get busy now; spread the holy gospel, and help others spread it; teach, speak, write, and preach [*lere / rede / schreyb vnd predige*] that man-made laws are nothing;" (LW 45:68; *Eyn trew vormahung*, Biii).

24. Amsdorf and Friar Petzensteiner were Luther's two companions who were allowed to escape when he was taken into custody at Eisenach. Luther also stayed at Amsdorf's home during the secret visit to Wittenberg in early December. See Eric W. Gritsch, *Martin—God's Court Jester: Luther in Retrospect* (Philadelphia: Fortress, 1983), 42.

25. Maria Grossmann, *Humanism in Wittenberg, 1485–1517* (Nieuwkoop: B. deGraaf, 1975), 82, shows Luther's preference for Augustine over Jerome ("theology over philology") on this issue.

# CHAPTER 4

1. The issues of controversy were obvious to everyone, but the plan for dealing with them was Luther's. Moreover, the urgency is a matter Luther redirects from an urgent need for reform to a lack of harmony and preparedness for difficulties.

2. We notice in Kesler's remarks not only which texts Kesler retained, but that he remembered them, especially in the manner in which he cites Paul.

3. In saying "dogmatic," I simply refer to Luther's accusation "departing from God's

ordinance and liberty" [*tretten vo(n) gottes ordenu(n)ge vnd freyheit*] (541.19).

4.  The sermon has only one unmistakable transition, which occurs where Luther turns directly to "images." All editors include the subheading "von Byldtnussen."

5.  Indeed, "vows" [*gelübte*] does not appear until late in the section (541.6). Luther takes up these clergy matters individually, as examples of the "must"/"free" principle, summarizing them as "vows" toward the end of the section.

6.  Despite the particular threat that Karlstadt posed for Luther, this is the only time in all the sermons where Luther mentions him by name. One does not need to mention often what is obvious to all. Crerar Douglas, *The Coherence of Andreas Bodenstein von Karlstadt's Early Evangelical Doctrine of the Lord's Supper: 1521–1525* (Ph.D. diss., Hartford Seminary Foundation, 1973), 155: "Luther's attack on Karlstadt was all the more effective because of his refusal to state publicly that Karlstadt was the object of attack: the impression was conveyed that Luther was concerned with principles, not personalities. Yet by lumping Karlstadt in with the most radical figures in Wittenberg, Luther in fact exaggerated whatever spiritualism or antinomianism, if any, Karlstadt had indulged in." Luther refers to Zwilling as "Gabriel," and the popular audience would never have thought of Gabriel Biel, to which Luther occasionally refers in theological writings.

7.  Augustus Steimle ed., *Luther's Works* (Philadelphia: A. J. Holman, 1918), 2:402, notes this allusion to Galatians and to the fact that Luther said something similar in a 1516 sermon. In a March 13 letter to the Elector, Jerome Schurff said that "Gabriel has confessed . . . ." He meant Gabriel Zwilling; see Preserved Smith and Charles M. Jacobs, *Luther's Correspondence and Other Contemporary Letters* (Philadelphia: Lutheran Publication Society, 1918), 2:102f. (Letter 534).

8.  Also at LStA 531.1 and 531.26.

9.  *NR*, 179ff.

10. This is in keeping with Luther's previous usage—the sun's two properties (532.16)—whereas he uses *exempel* twice in the Second Sermon (537.5, 22), both of which function as models for emulative action. Here (and earlier) *gleychnyß* functions as an analogy or lesson that makes no necessary implication that the audience comply, save to understand the analogy so it may enlighten the previous premise. *Exempel*, then, seeks persuasion through increased presence, while *gleychnyß* adjusts the focus to increased belief and understanding.

11. William J. Brandt, *The Rhetoric of Argumentation* (Indianapolis: Bobbs-Merrill, 1970), 127f.

12. Or it implies at least that Luther and the audience have gone as far as they can on this issue for now. Compare this to the ending of the Second Sermon.

13. Karlstadt's arguments in *Von Abtuhung* are summarized in Roy L. Vice, "Iconoclasm in Rothenburg ob der Tauber in 1525," *ARG* 89 (1998): 55–57. Cf. J. Travis Moger, "Pamphlets, Preaching, and Politics: The Image Controversy in Reformation Wittenburg, Zürich and Strassburg," *Mennonite Quarterly Review* 75 (2001): 325–54; and Neil R. Leroux, " 'In the Christian City of Wittenberg': Karlstadt's Tract on Images and Begging," forthcoming in *Sixteenth Century Journal*.

14. The first time Luther mentions "altar" is in the First Sermon (530.15).

15. "Foreshadowing" could be planned by Luther or be quite subconscious. It would probably be caught by the audience only in retrospect because that is how we catch it in analysis. If we had an audio text we might catch more. If repetitive form exists at all, then each succeeding repetition should become more significant.

16. If Luther can find contradiction in adjacent commandments, it would be, no doubt,

more disconcerting than to uncover it among widely separated texts. The Decalogue is a model of primordial, cohesive, progressive, structured legislation.

17. Besides, the audience hears it all.

18. Luther frequently uses *als* and *also* as demonstratives; hence, I added emphasis to both demonstrative and referent.

19. Luther did not do this in the Second Sermon, using *tempel* at LStA 536.29.

20. Passed over in the English translation (51:83).

21. Note how the expression parallels Luther's earlier phrase about a vow to strike one's father on the mouth.

22. C. A. Pater, *Karlstadt as the Father of the Baptist Movements: The Emergence of Lay Protestantism* (Toronto: Toronto University Press, 1984), 22.

23. All editions, German and English, put a section heading at the start of the "meats" section, which was in the original prints and was enumerated on the title page.

24. This personification of love is not explicitly developed in this sermon, but it foreshadows the "love" theme of later sermons. So this is not only recapitulation (from 530.7 [*hauptstück*]), but it is a subtle theme—here and to be developed later explicitly.

25. LW 51:84 misses the *repetitio* of "good."

26. See Luther's letter to Frederick "congratulating" him on his latest "find" (LW 48:386ff.; WABr 2:453–59, no. 455).

27. "*Not* enough" was previously used at LStA 531.13 [*nit gnugsam*] and at LStA 539.8 [*nicht genu(o)g*] (in reference to Wittenbergers). It is contrasted to Luther's actions ("enough" said) at the end of each sermon or serves to question whether Luther or Paul has spoken clearly or plainly enough.

28. Note the word plays among noun "goldpiece" [*gulden*], adjective "golden" [*gulden*], and verb "matters" [*gülten*] (544.17).

29. WA 10/3:33.3; also in Martin Luther, *Luther Deutsch: Die Werke Martin Luthers in neuer Auswahl für die Gegenwart*, 8 vols. (ed. Kurt Aland; Stuttgart: Ehrenfried Klotz, 1957–1974), 4:77. The text of the Invocavit Sermons in contemporary German is found in Luther, *Luther Deutsch*, 4:61–94.

30. Thus far it has always been a positive *exemplum*.

31. The rhetorical question is manifest in the word order [*Darumb wo(e)llen wir*] (545.1) and from Luther's immediate response.

32. LW 51:85, brackets "Ecclus. 19:2; 31:30," while WA and LStA cite nothing.

33. LW 51:87.

34. On Nov. 21, 1521, Luther had dedicated "On Monastic Vows" to his father, Hans Luther. In that letter of dedication, Luther argues that the cowl belongs to him, not he to the cowl; he is free to wear it or not (LW 48:335). In the *Table Talk*, Luther talks about how hard it was to give up his cowl (LW 54:337f, no. 4414).

35. Note doubled nouns at LW 51:71, 51:75 (three), 51:76, 51:78, 51:79, and 51:85, as well as doubled verbs at LW 51:72 (three), 51:75 (two), 51:83, and 51:85. For a discussion of doublets, see Neil R. Leroux, "Luther's Use of Doublets," *Rhetoric Society Quarterly* 20.3 (Summer 2000): 35–54.

36. LW 51:87 inverts Luther's syntax: "Thus St. Paul circumcised Timothy . . . because . . . ."

37. Luther had used these examples of Paul (circumcising Timothy but not Titus) in "A Sincere Admonition" (LW 45:73).

38. "And" becomes, in these places, not only a conjunction, but it often indicates causal or circumstantial connection.

39. LW 51:87.

40. Roland H. Bainton, "Pastor, Consoler, Preacher," in *Encounters with Luther, vol. 1: Lectures, Discussions, and Sermons at the Martin Luther Colloquia 1970–74* (ed. Eric W. Gritsch; Gettysburg, Penn.: Institute for Luther Studies/Luther Theological Seminary, 1980), 173: "So it is that Luther goes through Scripture from beginning to end. It is all so experiential and all so local. Whenever he talks about a river, or getting drowned, or anything connected with a flood, it's always the river Elbe, the one that went past Wittenberg. . . . The setting is always local. . . . It's all thoroughly *Deutsch*" (*Bainton's emphasis*).

41. The Weimar Edition follows the "a" recension and reads *Apostolische*.

42. Recall Schurff's letter (Smith and Jacobs, *Luther's Correspondence*, 2:102 [Letter 534]) that says, "Gabriel [Zwilling] has confessed." Kesler's remarks point to the Invocavit Sermons as the beginning of problems between Luther and Karlstadt.

43. LW does not translate the doublet.

# CHAPTER 5

1. Prior to the reforming activities in Wittenberg during the fall of 1521, Communion participation by the laity was generally only once a year, despite the fact that people often crowded forward enthusiastically to catch sight as the host was elevated; cf. Bernd Moeller, "Religious Life in Germany on the Eve of the Reformation," in *Religion and Society in Early Modern Europe 1500–1800* (ed. Kaspar von Greyerz; London: George Allen & Unwin, 1984), 13–42.

2. The general attitude of the communicant is the subject of the Sixth Sermon.

3. Robert Alter calls Nathan's approach the "rhetoric of entrapment." See Robert Alter, *The Art of Biblical Poetry* (New York: Basic Books, 1985), 144.

4. Yet Luther later defers to "custom" when recognizing priestly duties. Probably the more important imbalance he points to is between the flagrant human sin of sexual immorality and a mere piece of cloth.

5. See C. A. Pater, *Karlstadt as the Father of the Baptist Movements: The Emergence of Lay Protestantism* (Toronto: Toronto University Press, 1984), 183, for background on the various positions taken by reformers regarding the words of institution.

6. I am not arguing that "take" and "eat" are, in fact, two separate commands.

7. See Fred B. Craddock, *Overhearing the Gospel* (Nashville: Abingdon, 1978), 104ff., for explication of an "indirect" approach to an audience. Craddock's subtitle is "Preaching and Teaching the Faith to Persons Who Have Already Heard," and he takes Kierkegaard as his point of departure. The notion of "overhearing" is developed in Fred B. Craddock, *As One without Authority* (rev. ed.; Enid, Okla.: Phillips University Press, 1974), 119–41; and Fred B. Craddock, "Recent New Testament Interpretation and Preaching," *Princeton Seminary Bulletin* 66 (1973): 76–81. Eugene L. Lowry, *The Sermon: Dancing the Edge of Mystery* (Nashville: Abingdon, 1997), 11, claims that the "emerging new homiletical paradigm" in North America of the past 25 years owes its beginning to Craddock's first edition of *As One without Authority* (1971). The so-called new homiletic Lowry refers to has heavily stressed the process in which a preached sermon transpires for its audience, one that must not reveal ahead of time its conclusion or "punch line."

8. Luther's language echoes scriptural expressions from Eph 6:11.

9. *[S]eüberlich und weyßlich* are not merely synonyms; they touch both the knowledge and compassion poles of this section.

10. "Becomes *for me*" [*mir*] is representative, not personal.

11. LW 51:91 inverts the syntax: "Dear friends, you will not succeed . . . ."

12. Not *für*; see WA apparatus at 46.10.

13. The insult differs somewhat from that of John the Baptist: "You brood of vipers . . ." (Luke 3:7 RSV). Neither is Luther baiting his audience because neither of Luther's insults thus far is in second person. An interesting comparison would be to Jesus' stinging insult to the Pharisees (Matthew 23), which, though beginning with indignation, concludes with Jesus' emotional and communal "O Jerusalem, Jerusalem, . . . How often would I have gathered your children together as a hen gathers her brood . . ." (RSV). My point is that a speaker's bluntness with an audience has to be carefully examined in its context. Even then we can only speculate on what latitude an audience may grant.

14. We should not be surprised at Luther's vehemence because later sermons verify the importance with which Luther has already regarded the Sacrament. He considers these "high things" [*hochen sache(n)*].

15. Notice that the German text shows the doublet is asyndetic; hence, Luther no doubt carefully emphasized both terms, with a strategic pause between. Using a conjunction would dilute the emphasis on each term, running the two together.

16. These remarks are reminiscent of Paul's instructions in 1 Cor 11:34, though editors are silent on this. LStA editors call attention to similar disturbing events at Wittenberg and Eilenburg; cf. *WB*, 132. Surprisingly, Luther makes no reference to the biblical passage, though Paul's frustration and vehemence concerning Corinthian abuses of the Lord's Supper is quite similar to Luther's. Perhaps Luther was careful not to compare Wittenberg to Corinth, as well as cautious about not taking on too many apostolic roles.

17. LW 51:91; cf. apparatus of WA and LStA.

18. The other formula, "we have now heard," Luther has used just as often as this one.

19. The *auch welche* at 551.21 governs both predicates.

20. At 536.4; cf. the "ear"/"heart" dichotomy at 535.18 and the "outside"/"inside" dichotomy at 540.17.

21. Through the first three sermons, the whole expression was used [*hauptstück einen Christen*, etc.], but it has slipped in the last couple occurrences to the shortened *hauptstück*.

22. For some discussion of the motion/action distinction, see Burke, "(Nonsymbolic) Motion/(Symbolic) Action," *Critical Inquiry* 4 (1978): 809–38.

23. Such a circumscribing is similar to the crooner's expanding on his limitless affection for his beloved—". . . the north, east, west, and the south of you"—or Paul's "prayer" for the Ephesians that they "grasp how wide and long and high and deep is the love of Christ" (Eph 4:18) or Rom 8:38f. Read on for another allusion to Rom 8:31.

24. Frederic W. Baue, "Preaching as Explanation and Exclamation," *LQ* 9 (1995): 412.

25. Thus we see that "who are permitted" and "who belongs here" are synonymous. We realize that taking them as separate is expecting too much precision from a *distributio*. Probably the audience would catch the synonymy from Luther's voice.

26. Luther got the image from Augustine; see LW 51:94.

27. Participles are a more lively modifier of nouns than are adjectives. The latter tend

to be static and categorical, whereas participles are verbals that put action onto nouns.

28. Demonstratives, however, differ in the way they point attention. "That" tends to connote separation and remoteness, while "this" connotes nearness and agreement. The antithesis, then ("this, not that"), not only *informs* by asserting a difference, it *values* by making a choice.

29. LW 51:94, n. 27, says, "This is the first indication of a doctrine Luther later developed more emphatically . . . ."

30. I still recall the words of my ninth-grade history teacher, "Nothing creates allies so quickly as a common enemy."

31. William G. Moulton, *The Sounds of English and German* (Chicago: University of Chicago Press, 1962), 135f., distinguishes two types of questions: (1) "word" questions, where a clause contains a question word (interrogative), usually in first position, and has a finite verb in second position; (2) "order" questions, which are independent clauses with the finite verb in first position.

# CHAPTER 6

1. "Charity" [*caritas* (Vulgate)] would, perhaps, for us be a clearer term than "love," given the context of 1 Corinthians. It is used in the Authorized (King James) Version and in Robertson's translation of Augustine's *De Doctrina*; see Augustine, *On Christian Doctrine* (trans. D. W. Robertson Jr.; Indianapolis: Bobbs-Merrill, 1958). All of Luther's discussions on "love" in these sermons are about a *sharing*, an extension from one who has to one who has not. Luther, of course, is not nearly as theoretical as is Augustine in his definition of charity (see Augustine, *On Christian Doctrine*, 3.10.16).

2. In Scripture, what I call a "visitation" from an angel was often far from a euphoric experience for the earthly creature visited. Fear, trembling, and guilt were common constituents.

3. LW 51:95 has "we."

4. LW 51:95 reads "treasures." Timothy J. Wengert, "Luther's Catechisms and the Lord's Supper," *Word and World* 17 (1997): 56, says that by 1529 Luther had changed his name for the Lord's Supper from "sacrament" to "treasure," the latter term occurring 10 times in the *Large Catechism* (5:20–37 in *The Book of Concord* [ed. Theodore E. Tappert; Philadelphia: Fortress, 1959]). The images of "fruit" [*frucht*] and "oven" [*backofen*] seem conflicting, but if we understand "result" or "product" for *frucht*, it would be less awkward. The craft of these lines is not as tidy as their obvious effort to rejoice. I have said earlier that Section I functions to articulate a *definitio* of love. It does so by narrowing the focus—to the reciprocal relationship between believers and God by which believers express their love for God through their actions toward their neighbor—then by expanding the affect and appreciation (motivation) for God's role in love. The assertion, marked by *correctio* [*sag ich*], syntactically articulates the functional relationship of Sacrament to love (555.3).

5. The antithetical structure of 1 Cor 13:1–3 ("If I have . . . but not love . . .") is more effective as Paul expedites the comparisons through polysyndeton. This is clearest in the Vulgate as the four repetitions of *et* in verses 2f. permit Paul to prolong his "case" against love because he hauls in all the "heavy hitters," and, collectively, they prove futile against "love."

6. LW 51:96 reads "this is a terrible saying of St. Paul."

7. Cf. LW 51:70 ("these . . . you heard from me many days ago.").

8. Note the conjunction *vnd*, which starts a new paragraph in WA.

9. Luther had mentioned this very thing in his letter of March 12 to the Elector; see Preserved Smith and Charles M. Jacobs, *Luther's Correspondence and Other Contemporary Letters* (Philadelphia: Lutheran Publication Society, 1918), 2:100 (Letter 532).

10. Luther at least once told others at table about the importance of learning the art of finishing: "When I have nothing more to say I stop talking" (cf. LW 54:292 [WATr 4:4–5, no. 3910 (1538)]). On Luther's remarks about preaching, see James Mackinnon, *Luther and the Reformation* (London: Longmans, Green & Co., 1930), 4:304–18.

11. Luther's opening line makes it clear that he is near the finish.

12. To deal with confession earlier would, in any event, have been to imply the wrong idea: that confession is, indeed, a prerequisite to and should precede sacramental observance. In addition, after already discussing the importance of love for brethren, Luther may here have fewer difficulties with reformers' aversion to confessing to other human beings.

13. See David Myers, "Ritual, Confession, and Religion in Sixteenth-Century Germany," *ARG* 89 (1998): 125–43; see also W. David Myers, *"Poor Sinning Folk": Confession and Conscience in Counter-Reformation Germany* (Ithaca: Cornell University Press, 1996). For a different view, see Lawrence G. Duggan, "Fear and Confession on the Eve of the Reformation," *ARG* 75 (1984): 153–75. A glance at the traditional "agenda" is also helpful. This is Reminiscere Sunday, which comes from the Latin *reminiscere*, "to remember," spoken as an imperative as the first word of the introit. It set a mood for catechumens to reconsider all the instruction they had received. At the same time, the Gospel lesson for the day, Matt 15:21–28, suggests persistently looking to God for strength, a trait which Jesus had commended in the Syro-Phoenecian widow. Luther was more interested in scriptural themes than he was in tradition; cf. Paul Zeller Strodach, *The Church Year: Studies in the Introits, Collects, Epistles and Gospels* (Philadelphia: United Lutheran Publishing House, 1924), 112–15.

14. Thomas N. Tentler, *Sin and Confession on the Eve of the Reformation* (Princeton: Princeton University Press, 1977), 349. See also Leonhard Fendt, "Luthers Reformation der Beichte," *Mitteilungen der Luthergesellschaft* 24.3 (1953): 121–37; Bernhard Lohse, "Die Privatbeichte bei Luther," *Kerygma und Dogma* 14 (1968): 207–28; E. Fischer, "Die Neubelebung des Beichtinstituts durch Luther," chapter 3 in *Zur Geschichte der evangelischen Beichte, vol. 2: Niedergang und Neubelebung des Beichtinstituts in Wittenberg in den Anfängen der Reformation* (Leipzig: Dieterich'sche Verlags-Buchhandlung [Theodor Weicher], 1903). For background on confession in the Middle Ages, see Peter Biller, "Confession in the Middle Ages: Introduction," in *Handling Sin: Confession in the Middle Ages* (ed. Peter Biller and A. J. Minnis; Suffolk: York Medieval Press, 1998), 3–33; John Bossy, "The Social History of Confession in the Age of the Reformation," *Transactions of the Royal Historical Society* 25 (1975): 21–38; and John Bossy, "Moral Arithmetic: Seven Sins into Ten Commandments," in *Conscience and Casuistry in Early Modern Europe* (Cambridge: Cambridge University Press, 1988), 214–34.

15. Augustus Steimle, ed., *Luther's Works* (Philadelphia: A. J. Holman, 1918), 2:389f.

16. Kesler, an "eye and ear witness," [*als Augen=oder Ohrenzeuge*] provided his comments in a letter first published in 1533. He is fairly precise in what he says in *Sabbata* 1.1: *Am ersten sonnentag in der fasten stund Martinus widerumb uff zu predigen, ercleret das euangelion do uff disen tag nach altem bruch verordnet Mathei am vierten, wie Christus ist versucht worden. Demnach lietz er den text fallen und nam fur sich den gegenwurtigen handeln . . .* (WA 10/3:lii); cf. Johann Kesler, *Sabbata* 1.1.80, lines

20–25, in *Kesler's Sabbata* (ed. Emil Egli and Rudolf Schoch; St. Gallen: Fehr'sche Buchhandlung, 1902 [microfilm]).

17. In that context, reforms undertaken recently in Wittenberg reflected a swing from confession required by the pope to confession forbidden by the reformers.

18. Luther's diction shows a strong rhyming trend—namely, *erkündunge . . . sündiget . . . stünd*—that magnifies the presence of sin's severity. Prepositional prefixes highlight the relational aspects of the activity described—its spatial components of openness, gathering, separating. The rarely used separable preposition [*stünd . . . abe*] emphasizes the purpose of this form of confession—that the confessor "abandon his sin."

19. For those familiar with Matthew 18, the connection between the quoted instruction and the earlier *narratio* is distorted. Luther has connected separate phases of the entire episode from the Matthew pericope, which shows three stages of confrontation: (1) brotherly admonition in private, (2) brotherly admonition in the company of two or three witnesses, and (3) public accusation before the whole congregation. As Luther develops his narrative, he includes all three stages.

20. Luther does not say here that the measures are rehabilitative, though he does so later.

21. Note the prepositions conveying spatial placement: *vor dem gantze(n) haüffen* (556.21); *in bey wesen des volcks* (556.22); *vor der gantze(n) samlung* (556.28).

22. We have often closely examined syntactic sentence structure and vocal characteristics—rhyme and rhythm in assonance and consonance. But in this section, we notice even more. Throughout this section, Luther's vocabulary, in the description of this kind of confession, generates a repetitive and progressive form. In hearing the sound of the u-umlaut in several key action words, one can chart, through repetition and progression, "sin" and its consequences, with or without benefit of "brotherly admonition," which is the key term at 556.24. The action represented in these words suggests spatial vectors and boundaries, as indexed especially in the prepositional prefixes and phrases. These words show "love" (and rebellion) as actions, not merely as states. Observe: 556.5, "grounded" (in Scripture): [*gegründt*]; 556.6, "awareness" (of sins): [*erkündigunge . . . sündiget*]; 556.7, "abstains": [*stünd . . . abe*]; 556.18, 20 "abstains": [*abstünde*]; 556.25, "accuse": [*beschüldige*]; 556.27, "accusation": [*beschüldigu(n)g*]; 556.28, "exclude": [*absündern*].

23. To call the first kind of confession "interpersonal" and the second kind "intrapersonal" would be misleading. As I said previously, the first kind is commanded by God, horizontal, and Christian. The second kind of confession is more introspective than social, but it is not solipsistic. Luther speaks of communicating to God, not of soliloquy.

24. Four times (557.1, 10 [twice], 12).

25. The Vulgate reads: *et faciant iudicium et iusticiam*. The imperative that Luther quotes and the subsequent argument he develops reflect his preference for stressing the inner attitude of repentance. Like Erasmus, who, in the comments of his 1516 edition of the New Testament, diverged from the accepted meaning of Jesus' imperative of Matt 3:2 and elsewhere [μετανοεῖτε in Greek; *penitentiam agite* in Vulgate], Luther resisted the accepted notion of "do penance." Erasmus often rendered μετανοεῖτε as *respiscite* or *ad mentem redite* ("be mindful" or "come to yourself"). In his "Ninety-five Theses Explained" (1518), Luther denied that μετανοεῖτε means either the sacrament of penance or the purely inner attitude. See LW 31:83ff. and WA 1:530.

26. The *interpretatio* reveals the presumed dichotomy between *iudicium* and *iusticiam*, the former ("judgment") given the dual equivalents (infinitives—*accusare* and

*damnare*) connected by the conjunction *et*, which is not paratactic but linear, showing a progression from first to second verb. The latter noun, "righteousness," becomes the benevolent contrary of the former, with the single verb *fidere* and its object *misericordie dei* overshadowing through syntactic recency.

27. This section clarifies and diverges from the position Luther had taken in writing *Von des Beichte ob die der Papst Macht habe zu gebieten* (1521) during the Wartburg confinement. Whether what he wrote had been misunderstood or whether he changed his mind in light of subsequent disturbing events in Wittenberg, we cannot say, nor need we.

28. It is especially necessary to avoid this impression because Luther has already condemned similar hypocrisy in the Fourth Sermon (Peter and the Gentiles).

29. Later Luther will add another premise—that this confession, too, is authorized (he doesn't say "commanded") in Scripture.

30. Two other significant terms in the sentence are *sich darjnn* because Luther is battling a radical ecclesiology that would mistakenly (or callously) dismiss the need for (and concern toward) a brother in overzealous reforms designed to overthrow papal coercion. At 557.26f. the hypothetical-typical scenario that introduced this confession returns as Luther uses *seine(n) bru(o)der* and *seine(m) nechsten*. This time, however, the scenario is authenticated by Scripture, not by the pope.

31. The Latin *absolution* occurs at LStA 557.31; 558.12 [twice], 13, 19, 27.

32. Luther does not abandon the case of private confession; he broadens it—into an exhortation.

33. This would especially address audience members who are a little too sure of themselves.

34. In his 1522 New Testament, Luther does not use the same terms in Matt 6:14 and 6:12 as he does here. Hence, by here using the same word to describe one's own sins and those of others, he describes confession and forgiveness as a kind of horizontal "economy."

35. *Barmhertzigkeit* is a term occuring only once in the sermon series.

36. Luther avoided using these terms earlier, in the Fifth Sermon.

37. These are allusions to the "armor of God" motif in Ephesians 6, which was used by Luther in the First Sermon. In his 1522 New Testament, Luther uses the expression "armor of the Gospel" [*rüstung des Euangelion*].

# CHAPTER 7

1. LW 36:237–67; WA 10/2:11–41.

2. LW 49:3f. (Letter 120); WABr 2:489f., no. 470.

3. Preserved Smith and Charles M. Jacobs, eds., *Luther's Correspondence and Other Contemporary Letters* (Philadelphia: Lutheran Publication Society, 1918), 2:122 (Letter 548).

4. Smith and Jacobs, *Luther's Correspondence*, 2:120f. (Letter 546); WABr 2:505f., no. 478.

5. Verifying what was happening at that time is beyond the scope of my investigation. The social historians are battling those fronts. For example, see Susan C. Karant-Nunn, "What Was Preached in German Cities in the Early Years of the Reformation? *Wildwuchs* Versus Lutheran Unity," in *The Process in Early Modern Europe: Essays in Honor of Miriam Usher Chrisman* (ed. Phillip N. Bebb and Sherrin

Marshal; Athens: Ohio University Press, 1988), 81–96; Bernd Moeller, "Was wurde in der Frühzeit der Reformation in den deutschen Städten gepredigt?" *ARG* 75 (1984): 176–93. Most of those discussions pertain to a slightly later period than what I have in view.

6. The full title in the print I examined (designated *E¹* by the WA editor, who says the printer was Egidius Fellenfürst at Coburg) is *Uon beyder gestalt des Sacraments zu nemen: vnnd ander newerung. D. M. Luthers meynung* ("On the Reception of Both Kinds in the Sacrament: and Other Reforms, According to Doctor Martin Luther's Opinion." The WA editor identifies [WA 10/2:3] 12 editions printed at Wittenberg, Coburg, Augsburg, Zürich, and Strassburg).

7. Smith and Jacobs, *Luther's Correspondence*, 2:121 (Letter 547): "I had a private talk with Carlstadt to-day, and besought him not to publish anything against me . . . . They [University faculty] are trying to get him either to recall or to suppress the book, though I am not urging it" (from a letter from Luther to Spalatin).

8. LW 45:70–72.

9. LW 51:72f.

10. The only elements of the Wittenberger reforms of the January 24 ordinance that Luther did not roll back as a result of the Invocavit Sermons are the provisions for poor relief, which constituted 14 of the 17 provisions and which were not addressed in the sermons. See Carter Lindberg, *Beyond Charity: Reformation Initiatives for the Poor* (Minneapolis: Fortress, 1993), 200–02. David J. Lose, "Martin Luther on Preaching the Law," *Word and World* 21 (2001): 257, n. 11, comments: "This distinction between our life *coram hominibus* and *coram Deo* markedly shapes Luther's 'Sermon on Invocavit Sunday' (1522), where he divides the 'chief things' that all Christians should know into four parts—two pertaining to our relationship with God and two to our relationship with neighbor."

11. LW 48:394ff. (Letter 118 [bracketed items included by LW editor]); WABr 2:459–62, no. 456; see discussion of the letter in Martin Brecht, "Datierung, Textgrundlage und Interpretation einiger Briefe Luthers von 1517–1522," in *Lutheriana: Zum 500. Geburtstag Martin Luthers von den Mitarbeitern der Weimarer Ausgabe* (Archiv zur Weimarer Ausgabe der Werke Martin Luthers: Texte und Untersuchungen 5; ed. Gerhard Hammer and Karl-Heinz zur Mühlen; Cologne: Böhlaus, 1984), 389–90.

12. Roland H. Bainton, *Here I Stand: A Life of Martin Luther* (New York: The New American Library [Mentor Books], 1950), 162.

13. LW 48:394ff. (Letter 118 [bracketed items included by LW editor]); WABr 2:459–62, no. 456.

14. Smith and Jacobs, *Luther's Correspondence*, 2:99 (Letter 532).

15. LW 48:394ff. (Letter 118); WABr 2:459–62, no. 456.

16. LW 48:394ff. (Letter 118); WABr 2:459–62, no. 456.

17. Martin Brecht, "Luther und die Wittenberger Reformation während der Wartburgzeit," in *Martin Luther: Leben, Werk, Wirkung* (ed. Günter Vogler, Siegfried Hoyer, and Adolf Laube; Berlin: Adademie, 1986), 83.

18. Adam Weyer, " 'Das Euangelium wil nit alleyn geschrieben, ßondern viel mehr mit leyplicher stym geprediget seyn': Luthers Invocavit-Predigten im Kontext der Reformationsbewegung," in *Martin Luther* (ed. Heinz Ludwig Arnold; Munich: Edition Text & Kritik, 1983), 102.

19. Weyer, " 'Das Euangelium wil nit alleyn geschrieben,' " 103.

20. Smith and Jacobs, *Luther's Correspondence*, 2:102f. (Letter 534).

21. Luther to Spalatin, 13 March 1522, in Smith and Jacobs, *Luther's Correspondence*, 2:101f. (Letter 533). Karlstadt was incensed at what he saw as Luther's betrayal. See Karlstadt's letter to Hektor Pömer, 27 March, in Ulrich Bubenheimer, "Andreas Bodenstein von Karlstadt and seine fränkische Heimat," in *Quedenker der Reformation: Andreas Bodenstein von Karlstadt und seine frühe Wirkung* (Würzburg: Religion and Kultur, 2001), 15–48.

22. Smith and Jacobs, *Luther's Correspondence*, 2:115 (Letter 541); cf. *WB*, no. 102, 212–14, from which I quote here the portions in the main text that I have italicized: *Vir est, quantum ex vultu apparet, benignus, mansuetus et hilaris. Vox eius suauis et sonora atque etiam ita, vt admirer suauiloquentiam hominis. Piissimum est, quicquid loquitur, quicquid docet, quicquid agit, etiamsi ab impiissimis inimicis eius diuersum dicatur. Hunc qui semel audierit, modo si non fuerit saxo, iterum atque iterrum audire cupit, adeo tenaces aculeos infigit animis auditorum*; cf. also WA 10/3:liii. See James M. Kittelson, "The Transformation," chap. 4 in *Wolfgang Capito: From Humanist to Reformer* (Studies in Medieval and Reformation Thought 17; Leiden: E. J. Brill, 1975), 83–111.

23. Latin terms from Burer; cf. 1 Cor 3:1f. (KJV/Vulgate): "And I, brethren, could not speak unto you as unto spiritual, but as unto carnal, even as unto babes in Christ. I have fed you with milk, and not with meat: for hitherto ye were not able to bear it, neither yet now are ye able" [*et ego fratres non potui vobis loqui quasi spiritualibus sed quasi carnalibus tamquam parvulis in Christo, lac vobis potum dedi non escam nondum enim poteratis sed ne nunc quidem potestis adhuc enim estis carnales*]. Karlstadt also commented in his March 27 letter to Hektor Pömer that in the Invocavit Sermons Luther had taught the "first elements."

24. Smith and Jacobs, *Luther's Correspondence*, 2:62f. (Letter 511).

25. LW 48:390 (Letter 117); WABr 2:455.39–43, no. 455. In the italicized phrases (*my emphasis*), Luther clearly has in mind Gal 1:1, 11f.

26. For example, in the Eighth Sermon, Luther turned not only to Matthew 18, but also to Matthew 6 and the Psalms.

27. Consider particularly the proleptic dialogue over images in LW 51:82.

28. Luther was not shy about citing numerous Scripture passages in a few places in "A Sincere Admonition," particularly when arguing that he could discern God's apocalyptic judgment in this matter of possible rebellion. In the space of eight lines (LW 45:58 [*Eyn trew vormahung* Aii-Aii$^v$]), Luther cites Matt 5:24; Ps 36:14; Proverbs 27; Leviticus 26; and Deuteronomy 28.

29. For example, at LW 51:70: "Here we need a clear, strong text to bear out this point. Such is the saying of St. Paul in Eph. 2"; or at LW 51:71 (". . . as John declares in his first chapter . . ." and again "For without love faith is nothing, as St. Paul says in I Cor. 2 [sic]").

30. David S. Cunningham, *Faithful Persuasion: In Aid of a Rhetoric of Christian Theology* (Notre Dame: University of Notre Dame Press, 1991), 251, where, in examining the eucharistic controversy of 1526, he argues that it is the fight with the "enthusiasts" that prompted Luther to invoke the ambiguity of some Scripture passages. See 240–52 on "Luther's Argumentative Strategies" and "Luther as Rhetorical Theologian."

31. But see Clyde L. Manschreck, "The Role of Melanchthon in the Adiaphora Controversy," *ARG* 48 (1957): 165, where he points out a "paradox of adiaphora," saying that "if they were really non-essentials, a controversy could hardly arise." Luther does not use the term "adiaphora" in these sermons, however.

32. Perhaps, for example, at 542.24: "But they *worship* the images!"

33. LStA 530.26–531.5.

34. Jeanne Fahnestock, "Series Reasoning in Scientific Argument: *Incrementum* and *Gradatio* and the Case of Darwin," *Rhetoric Society Quarterly* 26.4 (Fall 1996): 37f., n. 7, argues that Paul uses a causal *sorites* in the form of a *gradatio* when he wants to show the interlocking consequences that follow from a falsification of Christ's resurrection. She is referring to verses 12–14: "We might unfold this sorites into the following [four] syllogisms: 1. Christ was dead/ The dead never rise/ Therefore Christ did not rise; 2. That Christ did rise is not true/ We preach that Christ is risen/ Therefore we preach what is not true. 3. Preaching what is not true is preaching in vain/ We preach what is not true/ Therefore we preach in vain; 4. Your faith comes from our preaching/ Our preaching is vain/ Therefore your faith is vain. St Paul, of course, made his premises hypothetical to show their disastrous consequences and then to contradict them firmly . . . ."

35. Verse 3 begins: "For [*gar*] I delivered unto you . . . "; *gar* is a conjunction that commonly signals an enthymeme or at least an explanatory reason.

36. Martin U. Brecht, *Doctor Luther's Bulla and Reformation: A Look at Luther the Writer* (Gross Memorial Lecture 1990; Valparaiso, Ind.: Valparaiso University Press, 1991), 7 (*Brecht's emphasis*). For a discussion of the context of Psalm interpretation, of which Luther was a vigorous participant, see. R. Gerald Hobbs, "Hebraica Veritas *and* Traditio Apostolica: Saint Paul and the Interpretation of the Psalms in the Sixteenth Century," in *The Bible in the Sixteenth Century* (Duke Monographs in Medieval and Renaissance Studies 11; ed. David C. Steinmetz; Durham, N.C.: Duke University Press, 1990), 83–99.

37. Eric W. Gritsch, *Martin—God's Court Jester: Luther in Retrospect* (Philadelphia: Fortress, 1983), 14.

38. "*Palaestra et exercitium*"; *Operationes in psalmos*, Part II, *Archiv zur Weimarer Ausgabe* . . . (Cologne: Böhlaus, 1981), 2:69.9 (LW 14:310), cited by Scott H. Hendrix, "Luther against the Background of the History of Biblical Interpretation," *Interpretation* 37 (1983): 235.

39. Luther surely also knew Psalm 22 in the Hebrew Bible. In his *Eyn trew vormahung* (Biii$^V$) he quotes Jesus' cry on the cross from Ps 22:2 in the Hebrew [*Eli, Eli*], as Matt 27:46 does, not in the Aramaic [*Eloi, Eloi*, or *Heloi, Heloi*, which the Septuagint uses] in which Mark 15:34 records it. Luther's use of this phrase in *Eyn trew vormahung* was in declaring the enemy already defeated: "Thus does Christ through us slay the papacy. Already it is singing, 'Eloi, Eloi'; it has been stricken; soon the word will be '*Expiravit*' " (LW 45:70). I have not checked WA to see if that is where LW found its reading.

40. Peter Auksi, *Christian Plain Style: The Evolution of a Spiritual Ideal* (Montreal: McGill, 1995), 208, quoting WA 5:499.

41. Helmar Junghans, "Rhetorische Bemerkungen Luthers in seinen 'Dictata super Psalterium,' " *Theologische Versuche* 8 (1977): 97–128.

42. Birgit Stolt, *Studien zu Luthers Freiheitstraktat mit besonderer Rücksicht auf das Verhältnis der lateinischen und der deutschen Fassung zu einander und die Stilmittel der Rhetorik* (Acta Universitatis Stockholmiensis: Stockholmer Germanistische Forschungen 6; Stockholm: Almqvist & Wiksell, 1969); "Germanistische Hilfsmittel zum Lutherstudium," *Lutherjahrbuch* 46 (1979): 120–35; "Neue Aspekte der sprachwissenschaftlichen Luther-Forschung," in *Martin Luther* (ed. Heinz Ludwig Arnold; Munich: Edition Text & Kritik, 1983), 6–16; "Revisionen und Rückrevisionen des Luther-NT aus rhetorisch-stilistischer Sicht," in *Stilistische-rhetorische Diskursanalyse* (Forum Angewandte Linguistik 14; ed. Barbara Sandig; Tübingen: Gunter Narr, 1988), 13–40; "Martin Luthers rhetorische Syntax," in *Rhetorik zwischen den Wissenschaften: Geschichte, System, Praxis als Probleme des 'Historischen Wörter-*

*buchs der Rhetorik'* (Rhetorik Forschungen 1; ed. Gert Ueding; Tübingen: Max Niemeyer, 1991), 207–20; "Rhetorische Textkohärenz—am Beispiel Martin Luthers," *Jahrbuch Rhetorik* 10 (1991): 89–99; "Martin Luther on God as a Father," *LQ* 9 (1994): 385–95.

43. "Pure and immovable" is rendered a doublet only in translating the single adverb *vnbeweglich*. This is the only doublet in this passage that Luther did not create. For more on doublets, see Neil R. Leroux, "Luther's Use of Doublets," *Rhetoric Society Quarterly* 30.3 (2000): 35–54.

44. LW 51:72 (*my emphasis*). LStA 2:532.15–22: "Merck ein gleichnyß / die Son hat zway ding / als *den glantz / vn(d) die hitze*. Es ist kein künigk also starck / der den glantz der sonne(n) *bygen oder lencke(n)* müge / sond(ern) bleybt in seine(n) stellen geo(e)rtert. Aber die hitz la(e)ßt sich *lencken vnd byge(n)* / vnd ist alweg vmb die sonne. Also der glaub mu(o)ß allzeyt reyn *vnbeweglich* in vnsern hertze(n) bleyben / vnd müssen nit dauon weychen / sonder die liebe *beügt vnd lenckt* sich vnser nechsten *begreyffen vnd volgen* mag Es sein ettliche die künden wol re(n)nen / etlich wol laüffen / etlich kaüm kriechen" (*my emphasis*).

45. Kenneth A. Hagen, "It Is All in the Et Cetera: Luther and the Elliptical Reference," *Luther-Bulletin: Tijdschrift voor interconfessioneel Lutheronderzoek* 3 (1994): 59.

46. *Rhet. Her.* 4.55.68.

47. Weyer, "'Das Euangelium wil nit alleyn geschrieben," 103.

48. Gerhard Ebeling, *Luthers Seelsorge: Theologie in der Vielfalt der Lebenssituationen an seinen Briefen dargestellt* (Tübingen: J. C. B. Mohr [Paul Siebeck], 1997), 7, quoted in a review by Friedrich Schweitzer, *Journal of Religion* 79 (1999): 301.

49. Heiko A. Oberman, "Holy Spirit—Holy Writ—Holy Church: The Witness of the Reformation," *Hartford Quarterly* 5 (1964): 58f. Michael B. Aune argues along similar lines with respect to Melanchthon's *theologia rhetorica* in " 'A Heart Moved': Philip Melanchthon's Forgotten Truth about Worship," *LQ* 12 (1998): 395–418.

50. William J. Bouwsma, "Renaissance and Reformation: An Essay on Their Affinities and Connections," in *A Usable Past: Essays in European Cultural History* (Berkeley: University of California Press, 1990), 231f.

# APPENDIX

1. In the *Open Letter to the Christian Nobility* (1520), PE 2, 61–164, and *The Babylonian Captivity of the Church* (1520), PE 2, 170–293.

2. Melanchthon.

3. Nicholas von Amsdorf (1483–1565).

4. A note in *MA³*, 4, 334 reads: "Luther correctly discerns that about the time of Jerome (*ca.* 345–420), the creator of the Latin translation of the Bible (the Vulgate), the peculiarly Roman character of the Christian church began to develop."

5. *Winkelmessen oder sonderlichen Messen.*

6. The contradiction of genders and the switch from impersonal to personal address reflects Luther's spoken style and is here retained.

7. Justus Jonas (1493–1555), dean (*Probst*) of the Castle Church and professor in the Wittenberg faculty, at this time a radical advocate of liturgical reform. However, the omission of the comma in the original text may indicate that Luther did not refer to Jonas at all, since Karlstadt was dean of the faculty. Cf. *WA* 10/3, 438.

8. Andreas Bodenstein Karlstadt (1480–1541).

9.   Gabriel Zwilling (Didymus) (*ca.* 1487–1558), Augustinian monk and champion of immediate reform of the mass.

10.   Zwilling's first name, Gabriel, probably suggested to Luther the addition of the name of the archangel Michael. Cf. Gal. 1:8.

11.   Namely, of the monasteries.

12.   As he does frequently, Luther here names the strictest of the orders.

13.   Luther has reference to the Iconoclastic Controversy, initiated by Emperor Leo III, who prohibited the veneration of images in 718, contested by Pope Gregory II, and finally settled in 843. Invocavit Sunday is the "Feast of Orthodoxy" in commemoration of the Seventh Ecumenical Council of 783, which dealt with this question.

14.   Duke Frederick is Elector Frederick the Wise of Ernestine Saxony (1463–1525). The "bishop of Halle" is probably Albrecht of Hohenzollern, archbishop of Mainz and of Magdeburg; the cathedral was located in Halle.

15.   *Kirchmess*: service for the consecration or commemoration of the consecration of a church, an occasion for placing images or embellishments in the church.

16.   For a discussion of this and related questions cf. also Luther's *Explanations of the Ninety-five Theses* (1518), *LW* 31, 86–87; 109–110.

17.   Reference to *On the Abuse of the Mass* (1521). *WA* 8, 477–563, especially pp. 508, 540.

18.   *Decretum Gratiani*, dist. 34, cap. 25.

19.   This law goes back to the Fourth Ecumenical Lateran Synod, 1215, under Innocent III. In the canon law: *C. 12, X, de poenitentiis.*

20.   A quotation from Augustine, cf. *Enarratio in psalmos* XXI. Migne, 36, 178. Also quoted by Luther in *Treatise Concerning the Blessed Sacrament, etc. WA* 2, 746; *PE* 2, 15.

21.   This is a first indication of a doctrine which Luther later developed more emphatically, the doctrine of *manducatio impiorum*, i.e., to receive the sacrament unworthily, without faith, is to receive it to one's damnation. Cf. I Cor. 11:27–29.

22.   Do judgment and righteousness. Cf. Gen. 18:19.

23.   To do judgment is to accuse and condemn ourselves; but to do righteousness is to trust in the mercy of God.

24.   *Von der Beichte, ob die der Papst Macht habe zu gebieten* (1521). *WA* 8, 138–204.

# FOR FURTHER READING

## INTRODUCTION

**From the homiletic tradition, on Luther as a preacher:** Yngve Brillioth, *A Brief History of Preaching* (trans. Karl E. Mattson; Philadelphia: Fortress, 1965), 103, confirms the lack of scholarship on Luther, citing Kiessling as a "short but interesting" exception; Brillioth's book was originally published in Swedish as *Predikans historia* (Lund: Gleerup, 1945). A. Skevington Wood, *Captive to the Word: Martin Luther—Doctor of Sacred Scripture* (London: Paternoster, 1969), devotes 10 pages to Luther as preacher, and he repeats (p. 85) the lament of Mackinnon without mentioning Kiessling. Harold J. Grimm, *Martin Luther as a Preacher* (Columbus: Lutheran Book Concern, 1929), 6, claims ambitious goals and is so broad that it does not (in 100 pages) provide any in-depth analysis. Doctoral dissertations on Luther's preaching are scarce in America, but see Glenn Don Smith, *A Rhetorical Biography: An Analysis of Selected Sermons Preached by Martin Luther* (Ph.D. diss., University of Nebraska, 1971), especially 128ff., which analyze the Invocavit Sermons; and Henry Steward Wilson, *The Speaking God: Luther's Theology of Preaching* (Ph.D. diss., Drew University, 1977). William Toohey and William D. Thompson, eds., *Recent Homiletical Thought: A Bibliography, 1935–1965* (Nashville: Abingdon, 1967), list more than 2,100 entries yet cite only one book (Kiessling) and no articles on Luther. A. Duane Litfin and Haddon W. Robinson, eds., *Recent Homiletical Thought: An Annotated Bibliography, vol. 2: 1966–1979* (Grand Rapids: Baker, 1983), in more than 1,900 entries, list one book (Kiessling), three articles, and two dissertations on Luther. Fred W. Meuser, *Luther the Preacher* (Minneapolis: Augsburg, 1983), presents his Hein Lectures of 1983, summarizing many of Luther's remarks on the importance of preaching and rhetoric. John W. Doberstein summarizes some of the reasons given for the lack of scholarship on Luther's preaching: "The reason for this lack seems to be the formidable task of studying and analyzing Luther's sermons of which more than two thousand are to be found in the Weimar edition (though it, too, does not contain all of the sermons of which transcripts are available)" (LW 51:xi); cf. Brillioth, *Brief History*, 104. The volume of extant preaching material in the WA takes up 16 volumes containing sermons exclusively, six containing postils. In LW two volumes (51–52) are devoted to sermons and postils.

**From the theological tradition, on Luther as preacher:** Shorter studies of Luther as preacher are easier to come by, and they tend to be one of two types: (1) summary treatments of Luther's career as preacher or (2) specialized topical investigations of some particular aspect of his preaching. Some examples of type 1 are

Harry F. Baughman, "Martin Luther, the Preacher," *Lutheran Church Quarterly* 21 (1948): 21–49; A. Skevington Wood, "Luther as a Preacher," *Evangelical Quarterly* 21 (1949): 109–21. Much more rigorous, but still wide ranging, is Emanuel Hirsch, "Luthers Predigtweise," *Luther: Mitteilungen der Luthergesellschaft* 25 (1954): 1–23. Some examples of type 2 include Horst Beintker, "Luther als Prediger des Evangeliums: Voraussetzungen in seinem Menschenbild," in *Luther als Prediger* (Veröffentlichungen der Luther-Akademie e. V. Ratzeburg 9; ed. Heinrich Kraft; Erlangen: Martin-Luther, 1986), 102–35; Ulrich Nembach, "Martin Luther als Begleiter auf dem Weg von der Exegese zur Predigt," in *Luther als Prediger* (Veröffentlichungen der Luther-Akademie e. V. Ratzeburg 9; ed. Heinrich Kraft; Erlangen: Martin-Luther, 1986),   42–52. Two short studies on the Invocavit Sermons are Hanfried Fontius, "Martin Luthers Predigt in aktueller Notsituation der Kirche: Die Invokavit-Predigten von 1522," in *Luther als Prediger* (Veröffentlichungen der Luther-Akademie e. V. Ratzeburg 9; ed. Heinrich Kraft; Erlangen: Martin-Luther, 1986), 77–88; Adam Weyer, " 'Das Euangelium wil nit alleyn geschrieben, ßondern viel mehr mit leyplicher stym geprediget seyn': Luthers Invocavit-Predigten im Kontext der Reformationsbewegung," in *Martin Luther* (ed. Heinz Ludwig Arnold; Munich: Edition Text & Kritik, 1983), 86–104.

**On the importance of preaching in the Reformation:** Histories of preaching have traditionally devoted more attention to Luther, for example, Yngve Brillioth, *A Brief History of Preaching* (trans. Karl E. Mattson; Philadelphia: Fortress, 1965), 103–18; cf. Edwin Charles Dargan, *A History of Preaching, vol. 1: From the Apostolic Fathers to the Great Reformers, A. D. 70–1572,* (repr. ed.; Grand Rapids: Baker, 1968), 358–91. See Joachim Dyck, "The First German Treatise on Homiletics: Erasmus Sarcer's *Pastorale* and Classical Rhetoric," in *Renaissance Eloquence* (ed. James J. Murphy; Berkeley: University of California Press, 1983), 221–37. Heiko A. Oberman, "Preaching and the Word in the Reformation," *Theology Today* 18 (1961): 16–29, shows that what the Middle Ages and the Reformation had in common was an emphasis on preaching but that what was new was a changed understanding of the function of the sermon and its relation to the sacraments. John T. Pless, "Martin Luther: Preacher of the Cross," *Concordia Theological Quarterly* 51 (1987): 89, points to Luther's 1523 treatise, "Concerning the Order of Public Worship," (LW 53:11) for Luther's insistence on renewed emphasis of preaching in the service.

**On the medieval art of preaching (*ars praedicandi*):** At or about the beginning of the 13th century, there was an explosion of handbooks on preaching (more than 300 hundred of which still exist in manuscript), exhibiting a fully developed theory of what was an essentially new rhetorical genre that was little known in the centuries since Augustine. For a thorough discussion of the history of preaching, including the rise of the *Ars praedicandi*, see James J. Murphy, *Rhetoric in the Middle Ages: A History of Rhetorical Theory from Saint Augustine to the Renaissance* (Berkeley: University of California Press, 1974), 269–356. Dorothea Roth, *Die* *mittelalterliche Predigttheorie und das Manuale Curatorum des Johann Ulrich Surgant* (Basler Beiträge zur Geschichtswissenschaft 58; Basel: Helbing & Lichtenhan, 1956), 17–55, is one of the most concise, yet careful, discussions on the early period: the fathers (Augustine, Gregory, Guibert of Nogent), Alaine of Lille, Guillaume of Auvergne, Humbert of Rome. A more recent and cogent summary of the history of sacred rhetoric is John W. O'Malley's 1984 Inaugural Bainton Presidential Lecture, "Erasmus and the History of Sacred Rhetoric: The *Ecclesiastes* of 1535," *Erasmus of Rotterdam Society Yearbook* 5 (1985): 1–29, where he argues that the *Ecclesiastes* is perhaps "*the* major monument" in the history of sacred rhetoric, rivaled only by Augustine's *De doctrina christiana*. On the university sermon, see Otto A. Dieter, "*Arbor Picta*: The Medieval Tree of Preaching," *Quarterly Journal of Speech* 51 (1965): 123–44; Harry Caplan, "Classical Rhetoric and the Mediaeval Theory of Preaching," *Classical Philology* 28 (1933): 73–87. The typical format of the "university" sermon, so-called because of its popularity at Paris and Oxford, is well known. As Murphy, *Rhetoric in the Middle Ages*, 331f., explains:

> The *ars praedicandi* specifies a special subject matter and then lays out a plan of arrangement for sermons, with 'protheme' or 'antetheme' followed by a 'prayer' and then statement of 'theme' (Scriptural quotation) with 'division' and 'subdivision' of that quotation 'amplified' through a variety of modes. Alexander [of Ashby] and Thomas [of Thetford] propose a final step, 'conclusion,' but, as we shall see, the later theorists generally abandoned this idea; it is not mentioned by other early writers like William of Auvergne.

Elmer Carl Kiessling, *The Early Sermons of Luther and Their Relation to the Pre-Reformation Sermon* (1935; New York: AMS, 1971), 27–29, traces the "pre-Reformation sermon" as more complex than only two types (homily or scholastic). The latter type he subdivides into two families—textual (based directly on the text, like branches rising immediately from the roots) and thematic (based on a theme deduced from the text, like branches rising from a trunk, which in its turn communicates with the roots). Textual further consists of two more types—textual pericope (dealing with a Scripture passage of some length) and textual verse (dealing with only a short verse). Thematic, Kiessling says, was far more numerous than the textual and can be divided into thematic-doctrinal and thematic-figurative (emblematic).

**On Luther's views of rhetoric:** See Birgit Stolt, "*Docere, delectare*, und *movere* bei Luther: Analysiert anhand der 'Predigt, daß man Kinder zur Schulen halten solle,' " *Deutsche Vierteljahrsschrift für Literaturwissenschaft und Geistesgeschichte* 44 (1970): 433–74, now included in Birgit Stolt, *Wortkampf: Frühneuhochdeutsche Beispiele zur rhetorischen Praxis* (Acta Universitatis Stockholmiensis: Stockholmer Germanistische Forschungen 13; Frankurt on the Main: Athenaeum, 1974); Helmar Junghans, "Rhetorische Bemerkungen Luthers in seinen 'Dicta super Psalterium,'" *Theologische Versuche* 8 (1977): 97–128; Eberhard Ockel, "Martin Luther und die rhetorische Tradition," *Müttersprache* 94

(1983–84): 114–26; Peter Auksi, *Christian Plain Style: The Evolution of a Spiritual Ideal* (Montreal: McGill, 1995), 204–16; Wolfgang Maaser, "Rhetorik und Dialektik: Überlegungen zur systematischen Relevanz der Rhetoriktradition bei Luther," *Luther: Mitteilungen der Luthergesellschaft* 69 (1998): 25–39. Andrea Grün-Oesterreich and Peter L. Oesterreich, " 'Dialectica Docet, Rhetorica Movet': Luthers Reformation Der Rhetorik," in *Rhetorica Movet: Studies in Historical and Modern Rhetoric in Honour of Heinrich E. Plett* (ed. Peter L. Oesterreich and Thomas O. Sloane; Leiden: E. J. Brill, 1999), 25–41. Klaus Dockhorn, "Hans-Georg Gadamer's *Truth and Method*," trans. and ed. Marvin Brown, *Philosophy and Rhetoric* 13 (1980): 164, says: "Luther knows exactly what he means by the *movere* of rhetoric. His opinion can be grasped very precisely because he delineates in detail what happens within the hearer of the word, when the Holy Spirit 'rhetoricatur.' The Holy Spirit acts like an orator, when it faces the most difficult task: to make present that which is past and that which is future; as when the Holy Spirit makes present the passion of Christ, and makes of that past the experience (*Erlebnis*) which is faith. Then faith happens as an affect." In "The Freedom of a Christian" (LW 31:357), Luther writes:

> Rather ought Christ to be preached to the end that faith in him may be established that he may not only be Christ, but be Christ for you and me, and that what is said of him and is denoted in his name may be effectual in us. Such faith is produced and preserved in us by preaching why Christ came, what he brought and bestowed, what benefit it is to us to accept him.

For further discussion on the compatibility of rhetoric to the Reformation concern for communicating with humans to change lives and on Luther's theology in particular, see William J. Bouwsma, "Renaissance and Reformation: An Essay in Their Affinities and Connections," in *Luther and the Dawn of the Modern Era: Papers for the Fourth International Congress for Luther Research* (Studies in the History of Christian Thought 7; ed. Heiko A. Oberman; Leiden: E. J. Brill, 1974), 127–49.

**On style in rhetorical criticism:** See Stephen E. Lucas, "The Renaissance of American Public Address: Text and Context in Rhetorical Criticism," *Quarterly Journal of Speech* 74 (1988): 241–60; Michael C. Leff, "Textual Criticism: The Legacy of Gerald P. Mohrmann," *Quarterly Journal of Speech* 72 (1986): 377–89. For a discussion of a renewed interest in close, textual analyses of rhetorical discourse, see Dilip P. Gaonkar, "Epilogue: The Rhetorical Text: The Enigma of Arrival," in *Texts in Context: Critical Dialogues on Significant Episodes in American Political Rhetoric* (ed. Michael C. Leff and Fred J. Kauffeld; Davis, Calif.: Hermagoras, 1990), 255–75. My approach to discourse and my critical methodology are sketched in Neil R. Leroux, "Perceiving Rhetorical Style: Toward a Framework for Criticism," *Rhetoric Society Quarterly* 22.4 (Fall 1992): 29–44; and "Luther's *Am Neujahrstage*: Style as Argument," *Rhetorica* 12 (1994): 1–42.

**On the use of rhetorical criticism in sermon analysis:** M. Eugene Boring recognizes the potential that rhetorical criticism has for homiletics:

> Rhetorical structure is a fundamental factor in the effectiveness of our own speaking and writing—a matter of homiletics. But rhetorical structure is also a fundamental factor for the normative text on which our preaching is based, the Bible—a matter of exegesis. Thus 'rhetorical criticism' is an (perhaps new) item to add to our kit of exegetical tools.

Cf. M. Eugene Boring, "Rhetoric, Righteousness, and the Sermon on the Mount," pages 53–75 in *Listening to the Word: Studies in Honor of Fred B. Craddock* (ed. Gail R. O'Day and Thomas G. Long; Nashville: Abingdon, 1993), especially 54. Ellen Monsma's dissertation, *The Preaching Style of Calvin: An Analysis of the Psalm Sermons of the* Supplementa Calviniana (Ph.D. diss., Rutgers University, 1986), is commendable for its accuracy and thoroughness in situating Calvin in the contexts of the rhetorical tradition and its Renaissance emphases and in a careful description of the broad features of the Psalter sermons. She provides important general findings (for example, Calvin having abandoned the thematic sermon, Calvin as mediating between Ciceronian and Senecan style, Calvin as employing virtually all the rhetorical devices, Calvin's discourse as manifesting the antithesis that was at the heart of his theology). The most interesting and informative sections of her analysis, however, are where she describes, thoroughly and carefully, what Calvin's discourse does, that is, how it works.

# CHAPTER 1

**On rhetorical criticism as an analytical tool in biblical studies:** The story of the "rhetorical turn" is usually said to have started in the 1970s in Old Testament studies by James Muilenburg, "Form Criticism and Beyond," *Journal of Biblical Literature* 88 (1969): 1–18; and in New Testament research by Hans-Dieter Betz, "The Literary Composition and Function of Paul's Letter to the Galatians," *New Testament Studies* 21 (1975): 353–79; and Hans-Dieter Betz's commentary in the Hermeneia series, *Galatians: A Commentary on Paul's Letter to the Churches in Galatia* (Philadelphia: Fortress, 1979)—see the review by David E. Aune in *Religious Studies Review* 7 (1981): 323–28. The story has been variously told by Vernon K. Robbins and John H. Patton, "Rhetoric and Biblical Criticism," *Quarterly Journal of Speech* 66 (1980): 327–50; Jan Lambrecht, "Rhetorical Criticism and the New Testament," *Bijdragen, Tijdschrift voor Filosofie en Theologie* 50 (1989): 239–53; Roland Meynet, "Histoire de 'l'analyse rhétorique' en exégèse biblique," *Rhetorica* 8 (1990): 291–320; Burton L. Mack, *Rhetoric and the New Testament: Guides to Biblical Scholarship* (New Testament Series; Minneapolis: Fortress, 1990), 7–48; and Duane F. Watson and Allan J. Hauser, eds., *Rhetorical Criticism of the Bible: A Comprehensive Bibliography with Notes on History and Method* (Biblical Interpretation Series 4; Leiden: E. J. Brill, 1994). What has provided the greatest momen-

tum and clarity (for New Testament studies) was a work that outlines not only theory, but a method—George A. Kennedy's *New Testament Interpretation through
Rhetorical Criticism* (Chapel Hill: University of North Carolina Press, 1984); cf.
the Kennedy Festschrift, Duane F. Watson, ed., *Persuasive Artistry: Studies in New
Testament Rhetoric in Honor of George A. Kennedy* (Sheffield: Sheffield Academic
Press, 1991). The sequential procedure that Kennedy lays out: (1) Identify the
rhetorical units comprising oral addresses, which can then be analyzed. (2) Determine the rhetorical situation. (3) Determine the dispositio, the arrangement of the
speech's parts. (4) Identify the features of style. (5) Assess the whole (Kennedy,
*New Testament Interpretation*, 33–38). C. Joachim Classen has now offered some
insights on Melanchthon, to which he has briefly referred in another article:
"Melanchthon's First Manual on Rhetorical Categories in Criticism of the Bible,"
in *The Passionate Intellect: Essays on the Transformation of Classical Traditions Presented to Professor I. G. Kidd* (Rutgers University Studies in Classical Humanities 7; ed.
Lewis Ayres; New Brunswick, N.J.: Transaction Publishers, 1995), 297–322. A
recent rhetorical critical study of the New Testament epistle of Jude shows how
serious attention to style can aid in the elucidation of a text, rather than allowing
it to be subsumed by prior classifications of genre; see E. R. Wendland, "A Com-
parative Study of 'Rhetorical Criticism,' Ancient and Modern—With Special Reference to the Larger Structure and Function of the Epistle of Jude," *Neot* 28
(1994): 193–228.

On lists, doublets, and other repetitive devices: On the matter of possible
strategic sequencing in lists, see Robert H. Gundry, "Mark 10:29: Order in the
List," *Catholic Biblical Quarterly* 29 (1997): 465–75. On doublet pairs, see William
K. Wimsatt Jr., *The Prose Style of Samuel Johnson* (Yale Studies in English 94; New
Haven: Yale University Press, 1941), 20ff., where he argues that in English prose
style there can be one or more of four expressive purposes at work when a writer
employs a pair of words with an equal relation to their context: (1) to give range
or scope, that is, to name the number of objects necessary to the whole meaning
of the context, either completely or illustratively—for example, "prince and
princess" (exact range), "pickles and conserves" (illustrative examples of homely
concerns); (2) to refer to the object under two ideas or aspects, both of which have
relevance to the whole meaning of the context; (3) a pair of abstract terms, where
it could be two objects or simply two aspects of one object; (4) pairs for emphasis,
where the closer the two terms come to being synonymous, the greater the
emphasis. See also Neil R. Leroux, "Luther's Use of Doublets," *Rhetoric Society
Quarterly* 30.3 (Summer 2000): 35–54.

On rhetorical figures: It is hoped that my functional classification is helpful
to the critic. The discussion in William J. Brandt, *The Rhetoric of Argumentation*
(Indianpolis: Bobbs-Merrill, 1970), is, of course, more pedagogically designed
and, thus, would be more precise. Yet his might prove awkward and confusing,
were I to use it here. His "Glossary" divides into argumentative figures, tropes,
stance figures, and other figures. However, prior to that (pp. 99–116), he recog-

nizes functions of "textual rhetoric," classifying "various distortions introduced into language to make it yield human truth": emphasis, division, definition, redefinition, comparison, position (stance), generalization, and particularization. Arthur Quinn, *Figures of Speech: Sixty Ways to Turn a Phrase* (Salt Lake City: G. M. Smith, 1982), approaches figures playfully, teasing out the plasticity of language for his readers. Each of his subsequent eight chapters produces examples that generate appreciation for language's functional effects. He skillfully challenges easy taxonomies and received notions, such as "deviance." See also Richard A. Lanham, *A Handlist of Rhetorical Terms* (2d ed.; Berkeley: University of California Press, 1991), and an online source: Gideon O. Burton, "Silva Rhetoricae: The Forest of Rhetoric" (1996–2001) (http://humanities.byu.edu/rhetoric/silva.htm).

**On syntactical structures:** An example of hyperbaton by inversion is the biblical shout in Acts 19:28, "Great is Diana of the Ephesians." For discussion of that sentence, see R. H. Carpenter, "Essential Schemes of Syntax: An Analysis of Rhetorical Theory's Recommendations for Uncommon Word Orders," *Quarterly Journal of Speech* 55 (1969): 164. In German syntax, however, verbs can be in first position—that is, at the start of a sentence rather than at the end, which is their usual position. This is not inversion for purposes of emphasis; it is grammatically required to form a question.

**On rhyme and the use of sound:** Rhyme, according to traditional prosodists, simply means likeness in word sounds. One term for end rhyme through variation is *homoioteleuton* ("like ending"). William Wimsatt distinguishes between *homoioteleuton* and rhyme. The former offers no "binding force" because in the sameness of the ending, the things are virtually alike. He sees rhyme as bringing together two things *unlike* (in meaning) that, through their sound, similarity can be found; cf. William K. Wimsatt Jr., "One Relation of Rhyme to Reason," *Modern Language Quarterly* 5 (1944): 323–38. Grant W. Smith, "The Political Impact of Name Sounds," *Communication Monographs* 65 (1998): 157f., argues that in contrast to vowels, "Studies of consonants have emphasized the relationship of sounds to the meanings of the words in which they existed" (157). Smith's study explores how the "comfort factor" plays a role in voter associations in selecting candidates. Thus, names (also epithets) can operate more independently of verbal context than other forms of language because they are "verbally opaque, their differentiation based more purely on sounds . . . [that] can be measured in terms of phonetic attributes" (156). Names used in live speech, however, may indeed be more affected by the verbal context than candidate last names, which seem so much more subject to the "comfort factor" alone. Winifred Nowottny, *The Language Poets Use* (London: Athlone, 1962), 4:

> [N]o *simplistic* view of a 'style of sound' is possible, for several reasons. One is that the systems capable of minicry are themselves various . . . and we might find if we set about relating the variety of mimicking systems to the variety of attributes it is possible to mimic, that the interest of the diverse kinds of relations between the mimicking and the mimicked might vary enor-

mously from one case to another even if only in response of the distance betweeen the medium and what it mediates. . . . But corporeality may be ordered in what looks like the reverse direction: that is, so as to focus attention on the most important conceptual relations in a situation. Features of sound and spelling *can* emphasize meaning. (*my emphasis*)

For some recommendations to preachers on using sounds of words constructively, see David Buttrick, *Homiletic: Moves and Structures* (Philadelphia: Fortress, 1987), 205–07.

## CHAPTER 2

**On the Augustinian order:** See Heiko A. Oberman, *Luther: Man between God and the Devil* (trans. Eileen Walliser-Schwarzbart; New Haven: Yale University Press, 1989), 53. The Saxon congregation was the only Observant house in Germany. The Observantists had returned to a more strict rule; cf. Agostino Borromeo, "Augustinians," in *The Oxford Encyclopedia of the Reformation* (ed. Hans J. Hillerbrand; New York: Oxford University Press, 1996): 1:100f. In 1515 Luther was appointed district vicar of the 11 monasteries in the Congregation of the Reformed Augustinians in central Germany; cf. Eric W. Gritsch, *Martin—God's Court Jester: Luther in Retrospect* (Philadelphia: Fortress, 1983), 12.

**On Wittenberg:** *Leucorea* is the Greek translation of the German word "Wittenberg" (white hill). Johann von Staupitz was also cofounder of the university, as well as its first theology faculty; cf. Helmar Junghans, "Wittenberg," in *The Oxford Encyclopedia of the Reformation* (ed. Hans J. Hillerbrand; New York: Oxford University Press, 1996): 4:282–86; Ernest G. Schwiebert, "The Electoral City of Wittenberg," *Medievalia et Humanistica* 3 (1945): 99–116.

**On the papal bull against Luther:** The bull *Exsurge Domine* ("Arise, O Lord") was delivered to Luther on Oct. 10, 1520. Not a bull of excommunication, it was a condemnation—in 41 articles—of Luther's errors and a threat that if he did not publicly recant and refute these errors within 60 days after receiving the bull, he and his protectors would be in danger of excommunication. After issuing his own "anti-bull," Luther and his students burned the papal bull in a public ceremony on December 10. In January, a bull of excommunication (*Decet Romanum*) announced the pope's final decision. The Diet of Worms was a confrontation with the emperor. The Edict of Worms was issued late in May 1521, a month after Luther was confined at the Wartburg. The edict was the imperial decision of Charles V—who had just been crowned emperor in October 1520—and the imperial diet [*Reichstag*], Charles's first, which convened on Jan. 27, 1521. For the facsimile text and English translation of a French version (Paris: Pierre Gromors, 1521?) of the Edict of Worms (and preceding events), along with a superb critical introduction, see De Lamar Jensen, *Confrontation at Worms: Martin Luther and the Diet of Worms* (Provo: Brigham Young University Press, 1973). On Luther's use of the *bulla* literary form, see Martin U. Brecht, *Doctor Luther's Bulla and Reformation:*

*A Look at Luther the Writer* (Gross Memorial Lecture 1990; Valparaiso, Ind.: Valparaiso University Press, 1991).

**On Luther's early devotional writings:** In 1519 three devotional writings were immensely popular: "Exposition of the Lord's Prayer for Simple Laymen, 1519" (LW 42:15–81) [*Auslegung deutsch des Vaterunsers für einfältigen Laien 1519*] (WA 2:75ff.) saw 24 editions (Benzing, no. 260–83); "Sermon on the Estate of Marriage, 1519" (LW 44:3–14) [*Ein Sermon von dem ehelichen Stand 1519*] (WA 2:162ff.] saw 20 editions (Benzing, no. 358–77); "Sermon on Preparing to Die, 1519" (LW 42:95–115) [*Ein Sermon von Bereitung zum Sterben 1519*] (WA 2:680ff.) saw 26 editions (Benzing, no. 435–60). In contrast, "Babylonian Captivity" saw only six editions in its German version (Benzing, no. 712–17). My thanks to Hans J. Hillerbrand (at a public lecture in Spicer, Minn., May 13, 1996) for initially calling my attention to Luther's early popularity as a devotional writer; cf. Hans J. Hillerbrand, "The Spread of the Protestant Reformation of the Sixteenth Century: A Historical Case Study in the Transfer of Ideas," *The South Atlantic Quarterly* 67 (1968): 265–86, which draws upon Louise W. Holborn, "Printing and the Growth of a Protestant Movement in Germany from 1517 to 1524," *Church History* 9 (1942): 123–37; and Hans J. Hillerbrand, "Radicalism in the Early Reformation: Varieties of Reformation in Church and Society," in *Radical Tendencies in the Reformation: Divergent Perspectives* (Sixteenth Century Essays and Studies 9; ed. Hans J. Hillerbrand; Kirksville: Sixteenth Century Journal Publishers, 1988), 31. See also Martin U. Brecht, *Doctor Luther's Bulla and Reformation: A Look at Luther the Writer* (Gross Memorial Lecture 1990; Valparaiso, Ind.: Valparaiso University Press, 1991), 13: "[I]nitially—that is, prior to becoming controversial—Luther viewed himself as an author who was writing on religious subjects for the common people. His sensitivity to the spiritual needs of the laity motivated his writing." In 1535 Luther wrote "A Simple Way to Pray: For a Good Friend" (LW 43:187–211; WA 38:351–75) and dedicated it to Peter Beskendorf, the barber and surgeon; cf. Martin Brecht, *Martin Luther: The Preservation of the Church 1532–1546* (trans. James L. Schaaf; Minneapolis: Fortress, 1993), 14: "Nowhere is the connection between order and freedom in Luther's practice of prayer so clearly seen as in his advice for Master Peter." Cf. Richard G. Cole, "The Reformation Pamphlet and Communication Processes," in *Flugschriften als Massenmedium der Reformationzeit: Beiträge zum Tübinger Symposion* (ed. Hans-Joachim Köhler; Stuttgart: Klett-Cotta, 1981), 139–61.

**On Luther's correspondence from Wartburg:** For Luther's letters from Wartburg, in English, see LW 48:200–399; cf. Preserved Smith and Charles M. Jacobs, eds., *Luther's Correspondence and Other Contemporary Letters* (Philadelphia: The Lutheran Publication Society, 1918): 2:21–100. In German, cf. Herbert von Hintzenstern, ed., *Martin Luther: Briefe von der Wartburg 1521/1522* (Eisenach: Wartburg, 1991), which does not include letters in February or March 1522. Luther made a secret visit of three days to Wittenberg on Dec. 3–4, 1521. He also needed to maintain communication to remain supplied with documents necessary for his writing and to keep abreast of his publisher Grunenberg; see Gottfried Krodel's "Excursus" in LW 48:237–43. But see A. Steimle, *Luther's Works*, 6 vols. (Philadelphia: A. J. Holman, 1916–43), 2:387, who says Luther was not fully informed. I am not debating the accuracy or timeliness of Luther's knowledge, that is, "how" he was kept informed; I am simply contending "that" he seemed to be aware of the situation in Wittenberg. See also Friedrich von Bezold, "Luthers Rückkehr von der Wartburg," *Zeitschrift für Kirchengeschichte* 20 (1900): 186–233.

**On the so-called Wittenberg Movement:** Accounts of the events are numerous and, for the most part, compatible regarding what occurred; who was responsible and what were the various motivations and agendas, however, is contested turf. Accounts can be checked by consulting James Samuel Preus, *Carlstadt's "Ordinaciones" and Luther's "Liberty": A Study of the Wittenberg Movement 1521–1522* (Harvard Theological Studies 26: Cambridge: Harvard University Press, 1974), 8–11; Harry Loewen, *Luther and the Radicals* (Waterloo, Ontario: W. Laurier University, 1974), 30–36; Mark Edwards, *Luther and the False Brethren* (Stanford: Stanford University Press, 1975), 6–23; and Steven E. Ozment, *The Reformation in the Cities: The Appeal of Protestantism to Sixteenth-Century Germany and Switzerland* (New Haven: Yale University Press, 1975), 138–45. Another highly reliable source is Wilhelm H. Neuser, *Die Abendmahlslehre Melanchthons in ihrer geschichtlichen Entwicklung (1519–1530)* (Beiträge zur Geschichte und Lehre der Reformierten Kirchen 26 [Melanchthon-Studien 2]; Neukirchen: Neukirchener Verlag des Erziehungs-vereins, 1968), 114–228. There is now a new short study on the Wittenberg Movement by Stefan Oehmig: "Die Wittenberger Bewegung 1521/22 und ihre Folgen im Lichte alter und neuer Fragestellungen: Ein Beitrag zum Thema (Territorial-)Stadt und Reformation," in *700 Jahre Wittenberg: Stadt, Universität, Reformation* (ed. Stefan Oehmig; Weimar: Hermann Böhlaus Nachfolger, 1995), 97–130. The documents collected by Nikolaus Müller were collected in response to Hermann Barge, *Andreas Bodenstein von Karlstadt*, 2 vols. (2d ed.; Nieuwkoop: B. deGraaf, 1968); see also Hermann Barge, "Luther und Karlstadt in Wittenberg: Eine kritische Untersuchung," *Historische Zeitschrift* 99 (1907): 256–324. Hermann Barge, "Zur Genesis der frühreformatorischen Vorgänge in Wittenberg," *Historische Vierteljahrschrift* 1 (1914): 1–33. Scholarly literature about Karlstadt, in English, seriously lags that on Luther; cf. Ronald J. Sider, *Andreas Bodenstein von Karlstadt: The Develoment of His Thought 1517–1525* (Studies in Medieval and Reformation Thought 11; Leiden: E. J. Brill, 1974); Ronald J. Sider, ed., *Karlstadt's Battle with Luther: Documents in a Radical-Liberal Debate* (Philadelphia: Fortress, 1978); and the bibliography in C. A. Pater, *Karlstadt as Father of the Baptist Movements: The Emergence of Lay Protestantism* (Toronto: University of Toronto Press, 1988), 301–27. See also Hans J. Hillerbrand, "Andreas Bodenstein of Carlstadt, Prodigal Reformer," *Church History* 35 (1966): 375–98. Bernhard Lohse, *Martin Luther's Theology: Its Historical and Systematic Development* (ed. and trans. Roy A. Harrisville; Minneapolis: Fortress, 1999), 144–50. Cynthia Grant Schoenberger, "Luther and the Justifiability of Resistance to Legitimate Authority," *Journal of the History of Ideas* 40 (1979): 5, says: "He [Luther] was shocked and frightened by the disorders he witnessed during his brief secret visit from Wartburg Castle to Wittenberg in 1521, as well as by the anarchic conditions he observed en route in Thuringia."

**On Karlstadt's evangelical Mass:** An English translation is available: Ronald J. Sider, ed., *Karlstadt's Battle with Luther: Documents in a Liberal-Radical Debate* (Philadelphia: Fortress, 1978), 7–15. Using Freys-Barge 78, Sider translates approximately 60 percent of the text—Articles 1, and 6–24. In a yet unpublished article, I have translated the remaining approximately 40 percent, which consists of portions of Article 1, all of Articles 2–5, portions of Article 23, and all of Article 25. In this sermon of 15 octavo pages (approximately 500 lines set off in 25 numbered articles of uneven length), Karlstadt first sets out to remind his audience that the clergy have no right to withhold the Sacrament from those who desire to partake but have not gone to confession, nor do the clergy stand on any legitimate authority when they try to scare people away by insisting that parishioners cannot partake until they have made themselves sufficiently fearful or sad. He then argues that only unbelief should prevent partaking, that proper belief is demonstrated when one boldly grasps the promises of Christ extended in the bread and the cup. Because forgiveness of sins is one of the two promises inherent in the Sacrament (through the cup; the other promise is victory over death through the bread), Karlstadt attempts to undercut any prohibitive power of priestly confession that might nullify people's preparedness for the Sacrament through unforgiven sin. He does warn people that their unbelief should keep them away. Therein does he hold responsible at one and the same time both (1) the oppressive clergy—for the problems of withholding the cup and obstructing partaking without confession—and (2) the laity—for the solutions that they should ignore confession and boldly partake in faith. Harry Loewen says 2,000 people attended this service and that this celebration "seemed to break the dam in Wittenberg"; cf. Harry Loewen, *Luther and the Radicals* (Waterloo, Ontario: W. Laurier University, 1974), 33. There is agreement that this service was public and controversial, but I can find no consensus as to where the service was held. Many scholars agree that the service occurred at the *Schloßkirche*, which is where Karlstadt had originally scheduled it (see Heinrich Böhmer, *Luther in Light of Recent Research* (trans. Carl F. Huth Jr.; New York: The Christian Herald, 1916), 162; Carter Lindberg, *The European Reformations* (Oxford: Blackwell, 1996), 103; Ulrich Bubenheimer, "Andreas Rudolff Bodenstein von Karlstadt: Sein Leben, seine Herkunft und sein inner Entwicklung," in *Andreas Bodenstein von Karlstadt, 1480–1541: Festschrift der Stadt Karlstadt zum Jubiläumsjahr 1980* [ed. Wolfgang Merklein; Karlstadt: Historischer Verein e.V. Evang.-Luth.Kirchengemeinde, 1980], 33; Martin Brecht, *Martin Luther: Shaping and Defining the Reformation, 1521–1532* (trans. James L. Schaaf; Minneapolis: Fortress, 1990), 34; and Hellmut Hasse, "Karlstadt as Prediger in der Stadtkirche zu Wittenberg," in *Andreas Bodenstein von Karlstadt, 1480–1541: Festschrift der Stadt Karlstadt zum Jubiläums-*

*jahr 1980* [ed. Wolfgang Merklein; Karlstadt: Historischer Verein e.V. Evang.-Luth.Kirchengemeinde, 1980], 65, to list a few). Moreover, Ronald J. Sider, *Andreas Bodenstein von Karlstadt: The Develoment of His Thought 1517–1525* (Studies in Medieval and Reformation Thought 11; Leiden: E. J. Brill, 1974), 159, n. 56, claims that Barge has proven that the historic occasion occurred at All Saints'. However, Leopold von Ranke, *History of the Reformation in Germany* (ed. Robert A. Johnson; trans. Sarah Austin; London: Routledge, 1905), 252, says it took place at the *Stadtkirche*, as does Ingrid Schulze, *Die Stadtkirche zu Wittenberg* (Berlin: Union, 1966), 20; and Thomas von der Heyde, in *Neue Zeitung*, a Dresden newspaper account compiled by Müller in *WB*, no. 72, 170. Luther was much more concerned about what took place at the latter—his own pulpit—than at the former—the University chapel where Karlstadt shared preaching assignments. In their 1524 face-off at the Black Bear Inn at Jena ("What Dr. Andreas Bodenstein von Karlstadt Talked Over with Dr. Martin Luther at Jena, and How They Have Decided to Write against Each Other, 1524")—in Ronald J. Sider, ed., *Karlstadt's Battle with Luther: Documents in a Liberal-Radical Debate* (Philadelphia: Fortress, 1978), 36–49—Luther confronts Karlstadt directly over the matter of his lack of jurisdiction at the *Stadtkirche*. There Karlstadt virtually admits that he preached at the *Stadtkirche*, but he argues that his right to preach *per se* is his right because of the archdeaconate. Further, he claims that the same people attend both churches. On page 44, note 18, Sider argues that Karlstadt's preaching and communion service on Dec. 25, 1521, was with the full cooperation of the parish priest [*pfarrer*] Simon Heims, according to *WB*, no. 63, 136. Martin Brecht, "Luther und die Wittenberger Reformation während der Wartburgzeit," in *Martin Luther: Leben, Werk, Wirkung* (ed. Günter Vogler, Siegfried Hoyer, and Adolf Laube; Berlin: Adademie, 1986), 79, says the Christmas service occurred at the Castle Church and that Karlstadt then held another service on New Year's Day at the City Church. For a review of the issues, see Hellmut Hasse, "Karlstadt als Prediger in der Stadtkirche zu Wittenberg," in *Andreas Bodenstein von Karlstadt, 1480–1541: Festschrift der Stadt Karlstadt zum Jubiläumsjahr 1980* [ed. Wolfgang Merklein; Karlstadt: Historischer Verein e.V. Evang.-Luth.Kirchengemeinde, 1980], 58–83.

**On the Zwickau Prophets:** See Theodor Kolde, "Ältester Bericht über die Zwickauer Propheten," *Zeitschrift für Kirchengeschichte* 5 (1882): 323–33; Harold S. Bender, "The Zwickau Prophets, Thomas Müntzer, and the Anabaptists," *Mennonite Quarterly Review* 27 (1953): 3–16 (originally published in German in *Theologische Zeitschrift* 8 [1952]: 262–78); Paul Wappler, *Thomas Müntzer in Zwickau und die "Zwickauer Propheten"* (Schriften des Vereins für Reformationsgeschichte 71; Gütersloh: Gütersloher [Gerd Mohn], 1966). A recent review of the literature is Olaf Kuhr, "The Zwickau Prophets, the Wittenberg Disturbances, and Polemical Historiography," *Mennonite Quarterly Review* 70 (1996): 203–14. The particular issue of infant Baptism, which the prophets raised (and which Karlstadt later also took up), is not an issue for the Invocavit Sermons; cf. Siegfried Hoyer, "Die

Zwickauer Storchianer—Vorläufer der Täufer?" *Jahrbuch für Regionalgeschichte* 13 (1986): 60–78.

**On Karlstadt's tract on images and poor relief:** See Neil R. Leroux, " 'In the Christian City of Wittenberg': Karlstadt's tract on Images and Begging," forthcoming in *Sixteenth Century Journal.* An English translation of Karlstadt's tract is Edward J. Furcha, ed. and trans., *The Essential Karlstadt: Fifteen Tracts* (Classics of the Radical Reformation 8; Waterloo, Ontario: Herald P, 1995), 101–28, whose translation of both articles is based upon the text in Hans Lietzmann, ed., *Andreas Karlstadt: Von Abtuhung der Bilder und Das Keyn Bedtler unther den Christen Seyn Sollen* (Bonn: Weber, 1911). Another modern German edition of *Von Abtuhung der Bylder* is found in Adolf Laube and Annerose Schneider, eds., *Flugschriften der frühen Reformationsbewegung (1518–1524)*, Band 1 (Vaduz: Topos, 1983). An earlier English translation of *Von Abtuhung der Bylder* is found in Bryan D. Mangrum and Giuseppe Scavizzi, eds. and trans., *A Reformation Debate: Karlstadt, Emser, and Eck on Sacred Images, Three Treatises in Translation* (Toronto: Victoria University Centre for Reformation and Renaissance Studies, 1991), 19–39. An earlier English translation of *Das Keyn Bedtler* is found in Carter Lindberg, " 'There Should Be No Beggars Among Christians': An Early Reformation Tract on Social Welfare by Andreas Karlstadt," in *Piety, Politics, and Ethics: Reformation Studies in Honor of George Wolfgang Forell* (Sixteenth Century Essays and Studies 3; ed. Carter Lindberg; Kirksville: Sixteenth Century Journal Publishers, 1984), 157–66. Karlstadt felt cornered by increasing popular demand for Communion in both kinds, but he also came to a crossroads with respect to images. Concerning the Wittenberg Ordinance of January 24, Martin Brecht, *Martin Luther: Shaping and Defining the Reformation, 1521–1532* (trans. James L. Schaaf ; Minneapolis: Fortress, 1990), 39, says: "A new element of the constitution was the planned removal of the altars and images of the saints. Karlstadt was behind this, and he had already announced that on 26 January he would deliver a sermon, 'On the Abolition of Images and That There Should Be No Beggars Among Christians.'" I have been thus far unable to ascertain what Brecht means by "deliver a sermon,"—whether he knows this material was delivered earlier in oral form. Thus, for the prior issue (Sacrament) Karlstadt moved forward to reinstitute a New Testament practice; in the latter issue (images), however, he attempted to undo what he believed were harmful, idolatrous behaviors. In fact, two years later ("Whether One Should Proceed Slowly and Avoid Offending the Weak in Matters that Concern God's Will"), he still likened the image situation to that of seeing an innocent child holding a sharp knife in his hand, to whom one's "brotherly love" surely would not allow that child to keep the knife. The argument responds directly— though without any explicit attribution—to Luther's argument in "A Sincere Admonition," which Karlstadt had surely read:

> Take an analogous case [*Merck eynn gleychnisz*]: If an enemy had tied a rope
> around your brother's neck, endangering his life, and you like a fool were to

fly into a rage at rope and enemy and frantically pull the rope toward you or slash at it with a knife, you would most likely either strangle or stab your brother, doing him more harm than either rope or enemy. If you really want to help your brother, this is what you must do: You may slash away at the enemy as vigorously as you please, but the rope you must handle gently and with caution until you get it off his neck, lest you strangle your brother." (LW 45:73)

**On the Jan. 24, 1522, Wittenberg Ordinance:** The "Order of the City of Wittenberg (1522)" is published in Carter Lindberg, ed., *Beyond Charity: Reformation Initiatives for the Poor* (Minneapolis: Fortress, 1993), 200–02. Lindberg's source is the modern edition of Hans Lietzmann, ed., *Die Wittenberger und Leisniger Kastenordnung* (Berlin: de Gruyter, 1935). I have consulted the earlier edition, Kleine Texte 21 (Bonn: A. Marcus & E. Weber, 1907). There is a growing body of literature on 16th-century poor relief and its connection to the Reformation. For a concise overview of the history of church thoughts on poverty, including the Reformation period, see Carter Lindberg, "Through a Glass Darkly: A History of the Church's Vision of the Poor and Poverty," *Ecumenical Review* 33 (1981): 37–52. For a general introduction to Wittenberg actions on the issues, see Carter Lindberg, *The European Reformations* (Oxford: Blackwell, 1996), chapter 5, 111–34, and his bibliography (Lindberg has been particularly prolific in the area of scholarship on poor relief). For information on Luther's ideas and contributions, see Susannah Hall, "The Common Chest Concept: Luther's Contribution to 16th Century Poor Relief Reform," *Social Thought* 5 (1979): 43–53; Richard P. Hordern, "Luther's Attitude Towards Poverty: Theology and Social Reform," in *Festschrift: A Tribute to Dr. William Hordern* (ed. Walter Frietag; Saskatoon: University of Saskatchewan Press, 1985), 94–108; Ole Peter Grell, "The Protestant Imperative of Christian Care and Neighborly Love," in *Health Care and Poor Relief in Protestant Europe 1500–1700* (ed. Ole Peter Grell and Andrew Cunningham; London: Routledge, 1997), 43–65; Harold J. Grimm, "Luther's Contributions to Sixteenth-Century Organizations of Poor Relief," *ARG* 61 (1970): 222–34; Abby Phyllis Knobler, *Luther and the Legal Concept of the Poor in the Sixteenth Century German Church Ordinances* (Ph.D. diss., University of California at Los Angeles, 1991); Jeffrey Philip Jaynes, *"Ordo et libertas": Church Discipline and the Makers of Church Order in Sixteenth Century North Germany* (Ph.D. diss., Ohio State University, 1993), especially chapter 1. For detailed studies on the church ordinances, see Jeffrey Philip Jaynes, "Church Ordinances," in *The Oxford Encyclopedia of the Reformation* (ed. Hans J. Hillerbrand; New York: Oxford University Press, 1996): 1:345–51; Hermann Barge, "Die älteste evangelische Armenordnung," *Historische Vierteljahrsschrift* 11 (1908): 193–225; Otto Winkelmann, "Die Armenordnungen von Nürnberg (1522), Kitzingen (1523), Regensburg (1523) und Ypern (1525)," *ARG* 10 (1912): 242–80; *ARG* 11 (1913): 1–18; Otto Winkelmann, "Über die ältesten Armenordnungen der Reformationszeit (1522–1525)," *Historische Vierteljahrsschrift* 17 (1914–15): 187–228; 361–400; Karl Pallas, "Die Wittenberger

Beutelordnung vom Jahre 1521 und ihr Verhältnis zu der Einrichtung des Gemeinen Kastens im Januar 1522," *Zeitschrift des Vereins für Kirchengeschichte in der Provinz Sachsen* 12 (1915): 1–45, 100–37; Karl Dummler, "Die Leisniger Kastenordnung von 1523," *Zeitschrift für evangelisches Kirchenrecht* 29 (1984): 337–53; Stefan Oehmig, "Der Wittenberger Gemeine Kasten in den ersten zweieinhalb Jahrzehnten seines Bestehens (1522/23 bis 1547): Seine Ausgaben und seine sozialen Nutznießer," *Jahrbuch für Geschichte des Feudalismus* 13 (1988): 133–79.

# Subject Index

# SCRIPTURE INDEX